The Meaning of Maryknoll

*Maryknoll's official symbol is the Chi Rho
(pronounced key row). It is composed
of a circle that represents the world
and the first two Greek letters
which begin Christ's name. It signifies
"Christ over the world."*

The Meaning of

MARYKNOLL

Illustrated with Photographs

ALBERT J. NEVINS

McMullen Books, Inc., New York

To those Maryknollers who have given
their lives to the fulfillment of
the Great Command, and in so doing
have established a pattern for our
missionary generations to follow.

Contents

1 The End Is a Beginning   1
2 The Man from the Tar Heel State   10
3 A Moment in Boston   21
4 Three Letters   30
5 Laying the Foundation   43
6 The Days of the Giants   52
7 Kongmoon—The River Gate Opens   62
8 A Small but Constant Flame   69
9 Korea—The Hermit Kingdom   80
10 Witness   87
11 Kaying—The King's Highway   96
12 Wuchow—From the Ground Up   107
13 Manchuria—Land of Many Masters   120
14 Philippines—Tragedy in the Pacific   131
15 Oriental Work in the United States   142
16 Kweilin—Land of Gingerbread Mountains   150

17 Calvary in China   161
18 Kyoto—The Banners Are Flying   167
19 Building with Japan   177
20 The End of an Era   187
21 Bolivia—High and Low   201
22 Peru—Reaching for the Sky   212
23 Chile—A World in Miniature   225
24 Guatemala—The Sun Shines Bright   238
25 Africa—Land of Promise   252
26 Formosa—Earthquake Island   264
27 Hong Kong—Doorstep of the Dragon   270
28 The Maryknoll Brothers   283
29 The Maryknoll Sisters   292
30 Valiant Women   302
31 The Training of a Missioner   314
32 Spreading an Idea   322

1

The End Is a Beginning

The gate of the People's National Prison on Canton's Yellow Flower Road slammed shut, closing off the outside world as effectively as if one had suddenly been transported to another planet. Momentarily a wave of relief passed over the two new prisoners, something akin to the feeling of a sailor who reaches a sheltered harbor after riding out a hurricane. Not that the prison was really a safe port. It was only a pause on the way to another Calvary. But at least for the time being, the humiliation of public spectacle was over.

Even the armed guards seemed relieved. They straightened their loose, ill-fitting uniforms, and waited for the prison officials to take over their charges. Now that their destination had been reached, the guards felt free to relax their attention, thus allowing one of their prisoners an opportunity to whisper to his companion.

"We're going to prison in honor of Christ," softly said the man. "It's no disgrace."

In the next moment, the prisoners were separated and taken off to different cell blocks. The woman was led to her part of the prison, the man to his. The ring of their footsteps on the stone floor of the corridors grew farther and farther away. The woman didn't know it then, but she was the last friend to hear Bishop Francis X. Ford's voice.

"We're going to prison in honor of Christ," he had said. "It's no disgrace."

It is difficult to pinpoint time and say, "This is where it began." A story can start at the end, or at the beginning, or at a thousand and one points along the way. So it is with Bishop Ford. His story could originate in Brooklyn on January 11, 1892, the day he was born to Elizabeth Ford and Austin Ford. Mr. Ford was the crusading editor of *The Irish World*, the first paper in America to reach a million circulation. Or it could commence weeks later in Sacred Heart Church, when the infant was baptized with the name of that great apostle, Francis Xavier. There are hardly any limits for the points of departure, the moments of decision, the borders of the threads that were not to be completely unraveled until years later in his prison in Canton. Francis' generous decision to become a priest, his formative years at Cathedral College in New York, his entrance into the newly founded Maryknoll Society in 1912, his departure for South China in 1918, his consecration as the first Bishop of Kaying in 1935—all of these are elements with a direct bearing on the end. So are other persons, other times, other places. Yenan and Yalta. Marx and Mao Tse-tung. Moscow and Montreal.

But this book is not solely about Bishop Ford. He is only one figure in a short but crowded line of marching men, a chapter in an unfinished book. For this reason no pretense will be made here to give a detailed study of his life. The reason for introducing his story at this point can be served well enough by starting that story at the beginning of its end, and ending it at the beginning that will have no end.

The locale is Kaying, Kwangtung, China, two days before Christmas, 1950. Bishop Ford sits in his cathedral rectory clearing up details because he knows that time is quickly running out. It has been a year since the Reds came to Kaying, and every day the noose draws tighter. Suddenly there are the sounds of cars driving up, the running of feet, and muffled shouts. Red soldiers, acting on a prearranged plan, surround the mission, and officials of the

Provincial Police hurry inside. Some officials detain Bishop Ford in a room downstairs, while others direct searches through the rest of the house. That night Bishop Ford sleeps on the dining-room table, as two soldiers stand guard over him. The next day he is moved to his room, never to leave it until April 14, with but one exception. For the first three nights, the whole house is lighted up until dawn. Around the clock a search goes on. Every inch of space is examined—the Cathedral, the Bishop's House, the mission, the convent, the combination water-and-bell tower, the student hostel, all the outbuildings. Every book in the mission is subjected to minute scrutiny; every marked passage is noted.

The people of Kaying are shocked by the action. They know the bishop as a man of charity, a neighbor who has long lived among them. A petition is drawn up for his release, and over a thousand names are signed to it. The names are recorded by the Communists, but the petition itself ignored. A non-Christian of Kaying, a Mr. Yap, is so upset at the treatment being given to the bishop that he journeys to Canton at his own expense in the hope of having the American released. But the trip is of no avail. The Communists have plans to use Bishop Ford as the keystone of their attack on religion in China. The Chinese newspapers are filled with the fabricated charges being made against him; and even *Pravda*, in far-off Moscow, takes up the attack. An investigator is brought to Kaying from Peking to prepare "evidence" for the trial. Unending questioning of Bishop Ford begins.

On February 2, Bishop Ford is able to have a note smuggled to some of his missioners who, also, are imprisoned in the house. The bishop writes: "They kept at me for five hours steady today, and I am exhausted. Mostly questions about money to support the native priests. . . . The Big Shot lost his temper when he asked me to name one country where people are allowed to stay away from home overnight (discussing the refugees from Kiangsi, found here at the church) and I began naming besides the U.S., England and France, the South American republics, Spain, Portugal, Mexico— practically every country in the world except Russia, China, and the Iron Curtain countries. That shows what kind of picayune charges they have to resort to. They have nothing serious on me and I refuse to worry."

Toward the end of February, the other missioners under arrest in Kaying watch the guards escort Bishop Ford to the front of the new cathedral—a building that he had begun erecting after the war. The cornerstone, ordered months earlier, has arrived, and Bishop Ford is taken down to give directions where it should be placed. The priests watching from the mission window grieve to see their bishop looking pale, gaunt, haggard. The hours of unending questioning are beginning to have effect. The trumped-up charges against Bishop Ford take legal shape and are solemnly printed in papers all over China: Head of the United States spy ring, would-be saboteur of the Communist national-church movement, harborer of agents of the Kuomintang, organizer of an army to overthrow the People's Government. The propaganda would be ridiculous, except that it is taken seriously by the Reds and their dupes.

On the morning of April 14, 1951, Bishop Ford and his secretary, Sister Joan Marie, are taken from the mission by a squad of thirty soldiers. The two Americans are bound like common criminals. The bishop's hands are tied behind his back; another rope is fastened about his neck, extending down his back, and looped around his hands. Every time the weight of his hands and arms pulls downwards, his head is jerked backwards. This awkward position is made all the more painful because he is forced to carry his bedding behind him. He does this by clutching in his fingers the thin strips of bamboo with which the bedding is tied. The bamboo cuts into his fingers, and they are bleeding.

The Communists lead Bishop Ford and Sister Joan Marie through the main streets of town. Students, soldiers, and ordinary citizens are lined up along the route, while cheer leaders direct a demonstration against the missioner.

"Death to the American imperialist!"

"Death to the betrayer Ford!"

"Death to the American spy!"

The party moves to the bus station, where transportation awaits to take it to Hingning, a large market town about two hours away. The Communists telegraph ahead to Hingning officials, telling them to arrange a propaganda demonstration. The opportunity presented by Bishop Ford's transfer to Canton is too good to be overlooked.

The bus carrying Bishop Ford and his secretary is halted on the outskirts of town, and the Americans are ordered out to go by foot the rest of the way to the local jail. The Hingning officials have done their work well. The road is lined with slogan-shouting students, armed with sticks, stones, and garbage. When the students spy the American, a great roar goes up, like the roar that swells up in a huge stadium when the home team makes its first appearance. The bishop looks down the threatening line but his step does not falter. He walks slowly and deliberately into the crowd. Behind him comes Sister Joan Marie, followed by the soldiers. The roar turns to shouts and screaming. Blows begin to rain down, stones hit the bishop with sickening sounds, garbage and refuse cover him. Because of the way he has been tied, he is unable to even raise his elbows to defend himself. Curses and profanity swirl about him. Students start running up towards him, so as to get their blows in sooner. Now he is in the center of the closely packed crowd. Blow after blow strikes him. A youth spits in his face. Another jams a stick between his legs, tripping him. As he falls, kicks and blows follow him down. He struggles to his feet, and calmly continues his march.

The frenzy and hysteria of the mob mount. All order has gone out of the demonstration. The students, possessed by inculcated hatred, get completely out of hand. The soldiers, fearing that their prisoners will be killed even before the trial that is being prepared can open in Canton, try to fight their way through the mob to rescue the missioners, but it is too late—the blood-maddened students are beyond reason. They strike out at the guards to the accompaniment of curses and shouts, and the soldiers retreat to safety. Bishop Ford calmly continues his course through the gauntlet, making no protest at the flagellation. Each time he is tripped, he somehow manages to regain his feet. At last, bruised, disheveled, and covered with filth, he stumbles into the comparative safety of the Public Security Office. Sister Joan Marie, who has undergone the same treatment, follows.

The two prisoners are locked up overnight in the Hingning jail. People are brought in to see the "leader of the American spies" and to heap abuse and insults upon both prisoners.

"Where is your God now?" they cry. "What is He doing to help you? Our god is the devil. Our god has power over your God!"

The next day the two Americans are taken to Laulung. The demonstration here has to be cut short because of rain, and Sister Joan Marie is able to persuade a guard to buy some eggs and milk for the bishop—his first food since he was taken from his house in Kaying. The prisoners are led aboard a boat for Ho-yun. Here one of the guards changes the bishop's ropes for heavier ones, adding a little refinement of his own—he soaks the ropes in water before trussing the bishop up. As the ropes begin to dry, they tighten up and bite deeply into the flesh.

From Ho-yun, the suffering captives are moved to Waichow; and then to Chengmautau, to entrain for Canton. The demonstration in Chengmautau is terrible in its ridicule. Two holes—one above the other—are cut in the back of the bishop's black *saam*, the cassock-like Chinese gown he wears. A rope is tied to his hands, pulled inside the *saam*, and then out through a lower hole. The rope has the desired effect—it looks like a monkey's tail. To the laughter and jeers of the crowd, the humiliated American is led through the streets to the train. At Canton the prisoners are met by another crowd of organized demonstrators, shouting the now familiar slogans, and waving placards that could have come from previously visited villages.

The federal prison of Canton is a sprawling, red stone, cruciform structure. It is an old building, erected for the purpose of punishing prisoners and not pampering them. It is two stories high, except over one wing where the Reds added a third story to house their interrogation and "persuasion" rooms. The four elongated wings lead into a sort of rotunda, where three guards with machine guns are on constant watch. The thousands of inmates include political prisoners, murderers, thieves, pimps, prostitutes, and perpetrators of every other sort of crime. One wing is set aside for women prisoners, the remaining three are for men.

After their arrival, Bishop Ford and Sister Joan Marie are taken to separate sections of the prison and locked in reception cells. These cubicles—like all the cells of the prison—are small, narrow rooms with very high ceilings. They are dark, and they give the effect of living at the bottom of an elevator shaft. There is no furniture, and prisoners must sleep on the stone floor. The cells are not private. Sister Joan Marie is placed in a cell with seventeen other women, many of them guilty of the crudest crimes imaginable. The cell is big enough for eight people; but with seventeen, it has the semblance of a subway car at rush hour. Two cups of water are given to each prisoner daily. No clothing is furnished; no blanket, soap, towel, or washbasin. The damp and dark interior of the prison is a breeding ground for mosquitoes, but of course, no such thing as a mosquito net is available.

For the first two months, the new prisoners remain in the reception section undergoing a systematic brain-washing. This psychological treatment lasts for about twelve hours a day, but occasionally extends longer, sometimes until two or three o'clock in the morning. The sessions are bitter, full of hysteria and violence, screams and denunciations. The prisoners are living on starvation diet, suffering from malnutrition and associated diseases that place a heavy strain on the nervous system. They are always on the edge of complete nervous collapse.

When the two Americans are moved to the main section of the prison, conditions are a little better. There are still the crowded cells, the filth, the poor food; but the long brain-washing sessions end, and only brutal interrogation periods remain. Prisoners are given work to do. Sister Joan Marie becomes a water carrier, a job that lets her move in a limited way around sections of the prison, and that enables her to catch a few last glimpses of her bishop. Thus she becomes the only available witness to his final days.

In July, she gets a brief sight of Bishop Ford and rejoices that he looks fairly well. True, dark circles ring his eyes and he seems tired, but prison life is not expected to be a health cure. Long months pass, during which she does not see the bishop. The year 1951 slips into 1952, and Sister begins to worry about her superior. Then by an odd accident, she sees him again.

One day early in January, Sister Joan Marie is going about her work. On the damp stone floor of the corridor, her foot slips, and she loses her balance. Prone on the floor, she looks up at a wooden door, the bottom of which has slanted slats to permit ventilation. Through the slats she can see a stairway down which a man is laboriously descending. He is a prisoner, and over his shoulder, like a sack of potatoes, he is carrying another prisoner. From the black cotton gown, she recognizes the carried man as Bishop Ford.

At the bottom of the stairs, the prisoner slips Bishop Ford off his shoulder and stands him on his feet. The bishop's hair has turned white, and his *saam* hangs loosely on his thin frame. He has a stick to use as a cane, but he seems unable to make his feet move. He puts both arms out, standing there wavering.

"Come on. Walk!" says the other prisoner, with a laugh.

"I can't," replies the bishop.

The Chinese turns and pulls the American, as if to help him along. Bishop Ford tries to take a step forward but loses his balance. He collapses like a limp rag on the stone floor. The other prisoner squats, and the bishop throws his arms about the man's neck. Then the prisoner straightens up and carries the bishop down the corridor, out of sight.

"He must be very light," the watching Sister thinks, "because it hardly takes any effort for the other prisoner to carry him."

Two days later, Sister Joan Marie sees the bishop again. This time he is walking slowly, one arm linked in the arm of a fellow prisoner. He is very feeble. His face is emaciated and terribly aged. The soft, long white beard that had grown in prison looks like cotton. He is talking to his companion, and his face seems peaceful.

Sister sees Bishop Ford once again in February. The bishop is being carried over a prisoner's shoulders, up the stairs. But by this time malnutrition has left her so confused that she notes only the main incident and not the details.

The year moves along. It is now August 16. A guard comes for Sister Joan Marie and leads her to the Red warden's office. There she is told that Bishop Ford is dead. The warden orders her to sign a certificate stating that Bishop Ford died of illness and old age and not from ill treatment. She tries to resist, but in her shocked and weakened condition, she is no match for the Communist. She signs the certificate, noting the day of death: February 21. That was six months earlier, and only a few days after she had last seen the weakened bishop.

The news of the bishop's death proves too much for the Sister, and she falls desperately ill. She is removed to a hospital, her captors fearing that she, too, will die and then suspicion will fall upon them for two murders. It now becomes important for them to get her out of the country alive. She was only to be a witness at Bishop Ford's trial; after his death she is no longer valuable. The Communists want no martyrs, unless they are their own. That is why the charges hurled against missioners are always political ones.

On September 2, Sister Joan Marie is brought before Communist officials again. They are very solicitous as to her health. They tell her that in a few days the whole story of Bishop Ford will be released to the public. Because of the bishop's many crimes, reaction will be hard to control. It will be difficult to save her from being torn apart by the people, so to protect her life they are deporting her at once. Two officers immediately escort her to the Hong Kong border, and Sister stumbles across the barrier to freedom.

With Sister Joan Marie's release, the news of Bishop Ford's death speeds around the world. Newspapers and magazines tell of the persecution. Radio broadcasts are beamed behind the Iron Curtain. Orators eulogize the dead prelate. Memorial masses are celebrated on four continents.

Upon announcement of Bishop Ford's death, many queries pour in on Maryknoll, the mission society to which he belonged. What kind of a man was he? What gave him his greatness? What formed his mind and heart to make him a victorious soldier of Christ?

It is to answer these questions and many others that this book is written. For the spirit of Bishop Ford is the spirit of Maryknoll. The traditions that formed him are the traditions of the Society to which he gave his life. Bishop Ford's story is the Maryknoll story, and one cannot be understood without the other. It is the purpose of this book, then, to tell that story—the *who*, the *what*, the *how* and the *why* of Maryknoll. The success of any society lies not in statistics but in the men it creates. The character, actions, and accomplishments of these men are the true index to success or failure. Thus, in defining the meaning of Maryknoll, the definition necessarily must be made in human terms. So in arriving at an understanding of Maryknoll, one also arrives at an understanding of the bishop who died in the prison on Canton's Yellow Flower Road; and an understanding not only of him, but also of others—some dead, more alive—in many and varied parts of the world. This, then, is to be the story of Maryknoll, told largely in terms of the priests and Brothers who compose the Catholic Foreign Mission Society—the men of Maryknoll.

2

The Man from the Tar Heel State

The little pier four miles below Wilmington, North Carolina, was a beehive of activity. It was the early morning of Friday, September 15, 1876, and the steam packet, *Rebecca Clyde*, had put in to pick up cargo and a passenger. No one on the dock had any reason to imagine that the people assembled there were unknowingly gathered to see the ship off on her last journey, or that they were to be witnesses to the beginning of a tragic disaster. Attention was focused not on the future but on the present, the immediate departure of the *Rebecca Clyde* for Baltimore.

Among those standing on the dock that Friday morning was a middle-aged widow who had come to put her youngest child aboard the ship. She was Mrs. Clarissa Bond Price, a handsome and intelligent woman, who belonged to a respected Tar Heel family that traced its forebears back through the American Revolution. At the age of eighteen she had been converted to Catholicism, an act which so enraged her parents that she was ordered from home and disinherited. The homeless girl found shelter with a Catholic couple, Dr. and Mrs. Frederick Gallagher, who lived in a nearby town. There she began a new life, and it was there that she met Alfred Lanier Price, the young newspaperman whom later she married.

The couple were very happy. Shortly after the marriage, they moved to Wilmington, where Mr. Price became editor of the *Daily Journal*, North Carolina's first daily newspaper. Ten children were born to the union, five boys and five girls. Mr. Price, an Episcopalian, was received into the Catholic Church in 1866, six years before his death. He had been converted by the example of his wife, a modest, devout and charitable woman who spent long hours in prayer.

Alongside Mrs. Price on the dock that fateful Friday morning was her youngest son, Fred—one month beyond his sixteenth birthday, having been born on August 19, 1860. The boy's full name was Thomas Frederick Price—Thomas after Mr. Price's father, and Frederick after Dr. Gallagher. His family and friends used the middle name. Fred was a smiling, cheerful boy, who had inherited the best characteristics of his parents—from his father, a keen mind and an inclination towards journalism; from his mother, something even more valuable, his deep religious sense. On his sixteenth birthday, Fred announced that he wanted to study for the priesthood, much to the delight of his gentle mother, who had already seen two of her daughters enter the convent. Arrangements were made for Fred to go to St. Charles College in Maryland, and thus it was for the purpose of traveling to Baltimore to begin his studies for the priesthood that young Fred Price was on the Wilmington dock that September morning.

A blast from the whistle of the *Rebecca Clyde* cut short the last good-bys. Fred kissed his mother and hurried aboard ship. Mrs. Price's heart was heavy, for this was her first separation from her son, and since the death of her husband she had come to rely on the boy. To the accompaniment of shouts of farewell, she waved to Fred as the little coastwise vessel pulled away from Wilmington, out into the center of the Cape Fear River, where another son, Joseph, had drowned some years earlier. The eight passengers, standing at the rail and watching Wilmington disappear, had no inkling of the tragedy that lay ahead. Down the river the little boat steamed, stopping at Smithville (now Southport) for additional passengers. On Saturday, it went past Smith Island, and into the open Atlantic.

A week earlier, winds had begun to form far out in the ocean opposite the Florida coast. Slowly they gained momentum, spinning around in a great circle, gathering up water and darkening the sky. A hurricane had been born and began moving northward, its path and that of the *Rebecca Clyde* destined to cross just below Cape Hatteras.

All Saturday the little steamer made its way northward, the anxious Captain Childs keeping a careful watch on the threatening sea. Dark clouds began to fill the sky, and gusts of wind roared down on the boat. Fred Price, an inexperienced sailor, stayed in his bunk. As the ship tossed and twisted in the rising swells, he had all he could do to keep from being thrown from his bed. On Saturday night the winds grew stronger and the sea rougher. Soon the full force of the hurricane surrounded the battered *Rebecca Clyde*. Foaming white water poured over her decks, some of it getting down into the cabins and hold. The boat became heavier and heavier, sinking lower into the water. Sunday morning came, and the storm continued unabated. Bruised and wounded, the *Rebecca Clyde* was almost impossible to handle. She no longer had sufficient power to be easily maneuvered. Deck cargo broke loose and smashed the steering gear. Four crewmen had been washed overboard. Suddenly near noon a man appeared at the head of the gangway and shouted down to the sick and frightened boy at prayer in his bunk.

"Abandon ship! We're going on the shoals! Abandon ship!" Fred heard the man scream against the background of roaring wind.

The continuous gyrations of the doomed ship made walking and balance difficult, but somehow Fred managed to get to the deck. Passengers and crew were already deserting the ship. It was impossible to launch a boat in the tempest, and the only way to escape was to jump overboard and pray that death would not come from being crushed on the Hatteras shoals, which lie far out from the mainland. But to his horror, Fred discovered that no life preservers were left on the vessel. It was every man for himself, and the crew had taken the life preservers. For the youth who couldn't swim, death seemed inevitable.

Fred made his way along the deck, seeking some sort of protection. He clung to the rail, and he hung on to ropes. Huge waves were washing over the stricken vessel. There was a grinding crunch as the boat struck a shoal. It began to keel over. At the same instant, a mountainous wave poured down on the boat. Its tremendous power bore the boy up and over the side, and away into the mad sea.

"Christ Jesus, save me or I perish!" cried the drowning boy as he disappeared in the waves.

The late Cardinal O'Connell, of Boston, who had been Fred Price's classmate at St. Charles, tells the rest of the story in his autobiography, *Recollections of Seventy Years*. He states that he had heard rumors of the shipwreck from one of the priests on the faculty and therefore persuaded his friend, Fred Price, to tell the story. Fred was at first reluctant, but finally agreed when the future Cardinal promised to keep the story in confidence.

"Bashfully, in a quiet but assured tone of voice, this young saint related the authentic story which thrilled me to the depths of my soul," the Cardinal reports. "I cannot here reproduce the simple yet tremendously moving picture then portrayed by him, but as I go back in memory, the same touch of mysticism which then I felt comes back to me."

The Cardinal next relates Fred's story up to the moment he disappeared into the sea, calling on Christ for help. Then the Cardinal continues:

"Like a flash the sky seemed to open, and out of a speck of blue came the clearest possible vision, as clear as he saw the howling waves about him—Mary, the Mother of Christ, appeared before his eyes. Upon her face was a smile, and, gently stretching forth her hand, she pointed to a great floating plank, which had been washed overboard from the sinking ship. With a few heroic strokes he gained the plank, and grasping a great ring on its upper surface, he swung, now up, now down, feeling nothing and thinking of the vision, which would always remain indelibly imprinted on his soul. He began the Litany of the Blessed Virgin, and as he said, 'In my joy I almost sang it.'"

Hour after hour Fred clung to the plank as the storm raged about him. At last the plank driven in towards land was tossed by a breaker on to shore. The half-dead boy pulled himself up over rocks and sand to safety before he collapsed from exhaustion. It was here that rescuers found him. He was brought to Portsmouth, a tiny village on the ocean side of Pamlico Sound where he learned that only seven others survived the shipwreck. Captain Childs, his two mates, two engineers, the steward, three seamen, two coal heavers, and a passenger had perished in the sea. Five days later, still shocked and sick from his experience, the derelict boy, bereft of all his possessions, arrived back at his mother's house in Wilmington.

One of those rescued was a young Wilmingtonian of a prominent family, Mr. J. M. Cronly. In a statement issued to the papers after the disaster, he said: "Mr. Price only let go of the hull when it was washed from under him, and on coming to the surface grasped a piece of the vessel which was near him and gradually drifted to shore. His escape was certainly miraculous as he was unable to swim."

Fred Price finally reached St. Charles College in time for the February term. He proved himself to be a solid student, not brilliant or extraordinary. He impressed everyone with his good humor, his generosity, his piety, and his remarkable devotion to the Blessed Virgin. In 1881, his college course finished, he entered St. Mary's Seminary in Baltimore. The years of classroom routine passed slowly. At last on June 20, 1886, he was ordained in Wilmington, the first North Carolinian ever to reach the priesthood.

Only one thing marred Father Price's ordination day, and that was the fact that his mother was not present. That good woman had died the year before. The devout widow had made many sacrifices to keep her son in the seminary, and Father Price felt sure that her many prayers had gained for him spiritual strength at the time he needed it most. He felt sure of one other thing, too, and that was the fact that his mother was in heaven.

Shortly before her death, Father Moore, her pastor, who was partially paralyzed and blind so that he was no longer able to say Mass or read the missal and breviary, had said to her: "Mrs. Price, you will soon be with Almighty God. When you see Him, will you ask Him to give me back my eyesight, so that I may be able to read Mass again?"

On the morning after Mrs. Price's death, Father Moore was able to read the missal and say Mass.

The following Sunday, during Mass at the parish church, Mrs. Price's eight-year-old grandson screamed and had to be taken out of church. "Mama!" he exclaimed, "I saw Grandma! She was up over the altar, and a man was there on one side, and a beautiful lady on the other. They were all dressed in spangles. Mama, Grandma was so pretty!"

The parish record reads simply: "July 25, 1885, died Clarissa Bond Price, full of good works and deeds."

Immediately after ordination, Father Price took charge of his home parish in Wilmington while his pastor, Father Moore, left on a visit to his home in Ireland. Upon the pastor's return, Father Price was given charge of a rural area in the eastern section of the state, embracing about three hundred square miles. He covered this territory by train, horse and buggy, and foot. The rural population was intensely prejudiced against Catholics, of whose doctrines and customs they were entirely ignorant; and work among such people was very difficult.

Riding on the train one day, Father Price was interrupted in reading his breviary by an elderly spinster sitting nearby.

"Aren't you a stranger in these parts?" asked the woman.

"No, I'm a Tar Heel," answered Father Price.

"Oh, I thought you looked like a papist priest," explained the woman.

"I'm a Roman Catholic priest."

"Is it true that you popish priests have horns?" inquired the woman.

With a flourish, Father Price removed his hat and pointed to a tiny pimple on his forehead. "I'm only a young priest," he answered with a straight face. "Mine are just beginning to come out."

Sometimes the opposition took stronger measures. One day Father Price stopped in a country store to buy some crackers and cheese for his lunch. As the storekeeper wrapped the purchase he studied his customer.

"You Priest Price?" he finally asked.

"Yes, I'm—"

"No sale!" exclaimed the man curtly as he unwrapped the package.

In 1888, Father Price took charge of St. Paul's Church in New Bern, and its seventeen missions. One of his missions was Goldsboro, where he built the first church of his own, dedicating it to the Mother of God, to whom he had very great devotion. He was an energetic and tireless apostle, with a deep understanding of Tar

Heel prejudices and customs. People soon began to overlook the fact that he was a Catholic priest and accepted him for the man he was. More and more came to hear his plain but touching sermons. Fallen-away Catholics were brought back to the practice of their Faith, and slowly the number of his converts began to grow.

In 1895, Father Price became pastor of Sacred Heart Church, Raleigh. Up to this time, he had not projected his thinking very far into the future. He covered his large mission territory, preaching and praying, administering the sacraments, and doing good work. He longed to see every Tar Heel a Catholic, but he had not worked out any systematic or long-range method. However, just before going to Raleigh, he had begun to think of new approaches to the apostolate of the South; and in his envisioning, he began to see a large-scale mission movement headed by some society or congregation that could specialize in training missioners. He had come to believe that the ordinary seminary training was not sufficient for a mission apostolate.

About this time he began to give missions to non-Catholics. Wherever bigotry was strongest, there was Father Price to explain doubts, answer questions, and create understanding of the Catholic Church. He soon sensed a new need—the need for a publication that could promote the ideas he was preaching. Gradually a plan took shape in his mind, and at last he approached his ecclesiastical superior, Bishop Haid, of the Benedictine Abbey at Belmont, and asked permission to start a monthly magazine.

Bishop Haid, a realistic man, pointed out the difficulties. There were only eight hundred Catholics in the whole State, and it would be impossible for them to support such a venture. The bishop himself had no money.

"I have thirty-five dollars," Father Price replied. "That's enough to get five hundred copies of the first issue."

"But what about the next issue, and the one after that?"

"God and Our Lady will keep it going," replied the priest firmly.

The bishop, who knew that God and Our Lady had settled other problems for Father Price, decided to let him go ahead. Thus the magazine *Truth* was born. By what means that monthly succeeded, was (and still is) a great mystery. Father Price was too busy to solicit subscriptions, and the writing and editing of *Truth* had to be done as he traveled around the State. But the magazine did succeed. Before long it had a circulation of five thousand; then twelve thousand; and it continued to grow until 120,000 copies were appearing monthly.

In his travels in North Carolina, Father Price encountered many impoverished families, unable to support their children. He also met homeless boys, wandering about the State, seeking to find a way to keep themselves alive. Something must be done for them, he reasoned, and he decided to do something. He would establish an orphanage. Again there was the problem of money with which to start, but once more Father Price showed that he was not depending for support solely on this world. No one knows how he purchased some six hundred acres on a hill overlooking the campus of North Carolina State College—a site that gave an impressive view to the east of the city of Raleigh. But he found the money somewhere, and he had his orphanage which he named Nazareth.

The orphanage prospered and grew. More and more boys were received. Sisters of Mercy were brought in to care for them, with Father Price's sister, Mother Catherine, as Superior. He began another publication, *The Orphan Boy*, for the purpose of raising funds to help support the orphanage.

Meanwhile, Father Price still carried on his apostolic work of direct contact with the people. At the turn of the century, two other priests were assigned to assist Father Price, and this gave him the opportunity to spread farther afield. New outmissions were attached to Nazareth, and new areas were added to the Sunday Mass schedule. In the year 1903 alone, Father Price built eight small rural chapels. His formula of "God and Our Lady" was working well.

But Father Price was filled with a divine unrest. His views were never constricted by past accomplishments, and as time progressed his horizons opened wider and wider. As his next move he purchased twenty acres of land across the road from Nazareth, and began to build a seminary where missioners for the rural districts of North Carolina would be trained, and if all worked well the priests might be spread throughout the needy areas of the entire South. The new building was called *Regina Apostolorum*—Queen of the Apostles. The seminary was not a large structure, although it was three stories high. He designed it to hold forty students. The building was still in an unfinished state when the first twenty-five students reported, in the fall of 1902.

With the Apostolate underway, Father Price then instituted a plan that had long been in his mind. He invited seminarians from Northern seminaries to spend parts of their summer vacations in North Carolina; he said that they could gain valuable experience, and in return would do badly needed catechetical work. Seminarians from St. Joseph's Seminary in Yonkers, New York, and from St. Mary's in Baltimore, responded. Working out of Nazareth, they conducted missions and taught catechism, often being away from the home base as long as two weeks at a time. The life was rugged and difficult, but the young seminarians thrived on it and edified the Tar Heels with whom they came in contact. Many of those seminarians eventually held important positions in their home dioceses, and all of them were noted for their apostolic spirit, the growth of which could be traced to Father Price.

A severe setback, from which the young Apostolate never fully recovered, was experienced early one Sunday morning in the fall of 1905. Father Price was aroused from sleep by one of the students, who was screaming that the building was on fire. Father Price hurried from his room and found the corridors filled with smoke and flames. There was no escape by the stairs. A few students had already managed to get out of the inferno, but the majority, together with the priests and a visitor, were trapped on the second and third floors. There was nothing to do but jump from the windows. No one perished in the fire, but one boy died from injuries sustained when he jumped from the third floor, and several others were seriously hurt. The building was reduced to broken walls. For all practical purposes, it was the end of the Apostolate. A new building was later erected, this time fireproof. But Father Price was rapidly approaching an hour of decision, and when that time came, the authorities allowed the Apostolate to fade out of existence.

During the immediate years that followed, Father Price's horizons expanded beyond North Carolina, beyond the South, beyond America, to the whole world. The pages of *Truth*, which had become one of the most important mission voices of the Church in America, revealed this world-outlook development. In one of his editorials, Father Price commented: "The mission movement seems to be gaining momentum all along the line . . . The foreign missioner is the very cream of Catholic life."

In 1908, Father Price met Father (later Bishop) John J. Dunn,

Propagation of the Faith Director of the New York Archdiocese. After the meeting he confided to his diary: "Both Father Dunn and I discussed the Foreign Mission Seminary and its adjunct, and the idea of our going into it came up. But I fear it is too faraway —running ahead of God's Providence, but oh! how I long to establish that work and lead a band to the foreign-mission field and die a martyr."

The founding of a seminary to train priests for foreign-mission work was being discussed in some parts of the United States, but little of a practical nature was happening. A Boston publication, called *The Field Afar*, and edited by a Father James Anthony Walsh, was promoting the idea. Father Price read this magazine avidly for nourishment of his own dreams, but its ideas seemed to be in the abstract—words on paper and nothing more. In his diary for 1909 he wrote, "The foreign-mission development is the true and full end of my work." That same year, he outlined in *Truth* some of his ideas on the subject. He saw a major seminary centrally located, with preparatory seminaries spread around the country— New York, Boston, Chicago, St. Louis and San Francisco.

"At the present time," he wrote, "the Church in the United States is sending out almost no missioners to foreign countries. In a few years this is likely to be changed. We look for the Catholics of the United States to become the greatest mission force in the world, and therein lies the salvation of the Church in the United States . . . The matter of missions will not down. It lies in the very essence of Catholicity, and it is shameful that we do so little."

Father Price had presented himself with a challenge. He was encouraging others to take active part in the foreign-mission movement, and he was enough of a realist to know that what he directed others to do, he must first do himself. He decided to seek out his answer in a retreat at Belmont Abbey, because it was in these hours when he was alone with God that he reached his real decisions. But before making the retreat, there was one other thing he must do. That was to pay his homage to his Eucharistic Lord at the first Eucharistic Congress to be held in the Western world. So in September of 1910 he journeyed north to Montreal on pilgrimage, hoping that God would bless him with sufficient grace so that he would know what to do with his life. All his reasoning told him that he must become an active part of the foreign-mission movement; but on the other hand, he realized the tremendous responsibilities he had built up over the years in North Carolina.

On the morning of September 10, he was breakfasting at the Hochelaga Convent in Montreal, preparatory to going to the great outdoor Mass at Fletcher Field. Other priests at the table were carrying on a conversation, when Father Price's own reveries were broken by the mention of a name—"Father Walsh."

"Father Walsh of Boston? The editor of *The Field Afar*? Is he here?" inquired Father Price.

"Yes," answered Father Conaty, who had mentioned the name. "He is staying with Mayor Michaud at Maisonneuve. I met him last night at a band concert."

"I must see him!" exclaimed the North Carolinian, hurrying from the table to a telephone.

Father Walsh was just leaving Maisonneuve when the call came through. When the Boston priest heard Madame Michaud at the telephone, he got a strange and sudden impression that Father Price of North Carolina was calling and asking for him.

He went to the instrument and heard an excited voice: "This is Father Price of Nazareth, Father Walsh. I must see you immediately!"

"I am just leaving for Fletcher Field," answered the Bostonian, "but if you can come at once, I'll wait for you."

"Don't leave!" begged Father Price. "I'll be there in five minutes."

Father Walsh agreed to wait, and Father Price hurried from the convent. It seemed to him that a prayer had been answered, as if the voice of God were in the chance remark that had been heard at the breakfast table. Father Price almost ran up the hilly Montreal streets. Ahead of him lay—he knew not what. Could it be China? Could it be the fulfillment of his dreams? Father Walsh would tell him what to do.

3

A Moment in Boston

When the benevolent but ill-fated Emperor of Brazil, Dom Pedro II, paid a visit to Boston in 1876, the whole town was organized in civic celebration to bid him welcome. Among the events scheduled was a reception in historic Faneuil Hall, at which a Boston schoolboy was to give one of those stilted and unnatural recitations so popular before the turn of the century. To select this young performer, an elocution competition was held in the city's public schools, and a nine-year-old student at the Dwight School was named the winner.

For young Jimmy Walsh, to whom the honor came, this was to be his first public appearance in a city in which he was to become something of a celebrity. As far as we know, it was also the boy's first contact with any foreign land. Neither history nor the press of that day records with what success the oration was delivered. Likewise, it is not chronicled just how the son of an Irish immigrant (even if he was a successfully prosperous Irish immigrant) should have been selected to greet royalty in a tradition-bound city of considerable class consciousness. We are only left to conclude that the boy won the honor through his own outstanding qualities which even at that early age must have set him apart from the crowd.

James Anthony Walsh was born in Cambridge, Massachusetts, on February 24, 1867, to James and Hannah Shea Walsh. Mr. and Mrs. Walsh had both come to Boston from County Cork, and at the time of James' birth were already American citizens. James was to be the second oldest of six children. A third son, Timothy, was destined to become one of the most prominent ecclesiastical architects of the country, and one of the founders of the firm of Maginnis and Walsh, which even today is designing buildings for all parts of our nation.

Mrs. Walsh was an educated, cultured woman of great refinement. She set high standards for herself and for her children, and was determined that they would all become proper ladies and gentlemen. She had a library full of good books, not for decoration, but for her children's use. She tested all her youngsters for musical abilities, found Jimmy to be the best, and saw to it that he developed a proficiency at the piano. She was not a martinet, however. Every Sunday evening the family gathered in the parlor for a session at singing, telling stories, and play-acting. Mrs. Walsh was raising a family of normal, healthy, happy, and well-mannered children. She was, in every sense of the word, a truly Christian mother.

When Jimmy was eleven years old, his mother became ill with pneumonia and died. It was a severe blow to the young boy. It is also testimony to the strength of his mother's character that she had so shaped her son during those few formative years that the remarkable qualities of James Anthony Walsh, the man, could be traced back to the direct influence of Hannah Shea Walsh, the mother.

Apart from the death of his mother, young James Anthony led an ordinary normal boyhood existence. He received good marks at the Dwight School without studying too hard. He was popular in his games. He became an altar boy at the Jesuit Church of The Immaculate Conception. When he finished public grammar school, he went on to the Jesuits' Boston College High School, where he did well in studies and was known for his extracurricular activities of debating and journalism.

In 1884 he entered Boston College. He was somewhat disorientated about what he wished to do with his life. For a long time he had been debating the idea of the priesthood but something seemed to be holding him back. He entered college, confused and uncertain. When his father suffered a financial reverse, young Walsh withdrew from college with a notion of supporting himself. But Mr. Walsh's business crisis was soon over, and his son no longer had that as an excuse for not continuing his studies. Still drifting like a rudderless boat, James Anthony signed up at Harvard University.

To those few intimates who knew something of the boy's doubts about his vocation, the choice of Harvard University seemed a clear indication that he had at last become settled in his mind. No one who wanted to become a priest would go to Harvard, for the University in those days was the center of a materialistic cult at which both Catholics and orthodox Protestants looked askance. Harvard certainly was no place to find a vocation, but it was a place in which one might lose his faith. Still drifting, young Walsh entered the Harvard Yard daily, but it was more of a physical than spiritual presence. His scholastic record at Harvard was far from brilliant. His highest mark was a 78 in Latin. But at Harvard, he did learn one important thing.

"I discovered," he said later in life, "that I did not belong there."

And with this discovery, came decision. He revealed it to his family at the end of the college year. He planned to enter Boston's two-year-old Seminary—St. John's, in Brighton—that autumn. He was going to become a priest.

The life of every man is touched by outside forces that mold and shape him—influences that direct the turnings of the road over which he must journey. James Anthony Walsh had three such influences: his mother, who formed his character; the Sulpician Fathers, who molded his thinking; and Father Thomas Frederick Price, who acted as a catalyst in an hour of indecision.

At the outbreak of the French Revolution, Bishop John Carroll had invited the French Sulpicians to Baltimore. They accepted the invitation and came to this country to staff St. Mary's Seminary. Men of towering vision and dedicated purpose, they spared no efforts in the training of the seminarians given to their charge. The priests they sent out were the men who built the Catholicism we know in America today. The young men they trained were the pioneers as religion and America moved westward across a

continent. When the Archdiocese of Boston opened its new seminary, it was only natural that the priests of Saint Sulpice should
be asked to take it in charge.

These were the men under whose influence came the young
Harvard dandy. They received a boy and fashioned a man.

The rector of St. John's Seminary was Abbé Hogan, a brilliantly
competent man of extraordinary personality. It was Abbé Hogan
who gave to young Walsh a live realization of the fact that the
Catholic Church extended beyond Boston, indeed even beyond
the United States to the whole world. Of course, everyone at
Brighton knew that he belonged to a world-wide Church. But
knowing the fact and having an active realization of it are two
completely different things.

Abbé Hogan spoke often of a young Frenchman with whom he
had been ordained in Paris. This young priest, named Theophane Venard, had joined the Paris Foreign Mission Society and
had gone off to Indo-China as a missioner, where he had met death
in one of the periodic persecutions that took place in that part
of the Asian world. It was a particularly violent death by behead-
ing, and also a very beautiful one. Through letters and diaries of
the martyr, Abbé Hogan made Theophane Venard come alive to
his students. The impression made on James Anthony Walsh was
a deep one, only partly to be gauged by the fact that he was to
publish a life of the martyr, visit the Frenchman's home and family, and name his first preparatory seminary after him.

Another Sulpician who had a tremendous influence on young
Walsh was Father Gabriel André. That French priest never tired
of talking missions, and he found a kindred spirit in the young
seminarian from Boston College and Harvard. Father André was
in correspondence with missioners all over the world, and teacher
and student spent many hours together perusing these dispatches.
One letter that James Anthony read at this time was to remain
long in his memory. He was to quote from it more than a quarter
of a century later during a conference to some Sisters.

"I am writing to you, my classmate," stated this letter. "It is
sixteen years since I left the seminary, with the fervor of youth
and a strong desire to shed my blood for Christ. These sixteen
years have passed in hard work, with very poor results. I have accomplished little and have come to the conclusion that nothing

can be done in this district until some man's blood has been spilled; and I tell you in all sincerity, as friend to friend, coldly, far from that fervor of the young apostle—that if tomorrow I were called upon to meet death for Christ and souls, I should be the happiest of men."

Father André and James Anthony Walsh entered into a partnership. Their capital was prayer, and this they invested in the foreign missions. Their odd hours took other practical bents, too. Between them they raised the money each year to support a catechist in Japan. Together they wrote a column for *The Sacred Heart Review*, a Cambridge publication; the column aimed at stirring up interest in the missions among Americans, whose own country was still under the jurisdiction of the Congregation for the Propagation of the Faith, which listed the United States as a mission land. The column brought in donations that were quickly dispatched missionwards.

In this manner the years passed quickly at Brighton. James Anthony Walsh had come to the Sulpician Fathers as a somewhat confused young collegian. On May 20, 1892, he was ordained a priest. He left the tutelage of the Sulpicians as a man—and what was even more important—as an apostle. Ahead lay a wide road. When he walked out onto it with his first assignment, he could not but wonder where that road was to take him.

Father Walsh's appointment was to St. Patrick's Parish in Roxbury, a very busy parish with over eighteen thousand souls, most of whom were of Irish stock. One resident of the parish was a man whose fame had spread far beyond Boston: the heavyweight champion of the world, John L. Sullivan. In addition to the regular parochial duties of counsel, confession, and other sacramental administration, the new curate was put in charge of the Holy Name Society, the Young Ladies' Sodality, the altar boys, and the altar itself.

With characteristic zeal, Father Walsh threw himself completely into the work, and with the initiative of youth he instituted a number of changes in the organizations in his charge. For the Holy Name Society he instituted an annual retreat. He put together a hymnal (containing a number of his own compositions) for the Young Ladies. Among his altar boys he looked for possible vocations to the priesthood; and when he found one, he did everything he could to encourage it. One vocational prospect was young William Finn, who was to become founder and director of the internationally famous Paulist Choir.

During those very busy years, a casual observer might think that Father Walsh had forgotten the foreign missions. Actually they were always close to his thoughts. When after several years he was able to take a vacation in Europe, a trip promised him by his father after his ordination, it was not merely a mere sightseeing jaunt. He visited the grave of Abbé Hogan, and spent fruitful days in Paris with Father André. When he returned to Boston, he gave a slide lecture of his travels, which showed the Paris Foreign Mission Society in France, Mill Hill's Foreign Mission Society in England, and the Milan Foreign Mission Society in Italy. He spoke about Theophane Venard and the seminary from which the young French missioner went forth to martyrdom.

In 1897, the Society for the Propagation of the Faith was started in the United States. Archbishop Williams, of Boston, immediately began a branch, and appointed a Boston priest, Dr. Joseph V. Tracy, who had been teaching in St. Mary's Seminary in Baltimore, as director for the archdiocese. For five years, Dr. Tracy fought an uphill battle trying to get the mission idea across to priests and people. Because foreign-mission work was a new idea, and the people were not trained to think about it, Dr. Tracy met with great difficulties. By the end of five years, his diocesan office had an annual income of $25,000, but the ex-professor was literally killing himself raising the sum.

One day in March of 1903, Father Walsh was reading the daily paper when he noticed an item reporting that Dr. Tracy's health had broken down and that he was being assigned to a parish.

"There wasn't any reason why the thought should come to me," related Father Walsh later, "but I said to myself, as soon as I noted the paragraph, 'I am going to be the next director of the Propagation of the Faith in the archdiocese.' I smiled and wondered why that thought should have come to me at all, and so strongly. Then I put it out of my mind.

"The following morning, Saturday . . . I went into the garden to say some Office. By this time I had quite forgotten about the Propagation of the Faith, but as I happened to look up, I saw a man with a beard go to the front door. As the maid opened it, I said to myself, 'That is Father Freri, the Central Director of the

Propagation of the Faith, and he has come to ask me to take Dr. Tracy's position.' "

A few moments later the maid called Father Walsh. The young priest's intuition was right. The bearded man was Monsignor Joseph Freri, and he had called to ask Father Walsh to take over the Boston office. When the latter learned that Archbishop Williams had given permission for the arrangement, he agreed. The next Monday the new director was at his desk. As he sat down in the office for the first time he said to himself, "I am going to stay in this work, in some form or another, for the rest of my life." It was a promise he was to keep.

Now that Father Walsh was on the "inside," he was amazed to discover how few English-speaking missioners there were in the foreign field. The thought began to weigh heavily upon him. The immediate problem, however, was one of funds, and to that he turned his full attention. In his first year, he doubled Dr. Tracy's income; next, he tripled it; and then quadrupled it. He made the Catholics of the Boston area aware of the missions. The amount of money he brought in during his first year as director was one fourth of the money contributed by the entire United States, and more than any other diocese in the world.

The celebrated Paulist missioner, Father Walter Elliott, wrote to Father Walsh: "Only yesterday I read the good news that Boston heads all Catholic Christendom in contributing to the propagation of our Holy Faith. Sincere congratulations to you, who are the chief cause under God, for so favorable a result. And I know that you will not 'let well enough alone'; but will set all so magnificent an example of zeal for souls, united to fine organizing methods . . . to place the Church in America . . . in the forefront of all Catholic missionary enterprise among the heathen."

Besides the lack of American missioners, one other need was bothering Boston's new director of the Society for the Propagation of the Faith. This was the paucity of good reading material on missionary topics. In 1906, he decided that the official publication, *Annals of the Propagation of the Faith*, was not interesting enough and suffered too much in being translated from the French. He recalled that in his travels among the Boston parishes, he frequently found piles of undistributed *Annals* in parish barns. He asked the National Director, Monsignor Freri, if it would be possible to have an American mission magazine. Monsignor Freri declared such a project impossible. Father Walsh then decided that, if he couldn't start such a magazine as part of his Propagation work, he would start one independently.

Father Walsh called together three of his friends: Father John I. Lane; Father James F. Stanton; and Father Joseph Bruneau, a Sulpician. They talked over the problem and decided to form the Catholic Foreign Mission Bureau and publish a mission magazine. In January, 1907, the first issue of *The Field Afar* appeared, and at the same time the monthly magazine *Catholic Missions* began in New York. The purpose of *The Field Afar* was ostensibly to spread knowledge of the missions, but in the records of the little group an unannounced purpose was set down: "To prepare the way for a Catholic Foreign Mission Seminary in this country."

It was not Father Walsh's opinion in 1907 that an entirely new society should be started. He envisioned the Paris Foreign Mission Society setting up a branch in this country. New York's Cardinal Farley, hearing that the anticlerical French Government might suppress the Paris organization, hoped to bring some of its priests to this country and start a mission seminary near Troy. But the Cardinal's invitation was declined. The English foreign mission society—St. Joseph's, at Mill Hill—likewise was not able to establish a branch in America. Father Walsh broached the idea of an American mission seminary to Archbishop Williams, of Boston, and was put off with the reply, "It will come in time."

Meanwhile the Catholic Foreign Mission Bureau was having great success with *The Field Afar*. The subscription list of the publication grew steadily, and circulation was nation-wide. Father Walsh was a great believer in photo-journalism long before *Life* made the term popular. For his magazine, he used all the pictures he could get, and besieged missioners all over the world for more. The Bureau also published a number of books: *Thoughts from Modern Martyrs*, a collection from the letters and reports of French missioners who had met violent deaths; *A Modern Martyr*, the life and letters of Theophane Venard; *An American Missionary in Alaska*, a biography of Father William Judge, S.J.

But through all those busy days, persisted the nagging conviction that something ought to be done about starting an American society for foreign missions. A society was needed, he believed, not only for spreading the work of the Church in distant lands, but also for the good of America. Without a sense of service and participation in the apostolic work abroad, the Church at home would suffer from lack of vocations and growth. Unless American Catholics were one hundred per cent Catholics, their spiritual lives were defective and incomplete. The logic was convincing.

In the spring of 1910, a French Dominican, Father Bertrand Cothonay, who had been a missioner in the Far East, called at Father Walsh's office. The two men had an interesting chat, during which the subject of a foreign-mission society in America was discussed. Father Cothonay then returned to Hawthorne, New York, where he was superior of a small community. When the Dominican was at home, he wrote to Father Walsh urging him to visit New York for the purpose of discussing several important matters.

It was August before Father Walsh was able to get to Hawthorne. He spent a week end with Father Cothonay, and the Dominican outlined a plan he had drawn up. He suggested that the permission of Archbishop Farley, of New York, be obtained to start a seminary on land adjoining the Dominican property in Hawthorne. Father Cothonay and his fellow Dominicans could arrange to teach at the seminary. The Dominican emphasized strongly, however, that control of the seminary should be in the hands of secular priests—that the new undertaking must be a movement of the American diocesan clergy. Then he asked Father Walsh if he would take over the direction of such a seminary.

Here was a challenge put bluntly to the Boston priest. Father Walsh was unable to give a definite answer. The idea appealed strongly to him, but he foresaw difficulties; a major one was that Archbishop O'Connell, the new head of the Boston Archdiocese, might be reluctant to release him for such a project. Then, too, he was doing remunerative work for the missions in Boston. Why risk all on a new venture that might or might not succeed? The Boston priest spent many prayerful hours over the project after his return to his usual duties.

Still undecided, Father James Anthony Walsh planned to attend the Eucharistic Congress in Montreal. There would be an abundance of grace there, and perhaps God would give him an answer. In this frame of mind, he journeyed to Canada, and his meeting in Montreal with Father Price—the meeting in which the Catholic Foreign Mission Society would be practically conceived.

4

Three Letters

When Father Price joined Father Walsh at Maisonneuve on that autumn morning of 1910, the two priests went immediately to Fletcher Field for the celebration of the outdoor Mass of the Eucharistic Congress. They were accompanied by Father Crane, of Boston, who took the first (and actually one of the very few) photograph of the cofounders of Maryknoll. When the Mass ended, Father Walsh and Father Price adjourned to the lobby of the Windsor Hotel to discuss their mutual interest. Friends of both men who passed them in the lobby later told how the two were so wrapped up in their own conversation that they noticed nothing going on about them.

The meeting of the two priests in Montreal was too short to cover all points needing discussion. It did, however, provide the stimulus for each priest to decide to enter the work actively. At the conclusion, Father Price agreed to go to Boston at the first opportunity to visit his former classmate, Archbishop O'Connell. The Southerner assured the Bostonian that the meeting with the Archbishop would probably remove any obstacles in the way of securing Father Walsh's release for the work.

In the weeks that followed, the two men entered into a correspondence in which each man fully revealed his mind. Father Walsh shows himself the practical organizer, weighing every factor. Father Price appears as a man of zeal and humility, who wants to put no obstacles in the way of success, even if success should mean his withdrawal from the work. The letters reveal, also, that there were several misunderstandings following the Montreal meeting.

Father Price to Father Walsh:

My dear Father Walsh,

I write you glad tidings of great joy. The unanimous decision of our conference in St. Mary's Seminary, Baltimore, was that I should begin this work of the Foreign Mission Seminary and I am now seriously making preparations which I trust will materialize into a formal opening of the work next fall. I cannot contain the joy of my heart or find words to express my great happiness. It is as though I had lived my life of 50 years to prepare myself for this which at length is at hand. There is another thing and it concerns yourself. We decided or rather gave our opinion, that you ought to come into this work with me; that you ought to get someone else to take your place in your present work and throw your lot into this. Now I want you to pray earnestly over this matter and examine it carefully before God to see if it be not the Divine Will that you do this thing. I will myself be praying earnestly for you and I will have all our people in my work do the same thing. I regard the settlement of this matter about yourself going in with me as one of the most important preliminaries and do not wish to take any vital step until a decision is made. So please let me hear from you in regard to it. I feel sure we could get your Archbishop to consent.

In the conference we were all of the opinion that the work should be started at Washington near the University but in such a way as to secure our own environment and purposes fully—that there at Washington we should begin with at least a preparatory course of classics; that the training of the young men and spirit be absolutely in our own hands; that as it would be impossible for us to have our own professors for some years we should send the students for classes elsewhere, and then when able should send our own men to establish our apostolic schools in Boston, New York and other places throughout the country.

What I think we should do is to begin in a humble modest

way and work forward as God in His own ways and times makes development clear. We could as a start either rent a place nearby or buy a small plot of ground in the neighborhood and erect what modest cheap buildings may be necessary until God opens the way for permanent location.

I have also spoken *confidentially* with Monsignor Shahan, Rector of the University, and he promises the most cordial support. We had a long talk last night of several hours and he went over the ground giving me his views, telling me he had for many years thought over the matter and heartily desired its being brought about. He affirmed substantially the same views we had all expressed in the Baltimore conference.

What I am doing just now is looking into the practical ways and means without taking any positive steps. When I have cleared these up, I will propose to my Bishop that it is necessary for me to establish this seminary and I have reason to be fairly certain that he will give his consent. You see for a number of years I have been carrying on our establishment in which we were training young men for our work and sending them to his Seminary at Belmont. Experience has demonstrated clearly that that mode of procedure is absolutely futile—I have worn it out to a frazzle—I am sure it is clear to him that it cannot go further. If I did not establish this Seminary for Foreign Missions the work at Nazareth would utterly perish. God has made that so clear that I am sure the Bishop cannot fail to realize it. When I have his consent, I will draw my own work at Nazareth in such shape that I can commit its running to other hands, though I will likely retain my grip on it. I have, however, some heavy works to finish there which will take some time and I doubt whether I will be fully free till next June.

When this is accomplished, I wish to go *with you* to Europe and study the Paris Seminary, Mill Hill and other places practically, and with you draw a definite plan and lines of action though I would like, as I feel sure it would be the true basis, to preserve as far as would serve our purpose the *Modus Vivendi* at Nazareth. Having drawn up our conclusions, and having obtained the approbation and blessing of the Cardinal of which I am sure, and also spoken to the Apostolic Delegate and obtained his good will, we will begin our work. It is I think our duty and the only proper and prudent thing to do to obtain the permission and good will of all the authorities before any vital step be taken and before the matter becomes known, and hence I think it necessary for us to preserve the greatest silence until after these approbations etc. be obtained and we decide that the time for proper announcement has come.

Whatever I write to you on this subject is, of course, confidential.

You may desire to know just why we thought the work ought to begin and center at Washington. Well—

(1) That is the only place that is *really national* and that can prevent the work from becoming local and diocesan. We thought the work ought to be placed at the beginning on the broadest and deepest lines possible and in building to build for all time.

(2) There are great helps to be obtained for such a work from the University which cannot be obtained elsewhere. You will easily realize these and we will talk them over some time.

(3) There our work will most likely be very directly under the supreme authority of the Church in the person of the Apostolic Delegate, who I understand is extremely desirous that such a work should have its fullest force and is not likely to allow any one to interfere with it. You understand how local authorities can easily hamper and handicap such a work which ought to be free, and our fullest and freest development is likelier to take place at Washington than anywhere else.

These are the principal matters you would like to know—so I think—though I have been obliged to write hastily and disconnectedly.

My heart is so full of joy and gratitude to God in regard to matters that it is continuously singing its *Te Deum,* and I trust your own heart will join me in that of which it is so full. I will be at Nazareth in two or three days. Write me there.

> Fraternally and sincerely your
> Servant in Our Lord
> Thos. F. Price

Shall I take *Truth* to Washington? Shall you take *The Field Afar* there? I am inclined to think we should and have our own printing press, etc. What do you think?

> T.F.P

Father Walsh to Father Price:

Dear Father Price,

Your long letter of September 21, has interested me greatly. I acknowledged the receipt of it by post-card and have delayed this answer so as to get time for reflection.

Our meeting in Montreal was unexpected and in that all too brief talk I felt that I could not have given you a very clear idea of my own position in relation to a prospective seminary for foreign missions. I will try to do so now before answering your letter in detail, as we should understand each other's views from the outset.

Ever since I entered on my present duties as Diocesan Director of the Society for the Propagation of the Faith, in the Archdiocese of Boston, I have realized the need of a Foreign Mission Seminary and looked forward to the establishment of one as the logical outcome of our effort here in Boston to develop the missionary spirit.

Gradually letters came from unexpected sources urging me to carry out the idea. These letters were all actuated by the most unselfish motives and were from saintly prelates and priests among others—Bishop Chatron of Osaka, Japan, a well-known Jesuit missioner in China, Bishop Benziger of Quilon, India, and Father Elliott of this country. The Superior-General of Mill Hill, during my stay with him in England, also brought up the subject and expressed the hope that I would consider this important work without delay.

At first I had not thought of personally inaugurating and directing such a seminary, but with the need evident and no one in sight to do so, I made up my mind to watch and pray for an opening. In the meantime prayers have been offered in many far distant missions and elsewhere for this intention. About a year before his death I mentioned the subject to the late Archbishop Williams, who replied, "That will come."

About this time I called together a meeting with three other priests, one a Sulpician, and together we four formed what we called the *Catholic Foreign Mission Society*, having for its immediate purpose the spread of Catholic literature, and for its ultimate end, the creation of a foreign mission seminary. The existence of this organization has never been made public. A thoughtful session was held and THE FIELD AFAR was settled upon as the organ of a future seminary. The publication of this paper, and of other mission literature, books, pamphlets, post-cards, circulars, etc., was begun at once under the name of the *Catholic Foreign Mission Bureau*—the word "*Society*" being suppressed as it would arouse curiosity and awaken needless inquiries. The little group is still interested but naturally the burden of work has been mine to carry, and practically I am the *Bureau*.

Shortly after Archbishop O'Connell came as co-adjutor to Boston, I had occasion to tell him the condition of our work for missions; and when I added that I looked forward to a *Foreign*

Mission Seminary as the logical outcome of this work—he commended the idea suddenly and warmly, implying that I had hit upon his own plan. On this occasion Archbishop O'Connell stated that if he were in full power he would at once convert the House of Philosophy into a foreign mission seminary and place me in charge of it. (I have never made this public. I tell it now in confidence.)

Since His Grace has come into power he has not alluded to the conversation just mentioned. Twice, however, he has suggested that I should look forward to a visit to the Far East so as to make personal observations of the existing need and opportunity. I brought up the subject of the Seminary again to His Grace, in the summer of 1909, but while he admitted that such an institution might come soon he did not appear at the time especially interested. It would not have surprised me at any time, however, in the past year, if His Grace had told me to start a *Foreign Mission Seminary*. He has the wide view of the Catholic Church, and if other important matters were not pressing him, and his attention happened to be centered upon this need, I believe that he would act with his customary vigor.

From all this you will understand that I have been regarding myself as the possible organizer and director of a *Foreign Mission Seminary*. I feel that you should know this but I hasten to add that I have been taking this view simply and because I have been urged on by disinterested and apostolic missioners.

I have been and am conscious of certain limitations of soul and body which would make me welcome the full assumption of this responsibility by another. On the other hand, the greatest movements in the Church have so originated that the beginnings were obscured (and thus God's glory rather than man's has prevailed).

I believe that such, if possible, should be the history of the United States Seminary for Foreign Missions. In this event, I would ask to share responsibility with one whose judgment and experience I would respect and who in turn would respect my own.

If this is your view we must know each other's mind as fully as possible before we think of uniting our forces.

You are fifty and I am well into my forty-fourth year. Both of us have, doubtless, certain settled habits of life and some fixed ideas. The proposed venture would be a tremendously serious change for me and the more I look into it the more difficulties I face. I have been praying for light and have offered Mass for that intention.

Before answering your letter in detail, therefore, I wish to get your replies to the following questions:

To whom do you refer when you speak of the Conference in St. Mary's Seminary?

Will you be alone in your project if I do not join you?

Do I understand that in associating myself under you, I shall be considering you at once as the organizer and director of the future seminary?

Or is it your mind that the origin of the seminary shall be quite impersonal (the outgrowth of a quickened mission spirit) and its direction undetermined for the present?

Your letter coming so soon after that conference, has given me a strong hope and made me share the joy of your *Te Deum*. I feel, however, that in justice to all concerned—to the cause, to you and to myself—I should know clearly your attitude towards me in this work.

I wish to make the best possible use of what practical experience and knowledge I have acquired in contact with foreign mission needs. If this cannot be through a foreign mission seminary, then, otherwise as I would see God's will. I have given this subject much thought since I saw you and very serious consideration since your letter arrived.

May God guide us both and others who in this country are waking slowly to this vital need!

Rev. James A. Walsh

P.S. A word in post-script and in answer to the more arbitrary recommendations in your letter.

I believe with you in a modest beginning.

The idea of sending students to a neighboring house of studies is practical and economical.

A study of the mission houses in Europe would be advantageous, in fact necessary.

I believe with you that Washington has many advantages as the site for a foreign mission seminary—although Massachusetts and New York ought to prove very desirable as sources of supply (for vocations and funds).

As to your *modus vivendi* at Nazareth, I cannot express an opinion because I do not know, except from an occasional comment, what it has been. If it has proved practical, adapted to the American youth, and can show fruitful results, it certainly ought to be considered.

You are free to take up the contents of this letter with Fr. Dyer.

Father Price to Father Walsh:

My dear Father Walsh:

Your note of October 7, acknowledging mine of September 29, brought me much pleasure. As I wrote you September 29, your letter surprised me as I was not aware of the matters contained in it and from these I infer you were yourself waiting for the development of circumstances to take up such an enterprise. I trust that we shall both together find such development in the present tide of affairs, but I write these words to explain the erroneous assumption I was under and under which I wrote you, as otherwise my attitude to you I fear must seem to you inconsiderate, harsh and arbitrary.

You say well that we should thoroughly understand each other at the outset and I shall try to make myself in this matter as clear to you as I can.

First of all allow me to make several general remarks which may enable you to understand me better.

(1) I will in no manner step in between you or anyone else undertaking such a work. I am quite sure that I would rather die any death than interfere with or prevent any work for God especially so great a work as one of this kind.

(2) Whatever part I might take in the formation of such a work I would consider the work purely in itself and its good only, and I would ruthlessly cast aside every consideration that might conflict with the greatest good of the work and throw myself—my whole soul—into the good of the work and that alone.

(3) I have so strong a conviction that the spiritual exercises of St. Ignatius are the true and proper basis for forming apostolic men and work that if left to myself I could place no other basis to such a work. These exercises however are for the interior and do not conflict with any external organization.

(4) I have almost a conviction that such a work ought not to exclude *Positis Ponendis* needy places in this country, such as North Carolina and other districts in the South and West. I say *Positis Ponendis* as I am aware of a danger in this of subverting the purposes of the work—a danger however, which can be averted by proper safeguards as for example by requiring all men to spend at least a certain number of years on the foreign mission first, and requiring a special permission from Rome to serve in this country

at all; or by placing the mission work at the absolute disposal of the Pope; or by other safeguards.

That I might understand you better—your position—you very kindly made known to me in your letter the various developments that have led you up to the present. The same mode of procedure may be necessary in my own case in regard to you.

Almost as far back as I can remember I have had two attractions in my life. One was to do what I could for the conversion of North Carolina, the other was for the foreign mission work with the possibility of dying a martyr in it. These two attractions grew stronger and stronger as I neared the priesthood. During my preparation for the priesthood a third attraction drew me strongly to the Jesuit life. With my Director I studied this third attraction closely and tried it long, but we could never come to any conclusion about it as it seemed irreconcilable with the other attractions. My Director advised me however not to give it up. These three attractions have wrought powerfully on my whole life and in fact have practically governed it.

After I had been above ten years in the priesthood in North Carolina a great despair came over me of ever being able, under the conditions under which I was working, to do anything really effective for the conversion of the place and I considered the matter of giving up the attempt. About that time Father Elliott began his work of missions to non-Catholics and my Director—Father Dissez—advised me to take it up and see what I could do with it. I followed his advice and gradually developed a somewhat different status from that of Father Elliott's and gathered around me some priests and students.

That was six years ago. Since that time whilst expending my efforts in doing what I could in a missionary way, I was studying the work and seeing what I could do. I have come slowly to the absolute conviction that it is not practically possible to develop priests for such a work as ours under the conditions that surround us here. Our life is built on lines of greater sacrifices than that of the ordinary Secular Priest. I became convinced that unless we could keep our own men during their preparation for the priesthood under conditions conducive to that life they were supposed to lead, it was impossible to turn out the men successfully, even if we could turn them out at all as priests.

In our own case at Nazareth I have seen man after man leave us glowing with the spirit of sacrifice for the priesthood, pursue his studies elsewhere and almost invariably have that spirit of sacrifice which was of absolute necessity for his life knocked entirely out

of him in a short while. I have become thoroughly convinced that
without a seminary of our own completely dominated by us, it is
impossible to keep up this work and make it a success. Now there
is nothing that Bishop Haid is more hostile to than such a seminary.
He has his own Benedictine Seminary here and I know he would
not for one moment consider the possibility of another here even
if one were practicable. At any rate it has become absolutely clear
to me that it is necessary for me to establish a seminary and that
it is necessary for me to go out of North Carolina to do it.

So far I have spoken of the developments which led up to the
time when I met you in Montreal. But I wish to call your attention
to the fact that my life and the work at Nazareth were built upon
the Spiritual Exercises of St. Ignatius and with the purpose of
developing into a work for foreign missions. It was owing to this
that I placed in the promises approved by Bishop Haid that
the men were to do "any mission work which is enjoined by the
Holy Father." Hence you understand that in beginning this work I
am beginning nothing new. I am only coming into the development which was looked forward to and designed and provided for,
to what extent was possible under the circumstances. I am merely
passing into a larger higher development of the same life. It is
like the silkworm developing into the butterfly. I am making no
sacrifices but on the contrary am coming into the fruition of a life
time. Hence you understand that my heart is full of continuous,
indescribable happiness and is singing a continuous *Te Deum*.
With this life and these ideas you may be sure that in the past I
kept an eye on the foreign mission work and seldom read of it
except with a burning heart. Some years ago I spoke to Father Dyer
of enlarging our work into the foreign mission seminary then but
I felt at that time that the season had not yet come for us. When
however it became clear to me that our work here could not
succeed without this development but absolutely demanded it and
that it could not be delayed longer, I asked Fr. Dyer and Fr.
O'Rourke, S.J., who had all along been more or less my advisers,
to take the matter under consideration. A meeting was arranged
amongst us, the result of which you know.

And now regarding your questions:

Leaving aside the two points (1) the matter of the Spiritual Exercises as a basis, and (2) not excluding needy places in this
country, the answers are as follows:

(1) Those who composed the conference at St. Mary's Seminary,
Baltimore, were Fr. Dyer, Fr. O'Rourke, S.J., and myself and the
object of the conference was to determine whether I should

establish a foreign mission seminary or not. By way of necessary and preliminary incidence we came to the conclusion that the work was necessary and opportune.

(2) If you do not join it is likely that I will be practically alone though I should try to associate one or two others with me.

(3) You would not "be expected to place yourself under me considering me at once as the organizer and director of the future seminary." Leaving aside the two points mentioned (1) the Spiritual Exercises as the basis and (2) not including needy places in this country for consideration for the moment, I would propose that we study together the points of organization and with much prayer and study draw up a plan of organizing and carrying on. Such points as we should differ about we could refer to some third party or parties in whom we would have confidence and commit the decision to them. The manner of choosing a Superior and the direction of the seminary would I suppose be provided for in the plan of organization itself.

After the seminary was organized and put on an assured basis it would be a matter of indifference to me what position I should occupy—the most obscure the best—seeking only to spend myself to the fullest extent for God's glory. I might here mention that once the work were on an assured basis, I would wish to go on the foreign missions myself, where I would trust that God would grant my daily prayer for martyrdom.

(4) I am not sure that I understand you about "the origin of the seminary being" quite impersonal (the outgrowth of a quickened mission spirit). The work is here calling for birth in agonizing cries and why we should sit down and wait for something further to turn up is not clear to me. I am not unmindful or without fear of running ahead of God's grace and so doing not God's but man's will, but I am inclined to think that if we went forward carefully, noting God's will as He developed the way, it would be the proper thing, and it might be, in the pressing need for priests in the Philippines and elsewhere more sinful to hang back than go forward. Furthermore, I am inclined to think that the authorities of the Church would urge us more vehemently to press the work as quickly as possible and this in itself is a strong indication of the divine will not to wait further.

Sincerely your Servant in Our Lord,
Thos. F. Price

P.S. I think it might be good to put before you the following which contains a plan which has been long incoherently in my mind and ask you to think over it:

After we have settled favorably the matter spoken of in this letter (and I feel that we shall unite) we might associate with us on the same basis Fr. Dunn and after doing so proceed as follows: With much prayer, study up thoroughly this work, going if necessary to Europe, Asia or Africa for that purpose, and plan out together—all three of us—a thorough organization not only of the higher seminary but of the supply and apostolic schools or small seminaries and have this plan approved by Rome. It might be good to begin as soon as possible and simultaneously (but in a modest way) small seminaries or supply schools—one at Boston and one at New York, and the higher seminary at Washington. As to who would be directors of the seminaries after we have organized we would determine the rules for settling that in the plan of organization itself. In a sense, the direction would be under all three of us as a body, as nothing could be done in any of these places without first being approved by the Association composed of us. As to who would be the actual director in such and such a place, that would be determined by rules drawn up in the plan of organization itself. We three could form a governing board or elect one as Superior. The reasons which may be urged for this plan are:

(1) If it can be done it ought to be done, for there is such an appalling cry for priests from the Philippines and elsewhere, that it seems almost sinful not to do it if we can—and can it not be done?

(2) My experience in life has taught me that it is a mistake not to throw your work on the largest and most permanent lines possible. Now sooner or later I feel sure that the higher seminary must be at Washington and the supply schools situated where the supplies come from—that is in large Catholic centers.

P.S. Since writing the above I have obtained from Bishop Haid to be free for this work after a little while, provided I see that the work of Nazareth is preserved. There is not much difficulty in this but it is hard to see how this can be done, unless you could admit in our basis for uniting the point of not excluding needy places in this country, as I have explained. Bishop Haid's permission was the thing I feared might be the most difficult thing in this work for me to get, and I look upon it as a most remarkable answer to the prayers I had many persons offer up for the matter—I feel almost in an ecstasy of happiness these days.

These papers as you know are confidential and contain matters about my life which I would not permit any one to read, and I only send them to you on account of the circumstances, and when you have made such use of them as you find necessary for your personal needs, please return them to me that I may destroy them.

T. F. P.

December 8th. The above papers have long been delayed partially by Fr. Dyer's absence as you will see from the enclosed letter from him, and partially by some important matters which have absorbed all my time; and hardly left me time to breathe. I have seen and talked with Fr. Dyer since receiving his letter and I think I can follow out his suggestions—that the work in North Carolina need be no bar to our union that if it does not fit in with what we judge to be best for the work, we can make it a special matter— and that the Spiritual Exercises of St. Ignatius need be likewise no bar to our union, but that we would adopt whatever the good of the work required. So that from my side I see no reason why we should not unite.

Sincerely your Servant,
T. F. Price

5

Laying the Foundation

Through such correspondence, Fathers Walsh and Price clarified
their ideas and worked out a set of principles on which they could
agree. In this stage of the negotiations, Father Price took the
initiative and carried the major share of the work.

It was after Christmas before Father Price had his own work
cleared up and could head northward again. He traveled to Boston to see Archbishop O'Connell, who greeted him as an old
friend. The Archbishop listened carefully to the plan and gave his
approval. He disagreed with the proposal that the new society
should be located in Washington but felt that it ought to be established in the North, near a strong Catholic center where mission
promotion had already been done. He suggested his own archdiocese as a possible location. He did not believe that professors
from foreign societies should be brought in to teach.

The two organizers decided (and in this the Archbishop agreed)
that they were not starting a new religious order or congregation.
Their movement found its source in the American clergy and
people, and therefore they felt that their new society must continue this identification. It would be composed of secular priests,

representatives of the American clergy as a whole, who were banded together for foreign mission work. The sole purpose of the foundation was to give American Catholics representation on the foreign mission fields by training American youths as foreign missioners. Father Walsh assured Archbishop O'Connell that this identification with the general body of American clergy would be drilled into the members of the new society; his mission priests would consider themselves the partners of every diocesan priest in America.

Father Price left Boston for New York to see Cardinal Farley, but somewhere along the way received an inspiration not to stop in the metropolis but to go directly to Baltimore, where he visited Cardinal Gibbons. He had known the Cardinal for many years, in fact America's most prominent churchman had at one time been his pastor in North Carolina. The Cardinal expressed his approval of the plan but added a caution. Since the new society was to be national in scope, it would need the support of the entire American hierarchy. The first step would be to consult with the Apostolic Delegate, Archbishop Diomede Falconio.

Off to Washington hurried Father Price, his well-worn beads slipping through his fingers faster than ever. The Delegate gave prompt encouragement, and repeated to Father Price the same advice that had been given by Cardinal Gibbons. The hierarchy must be persuaded to back up the project, otherwise the new society would be just another organization with its future growth restricted. If the mission priests were to be representatives of the entire American clergy for the extension of their vocations, the support of the hierarchy had to be gained. The best place to do this was in the bishops' annual meeting in Washington. Back to Baltimore to report to Cardinal Gibbons traveled Father Price, and then on to Boston to see Archbishop O'Connell again, and of course Father Walsh.

The two pioneers drew up a plan of the proposed society and forwarded it to Cardinal Gibbons. On March 25, 1911, the Cardinal wrote to all the archbishops in the United States, outlining the project and asking them to consult with their suffragan bishops on it. The Cardinal pointed out the need for such an organization and admitted that while requirements at home were great "the surest way to multiply our own material means for work at home, is by not limiting the expansion of charity and by not paralyzing the zeal of self-denial." The Cardinal pointed out that American Catholics could not delay participation in foreign missions "lest our own faith should suffer."

Cardinal Gibbons also emphasized that the American Foreign Mission Seminary ought to be established by the American hierarchy if it hoped to receive the sympathetic support of American Catholics. He proposed to place two questions before the archbishops at their next meeting:

1. Would they commend the proposed idea?
2. In the event of their favorable consideration, would they fix, or at least suggest, "one or more desirable locations from which a choice might be made, both for a provisional and a permanent seminary."

The Cardinal concluded his letter by stating that the decision of the hierarchy in this matter would be made known to Rome and to the American Catholic people.

Between the end of March and the end of April, Father Price was back on the road promoting the project. He traveled through the East and Midwest visiting bishops and explaining the plan to them. Everywhere he met with approval, and when the archbishops finally met at Caldwell Hall of the Catholic University of Washington, on April 27, 1911, Father Price felt quite sure that the plan would be accepted. Nevertheless, he left nothing to chance. All during the private meeting he was seen pacing the corridors of the building reciting his Rosary. It was a great relief when news was brought to him that the plan had passed with unanimous approval, and that the hierarchy had issued the following approbation and instructions:

"We heartily approve the establishment of an American Seminary for Foreign Missions as outlined in a letter sent by His Eminence Cardinal Gibbons to the Archbishops.

"We warmly commend to the Holy Father the two priests mentioned as organizers of this seminary, and we instruct them to proceed to Rome without delay, for the purpose of securing all necessary authorization and direction from Propaganda for the proposed work."

"Instruct them to proceed to Rome without delay." Father Price rushed to a telegraph office to send the good news to Father Walsh who was waiting in New York. Then he hurried back to the rectory where he was staying to write in more detail to his partner. He began his letter with these heart-soaring words, "This is the day which the Lord hath made: let us be glad and rejoice therein." He closed the letter with the simple statement, "I am very happy."

The days that followed were frantically busy ones. Father Price had to transfer all the projects at Nazareth. He left the arrangements for the trip to Rome in Father Walsh's hands. He only desired that the trip abroad would leave him sufficient time to make a pilgrimage to Lourdes to honor the Blessed Mother and Bernadette Soubirous, the little peasant girl destined to be canonized as a saint, and to whom he had great devotion.

Father Walsh was equally busy. He obtained from Archbishop O'Connell his release from the Boston Archdiocese; turned over his office to his successor, Father Joseph McGlinchey; and arranged for the printing of *The Field Afar* at a new press. Since the magazine belonged not to the Propagation of the Faith Society but to the Catholic Foreign Mission Bureau, he intended to use it as a means of promoting the new seminary.

On May 30, Father Walsh stood aboard the *Franconia* waiting the arrival of his partner. It was not until the gangplank was being raised that Father Price came hurrying on to the dock carrying his little bag. He apologized for his lateness with the simple explanation that he had been praying before the Blessed Sacrament and had lost track of time. Then he took all the money he had and handed it to Father Walsh saying, "You'd better be treasurer." Father Walsh was to be the man of business. He was to be the man of prayer.

Father Price's trip abroad was a source of wonderment to him. Used to the rough backwoods life of North Carolina, he found it very uncomfortable to be rubbing elbows with fashionably gowned ladies and polished gentlemen. He confessed to Father Walsh that he dreaded going into the dining room. There was too much formality.

When the boat arrived at Liverpool, the two priests went to the Mill Hill college at Freshfield, and then to Mill Hill headquarters outside London. After this they proceeded to Paris to visit the

famous mission society there, and to pray before the relics of
Theophane Venard who had just been beatified. The next stop
was in Italy at the headquarters of the Milan Foreign Mission
Society. On June 19, they arrived in Rome.

The days in the Eternal City were busy ones. There were calls
to be made, interviews to be had, and reports to be prepared. They
saw prelates in all ranks, and to each they explained the project
that had brought them from America. On June 29, 1911, the
Feast of Saints Peter and Paul, they were summoned to appear
before Cardinal Gotti, Prefect of the Sacred Congregation of
Propaganda. It was the third time that they had been called to
see that distinguished ecclesiastic. From the Church of San Sil-
vestro, where they were staying, the two Americans marched across
Rome to the Vatican. They went to the old and battered building
that housed the Propaganda offices, and ascended one by one
in the tiny, creaking elevator that rose to the Cardinal's apart-
ment.

His Eminence greeted his American visitors with a smile. After
the usual introductory remarks, the Cardinal came directly to the
point. The Sacred Congregation of Propaganda had studied their
proposal and decided favorably. They had formal authorization to
proceed, to open a house and recruit students. They should keep
the Sacred Congregation informed of progress. On their return
to the United States, they should present themselves to the Apostolic Delegate and to Cardinal Gibbons.

Overjoyed at the success of their long planning and arduous
work, Fathers Walsh and Price quickly made their departure. This
time they did not wait for the decrepit elevator, but hurried down
the rickety stairs. They went immediately to the tomb of
the Apostles for a prayer of thanksgiving on this, the first day of
their Society's foundation. On the following day, they had a private audience with the Holy Father, Pope Pius X, who blessed
the work and its founders. That audience over, the two pioneers
made plans to leave Rome. Father Walsh intended to go to a Mill
Hill Seminary in the Tyrol, and then on to France to visit Blessed
Theophane Venard's brother. Father Price planned a visit to
Lourdes, where he was to stay with Bernadette Soubirous' brother,
and then a trip to Nevers, where Bernadette had died as a Sister.
The two priests were to meet in Liverpool at the end of September.

One more task remained to be done before leaving Rome. That was to send a full report to Cardinal Gibbons. They told the Cardinal that they had chosen a name for their new organization: Catholic Foreign Mission Society of America: *Catholic* to distinguish it from Protestant mission groups; *Foreign* to define its purpose; *of America* because it had received the official sanction of the American hierarchy, and because the term would distinguish it from European groups and let people of mission lands know that Catholic Americans were interested in them.

When the two founders returned to America at the end of September, they realized that despite all their previous work they had only begun their task. Now came the proving. Father Walsh was full of ideas after seeing the mission operations of European societies. Father Price was a changed man. At Lourdes, he had undergone some profound mystical experience which he never revealed. He did confide in his diary that "I learned more in a few hours at Lourdes than I ever learned in my whole life . . . Truly, Mother, at Lourdes you CHANGED MY WHOLE LIFE." At Nevers, he had received the unusual permission to spend the whole night alone with the body of Saint Bernadette. But what specific revelation was made to him was a secret he was to take to his grave.

The founders approached the problem of their first location scientifically. After research and analysis they learned that within a four hundred mile radius of New York City there were seven and a half million Catholics. At a conference with Archbishop Farley on October 13, 1911, the founders were invited to establish their Society in his archdiocese. They accepted, and a site at Hawthorne, N. Y., was chosen.

Hawthorne is a quiet little community in Westchester County, lying at the head of the Saw Mill River valley, about thirty miles north of New York. Nearby was the Pocantico Hills estate of John D. Rockefeller, and just beyond is Washington Irving's Sleepy Hollow country. The town itself had been named after Nathaniel Hawthorne, the famous American author. Hawthorne's daughter, Mother Rose Hawthorne, a Catholic religious, conducted a cancer hospital within the town's limits.

While the Dominicans extended every hospitality to the new arrivals, Fathers Walsh and Price realized that they could not continue to live in the Dominican house for any length of time. Then, too, a place had to be found for the young ladies who aided Father Walsh in publishing *The Field Afar*. Two small houses were rented, and certain renovations and repairs were made. The Secretaries, as the Boston women were called, arrived in Hawthorne on January 5, 1912. Father Walsh and Father Price took occupancy of the second house a few days later; they were accompanied by a newcomer from Boston, Father John I. Lane, who with Father Walsh had been one of the founders of *The Field Afar* and the Catholic Foreign Mission Bureau.

Once settled, the new Society turned to the arduous task of sinking permanent roots. The group was incorporated under the laws of New York State, and Father Walsh was elected Superior. The two founders realized that Hawthorne did not offer the possibility of development, so they began to search for a suitable piece of land in the vicinity. Father Walsh had already named this nonexistent property "Maryknoll." Two young men, Ernst Hollger and Thomas McCann, arrived to begin the band of Auxiliary Brothers, which was to be formed to help the priests.

Since no seminary could be started without seminarians, the cofounders turned to this problem. While visiting Cathedral College in New York City one day in January, Father Walsh met a young student who then and there declared himself as the first seminarian for the new enterprise. The boy was Francis X. Ford —destined to become a bishop and to meet death at the hands of Chinese Communists. Father Price, meanwhile, was on the road making the new work known. In Emmitsburg, Maryland, he signed up a young graduate of Mount Saint Mary's College, James Edward Walsh, who was to become the first Maryknoll bishop and the second Superior General. The little community began to grow.

When spring broke upon Westchester, Father Walsh speeded up the search for a permanent property. Among the Pocantico Hills, he found a knoll, looking down on the majestic Hudson, which seemed to be an ideal place to locate his new Society. Upon inquiry, he learned that the property was for sale. It was Saturday afternoon, too late to have legal papers drawn up, but Father Walsh gave the owner a check for $10,000 as down payment. When he returned on Monday to complete the legal details of the transaction, he learned that over the week end the property had been sold to another buyer.

Investigation revealed that the new owner was the multimillionaire, John D. Rockefeller, who had turned most of Pocantico Hills into his own private estate. During the week end Mr. Rockefeller had heard that a Catholic organization was buying property adjoining his estate, and he had immediately moved to prevent the sale. A great lover of privacy, Mr. Rockefeller had once moved a railroad that disturbed his tranquility, and for some time had been endeavoring to buy out the Christian Brothers' property in Pocantico Hills (at which he was to succeed some years later).

Disappointed and angry, Father Walsh began legal action against Mr. Rockefeller, pointing out that his Society had given a binder on the property, and that its subsequent sale was a breach of contract. Mr. Rockefeller claimed that he was unaware of the down payment; but after much discussion and stalling, the oil magnate settled for $8,000 in damages. The money when it came was useful to the struggling new Society, but the loss of the property was temporarily grave. The summer was speeding by, and the fall term of the new seminary was scheduled to begin in September. It was imperative that a permanent location be quickly found.

July faded into August, and still no site was discovered. On the eve of the Feast of the Assumption, August 14, Father Walsh was driving back to Hawthorne. All day, high above the Hudson River, he had been searching the area north of Ossining. As he came along Pines Bridge Road, he passed a farm overlooking Ossining and the Hudson. It was the highest place around and the view south toward New York City, and west over the Palisades and Ramapo Mountains was truly magnificent. Here was a place that would make a worthy headquarters if he could obtain it. The property consisted of ninety-three acres, three houses and a barn. There were fields for crops and acres of woodlands. Discreet inquiries also elicited the fact that it was for sale.

Remembering his experience at Pocantico Hills, Father Walsh decided to take no chances on losing this property. He arranged for one of the Boston secretaries, Miss Mary Rogers, a former teacher at Smith College, to act as purchaser. On August 18, disguised in a linen duster and goggles after the fashion of automobilists in those days, and accompanied by Miss Rogers and two real-estate agents, Father Walsh drove to Ossining. Up Sunset Hill they went, past the sign "Ossining—High and Dry—No Malaria," to the farm.

The property was deeded to Miss Rogers, and later that day for consideration of the sum of one dollar, Miss Rogers signed it over to the Society. Maryknoll was at last more than just a name.

On September 9, 1912, the Society began to move to its new home. Father Price was away at the time on his second pilgrimage to Lourdes, and Father Walsh handled all the arrangements. Bit by bit the goods were transferred from Hawthorne. On September 18, a carriage drew up in front of the Hawthorne house. Built to carry four, almost the entire personnel of the Catholic Foreign Mission Society crowded into it. Besides the driver, there was Father Walsh; three students, Francis X. Ford, of Brooklyn, James E. Walsh, of Cumberland, Maryland, and William F. O'Shea, of Hoboken, New Jersey; and the two lay brothers. In the growing darkness, behind a lame horse, the crowded carriage began a creaking six-mile journey to the new home.

The pioneer band traveled in sublime faith. They had little of the goods of this world. The infant Society was already thirty thousand dollars in debt, undertaken to purchase the Ossining property. A lawsuit with the great Rockefeller was hanging over the Society's head. Professors and more candidates for the new Seminary were needed. The Society, as such, was still largely unknown to America. There was yet an uphill battle to be fought to make Catholic Americans mission-conscious. By all worldly standards, there should have been gloom and discouragement. But as the carriage wound its way through the Westchester hills, Father Walsh's heart was singing.

Maryknoll was real. Maryknoll had a home.

6

The Days of the Giants

When present-day Maryknollers look back to those early years and recall the struggles and trials they produced and the heroic figures who trod through them, the period is referred to as "The Days of the Giants." Progress was being made, slowly but surely. The Sunset Hill property was gradually taking shape. The secretaries moved over from Hawthorne, were given the name "Teresians," adopted a distinctive dress, and began to prepare for the day when they would be a community of missionary Sisters. The Brothers increased by one that first year, and took the title "Auxiliary Brothers of St. Michael." In the first year at Maryknoll, the student body increased to six. In addition to the three students who had emigrated from Hawthorne, there were Daniel L. McShane, of Columbus, Indiana; Alphonse S. Vogel, of New York City; and a third student who later dropped out.

Seminarians McShane and Walsh were ready for theology, and they attended classes at St. Joseph's Seminary in Yonkers. The four remaining students prepared at Maryknoll. There were as many professors as pupils. Father Joseph McCabe came from England on loan from the Mill Hill Fathers. Doctor Barile, fresh from

Rome, taught philosophy. Father Walsh and Father John I. Lane rounded out the faculty. Dr. Paluel J. Flagg came to give lectures on mission medicine.

In those early years traditions were formed that today are in the bloodstream of Maryknoll. Manual labor was introduced as a regular part of seminary routine. A stranger coming to Maryknoll might be surprised to meet one of the seminarians laying drain pipe, or scrubbing a floor. Father Walsh imposed such duties to test the humility and hardihood of his students. The daily chores became part of the training, and lessons learned at Maryknoll during the daily manual-labor period proved very useful in later life. The students received, also, other practical experience. Father William Cashin, chaplain at nearby Sing Sing Prison, arranged for them to teach catechism to the prisoners.

All the students at Maryknoll were philosophy students, and it became apparent to the Maryknoll founders that, if the Society was to develop, they would have to found a preparatory seminary, offering both high-school and college courses. Bishop Hoban, of Scranton, Pennsylvania, had once invited Fathers Walsh and Price to locate their new Society in his diocese. For many reasons, New York had been chosen instead. But now that a second foundation was planned, there was no reason why it should not be located in Scranton. In 1913, the Venard Apostolic School was opened in that city.

In a different connection, the year of 1913 was a disappointment to many who were watching the progress of Maryknoll: not a single new student was enrolled that year. Many Europeans, who had openly said that Maryknoll would never succeed because American boys were too luxury-loving and did not have the stamina that makes a foreign missioner, then nodded their heads in gestures that could only mean "I told you so!" However, Father Walsh was not dismayed. He had confidence that the cause would appeal to American youth, and he preferred to move slowly in the first years.

Father Walsh's judgment proved correct. The student body doubled in 1914, and there was a continuous steady growth thereafter. In 1914, Cardinal Farley ordained Daniel McShane—the Society's first seminarian to become a priest. In the following year, the Rule of the Society was approved by Rome. In 1916, the Scranton school was moved to newly purchased ground in Clarks Summit, and two years later the first ground was broken for the building of a permanent college. By 1917, the young Society numbered eleven priests, twenty-five major seminarians, and thirty-five minor seminarians.

The pages of *The Field Afar* give an intimate and heart-warming picture of those early days. Father Walsh prepared practically all the copy for the magazine himself. He had a warm, friendly style that made the young Society come alive to readers. No detail of its progress was too small or insignificant to be reported. Subscribers of the magazine felt that they were part of the growing movement.

When Billy, the horse, died one day while climbing Sunset Hill, readers all over America felt Maryknoll's loss. When Billy was replaced by a decrepit Ford, the same readers knew that Father Walsh had christened it "Tin Lizzie." A sewer put in to join the town sewer was called the "Sea Serpent's Grave." One reader wrote complaining about this sewer, stating, "Once I helped you when you were buying land by the foot, now you want money so that you can throw it away by the shovelful."

There were many events that never made the pages of *The Field Afar* but that did give zest to the early life. One such occurred the day Francis Ford challenged a visiting relative of Father Walsh to a cider-drinking contest. Ford managed to lose, but the visitor turned white and green and was never the same again. Enjoyed, too, were the many times that the skeleton from Doctor Flagg's medicine class turned up in someone's bed or closet. Or the impasses in which Father Walsh sometimes found himself when he tried to correct one of his future apostles. Bishop Raymond A. Lane, a student during those early days, tells about one such occasion when, during refectory reading, a student from New Jersey read about St. John the Apostle being put in a caldron of boiling oil. The student read it as "burling earl."

"What was that, Brother? What was in the caldron?" asked Father Walsh after he had tapped his little bell for attention.

"Burling earl," answered the confident student.

"How do you spell it?" Father Walsh inquired.

"Burling, b-o-i-l-i-n-g—"

"Just a minute, please," interrupted the harassed Superior. "How do you pronounce e-a-r-l?"

"Oil," was the prompt reply.

It was outside the classroom that the young Maryknollers received their greatest lessons, however. The two founders were extraordinary men, who complemented each other. In those first years, Father Price was often away. While Father Walsh remained at home to look after the Seminary and Society affairs, and to raise funds by the magazine and direct-mail appeals, Father Price was traveling the roads of the United States, buttonholing bishops, speaking in schools and parishes, and doing what he could by direct contact to make the Society known. When he was at Maryknoll, he acted as spiritual director for the seminarians.

Father Price was a man of deep spirituality. His humility was so great that he asked Father Walsh never to mention his name in the pages of *The Field Afar*—a request Father Walsh observed although it caused considerable embarrassment at times when friends wrote to Maryknoll to ask if the North Carolinian was dead. Father Price continually exhorted the young students to perform every act of the day for God, a practice he followed in his own life. He was constantly praying, and there was hardly a time when the rosary beads were not in his hands. When the treasury was low, or some other crisis imperiled the young Society, Father Walsh counted on Father Price's prayers to pull them through.

Contrary to priestly custom, Father Price wore a ring on the third finger of his left hand. It was a silver ring covered with black leather. The ring naturally provoked much curiosity, but Father Price would never speak about it. Sometimes a new student would ask him why he wore the ring.

"Can you keep a secret?" Father Price would ask in return.

"Yes," would come the expectant reply.

"Then—so can I!"

In his spiritual diary, he mentions the ring several times, but even there does not reveal its meaning. "I thought of covering the ring with a piece of black glove kid—so that it is little noticeable, and if one asks what it is, I will tell him it is a means to remember certain things—which is true."

The ring had some connection with the mystical experience Father Price underwent on his first journey to Lourdes. After his death the ring was examined. In the center was an engraved I H S. Then "MB + to MB." This is followed by a bracket enclosing initials and dates: DM April 7, 1915; SM March 25, 1917; ND Aug. 15, 1918. Crosswise runs this date: July 2, 1917. A lily is engraved, and on the petals appear the initials MB twice. Evidently the ring represented some sort of pact he had worked out with the Blessed Virgin and her protégée, Bernadette. In his diary he refers to himself always as "Marie Bernadette," a name he adopted at Lourdes. Father Walsh believed that the ring was a symbol for a mystical union between Father Price and the simple child whom The Immaculate Conception had chosen to confound the world.

Father Price's devotion to our Blessed Mother was childlike and inspiring. When he talked about the Blessed Virgin, he had no concept of time. Once he addressed a group of Sisters on the subject of Lourdes. He spoke two hours past dinner time, before the Mother Superior finally had to call a halt. He published a volume called *Bernadette of Lourdes* and a smaller one called *The Lily of Mary*, and spread devotion to the holy maiden in America at a time when she was very little known.

Father Price spent long hours at prayer. He had several secluded spots in the Maryknoll woodlands, where he was wont to retire alone. In 1913, in Nevers, France, he had put on two chains binding his body, and had made a pledge not to remove them for a second. In 1915, he wrapped a chain about his ankle, secured it with a small padlock, and threw the key away. It was his custom to make a one-hour visit to the Blessed Sacrament shortly after midnight. He never allowed anyone to make his bed or clean his room, probably because he slept on the floor with a stone for a pillow. He recited the Divine Office on his knees before the Blessed Sacrament, and in addition said the Little Office of the Blessed Virgin each day.

He wanted nothing for himself. His possessions were few, and practically everything he wore was a hand-me-down. He did not use tobacco or liquor. He would eat whatever food was put before him, with one exception—apples. Apples had played a part in the fall of man, Bernadette did not like them, and therefore he would have nothing to do with them. When he was alone, he sprinkled his food with ashes. He scourged himself with a lash. He was a man who practiced great penance, but as spiritual director he rarely gave permission for any of his charges to do likewise.

"He not only loved and worked for God," wrote a Maryknoll bishop summing up Father Price—"he also lived with God."

Father Walsh's modest saying was that Father Price was the "Mary" of the new Society—the prayer partner—while Father Walsh was the "Martha"—the work partner. Because the latter

was at Maryknoll more, and in closer contact with the seminarians, he had greater influence upon them. Father Walsh was a
perfectionist. He insisted on perfection in the seminarians' speech,
manner, and dress. He trained his students here to be writers, so
that when they should be in the missions, they would be able to
send back interesting reports. He was a gentleman and demanded
that all his priests be gentlemen. He could not endure having anything out of order. Once in speaking of the Resurrection, he described Saint John's hurrying into the tomb and finding the linen
cloths folded up, and the napkin, which had been placed about
Christ's head, folded in a separate place. "Please note," he told his
students, "that the napkin was *folded* and in its proper place." He
impressed upon everyone the necessity of saying, "Thank you" for
every gift.

Father Walsh's conferences to the students, given usually on
Sunday evening, were the high spot of the week for every seminarian. He would report the state of the Society, tell what he had done
during the week, speak about the future, make corrections when
necessary, give advice and always end on a spiritual note. Father
Walsh was a great believer in God's providence, and strove constantly to inculcate in his students a similar belief.

A maker of maxims, one of his favorite was "Think of the man
who comes after you." His most popular Scriptural quotation was
"Seek first the Kingdom of God." He put a small bulletin board
in the corridor of the Seminary on which he posted a maxim every
day. Other cards were made for the refectory and were displayed
one at a time, beneath the crucifix there. Through these daily
reminders he exhorted his students to become nobler and more
spiritual.

He was a real father to the students. They had their own nickname for him—"Papa," being careful always never to use it in his
presence. He was interested in their problems and in their families.
If a seminarian was ill, he was solicitous. Once when a seminarian
was suffering from an infected hand, Father Walsh summoned a
doctor from a banquet to give medical relief. If a student was in
need, the Superior was the first to offer help.

Although he was keeping a full daily schedule in caring for the
details of his own Society, he had a truly Catholic interest in the
whole world. He continued his activities of spreading general
mission ideas throughout the United States. *The Field Afar* in

addition to being an organ for gaining support for Maryknoll was also designed to provide mission education for its readers. He published books and pamphlets on the general mission cause. He was intensely interested in the work of other mission groups and gave them every encouragement he could. He continually exhorted his men to assist other Societies. "We are all working for God," he frequently said. "It doesn't matter who does the work." He never imagined America as being the sole province of his own Society. There was plenty of work to be done throughout the world, and the more groups doing it the better.

Archbishop McNicholas, a close personal friend, summed up Father Walsh in the following tribute: "His demands made on the young members of his Society were exacting. He required simplicity, a prayerful spirit and trust in God, great reliance on the Holy Ghost, a devotion to our Blessed Mother, a sensible observance of poverty in the manner of living, resourcefulness, self-immolation, joy in action, and a corporate resolution to carry out decisions reached. He made all its members realize that his religious family was approved and permitted to exist in order to serve the Church, that Maryknoll was only a small part of the missionary world, that its interests were therefore subordinate to the greater interests of the Church and the general welfare of the whole mission field. His solicitude for every member of his Society was deeply paternal."

A big order! But Father Walsh was a man who practiced what he preached. He was a practical idealist, a man of great vision, a marvelous organizer, an outstanding general. But greatest of all, he was a true father.

With the continued growth of Maryknoll, Father Walsh felt that the time had come for plans to be made for actual mission work. On September 3, 1917, the Maryknoll Superior set out for the Far East to find a mission field, and to observe mission operations first hand. He paused his journey in San Francisco to establish a mission procure, which would serve the double purpose of being a Maryknoll headquarters in the Far West, and a stepping-off place for the missioners to come.

He arrived in Japan early in October, traveling about the country, visiting mission bishops, looking for an invitation for his Society to take up work there. But no invitation was forthcoming.

From Japan he proceeded to Korea. Bishop Mutel in Seoul was interested in obtaining Maryknollers, but would not commit himself definitely. The Americans were just infants, untried and unproven. Father Walsh began to realize that his task was not going to be easy. He traveled to Manchuria and then down into China. He was counting on Bishop de Gúebriant, of Canton, to give Maryknoll a field in his mission. Some years earlier, the bishop's predecessor had promised a field when Maryknoll was ready. But did the promise hold after all the years, and would Bishop de Gúebriant feel the same way as the man he had succeeded? As Father Walsh picked up a remark here and there he began to have his doubts. In Shanghai Bishop Paris said that he was uncertain whether Americans could "accommodate themselves to Chinese life with its quaint customs and slow movements." The old doubt about the quality of the American missioner was still present.

When Father Walsh arrived in Hong Kong, he was surprised and delighted to learn that Bishop de Gúebriant was in the city. With trepidation the American superior arranged a meeting. Would Bishop de Gúebriant give Maryknoll a territory to begin work? Of course he would. Had it not been agreed long ago? An area had been set aside and was now ready. If Father Walsh would come to Canton the matter would be arranged at once.

On Christmas Day in Canton, Father Walsh signed an agreement by which Maryknoll was entrusted with its first mission field, a territory embracing Yeungkong and Loting, in Kwangtung Province. The agreement was dispatched to Rome for approval, and Father Walsh hurriedly sent a cablegram to Maryknoll announcing the good news. Later he recalled that his feelings were similar to those experienced in Rome years before when Cardinal Gotti gave approval to the young Society. Then he hurried to a map to study the new area.

Before returning to America, Father Walsh visited the region that was to be entrusted to Maryknoll. He made a first-hand study of the conditions under which his missioners would labor. Then he went on a private pilgrimage to Tonkin where Blessed Theophane Venard had worked and been martyred, and to Sancian Island where Saint Francis Xavier had died while trying to enter China. After a brief stop in the Philippines, he turned homeward, arriving back at Maryknoll shortly after Easter. He was hardly home when word came from Rome that the agreement with Bishop de Gúebriant had been approved.

On May 21, 1918, a meeting of the Maryknoll Council took place to discuss the personnel to be assigned to the new territory. Father Price asked Father Walsh to be permitted to go since he had had much mission experience in North Carolina. The other members of the new Society did not feel that Father Price stood much of a chance—his age and health were against him. But when the June assignments were announced, Father Price's name headed the list. To accompany him were Father James E. Walsh; Father Francis X. Ford; and Father Bernard F. Meyer, of Stuart, Iowa, who had come to Maryknoll in 1914.

Maryknoll's first Departure Ceremony took place on the evening of September 7, 1918, in the little chapel of the converted farm-house that served as Seminary and headquarters. It was strictly a family affair with only a few close Society friends, such as Monsignor Dunn, Father Bruneau, and Doctor Flagg, also present. The call for the ceremony to begin was sounded by a huge bronze temple bell that had been presented to Father Walsh in Japan, and which was to announce from then on the beginning of every Maryknoll Departure.

The four departing missioners filed into chapel. The Church's prayer for a safe journey was recited. Father Walsh gave a few parting words. Then each missioner took a pledge of obedience, received his assignment and a missioner's crucifix, and filed out to the sound of Gounod's *Departure Hymn*:

> Go forth, farewell for life, O dearest brothers;
> Proclaim afar the sweetest Name of God.
> We meet again one day in Heaven's land of blessings.
> Farewell, brothers, farewell.

The first Departure Ceremony set a tradition that was to be followed down the years.

After the ceremony, the entire community gathered on the front porch. The little band of missioners came out the main door. Two automobiles stood ready to whisk them to the train. A photograph taken at the time shows Father Price in the lead, hurrying, so it seems, to fulfill the vocation that had led him over the dusty roads of North Carolina, through the highways and byways of

America, and was now to lead him to a new and strange land. The missioners climbed into the cars. There were cheers and the blowing of horns as the cars started up—and then the silence of expectation and accomplishment, as the red taillights faded into the distance.

There is no record of the thoughts of Father Walsh when he saw his first little mission band drive away that cool September evening, but it is not too difficult to imagine those thoughts. Years of waiting, trials, and disappointment had prepared that day. At last a line had begun—an unbroken line of men who each year would march out from the quiet hills of Westchester to the turbulence of far corners of the world. Maryknoll had fulfilled its purpose. It was now in the complete sense of the term a missionary Society.

"Go forth, brothers. Farewell."

7

Kongmoon—The River Gate Opens

Father Price and his little band of missioners arrived at Yeung-kong shortly before Christmas, 1918. They had come to an historic mission territory. In 1552, Saint Francis Xavier had died on nearby Sancian Island while attempting to enter China. Thirty years later the celebrated Jesuit, Father Matteo Ricci, traveled through the region and began work along the West River. By 1704 there were 40,000 Catholics in Kwangtung Province. Then persecution broke out and the work lapsed for over a century.

In 1849, the Paris Foreign Mission Society re-entered the area. The new missioners found 8,000 Christians, most of the Christian families had fled to the Portuguese colony at Macao to escape the persecution. The French missioners set to work re-establishing the Church; and by the time the Maryknollers arrived, Kwangtung had a sizable nucleus of Christians. The area in which the Americans began work counted 5,000 Catholics. The former pastor of Yeung-kong, Father Alphonse Gauthier, was assigned to guide the Mary-knollers through the early days of adjustment.

By Easter, things at Yeungkong were so well organized that the first division of the Maryknoll forces took place. Fathers Walsh and Meyer left to open new missions at Loting and Tungchen, while Fathers Price and Ford remained at Yeungkong. Father Price was not in the best of health. The damp, tropical heat of South China aggravated his arthritis, and he was in constant pain. In August he finally agreed to go to Hong Kong to have a badly ulcerated tooth and a troublesome stomach condition treated.

After he arrived in Hong Kong, the tooth was taken care of without difficulty but his stomach condition created a greater problem. The doctor diagnosed a bad appendix, and ordered the veteran North Carolinian to St. Paul's Hospital for observation. For some days there was debate about the necessity of surgery, and finally the staff decided to make an exploratory operation. The date appointed was the Feast of the Nativity of Our Blessed Mother, September 8.

On the morning of Mary's birthday, Father Price offered Mass in the hospital chapel. Then he prepared for the operation. A Sister who was getting him ready noticed that he had small chains on his arms and one leg. She wanted to remove the chains, saying that the Protestant doctor might not understand. Father Price told her that it was impossible because he had long ago thrown away the keys to the padlocks. Then he was wheeled up to the operating room. Sister Eusebe, who was present at the operation, reported: "When the three doctors who operated opened Father Price's stomach, a great deal of pus came out. The whole stomach was gangrenous. Although the doctors used antiseptics and gave serum to save him, they knew it was useless."

Then followed three days of terrible suffering and pain, all of which Father Price bore without complaint. He felt that he was going to die, and even before the operation he had prepared a sealed envelope marked "To be opened after my death." One of the Sisters chided him when he mentioned death, saying that there was a great deal of work to be done in China.

"I like to work," answered Father Price, "but I am old—too old to work. All I can do is pray, and surely I can pray better in heaven."

On the evening of September 11, he called the Sister in charge and asked if on the morrow a priest could give him Extreme Unction. When the Sister gently reproached him about his desire to get to heaven so quickly, Father Price answered her by saying that the morrow would be the Feast of the Holy Name of Mary, a perfect day for a trip to see the Blessed Mother. In the morning he received Holy Communion and Extreme Unction.

About nine o'clock, his spiritual director, Father Jean Tour, arrived. "The time is coming. I am finished. I am going," Father Price said to him.

"Father Price," asked the French missioner, "will you kindly bless your friend, Father Tour, and in his person, dear Father Walsh and all Maryknollers?"

"Willingly," replied the American.

"You offer now your sufferings, and even your life, for the prosperity of your beloved Society?" continued Father Tour. "You pray that they all may do the work of God in a truly apostolic spirit?"

"Most certainly," said Father Price faintly.

While Father Tour bowed at the side of the bed, Father Price placed his weak hand on the kneeling priest's head and blessed him. The time was then nine-thirty. A few minutes later the dying man said, "Tell Father Walsh my last thoughts were for them all, and that I die in the love of Jesus, Mary, Joseph, and of Maryknoll." Father Tour began the prayers for the dying, but Father Price's voice failed and he was unable to join in. At five minutes past ten Father Price's pain-racked body ceased its struggle for life, and his soul hurried forth to meet the Mother he had so long loved and served. He died as he wished, on her feast day. It was September 12, 1919.

After Father Price's death, the sealed envelope was opened and it contained a letter expressing the wish that his heart be removed and sent to Nevers to be placed near the body of his favorite little saint, Bernadette. His body was buried in Happy Valley Cemetery, Hong Kong; and, when conditions permitted, his heart, enshrined in a suitable receptacle, was sent to Nevers where it was placed in a small niche in the chapel wall, according to arrangements Father Price had made years earlier.

In 1936, Father Price's remains were taken from the temporary resting place in Happy Valley Cemetery and were transferred to Maryknoll, at the edge of the woodland where he had so often gone to pray in solitude and silence. To this little plot of land called God's Acre, Maryknollers and lay folk journey for silent prayer beside the simple grave of the saintly Tar Heel whose dream led him across the world.

The Maryknoll mission in Yeungkong was under the jurisdiction of Bishop de Gúebriant, of Canton, until 1924. On January 31 of that year the territory was enlarged and formally transferred by Rome to Maryknoll under the title, Prefecture Apostolic of Kongmoon. It was the first territory ever to be placed in the charge of American priests, and the event marked another milestone in the history of Maryknoll and America's foreign-mission movement. The new mission consisted of an area the size of Ohio with a population of about six million. Kongmoon City was made the mission center, and it gave the whole prefecture its name. There were six other mission stations and a total of forty outstations. Father James Edward Walsh was appointed prefect of the new territory. Three years later, Rome, satisfied with the development of the work, raised the prefecture to a vicariate and named Monsignor Walsh to be its first bishop.

The new bishop, who had become superior of the Maryknollers in China after the death of Father Price, was an industrious and scholarly man. Despite many handicaps, the mission had grown steadily. There were almost twenty-five Maryknoll priests in the area, and three Maryknoll Brothers. Fifteen missions were established by this time, and the number of outstations had increased to 188. Twenty-eight schools had been opened, and six dispensaries established. The number of Christians was a little over 7,000 and more than 1,000 catechumens were being instructed for baptism.

One source of joy to all Maryknollers, and a sign of confidence given by the Holy See, was the fact that the new vicariate had been entrusted with the custody of Sancian Island, where a large shrine had been erected marking the spot where Francis Xavier had died and been buried. Two priests were assigned to the island to care for 1,300 Christians. The island was a place of pilgrimage, and it was there that Bishop James Edward Walsh was consecrated on May 22, 1927, the first native-born American to reach the episcopate of China.

All the Maryknollers in South China were at Sancian for the consecration except one—Father Daniel L. McShane. He had been ordained in 1914, the first Maryknoll seminarian to become

a priest. He had come to China in the second mission group in
1919. His absence was explained when a note reached Father
William Downs, a Maryknoll priest in Hong Kong, a few days
after the consecration. It said:

Thursday
(June 2, 1927)

Dear Father Downs:

I'm over a week on my back with smallpox. Thank God, I did
not go down to spread it to the others.

Please tell Bishop Walsh I'm trying so hard to offer my sufferings for his many new responsibilities. I give him everything I have.
God love him and dear Father Superior, my mother and brothers
and sisters. Tell them I'm praying for them. I hold no grudge
against anybody. I am thinking of the Sisters and Brothers also.
Dr. Dickson (of the American Presbyterian Mission) has been
especially kind to me. Can't retain the least food and the heat
is intense.

God's blessed will be done. No mail seems to be coming
this way.

Pray for me.
McShane

Father Daniel McShane had been born in Columbus, Indiana,
on September 13, 1888, the youngest of six children. After attending schools in Indiana, he entered St. Mary's Seminary in
Baltimore, and in 1912 transferred to the newly founded Maryknoll. As a young priest, he directed the small Maryknoll preparatory seminary in Scranton, Pennsylvania, and later was transferred
to open the Maryknoll procure in San Francisco. In 1919 he was
named to lead the second mission group into China. His first assignment was to Tungchen where he was to study the language
and become orientated under the guidance of Father Bernard
Meyer, himself only a veteran of one year.

At the end of the first year, Father McShane was assigned as
pastor to Loting, a bustling town in the northwest part of the
mission. Loting in ordinary times would have been a pleasant
enough place in which to live and work but when Father McShane
arrived it had several serious drawbacks. First of all, there was a
marked hostility towards the Catholic Church. Next, the town was
the center for a civil war then going on, and it frequently changed
hands. Finally, it was an area where poverty and superstition

compelled many families to abandon infant girls. About the civil war, Father McShane could do little except stay out of the way of bullets. But on the two remaining items he went to work with typical Hoosier vigor and perseverance. After some false starts he finally had the Church organized in Loting, and started building for the future.

To handle the matter of abandoned babies, he opened an orphanage. Immediately, the Catholic mission became the center for everyone who wanted to get rid of a child. The greater number of infants brought in were in such a neglected and starving condition that few managed to survive the first day or two. Father McShane baptized the dying children and felt secure in the belief that his work could not help but succeed, having so many innocent advocates in heaven.

The Chinese, despite the charity of the American, did not flock to join the Church but Father McShane felt that his roots were firmly enough established in Loting so that he could look around for another place to broaden his work. He chose the market town of Lintaan and set about beginning an orphanage and outmission there. He had great difficulty renting a house because the superstitious people had no desire to have deaths take place in any houses they owned. But he finally secured a mudbrick shop, and the project was begun.

Father McShane was hardly back in Loting when he received a call for help from the catechist he had left behind in Lintaan. Some of the Lintaan citizenry were making threats against the orphanage. The missioner hurried back to the market town to be greeted by a shower of stones and abuse. But the Hoosier showed no fear, and the innate sense of fair play of the people restrained the troublemakers. The orphanage was left alone.

One day towards the end of May, 1927, Father McShane found another abandoned baby near the mission. He carried it home and baptized it. The child was number 2,483 on his baptismal register. It was also to be the last he was to record. The infant had smallpox and the priest contracted the disease. On June 4, Father McShane died, a victim of his own heroic charity.

Bishop Walsh, after his consecration analyzed the situation of his vicariate in this way: "The status of Kongmoon comes to this. The Vicariate has realized: (1) Its first indispensable bit of building, (2) its business organization, (3) occupation of its territory.

What it must now turn to is mission work proper, which entails: (1) Its mission organization of native help, (2) its larger building program of training school and central establishments, and (3) its propaganda—direct and written—to establish contact with its six million souls. When these activities get fairly under way, Kongmoon will be a functioning Chinese Mission."

Bishop Walsh realized that his territory would never be really successful without a seminary. Like all his missioners, he held that Maryknoll had only come to the Kongmoon area until the Chinese themselves were strong enough to take over. In 1923, he had begun a *probatorium* in Yeungkong which was designed to provide elementary education preparing boys for the minor seminary. At the time of his consecration in 1927 the vicariate had more than thirty boys in the seminary that he had opened a year earlier. It is significant that in a struggling mission, less than ten years old, he should place such emphasis on the training of native vocations. But it was a policy that was to bear rich dividends when in another decade the Japanese Army poured into South China, and still later when the Communist hordes took control of the region.

Another project of the Kongmoon Vicariate which was started early was the novitiate for native Sisters. In 1928 Bishop Walsh began the novitiate in a rented building. Maryknoll Sisters were brought in to train the native girls. Two years later a permanent convent was erected, and seven girls were accepted, and in the next two years the number doubled. In 1933, five of the novices were clothed with the religious habit, and three years later those novices pronounced their first vows as Sisters of the Immaculate Heart.

8

A Small but Constant Flame

In October, 1933, Father Joseph A. Sweeney, of New Britain, Connecticut, was assigned to begin work among the leper beggars of the Kongmoon area. His first scene of operation was in a bamboo grove near the city of Toishan, the place of origin of a very large percentage of Chinese who had emigrated to the United States. He reported his first visit in these words: "Sitting around in that jungle darkness were deformed creatures with only stumps where hands and feet should have been. Many had distorted faces. I saw one afflicted Chinese woman, hideous to behold, with a beautiful eight-month-old baby girl in her arms. The child, as is often the case with the children of lepers, was spotless."

Father Sweeney, with his zealous confrere Father Frank Connors, set about to transform the place of death and corruption into a little park. At first he was misunderstood because a pagan mentality found it difficult to comprehend why a white man should wish to come among them. But Father Sweeney has a way with him, and he soon won the lepers over. He built toilets, a kitchen, and a dispensary. He distributed clean clothing and helped with obtaining food. Soon the lepers took a new interest in life and even planted flowers to beautify the bamboo grove.

Next, Father Sweeney heard about fifty lepers living in a cemetery near Sunwui. These unfortunates had built crude shacks from discarded coffin boards and lived cut off from humanity. Occasionally bands of soldiers would raid the makeshift colony and shoot any lepers found. Father Sweeney went to Sunwui, erected clean bamboo houses with palm roofs. He then moved the lepers to these new quarters and burned down their former hovels. The whole area was disinfected and all the rats were killed. He built a kitchen and a mudbrick dispensary, and in this latter building he gave daily treatment to each leper.

Within a year, Sunwui was a transformed place. Truck gardens supplied fresh vegetables; banana, papaya, and orange trees gave abundant fruit; beds of tropical flowers made the once decaying graveyard a place of beauty. Father Sweeney's work won recognition and in 1936 the Chinese Government deeded a large tract of land at Ngaimoon for a permanent colony. Once again Father Sweeney began transforming a wilderness. He started building new homes, a hospital, a chapel and kitchens. Before the construction was finished the worst typhoon ever recorded for the region struck and devastated the colony. So Father Sweeney had to begin anew. By this time the Japanese military had flooded into the South China area and complicated his problem. But in 1938 the colony was ready and all the lepers at Sunwui and some other parts of the Kongmoon area were brought to Ngaimoon, to the colony named Gate of Heaven.

The new leper colony was a veritable paradise for the afflicted Chinese. In it they were able to return to some semblance of normal life. The rich bottom lands produced good harvests of rice and vegetables. The river offered fish for the taking. The brick buildings of the colony presented an over-all impression of stability and permanence.

Father Sweeney was also enabled to develop his work through the aid of Catholic doctors. First came Dr. Harry Blaber, fresh from internship in Brooklyn. After five years of service he returned to America, married, and took his wife back to China. He remained at the colony until conditions caused by the proximity of the Japanese troops became so intolerable that he had to return with his wife to the United States.

Another doctor was Artemio Bagalawis. As a young medical student in Manila, Bagalawis had come into contact with the Maryknoll Fathers. He was a member of a prominent Filipino family, and his father was one of the leading supporters of the Apostate Bishop Aglipay who had set up an independent Filipino Church. Bagalawis had been baptized and brought up in the Aglipayan sect. Impressed by the work of Father James Drought and other Maryknollers in Manila, young Bagalawis renounced the schism and was received into the Catholic Church. Following his graduation from the University of Santo Tomas in 1934, he volunteered for mission work in China. In 1939 his fiancée came from the Philippines, and the couple were married at the Gate of Heaven Leper Asylum.

During the war he moved from place to place ahead of the invaders. After the war he was engaged by CNRRA to work in Canton. When CNRRA finished its work he went to Toishan with his wife to be surgeon at the new Sacred Heart Hospital opened by Bishop Paschang. He stayed on until he was stopped by the Communists and deported. He lost all his precious medical books and instruments. He is now back in the Philippine Islands but will be ready to rejoin the Maryknollers when they return to the mainland.

Another doctor who joined Father Sweeney's staff was an Irishman, Dr. John J. Sherry. Before the first World War he had a flourishing practice in London. During the war he served in front line hospitals in France. After the war he suffered a period of ill health and went to Lourdes for a rest. Impressed with the devotion shown at Lourdes, he had remained to join the Medical Board there, even though he had regained his health. In 1932 he decided to spend the rest of his life in a place where he could "do the most for mankind," and his search for this spot brought him to the abandoned lepers in the former graveyard at Sunwui.

In 1936, at Maryknoll's First General Chapter held in Hong Kong, Bishop James Edward Walsh was elected Superior General of Maryknoll. Since his new duties took him to the Maryknoll headquarters in America, a replacement had to be found to succeed him as head of the Kongmoon Mission. The priest selected was Father Adolph J. Paschang, a Kongmoon missioner from Martinsburg, Missouri. On June 17, 1938, the Holy See formally named Father Paschang, Vicar Apostolic, and he was consecrated bishop in November.

Bishop Paschang took charge of the Kongmoon territory at a

time when the area was being invaded by the Japanese. Those were difficult days, ones that brought many sufferings to the people. The bishop worked and organized to give what help he could. Relief stations were set up and new dispensaries were opened. It was not long before the American superior was being referred to as the "little bishop of charity." In the first year after his consecration the Kongmoon dispensaries gave 40,000 free treatments at 17 stations. There was an old folks' home, a home for the blind, a hospital, and 28 schools. The population at the leper colony had grown to 271. The mission staff numbered 32 priests, 4 Brothers, 15 Sisters, and there were 72 seminarians being trained. If the times were ordinary ones, those would have been the years of great progress.

But the times were far from ordinary. Already in those first days incidents were beginning to develop that made the future uncertain. A Japanese warship steamed into the harbor of Sancian Island. Soldiers and sailors streamed ashore to de-activate any military potential the island had. During a search a gun was found in the home of one of the Christians, and the terrified man was dragged off to be punished. Father John J. Joyce, assistant to Father Robert J. Cairns, Sancian's pastor, hurried to the man's aid. A Japanese officer ordered the priest to be shot for his interference.

Father Joyce, who had experienced close calls before from pirates and tropical storms, was pushed up against the mission wall. The officer drew his gun and fired point-blank at the tall New Yorker. The bullet went through the priest's cassock but fortunately did not touch him. The officer wheeled about and left the mission yard without firing again. Later Father Joyce confessed to friends that in the excitement of preparing to die he had found himself reciting "Grace Before Meals" instead of the "Act of Contrition" he intended.

The Japanese blockade cut the leper colony off from its supplies of medicine. Malaria began to take a toll of victims and an epidemic of anemia broke out. Father Sweeney, who had gone to Hong Kong for an operation, found a boat owner who was willing to run the blockade. A quantity of medicine was put aboard and under cover of darkness the two set out to get through the Japanese net. Suddenly the darkness was split by the beam of a Japanese patrol boat. The soldiers opened fire with a machine gun and their patrol boat came rushing in to ram the block-ade runner. Father Sweeney knew that all was lost. He jumped into the South China Sea. For six hours he swam in the darkness. When daybreak came, he stumbled, exhausted, on a small unin-habited island.

"Two weeks went by, and the numb ones at Gate of Heaven were desolate," stated *The Reader's Digest*, reporting the incident to its millions of readers. "They prayed for Big Joe's return, with-out much hope. Then, one morning, the Japanese across the river were startled by the shrill rejoicing that swept the leper colony. A Chinese fisherman had found Father Sweeney, and Big Joe had come back to Gate of Heaven."

Following Pearl Harbor, the Americans who had been tolerated in the Kongmoon area by the Japanese became enemies. Once again a warship put in at Sancian. This time Father Joyce was away at the leper colony and Father Cairns was alone. The Jap-anese took him off the island. His fate is not known, though local Chinese say he was bound in a pig crate and thrown into the sea. Father Cairns, a native of Worcester, Massachusetts, thus became one of the first Americans to die in a war that was to take so many lives.

Father Joyce, on the mainland, had his own troubles with the Japanese army which was entrenched on the opposite side of the river to the leper colony. The soldiers lobbed shells into the com-pound and whenever anyone was seen moving in the Gate of Heaven Colony, the soldiers used the moving figure as a target for rifle practice. One day a leper caught in the open was hit by bullets. Father Joyce, who saw the incident, rushed from his place of safety, dodged through a hail of bullets, picked the leper up and carried him back out of the line of fire. Father's heroism, however, was useless. The leper's blood stained the priest's cloth-ing, and the poor man died as Father Joyce gave him the last absolution.

The Japanese pressure became so strong, and threat of capture so great, that the Maryknollers were finally forced to withdraw from the colony to avoid being taken prisoners. Father Sweeney joined the United States Army Air Force as a chaplain and began marking time until he could get back to his lepers.

The Japanese had moved even earlier against Bishop Paschang. On the morning of Pearl Harbor, while the bishop and three of his priests were feeding nearly a thousand refugees at the mission, Japanese soldiers arrived to break up the distribution. The next day the four Americans were taken into detention. After some discussion it was finally decided to expel the bishop and his three priests to the Portuguese colony of Macao. The Japanese had Macao surrounded, so it was as restrictive as a prison, yet the Japanese did not have to provide food for the Americans.

Macao was a tiny island of freedom, full of sick and suffering refugees. Bishop Paschang and his priests set about helping the ill and dying. All the time the bishop prayed for a way to get back to his own mission territory. At last he made contact with Chinese guerrillas, and a plan was made. One dark night the bishop and Father Anthony J. Paulhus, of Fall River, Massachusetts, who was the rector of the Kongmoon seminary, slipped from their house and made their way to the waterfront. They hid behind some barrels until a rowboat came into the dock. Then at a prearranged signal, they left their hiding place and hurried to the rowboats.

"Come quickly! There are many blackbirds (Japanese) around tonight," whispered a young Chinese guerrilla holding a submachine gun.

Two other guerrillas were in the boat, both heavily armed. The priests climbed in the frail craft, and by oars muffled with rags the soundless boat was propelled away from Macao. Once a patrol boat passed within a hundred feet. The escapees were almost to the shore of China when a searchlight caught them in its full glare. A Japanese patrol boat roared down on them firing from a machine gun in the bow.

The guerrillas rowed like mad, and the bishop and his friends stumbled ashore under a hail of bullets. They leaped behind a mass of debris on the beach from where the guerrillas returned fire. The battle went on for a half hour. The Japanese did not land because they feared a trap, and at last the besieged men were able to get away in the darkness. For weeks Bishop Paschang and Father Paulhus were transferred from one guerrilla band to another, until at last they reached Free China. Then bishop and priest made their way back to the Kongmoon territory. They could not go to Pakkai which was in the hands of the Japanese, so Bishop Paschang made his headquarters at the Loting mission, and there he remained helping the people for the rest of the war.

As soon as peace came, Bishop Paschang set about the gigantic task of relief and rehabilitation that was needed in his mission. In the city of Toishan fifty people a day were dying of starvation. On one day, 102 emaciated corpses were picked up off the city street. In the vicinity of Toishan, 25 congee kitchens were opened. Congee is a rice gruel, fortified with vegetables. More than a quarter of a million people were fed during the famine. In Hoignan the missioners started to feed two hundred, and were soon up to a thousand. The Hoignan orphanage took in about a hundred children. Father Lawrence A. Conley, another Massachusetts Maryknoller, began a Boystown in an abandoned temple near Toishan.

Bishop Paschang received a strong assist in his reorganization work from an unexpected source. When he had first come to Kongmoon Mission, Bishop (then Father) Paschang had been stationed in Kochow. There, one day, the son of a wealthy and cultured family was brought to him and Father was asked if the boy might be enrolled in the mission school, even though he was not a Catholic. Father Paschang was doubtful about the boy when he heard that no school in the Kochow area had been able to keep him because of his wild ways and his refusal to study. But the young priest decided to take a chance.

Young Wong may have had the idea of entering the mission school to continue his ways of violence and havoc, but something about the Americans restrained him. Besides the school was different. For the first time he learned what discipline meant. Instead of having teachers who fawned upon him because of his social position and who begged him to do school work, he had masters who told him what to do and expected it to be done at once. In this environment the boy found himself. He became a leader in the school both in study and in sports. Upon his graduation he took all the first prizes, even in religion.

Then Wong dropped a bombshell into his family circle. He announced that he was going to become a soldier. His parents pleaded with him not to disgrace the family name. They repeated the classical saying, "Good metal is not used to make nails; good men are not soldiers." They begged Father Paschang to intervene. The missioner, however, sided with the boy. He urged that young Wong be allowed to decide his own career. So off went the boy to become a soldier.

By the time the war with Japan broke out, Wong had become a brigadier general. His feats in the field were legendary. After

America entered the struggle, General Wong was assigned as the liaison between Chinese and American forces. At war's end, the general returned home to the Kongmoon area. He sought out Bishop Paschang and offered his help. When the new Morning Star School was opened, General Wong, head of the board of trustees, declared at the formal opening: "The training I received as a student in this Catholic school was the best preparation I could have for life. I want other young men of my country to have the same opportunity I had, to know the Catholic priests, to learn the great lessons they teach."

In that postwar period, other mission schools were opened, too. Brother Albert Staubli began a Catholic trade school in Pakkai to teach Chinese boys carpentry and woodcarving. Brother Albert had built many of the mission buildings of Kongmoon Vicariate, and in his trade school he set boys to fashioning woodwork for the new memorial chapel that was planned for Sancian Island.

Father Sweeney went back to the Gate of Heaven leper colony. After the Japanese occupation he found the place a mass of filth, broken furniture, and ruined buildings. As he had done so many times in the past, he rolled up his sleeves and started rebuilding. Lepers returned to Ngaimoon, and soon the Connecticut Yankee had a family of two hundred. Dr. Bagalawis, who with his wife and young son had been forced to flee the colony to escape capture, had spent the war years helping Maryknollers in Free China. Now he, too, returned. Once more the colony was brought to efficient condition.

Since the Maryknollers had been in Kongmoon, they had gone through civil wars, flood, famine, and international war. After World War II they looked for peaceful years and the reaping of the harvest. But in the north a new threat had formed. Communists overran Manchuria, and then North China. Like a bloody, devastating sickle they swung southwards towards the rich rice lands. They marched under banners reading "Liberation" but theirs was the liberation of the firing squad and garrote. Wherever the Communists held sway, men were terrorized, murdered, and religion was strangled.

At the end of 1949 the Reds reached Kongmoon, and at once began their program of "reform." Missions were closed, priests and Sisters imprisoned. The native Chinese priests who had been trained in the Kongmoon seminary suffered first and hardest. They were beaten and tortured. Some were publicly exhibited in stocks and chains, wearing about their necks signs that proclaimed them "running dogs" of the Americans. They were condemned to penal servitude. Then the noose tightened. Public trials against the Americans took place. After months of imprisonment, the Maryknollers began to be expelled. Sisters, Brothers, and priests—one by one the Reds exhibited them, sentenced them and drove them out.

A large trial was held in Loting where Father Robert P. Kennelly, of Norwalk, Connecticut, who had taken over the direction of the Loting orphanage following the death of Father Mc-Shane, was accused of putting thousands of babies to death. The Reds had previously expelled the priest but the trial was held *in absentia* for propaganda purposes, and Father was found guilty and sentenced to two years in prison. Father Raymond A. Gaspard, his assistant, was in the hands of the Reds and was confined to prison. A public trial was held in Kongmoon City to humiliate Brother Albert and put him in jail as a common criminal.

It was twenty months before the Reds put the screws on the little bishop of charity. He was too popular for them to proceed hastily. First, the "squeeze" was put on him for taxes. Then he was urged to leave China. But the man who had run the Japanese blockade to get home to his mission was not going to run away because of a few threats. So pressure was applied. On three different days the Reds forced Bishop Paschang to contact Maryknoll headquarters in Hong Kong by telephone to say that local Chinese officials were demanding money from him under torture. On the first two days the amount stated was $40,000; on the third day it was reduced to $22,000. The Papal Internuncio to China, Archbishop Anthony Riberi, gave orders that no ransom should be paid; if the Church should once pay ransom, there would be no end to the demands from all over China.

When the money was not forthcoming, Bishop Paschang was dragged to public trial. His hands were tied behind his back and a noose circled his neck. Some twenty Reds beat and kicked him, and forced him to kneel before a crowd of people while men and women struck him about the head for three hours. The Communists shouted accusations of all sorts of crimes. What must the decent people of Kongmoon have thought? They knew their little bishop. They knew that long before the Reds came he had sold much of the mission's property and had used the money for the poor. They knew that he had taken his own episcopal garments and transformed them into dresses and coats for the orphans. They knew that he had introduced farming techniques to help the farmers better to earn their daily bread. They knew how he had started a knitting mill to aid the unemployed. They knew about the boys he had sent to Peking and Shanghai to study and thus be ready to lead their own people. They knew how during the war he walked all over the mission area giving assistance and help to those in need. They knew how much he loved the Chinese people and how cheerfully he gave of himself, for in their hour of need they had seen him doing coolie work, carrying bags of rice on his shoulders, and unloading medical supplies from the river boats. All of this they knew was done for them.

On the next day the bishop was paraded through the town, dragged along by the noose about his neck. After that his wrists and knees were rubbed on rough bricks until they became raw and bloody. Now the noose would jerk him upwards; next it would allow him to fall down again on the broken stones. The blood ran through his trousers. His hands were numb from pain. For hours the torture went on. This terrible day was the fourteenth anniversary of his consecration as Bishop of Kongmoon.

"When they beat me," he recalled later, "the men hit me on the back of the head until my neck was badly swollen. The women hit me in the eyes until they were black."

But the Reds were unable to break his will, and at last worn out by their own efforts to obtain a false confession, they seized all the money and property he held for the mission and took him to the Macao border. Once before Macao had been his prison, now it was to be his path to freedom. From Macao he made his way to Hong Kong to await the day when he could get back to his people and diocese.

And so they went, one by one, into prison and into exile. Priest, Brother, and Sister went, and gradually the organized religious life of the diocese slowed down. At the Gate of Heaven leper colony, the Reds allowed work to continue. They were hard put for an excuse to close the colony; they could not call life among the living dead a form of American imperialism; their indoctrination had given them no way to fight the tall priest from Connecticut and his young assistant from Maryland, Father Carroll Quinn.

When the Reds first came Dr. Bagalawis sent his wife and son to Hong Kong. He continued his work of mercy among the Kongmoon stations but the strain of life under the Communists began to tell. Each time he operated, Red soldiers held bayonets at his back and threatened to kill him if the patient should die. Under such conditions work was impossible, so he rejoined his wife and son, and returned to Davao in the Southern Philippines to open a clinic for the Chinese there until the time when China should be free again.

Father Sweeney and his assistant, Father Carroll I. Quinn, of Baltimore, remained behind. They had no actual control of the colony—it was in Red hands. They lost their house to the "liberators" and took up residence in the sacristy of the church. But they were still able to help their patients. Later Father Sweeney said that the year 1952 was the happiest year he had ever spent in China. Not because of the Reds, but because of the loyalty of his lepers under Red rule.

Then in August of 1953, the Communists took Father Sweeney and Father Quinn from the colony on the pretext of having them register at the county seat. The conquerors promised the lepers that their priests would be back almost immediately. But the Reds had other plans that did not include a return trip to Gate of Heaven. The Reds moved the two priests on and on until the Hong Kong border was reached, then they pushed the Americans across to an undesired freedom.

With the expulsion of Fathers Sweeney and Quinn the last two Maryknoll Missioners of Kwangtung Province were driven out. The area that had seen the arrival of the first mission band in 1918 was now for the first time in thirty-five years without a Maryknoller. Flood, war, pestilence, and famine had not been able to halt that work, but now under the Communists the Christian advance is stalled. Yet though Kongmoon Diocese officially has come to a standstill, a small but constant flame of faith still burns within.

9

Korea—The Hermit Kingdom

Korea has become a household word to the people of America, because on the peninsula's hillsides and in its fertile valleys American youth has made the greatest sacrifice that can be asked of man. Within its mud-locked and sometimes frozen earth, thousands upon thousands of American boys spend the long sleep before the day of general judgment. Yet just a few short years ago Korea was a tiny splotch on the map, a spot that only a rare American could properly locate. And even today when the name itself has been burned into so many hearts and minds, not many more know much about the Koreans—their peacetime life and their customs.

Of all the inhabitants in the modern world, the Koreans are unique. For they are a people who did not wait for missioners of Christianity to convert them, but who started their own conversion and then asked for priests. Korea had long been known as The Hermit Kingdom, a name given because of its inaccessibility to the rest of the world. Korea's citizens lived behind walls, preserving their own customs and language. Contact with the outside world was little sought, and foreigners were barred from The Hermit Kingdom under penalty of death.

Now it had long been the custom for the Korean King to send an embassy to Peking each year with tribute for the Emperor. As early as 1631 these ambassadors had been in touch with the Jesuit missioners in the Chinese capital and by 1700 Father Ricci's *True Principles Concerning God* was already known in Korea. Thus it was that when in 1777 a group of Korean scholars retired to a mountainside to study books on nature, they examined among others some of these Christian doctrine books brought to Korea years before. They found the doctrine on the Providence of God, the soul, virtue and vice so beautiful that they at once began to conform their own morals to these Christian precepts.

One of the scholars named Pyek prevailed upon a friend, Ri Syeng Houn, who was going to China with his father, the ambassador, to investigate this Christian religion and to bring back additional information. The friend returned with a new name, Peter Ri, received when his investigation in Peking had led him into the Catholic Church. In Korea Peter baptized his friend Pyek, "John the Baptist," and a scholar named Kouen was baptized "Francis Xavier."

The three new Christians set about preaching their Faith, and made many converts, all of whom they baptized. The converts became so numerous that a secret message was forwarded to the Bishop of Peking asking for clergy. In 1794 the bishop sent a Chinese priest, who found more than 4,000 Christians awaiting for his arrival. A mass convert movement was soon underway, and 6,000 more Christians were added. But the pagan rulers of Korea had other ideas, and in 1801 began the first of the many terrible blood baths leveled against Christianity. Among those martyred was the zealous Chinese priest, Father Tsiou. Nevertheless, the Korean Church continued to grow. French missioners entered Korea from Manchuria through drains beneath the city walls of Wiju on the Yalu and many of them met death along with their converts.

One heroic figure of that early period was Blessed Andrew Kim, who belonged to one of Korea's first Christian families. Andrew's grandfather had died after eleven years in jail, and his father had to flee Seoul in order to remain alive. Andrew studied at Macao and was ordained, the first Korean priest, but he had hardly returned to his own country from China when he was arrested. Only twenty-five years old, he was led from his prison cell one September day of 1846 to a field outside Seoul. There he found martyrdom from eight hacking blows of the executioner's sword.

In 1922, the Holy See assigned Maryknoll a territory in Korea. The young Society was then only a decade old and hardly four years had passed since its first mission band had set out for China. In presenting the mission to Maryknoll, the Holy See was giving a definite sign of confidence. The new territory had formerly been entrusted to the Paris Foreign Mission Society, which because of the war just ended in Europe was unable to staff it. The area was in the very north of Korea, bordering Manchuria, along the Yalu River. It was a region that included one-fifth of all Korea, about the size of Massachusetts, Connecticut and Delaware combined.

Father Patrick J. Byrne, of Washington, D.C., was assigned to pioneer the field. Father Byrne had gone to Maryknoll after his ordination at St. Mary's in Baltimore in 1915, and thus became the first priest to join the new Society. Gifted with a wonderful sense of humor and intellectually talented, he had served as director of the preparatory seminary in Clarks Summit, Pennsylvania; as director of the Major Seminary at Maryknoll; and had filled other responsible positions. He arrived in Korea early in 1923.

Father Byrne's first task was to make for Maryknoll headquarters a survey of the new territory. He found that the French missioners had established five centers with sixty stations, and developed a body of faithful numbering 4,890. There were three primary schools, poor and crowded, but schools none the less. He drew up a program for expansion which called for more schools and a seminary, and he ended his report by saying: "We shall do our building in the imagination, while working at the language. However, we shall also pray for the coming of a millionaire."

Before the year was out, Father Patrick H. Cleary, of Ithaca, New York, and Father John E. Morris, of Fall River, Massachusetts, joined Father Byrne. The group took up residence at Gishu on the Yalu River. In the spring, Father Byrne went to Shingishu, and Father Morris to Yengyou.

Father Byrne continually marveled at that first winter (and all winters thereafter). The temperature sometimes went to thirty-five or forty below zero. "No matter how cold the day, nor how early the Mass," he wrote in a diary to Maryknoll, "the village community turns out. One of the Fathers here has christened the churches 'holy refrigerators;' but the Christians will come before Mass, to remain after, and should there be more Masses, remain for all. At times the Sacred Species will freeze in the chalice before Communion, and must be thawed by holding the cup in the hands and breathing upon it."

The old adage that the blood of martyrs is the seed of Christianity proved true in the Korean mission. Growth was steady. In 1927, the mission was raised to a prefecture with Monsignor Byrne at its head. The name assigned was the Prefecture Apostolic of Pengyang. Today the city is known as Pyongyang. The mission staff consisted of seventeen priests, two Auxiliary Brothers, nine Maryknoll Sisters, and six Korean Sisters. Eleven districts were staffed, and there were eleven schools, three dispensaries and one home for the aged. Special work had been undertaken among the 50,000 Japanese in the mission, for Korea at this time was under Japanese control.

In 1930, Father Peter Ryang was ordained, the first native to become a priest for the Pengyang Mission. That year, too, saw Monsignor Byrne turn over his duties and return to the United States for other important work, which was to lead him eventually to found the Maryknoll work in Japan, as he had done in Korea. Two years later in Pengyang City, the second native priest, Father Francis Hong, was ordained.

By the end of 1935, Catholics in the mission had increased to almost 18,000. In that year there were twenty-six Maryknoll priests, four native priests, four Maryknoll Brothers, twenty-two Maryknoll Sisters, and fourteen Korean Sisters. Another sign of progress was the fact that fifty-seven Korean boys were preparing for the priesthood. Two of these were sent to the international seminary of Propaganda Fide in Rome. They distinguished themselves in their studies and were very popular among the students. Fathers Kim and Paak were ordained in Rome and returned to Korea in 1940. At the outbreak of the Korean war they were taken prisoners by the Communists and have never been heard of since. They are presumed to have been put to death for the Faith. At this time, too, the prefecture had thirteen schools.

The mission at Chinnampo, a seaport on the southwest coast, was a good example of what was being accomplished. When the first Maryknollers entered the city, they were insulted, derided as "foreign devils," and treated with hostility. By 1935, they were met everywhere with respectful salutations and were among the most honored people in town. The reason for the change was to be found in the works of charity and education that had been established there by Father Leo W. Sweeney, of New Britain, Connecticut, who was the brother of Father Joseph Sweeney of the leper colony in Kongmoon, and by Father Hubert M. Pospichal, of Elma, Iowa. Those two priests had begun a six-grade Government-recognized school, a four-grade school for poor children, a night school for poor adults, a dispensary, and an old folks' home. The schools alone gave education to 1,700 pupils. Within a few years, this mission was able to record 658 adult baptisms within a single year.

In 1938, Father William F. O'Shea, one of the first four Maryknoll students, was appointed Prefect Apostolic of the Korean mission; and in the following year, a cable from Rome announced that the mission had been raised to the rank of vicariate and Monsignor O'Shea named as the first bishop. He was listed among twelve missionary bishops to be consecrated by Pope Pius XII himself, at St. Peter's in Rome. This high honor was an indication of the Holy Father's paternal interest in world-wide mission development. The consecration took place on October 29, 1939.

Bishop O'Shea hurried back to Korea, and in the following year ordained his first priest, Father Callistus Hong, who had been sent to the seminary years earlier by Father Morris. Six other native Korean priests of the mission were in the sanctuary for the ordination. The growth of the Korean clergy was a matter of great satisfaction to the Maryknollers. The times were becoming unsettled, and the native priests could be counted to carry on the work if the restrictions being placed on the Americans by the Japanese should grow worse.

Only a short while earlier the first novices in the new native Korean congregation of the Sisters of Our Lady of Perpetual Help, sixteen in number, received the habit of their new society. These Sisters had been trained by Maryknoll Sisters. Half of the novices came from families in which one or both parents were pagan. Five of them were qualified teachers, others had received high-school education under the Maryknoll Sisters.

The spiritual report for 1940 which was sent to Maryknoll was very encouraging. The 5,000 Christians of fifteen years earlier had now grown to 25,000, and 3,500 catechumens were being pre-

pared for baptism. The mission at this time had 35 Maryknoll
Fathers, 7 Korean priests, 3 Maryknoll Brothers, 21 Maryknoll
Sisters, 29 Korean Sisters, and 112 Korean catechists. A Maryknoll Sister-doctor, Sister Mary Mercy, was in charge of the mission's three dispensaries.

Then on the Feast of The Immaculate Conception, 1941, the
blow fell. What happened at the Japanese mission in Chinnampo
that day is typical of the occurrences throughout the entire territory.
Big preparations had been made for the feast, and when Sister
Gregoria, a Maryknoller from Chicago, went out to organize the
choir for Mass she was amazed to see only one person in church.
Sister didn't know it but halfway across the world, on the other side
of the international date line, Japanese planes that morning had
just bombed and strafed Pearl Harbor.

It was not long before Japanese officers appeared and explained that Japan was at war with the United States. Father
Joseph A. Hunt, of Brookline, Massachusetts, the pastor of the
Japanese mission, was already arrested and at police headquarters.
Sister Gregoria and her superior, Sister Elenita, of Elizabeth, New
Jersey, were taken to the police station and questioned for most of
the remainer of the day before being taken back to the mission
and confined to the convent. Father Hunt was not sent home but
placed in jail. The next days were troubled ones. There were con-
tinual searches made of the mission, and more long hours of questioning. On December 11, Father Hunt managed to send word
that Sister Gregoria should consume the Blessed Sacrament. He
had been arrested so quickly that he had been unable to care for
It. This was a privilege that came to many of the Sisters in Korea.
In Yeng You, for example, the Sisters had to consume the Hosts of
three large ciboria.

For long months the Maryknollers were either in prison or interned. Example after example could be furnished of the loyalty
and generosity of the Korean Christians during this period. Time
after time from their own scant store of provisions they smuggled
food to the Americans. On many occasions, although desperately
poor themselves they sent small gifts of money to the missioners.
At last in 1942 the Americans were repatriated to the United
States aboard the exchange ship *Gripsholm*.

Meanwhile, affairs of the vicariate were taken over by Bishop
Paul Ro, of Seoul, a Korean. He sent six Korean priests from Seoul

to help the eight Korean priests in the Maryknoll territory. The native Sisters were placed under the direction of Sister Mary Agneta Chang, a Korean Maryknoller. Thus, providentially, despite the expulsion of the Maryknollers, the mission's work could go on. Christians would still receive the sacraments and be able to attend Mass. Once again the wisdom of the Holy Fathers in urging the rapid development of a native clergy was demonstrated.

The Maryknollers who had been sent home by the Japanese marked time in temporary work waiting for the war to end, and for the time they could get back to their posts. In 1944, Bishop O'Shea resigned his post so that one of his own priests, Father Francis Hong, might succeed him as vicar apostolic. There was no indication when the war with Japan would be over, and the Christians of Pengyang needed a shepherd. Once again God's hand could be seen in the move for in less than a year, Bishop O'Shea died suddenly and unexpectedly of a heart attack while hurrying to catch a train for Maryknoll in New York's Grand Central Station.

Then in 1945 came the atom bomb and the dramatic end to the war with Japan. But before American forces could move into that country the Soviet armies had sliced the nation in half, after entering the war in its very last days. As soon as the military permitted, Maryknollers returned to Korea. Their own mission territory of Pengyang was above the 38th parallel, and thus effectively sealed off by the Communists. The American missioners took up work in the diocese of Seoul, until such time as they might be allowed to go north.

10

Witness

In 1947, Monsignor Byrne, who had pioneered Maryknoll's work in Korea, was named Apostolic Visitor to the new South Korean government. He immediately left his post in Japan for the South Korean capital at Seoul. Monsignor Byrne brought much prestige to the Church in South Korea. He was on excellent terms with the South Korean President, Syngman Rhee. One of the high officials of the new government was a Catholic from his former Pengyang mission, Dr. John Chang. This scholarly Korean had been educated at Manhattan College in the United States with the help of Maryknoll, and for some years had taught in Maryknoll schools in Pengyang. After the war, he was elected to the National Assembly with a majority exceeded only by that of Mr. Rhee. In the months that followed he was given successively more important posts: head of the Korean delegation to the United Nations, ambassador to Washington, and finally premier of South Korea.

In 1948, Monsignor Byrne received a long report from an American Army official on the state of religion in North Korea. It was a gloomy picture. More and more restrictions and embarrassments were being directed against the Church.

The constitution adopted by the Communist government of North Korea in 1948, while stating that freedom of religion was assured, effectively limited religious activities. It prohibited the teaching of religion to any child until he reached the age of twenty-one, and it ordered all children to attend public school on Sundays. Christians were not given jobs in government factories and schools. But the devotion of the Korean clergy and the faith of the Christians were edifying. The Pengyang Cathedral, which had been destroyed in the war, was being rebuilt by funds collected from the faithful by Bishop Hong. The labor for the cathedral was almost completely volunteer. People came in for a week at a time from all parts of the mission, bringing their own rations, and working from dawn to dusk. At night they slept on the ground around the cathedral. Men, women, and children worked carrying bricks and mortar, mixing cement, and building scaffolding. It was not unusual to see the Korean Sisters climbing the runways to the top of the walls, each with a load of bricks on her back. And also just as heartening was the news that 27 Korean seminarians were under instruction.

In 1949, Monsignor Byrne was appointed Apostolic Delegate and raised to the rank of bishop. During the ceremonies attending Bishop Byrne's consecration in Seoul, President Rhee publicly declared: "Your Excellency is fully aware that we, the Korean people, are deeply grateful to the Supreme Pontiff and the other leaders of the great Catholic Church who have shown, on various occasions, unqualified sympathetic interest in our fight for freedom and independence. The very fact that they made it possible for you to be here as an official representative of the great Catholic Church, even before this Republic of Korea was born and before your recent consecration as bishop, is a clear manifestation of the unshaken faith of the Catholics in the ultimate victory of a cause dedicated to justice and freedom for mankind."

That same year, the Reds, having solidified their position in the north, began open attacks on the Church. Bishop Hong was arrested while on a journey to visit some of his Sisters. One by one the native priests were arrested and disappeared. Two young seminarians from Pengyang succeeded in crossing the border to freedom, so that they could continue their studies in Seoul. They reported that six more priests had been seized by the Reds. Their arrest precipitated a bloody battle between soldiers and 200 parishioners

Major seminary and international headquarters for Maryknoll are at Ossining overlooking the Hudson, 35 miles from New York City. In the seminary quadrangle the annual departure ceremony is held

The eyes have it! Father Bernard J. Hesler, of Schenectady, N. Y., holds the rapt attention of these Japanese youngsters at the Maryknoll mission in Kyoto, which was founded in 1935.

The world's poor and needy, particularly children and the aged, have a large corner on the heart of every Maryknoller. Japan's war-torn areas have spawned sad boys like Kano,

Father James Anthony Walsh was Propagation of the Faith Director in Boston when with Father Price he founded Maryknoll in 1911. He was Superior until he died in 1936.

Thomas Frederick Price, the other cofounder, was well known as a missioner in North Carolina. He headed Maryknoll's first mission band in 1918. He died in 1919.

A Communist jail in Canton, China, became the death-place for Bishop Francis X. Ford, of Brooklyn. He went to China in 1918, and became head of Kaying mission.

Pioneer of two Maryknoll mission territories was Bishop Patrick J. Byrne, of Washington, D. C., who met death in Korea as the result of cruel treatment by Red captors.

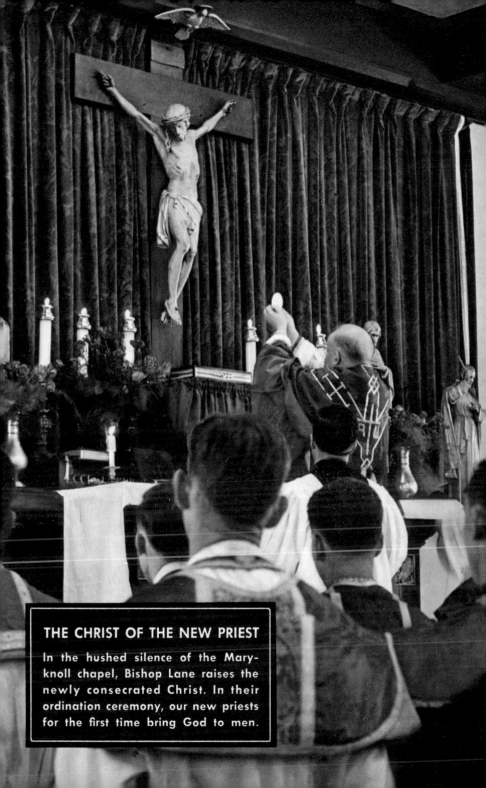

THE CHRIST OF THE NEW PRIEST

In the hushed silence of the Mary-knoll chapel, Bishop Lane raises the newly consecrated Christ. In their ordination ceremony, our new priests for the first time bring God to men.

These Maryknoll seminarians find a beehive full of activity. Manual labor period trains the seminarian in many occupations.

The Maryknoller's parish becomes the world. Father Robert Kearns, of New York, (above) witnesses an Andean wedding. Six nationalities are represented (below) by a typical group of student Maryknollers.

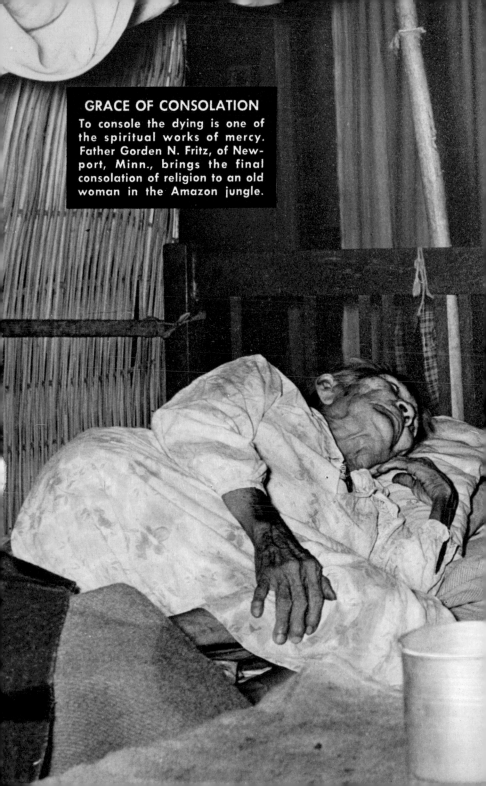

GRACE OF CONSOLATION
To console the dying is one of the spiritual works of mercy. Father Gorden N. Fritz, of Newport, Minn., brings the final consolation of religion to an old woman in the Amazon jungle.

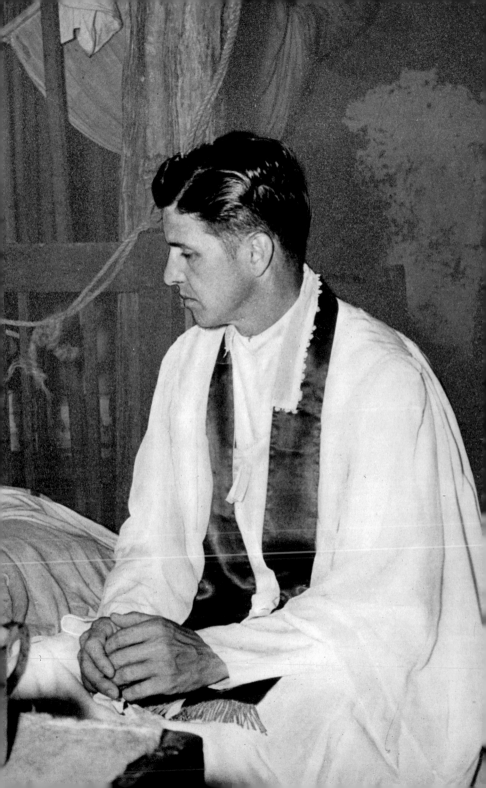

Hong Kong refugee boy — he searches the city dumps for his supper.

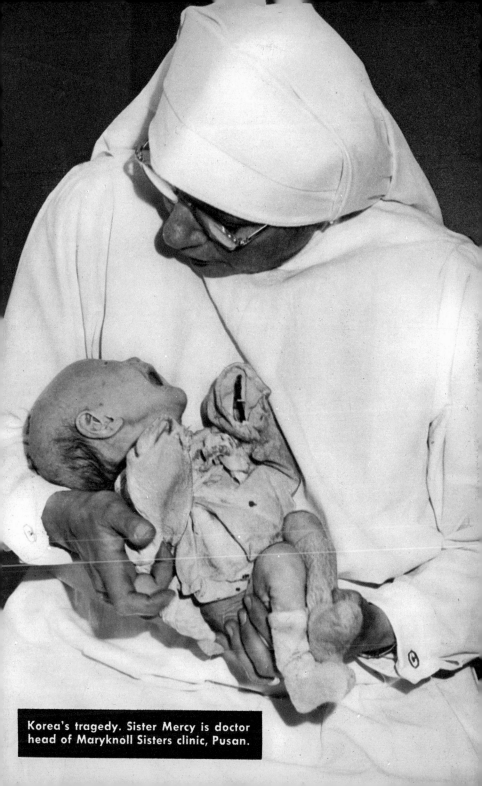

Korea's tragedy. Sister Mercy is doctor head of Maryknoll Sisters clinic, Pusan.

The first four missioners of the Catholic Foreign Mission Society of America to leave for China in 1918 were (front) James E. Walsh, Thomas F. Price, Francis X. Ford, and (standing) Bernard F. Meyer.

THE "RED" LOOK

The effects of Communist brain-washing show in the altered face of Father Robert W. Greene, Jasper, Ind., photoed before and after his public trial in Tungan, China.

AFTER

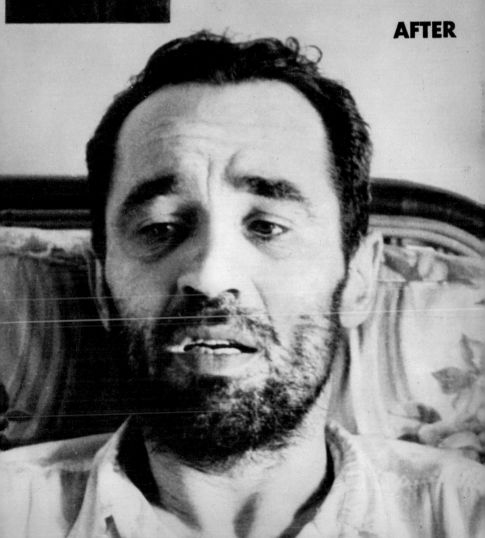

When a dormitory at Kyoto University went up in a blaze, Father John Murrett, of Buffalo, opened his tiny cottage to burned-out students. For years his "sardine can" served as a happy home to many young men

St. Theresa's was first convent, cradle of Maryknoll publications.

"No room!" says Father Justin Kennedy of New York, now in the Philippines.

who came to the aid of their priests. The fight ended only when two of the Fathers voluntarily gave themselves up. The seminarians said that only six priests were left in all of North Korea, and that 10,000 Korean Catholics had been put to death.

The Maryknoll group in Korea at this time consisted of eight priests and four Sisters. Bishop Byrne as Apostolic Delegate was independent of actual Maryknoll work, but he had a Maryknoll priest, Father William R. Booth, of Brooklyn, with him as secretary. The Society's activities were directed by Father George M. Carroll, of New York City, a veteran Korean missioner. Father Carroll was also representative for the American Catholic War Relief Services. He and his fellow priests were busily engaged in many works of charity, as well as in caring for regular parish duties. Then overnight the work in South Korea was shattered. Father George Carroll came hurrying on the morning of June 25, 1950, from the Sabingo base where he had gone to say Mass for the soldiers.

"The officers have all been called out," he told Bishop Byrne. "The North Koreans crossed the parallel this morning at four o'clock. A big army is marching on Seoul."

On Tuesday Father Carroll ordered all his priests to evacuate in order to avoid capture. Bishop Byrne, who was directly under the Holy See, felt that it was his own duty to remain and offer what support he could to the Korean Christians and clergy especially as Bishop Ro of Seoul was in Rome on his *ad limina* visit to the Holy Father when the Reds attacked. Father Booth obtained permission from Father Carroll to stay with the bishop. On Wednesday the Reds came, and armed looters began stripping the residence of the Apostolic Delegate. When Bishop Byrne and Father Booth were finally arrested, they were carried off to jail in their summer clothing, a fact that was to cause them much suffering later on.

For eight days they were confined in the stifling heat of a crowded and makeshift jail; given only a handful of barley and rice, and a little water, each day. They were forced to watch thousands of Koreans being brought in, interrogated, and sentenced to be shot. With them were other missioners: Father Ryou, a Korean, who volunteered to accompany the bishop to jail; Father Villemot, an 83-year-old French priest; the two aged Gombert brothers, one 76, the other 74, both priests; Sister Beatrice, the French superior of the St. Paul de Chartres Sisters; Monsignor

Francis Quinlan, Irish-born Columban Father; and many others.

On the ninth day, the prisoners were taken north to Pengyang, and the very area Bishop Byrne had pioneered and governed. All the rest of the captivity was to be spent in his former mission, the territory that the Maryknollers were so anxious to re-enter. Conditions at the Pengyang prison were very bad. The prisoners received a few ounces of rice and a little water each day. They slept on the floor, and were forbidden to talk to prisoners in other rooms than their own. When, in September, General MacArthur began to counterattack the Reds from his Pusan perimeter and made his surprise landing at Inchon, the prisoners along with captured American soldiers were taken north to the Yalu River, traveling in crowded boxcars by night.

At Manpojin on the Yalu River, Father Booth had an experience he was never to forget. At daybreak the prisoners were taken off the train and confined in a schoolhouse. Father Booth sat down at a desk and fell asleep, but soon was awakened by a gentle shaking.

"Aren't you Boo Sin Poo?" asked a young man in civilian clothing. "Boo" is the name Father Booth had been given in Korea when he came as a missioner to the Pengyang territory. "Sin Poo" means "Spiritual Father."

"Yes," answered the surprised missioner.

"Don't you know me?" asked the young man.

"I'm sorry. I don't think I do."

"I'm John Ri. You confirmed me here twelve years ago."

Then Father Booth remembered. He had been administrator of the area at the time and had gone to this village to confer the Sacrament of Confirmation. John had been about twelve years old then.

"How did you get in here?" asked Father Booth.

"The guards think it is good for us to see the foreigners who have been humiliated," he replied. "No one stopped me. One of the Christians saw you being led through town."

"But you'll get in trouble if you are seen talking to me."

"They think I'm trying to sell you these." He pulled a string of ten eggs from behind him. "They are for you, Father."

The starving missioner was almost ready to cry at the gift. The young man also presented a package of tobacco. Then he left to tell the Christians that the prisoner was indeed Boo Sin Poo. He came back a half an hour later and pressed five dollars into the missioner's hand, a gift the poor Christians had collected. He said that the Christians would be at the railroad station when the prisoners left, and asked if the Christians could have absolution since there was no knowing how soon they would see another priest.

When Father Booth went back to the train with the other prisoners, he saw the little group of Christians gathered close to the railroad station. They made no sign to attract the attention of the Red guards. As Father Booth passed he said the words of absolution and made the sign of the cross close to his breast so that only the Christians could see it. Not a word was spoken, but he could read the gratitude in their eyes.

On October 21, 1950, the prisoners began a forced march to avoid the advancing American troops. The route was along the Yalu River, over mountains that were already covered with snow. The weather was cold, and snow flurries and Siberian winds beat about the sick and weak marchers. The Korean commander, a major called The Tiger, had ordered that anyone falling out of line should be shot. The march was an unending purgatory. The Carmelite Sisters, who were walking in bare feet, left a trail of blood in the snow.

On one day of the march, twenty-one American soldiers were shot. On that day, too, Sister Beatrice collapsed and was shot. So was a White Russian woman. Someone would fall from exhaustion, there would be an explosion of a gun, the guards would roll the body off the trail, and then continue along laughing and joking. On two occasions Bishop Byrne gave general absolution. After eight days the group reached Chunggangjin, far up the Yalu. Over a hundred people had died on the march, and its effects were not over. Old Father Villemot, who never once complained, passed away in his sleep the next day. The two elderly Gombert brothers died within a day of each other. Sister Mary Clare, an Anglican nun, died the day the march ended. And it was at Chunggangjin that Bishop Byrne caught pneumonia.

The Tiger, the day after the march had ended, ordered all the prisoners out at seven in the morning to exercise. The weather was ten degrees below freezing. Bishop Byrne was required to strip down to his shirt and do calisthenics. That night he developed pneumonia. Four days later The Tiger ordered his prisoners to a new camp about four miles distant. The order came at midnight and Bishop Byrne, although very sick, had to walk all the way.

About twenty prisoners were crowded into one small room. Bishop Byrne was very weak by this time.

"I consider it the greatest privilege of my life," he said to his priest companions, "to have suffered together with you for Christ."

The next night the guards came at midnight and demanded that Bishop Byrne and Father Coyos, a Paris Foreign Missioner suffering from tuberculosis, be removed to another building. The wind was blowing and it was freezing cold, so Monsignor Quinlan tried to talk the guards out of the move, but they stood firm. Monsignor Quinlan and Father Booth helped the two sick men to the assigned house. It was a miserable place without heat. It had no windows, so it was perpetually dark. A straw mat served as a door, and there was only a little loose straw on the floor. For four days the bishop lay in this poverty. Father Coyos gave him final absolution on November 24. The next day Bishop Byrne died early in the morning.

Monsignor Quinlan, Father Booth, and two others, received permission to bury the bishop. They hewed a shallow grave in the frozen ground, and then laid the shriveled, shrunken body to rest. Bishop Byrne was wrapped in Monsignor Quinlan's cassock. The grave was covered with stones, a fortunate decision because in the spring crows came and ate the bodies of many who died over that terrible winter. For three years, Monsignor Quinlan and Father Booth were held prisoners. Then they were released by the Reds in 1953 and sent home through Soviet Russia. Monsignor Quinlan is now back in Korea and has been appointed Regent of the Apostolic Delegation to continue the work Bishop Byrne was doing when he was taken prisoner.

When the United Nations drove north in 1950 to rout the Korean Reds, Father George Carroll followed right behind. From Pengyang he sent word to Maryknoll headquarters that priests were urgently needed. "The situation is most serious," he wrote. "Every priest in the two northern provinces has been taken."

There was no trace of Bishop Hong and his clergy, and it was presumed that they were all dead. Christian families who knew Monsignor Carroll greeted the American so profusely that tears were brought to his eyes. The cathedral in Pyongyang that the people had been building at such a great sacrifice had been confiscated by the Reds, who had altered it, and turned it into a school. The Christians however had been able to save the sacred vessels and altar equipment which they had hidden. They immediately began clearing up the red-brick cathedral so that Mass might be offered.

The native Sisterhood which had been disbanded by the Communists six months earlier began to reassemble. The superior, Sister Mary Agneta, who had been left in charge when years earlier the Japanese had interned the Maryknoll Sisters, had been arrested by the Reds on October 4, 1950. Sister Agneta was the sister of John Chang, who was playing so prominent a rôle in the new South Korean Government. Rumor, fairly well substantiated, said that Sister Agneta, along with other Korean women, had been taken to the outskirts of Pengyang and shot.

Monsignor Carroll received word from Rome that the Holy See had appointed him Apostolic Administrator of the Pengyang Vicariate. Word also came that Maryknoll was sending two veteran missioners to assist him in reorganizing the mission: Father James V. Pardy, of Brooklyn, and Father Joseph W. Connors, of Pittsfield, Massachusetts.

Then overnight the situation changed. Chinese Communist "volunteers" poured over the Yalu River. The United Nations forces were driven back, and the long months of bitter warfare began. North Korea was once again Communist-controlled. Once more the Iron Curtain had fallen.

The Maryknollers did not desert Korea. The embattled Republic of Korea stood in great need. Millions of refugees had poured into the zone of freedom. There was a tremendous amount of work to be done. Some of the Maryknollers became chaplains in prisoner-of-war camps, for among the North Korean prisoners were some drafted Catholics. Those Christians were used as a nucleus for reaching their companions; soon Father Roy D. Petipren had close to a thousand prisoners under instruction. Catholic life began developing in camps that were once thought to be completely Communist.

Other Maryknollers entered parish work. Father Connors became pastor of a newly established parish in Pusan, and carried on relief work along with his other duties. One distribution alone saw 250 bales of clothing distributed to the poor and needy. Monsignor Carroll directed relief operations as Korean representative for the American Bishops' War Relief Services. By 1953, thirteen Maryknoll priests and eighteen Maryknoll Sisters were at work in South Korea.

The work of the Maryknoll Sisters during the war-ridden years attracted international attention. In 1950, three Maryknoll Sisters left the United States for medical work in Korea. Through the good offices of General MacArthur, the way was cleared for them to take up medical work in Pusan, then in the war area. When the war erupted, the Sisters were evacuated to Japan, and it was not until 1951 that they were able to get military permission to return to Pusan. Early that year they resumed work in a small dispensary, and began visiting the refugee camps. Within six months they had the largest dispensary and children's clinic in all Korea. More and more Sisters were sent from America to assist in the work, and native Sisters were brought in to help. The clinic was enlarged through the generosity of His Eminence Francis Cardinal Spellman, who visited the Pusan Clinic in 1952, and gave the Sisters a substantial donation. It has been of extraordinary service in treating an average of 2,000 patients daily. In 1953, three Sister-doctors and a half dozen nurses and pharmacists were busy from dawn to dusk. The work was initiated and directed by Sister Mary Mercy Hirschboeck, a native of Milwaukee, who received her medical degree at Marquette University. She and her assistants hope to serve as long as the Korean people need them.

In late 1953, Father Pardy was appointed superior of all Maryknollers in Korea, and at the same time it was announced that the Society had made an agreement with Bishop Ro, of Seoul, to take over the spiritual care of the entire Chung Chong Pouk To Province and to develop it as part of the Seoul Vicariate. The area, some ninety miles wide and a hundred miles long, contained 1,400,000 people, of whom 12,000 were Catholics. There were five central missions in the territory. In addition to Father Pardy, four other Maryknoll priests were assigned to the work there.

The Catholics made Father Pardy feel at home when he arrived at his Chang Ho Wun parish in the new area. In them he found the same sterling faith that he had known in North Korea.

"The Communists held this section for four months in 1950," some of the Christians told him, "and at first they met in Holy Rosary Church, up there on the mountainside, but we soon fixed them. Some of the Catholics carried rocks up to the top of the sixty-foot church steeple, and then hid in the steeple until the Reds had gathered for their nightly meeting. Then the Catholics dropped the rocks on the church roof and in the yard. Those Reds ran out of the church screaming about some imperialist secret air weapon! From then on the Reds held their meetings in old buildings at the foot of the hill, which they felt were better protected against secret air attacks."

This is the spirit of the Korean Catholics, a spirit inherited from ancestors who were the first Koreans to die for the Faith. It is the spirit of the South Korean Catholic and of the North Korean Catholic. It is the spirit that led young John Kim to brave Red guards in order to see and help Father Booth. It is the spirit attested to by many of our American soldiers who were prisoners of the Reds, and who were exchanged in 1953.

"During the bitterly cold first winter of the war," one of these former American prisoners told Father Connors in Pusan, "we were quartered in a confiscated Maryknoll mission at Pyongyang. Regularly an old Catholic Korean woman risked her life to smuggle us food and tobacco. She knew only a few words of English, but she spoke a universal language of prayer. Every time we saw her, she was calmly reciting the Rosary. We never knew her name. We just called her *Mama-san*. If the four of us who survived ever find her, she will have no worries the rest of her life!"

11

Kaying—The King's Highway

Grant us, Lord, to be the doorstep by which the multitudes may come to worship Thee. And if, in the saving of their souls, we are ground underfoot and spat upon and worn out, at least we shall have served Thee in some small way in helping pagan souls and we shall have become the King's Highway in pathless China.

This beautiful prayer was composed by Father Francis X. Ford during the early days of his apostolate in China. It became an invocation, in the spirit of which he was to live and to die, a petition touched with prophecy.

Father Ford went to South China as a member of the first Maryknoll mission group. His assignment was the city of Yeungkong, Maryknoll's first mission. His first major decision as pastor of Yeungkong was to open a boys' school that would care for both boarders and day pupils. As the years passed, his works grew: a home for old women, a girls' school, a home for blind children, and an orphanage. He built the first three-story building in Yeungkong, a convent to house the first group of Maryknoll Sisters to arrive in China.

In 1925, when the Paris Foreign Mission Society offered Maryknoll a part of its Swatow Vicariate, Father Ford was assigned to
pioneer the territory for Maryknoll. He entered the new mission
field on October 4, 1925, accompanied by Father James M.
Drought, of New York City, who was later to work in the Philippines and then become vicar general of the Maryknoll Society.
The territory lay in the northeast corner of Kwangtung Province,
had a population of about two and a half million, and boasted
4,456 Catholics—the fruit of many years of hard labor by the
French missioners, whose pioneers had arrived in 1849.

The new territory was a region inhabited by the Hakka people.
Hakkas are not aborigines, but descendants of northern Chinese
who were moved south by successive migrations. They are a proud
and intelligent people who cling to their own customs and language as much as do the Basques in modern Spain. Father Ford
chose for his mission center the city of Kaying which was less a
business center than other cities of the region but was the cultural
capital of the Hakka people. This city lent its name to the whole
mission.

Father Ford had hardly arrived in Kaying when he began a
seminary. It was a makeshift one to accommodate a dozen boys.
The dormitory was the front porch of his own rectory, and the
classroom was his own dining room. The establishment of this
seminary before any other mission work was started was not without good reason. Speaking of the native clergy, Father Ford said:

"They are the backbone of the local Church and will guarantee
its permanency; they are the pledge by which the native Christians
are bound to the eternal Church. A country without a native clergy,
or having an insufficient native priesthood, is always in danger of
being stranded for lack of a pilot. In time of persecution, the first
to be wiped out or driven out is the foreigner."

With such reasoning in mind, the first structure to be erected in
the new mission was a permanent seminary—a solid, earthquake-
proof building along Oriental architectural lines, and capable of
holding forty boys. At first Father Ford himself conducted the
classes, but as the mission grew and more missioners arrived, he
assigned regular seminary professors. Nevertheless, he was still always available for special instruction of any student desiring it.

The first student of the Kaying seminary was a thirteen-year-old
boy, John Yap, who came from one of the "better families" of the

mission. Young Yap set example and helped establish traditions for the new institution. In all his time at the seminary, he was never known to commit a deliberate violation of any rule; and for his classmates, he was a model of humility and mortification. Then suddenly John developed serious lung trouble. He grew progressively weaker, until at last death was not far off. John's father was at the bedside, and the boy begged the man to be resigned to God's will. When Mr. Yap finally gave his assent, John, as though waiting for his permission, quietly closed his eyes. "God chose our worthiest," Father Ford wrote. "It is a reassuring thought that we are represented in the Eternal Sanctuary by one who was so grateful here below for what we gave him."

In 1929, word came from the Vatican that the mission territory had been erected as a Prefecture Apostolic, and Monsignor Ford named its first prefect. In the following year, the new prefect sent a group of young women from his mission to the Maryknoll Sisters in Hong Kong. The Kaying young women were to be trained as a nucleus for the foundation of a Chinese Sisterhood. Three years later he opened a novitiate for this Sisterhood in Siaoloc.

Many Americans are under the impression that Communists, particularly Chinese Communists, are a postwar scourge sent by Moscow to harass the world. It will be surprising to many to learn that, from the time the Kaying mission was started, it was disturbed by Communist threats and attacks. Christian villages were frequently besieged, and more than one Christian died protecting his home from Red bands. The Kaying Vicariate's report in 1929, for example, is full of the doings of Communists. Here are some of the data: Eighteen Fukien Christians arrive in Kaying as refugees from the Reds; a bulletin tells that the Reds have taken over Chungyen, one of the Kaying outstations; some seminarians are sent home, lest they be cut off from their families; the annual Kaying retreat is postponed until the situation will be stabilized; the American consul at Swatow informs Monsignor Ford that Americans in the Kaying section are in possible danger from the Reds, and he suggests withdrawal to Swatow. Bishop Ford's correspondence of this period was used two decades later by the Reds, in an attempt to justify their arrest and imprisonment of the Kaying superior.

The German Dominicans in adjoining Fukien Province were driven from their missions by the Communists during these years, and they became guests of the Maryknollers in Kaying. One of them—Father Ludwig—a slender, scholarly man, heard that the Reds had withdrawn from the village where his mission was located. He immediately set out to re-gather his scattered Christians, and to build another church where the old one had stood before it was desecrated and burned by the Communists. The very night Father Ludwig returned, when the Christians had come out of hiding and Father was leading them in prayer, he was seized by the Reds, dragged into a mountain camp, and imprisoned in a cage. Weeks passed before word finally came that the Reds had killed their captive.

Then the Communist threat struck nearer home. A large band of Reds invaded the village where Father Patrick F..Malone, of Brooklyn, was stationed. Father was dressed in Chinese clothes, and with the aid of an umbrella to keep off the sun, he managed to get away through the fields, under the guns and stares of the Communists, who thought he was a Chinese. The Reds desecrated and smashed his chapel, leaving nothing intact or usable.

On April 30, 1935, Father Harry M. Bush, of Medford, Massachusetts, accompanied by a Chinese seminarian and one of the mission workers, was on his way to visit a village in his area. Suddenly his group was surrounded by men with drawn guns. Taken captive, priest and friends were led into the mountains, where they were secured with iron chains and shackles. The next morning their captors turned the prisoners over to a large body of Reds. The mission worker was released with a ransom note because the Reds needed money to carry on their outlaw operations. However, it was a firm policy of Maryknollers not to pay ransom. If money were given for one priest, every other priest would be endangered. Although no money was forthcoming for Father Bush, the ransom note did have the effect of putting the Government troops on the trail of the Communists.

Then followed a period of about forty days, during which the Reds traveled through the mountains in rapid marches, all made at night. The daylight hours were spent hiding in caves or other secluded spots in the hills. All cooking was postponed until dusk; and being always on the run, the Reds had little food, and even less variety in it. Often the group traveled barefooted, so as not to leave tracks. Priest and seminarian were continually bound, and the American, completely unused to such a rough type of life, was suffering greatly. After six weeks of this existence, Father Bush had become so weak and exhausted that he knew if he were ever going to escape he would have to do it quickly. Otherwise he would not have enough strength.

He talked over an escape plan with the young seminarian. The next morning, after another all-night march, the entire camp was exhausted—even the guard was not alert. For the captives, it was now or never. Slowly the two slipped away. Once clear of the camp, priest and boy separated. Father Bush made for a hill near by; he believed that, if he could get over its top, he would be safe. As he was scrambling up the hill, he heard a shout from the camp. His escape had been discovered. He hastened his step; a bullet went whistling past him. He was almost to the top when, in his haste, he lost his glasses. He was very nearsighted, and without glasses was practically blind. He hid in some bushes, but one of the soldiers found him and beat him with a rifle butt. The Reds were furious; they knew that the seminarian who escaped would set soldiers after them. They had to get away from the place immediately. Another march began. Why Father Bush was not killed on the spot, he will never know this side of heaven. The best guess is that the Reds were holding him as their trump card. If they should be caught, they might be able to buy their freedom by giving him his. It was hardly any time before the Government soldiers, tipped off by the seminarian, were in pursuit. The marches became longer, food less. At last, the Reds were in a desperate position. The Government troops were closing in about them. A hurried meeting was held. The main party of Reds would go ahead; two guards would bring Father Bush and several other prisoners behind. There was considerable argument. After the main body of Reds had left, one of the guards killed the leader and led the prisoners to the pursuing soldiers. Thus Father Bush returned to freedom, while the friendly Red guard guided the Government troops after his former comrades.

Yet despite these troubled times, the Kaying mission was steadily growing. In 1935, the vicariate had 26 Maryknoll priests, 6 Chinese priests, 12 Maryknoll Sisters, 15 postulant Chinese Sisters, 44 seminarians, and 87 catechists. There were 18 districts staffed by the mission, 385 outstations, a minor seminary, a Sisters' novitiate, 3 student hostels, 15 schools, and a Catholic monthly

paper that had a circulation of 2,300. The Catholic population of
the mission had doubled in ten years.

That the Holy See was satisfied with the progress, seemed evident. On June 18, 1935, a decree was issued raising the mission to
the status of a vicariate, naming Monsignor Ford as its bishop. The
consecration of Bishop Ford took place that September at Maryknoll, New York.

Bishop Ford chose for his episcopal motto the Latin word *Con-
dolere*—"To suffer with." It was a word that identified him with
his people. He felt that China was his true earthly home, and he
looked on the Chinese people as a mother looks on her children—
he saw their beauty and their good qualities, and never considered
their faults. Long years earlier, he had given his life to their service, and he was never to withdraw any of the gift. He impressed
this wholehearted devotion on all his missioners, urging them to
reach the hearts of the Chinese people through understanding and
kindness. He wanted his missioners to study the customs of the
Chinese—particularly the Hakka group—their history, their philosophy; and he wanted the missioners as much as possible to identify
their own lives with those of the people they served.

Bishop Ford's approach to mission work was always well planned
and rooted in basic fundamentals. The way he used the Maryknoll
Sisters in the apostolate was a good example of this. He did not
regard the Sisters solely as schoolteachers or hospital nurses; he
wanted them to be apostles. He sent them out two by two into
the country villages to visit and live among the people in native
homes, to talk with non-Christians, and to teach by example. This
departure from the ordinary activities of Sisters was so successful
that Chinese bishops in the north asked permission to send their
Sisters to Kaying for training. The Papal Internuncio to China
commended the plan, and stated that the Church would grow
much faster if more Sisters were assigned to participate in the direct apostolate of conversion.

Bishop Ford had a great appreciation for the intellectual apostolate. For this reason, he felt a strong interest in students. He began
student hostels for the many boys who were studying at various
schools in Kaying, devoting much time and attention to those
young Chinese. The Kaying Vicariate had long been in need of a
central house for its priests, and at last Bishop Ford began to build

one; but before it was finished, he decided to turn it into a student hostel. Many Catholic boys received from Bishop Ford the chance for higher education. He sent boys to universities in Shanghai and Peking. He was determined that the Church in Kaying should be built on faith, but not blind faith; rather a faith that would be intelligent.

Bishop Ford also organized an apostolate of the printed word. Father Charles P. Hilbert, of Rochester, New York, was made editor of *The New Southern Star*, a monthly magazine written entirely in Chinese, and distributed widely throughout the Far East. There was a steady demand for a score of doctrinal books published in Kaying, some of the works going into two and three editions. Orders for the books came from all parts of China, and from Java, Sumatra, and Borneo.

During World War II, Kaying became a large refugee center. The area was mainly free of fighting, and most of the work of the mission went on without much dislocation. Many Chinese colleges, forced to flee the war zone, set up temporary quarters for their refugee students in the Kaying region. Bishop Ford welcomed those students to his hostels and aided them in every way possible. He began the erection of a cathedral, but progress was slow because of the difficulty in obtaining money and materials. The last years of the war with Japan brought on famine—caused by drought, the difficulty of getting rice into the region, and the influx of refugees from the war zones. With starvation came epidemics of typhus and cholera. There are no statistics available as to the total number of deaths, but Bishop Ford observed in one report that, in a single month, coffin shops reported a 600% increase in the demand for their goods. The missioners themselves, like their neighbors, were on reduced rations during all that time.

Because war conditions prevented Kaying's young seminarians from leaving the area and going to major seminaries, Bishop Ford set up a major seminary under the direction of Father Hilbert. Six priests of the Milan Foreign Mission Society served as professors. These men were Italians of the Waichow area of the Hong Kong Diocese. Because their country was at war with China they were rated as enemy aliens of China. Bishop Ford went guarantor for them, and thus they were able to render invaluable service for the Church all during the war. Among them was Father Bianchi who is now Bishop of Hong Kong. The Kaying Seminary was one of the few seminaries able to operate in China during those years, and Bishop Ford opened it to other bishops, making it a regional seminary.

In 1944, the Kwangtung International Relief Committee was set up. This committee was composed of the Kaying mayor, the local chamber of commerce, and the Catholic mission. Bishop Ford appointed Father John Donovan, of Newport, Rhode Island, to represent him on the committee, and Father Donovan was made chairman. The American priest had had much experience in relief work, having served on the Emergency Relief Council in Hong Kong in 1939. As part of the relief operation, Maryknoll Sisters set up *congee* kitchens, from which rice gruel was served daily to the needy. During this time the bishop developed a bad case of sprue, brought on by the poor diet.

Bishop Ford encouraged his missioners in social works of mercy. Some of them did outstanding work in this regard. Father James A. McCormick, of Clarks Summit, Pennsylvania, worked in the Siaoloc farming area. Hunger was so acute in his region that the people were forced to eat seed rice needed for the next planting. As a result, they had to borrow money from loan sharks to buy seed rice, and it was a standard practice for the farmers to be charged 300% interest. Naturally, the people could not repay such a high rate, so many of them lost their land to the money lenders.

Father McCormick decided to set up a rice bank co-operative, which would lend rice seed. Father felt that the way to make the rice bank a success was to have a large committee decide on loans —thus avoiding favoritism, personal enmities, or dishonesty. Eleven young farmers were elected to the bank's board of directors, and seven older men formed the board of auditors to check the younger men. Through some friends in America, the missioner raised half the capital needed, and Siaoloc farmers who joined the co-operative put up the rest in rice. The interest on loans was 20% per harvest, each loan being paid back with its interest after harvest. When a bad harvest came along (less than half of normal), the rice bank had its first real test; but there was no default in payment. The people of Siaoloc were proud of the record of their bank.

The rice bank solved one of the basic problems of the region, and Father McCormick turned next to unemployment. He decided that the establishment of home industries would be best for that farming area. A weaving co-operative seemed to be the answer. A master weaver from one of the factories near Kaying was hired to teach the fifteen students in the first group. Each student was asked to pay a share of the teacher's salary; and if any student did not have the money, he was able to borrow it from the co-operative. In addition each student paid for his own machine—which was built by local carpenters, thus spreading employment. Students were taught how to dye thread, wind it, set up their machines, and weave. A student graduated after he (or she) had woven ten bolts of cloth, each 72 feet long. The first bolts produced were a bit rough and irregular, and were sold for children's clothing at a price to cover materials. But experience soon remedied the defects, and future production was excellent. The next lots of cloth sold at a substantial profit, and the Siaoloc cloth was in so great demand that the co-operative couldn't keep up with orders. The success of the project brought other students into the co-operative, and the business grew.

Father McCormick also started a soap-manufacturing co-operative, and an irrigation project through a system of small dams that made the Siaoloc farmers independent of rainfall. When the Communists took over the Kaying mission, the Siaoloc missioner was just preparing to begin a glass-making co-operative.

Another missioner who had an active social-action program was Father Maynard Murphy, a Maryknoller from Montreal, Canada. He was stationed at Petteoutsai for over twenty years. In the period of hard times, he set up a rice bank very similar to the one in Siaoloc, and his bank forced merchants in the area to lower their interest rates. His second project was agricultural. Father Murphy had mission workers plant banana, pomelo, and papaya trees. Seven to ten stalks of bananas purchased seventy pounds of unhulled rice; the other fruit was exchanged for rice and eggs. The trees helped support the mission and provided the means of obtaining food for charity cases. This missioner also set out large vegetable gardens that provided the mission with fresh vegetables the year round and a surplus that was given to the poor. Soon a canning outfit to put up vegetables was imported.

A third project began when Father Murphy persuaded the people of Petteoutsai to cut down their unproductive trees, promising that he would buy the wood and pay for it in rice. Then he imported olive trees to take the place of the destroyed trees. The olives furnished a steady income, and provided money for the rental of additional orchard space to be assigned to poor families. Through these agricultural projects, the standard of living of the local people was raised. The fourth project was begun by the Petteoutsai mission to combat seasonal unemployment. During the starvation months before the rice harvest, when no work was available, the poorest families were employed by the mission. They were put to building and repairing roads and paths, and constructing walls. This enabled them to exist until harvest time, and also gave them the assurance that they were earning their rice and not depending solely on charity.

Bishop Ford encouraged all such projects, and lent them every assistance. He saw them as not only a means of helping the people, but also a clear demonstration that the Church is interested in all forms of social activity. He continually told his missioners to adapt their work to the needs of the local people. For example, in Kaying, when he found that men could not attend the daytime instruction classes, he immediately set up classes in the evening. The men—bankers, merchants, doctors, newspapermen, and manual workers—studied from half past eight to half past eleven. The 1950 class had more than one hundred members who took the three hours of study after a hard day of work.

The officials of Kaying knew that they could always count on Bishop Ford's help in any civic project, and they consulted him on all sorts of problems. When civil authorities wanted a bridge across the Moikong River, they approached the bishop. He contacted Father Joseph Constancis, of the Paris Foreign Mission Society, who was a well-known architect. Father Constancis drew up the plans and Bishop Ford paid for one of the ten spans of the bridge. The foundation of reinforced concrete was sunk below the water to a depth equal to its height above the water. During the war it remained intact, although bridges built at much greater expense, but less solidly, were destroyed.

Bishop Ford's report for 1950, the last report issued from Kaying, gave a picture of the mission before the coming of the Communists. There were 23,000 Catholics with over 1,000 catechumens preparing for baptism. The mission had 26 parishes, and 349 outstations. There were 6 student hostels, 18 elementary schools, and one high school, as well as seminary and Sisters' novitiate. Personnel of the mission numbered 19 Chinese priests, 16 Mary-

knoll priests, 16 Maryknoll Sisters, 26 Chinese Sisters, 42 seminarians, 92 catechists, and 39 teachers. It is interesting to note from
these figures how substantially developed the native clergy had become. Six of the nineteen in 1950 were refugee priests from the
north. All but one returned north before Bishop Ford's arrest.
When the Communists began searching for this sixth, Bishop Ford
helped him get to Singapore where he now works among the
Chinese.

Yet the Chinese personnel of the diocese promised soon to out-
number the foreign. Bishop Ford's hope that he would be the last
foreign bishop of Kaying was beginning to promise fulfillment. In
1950, too, Bishop Ford inaugurated a new building program for
the seminary.

Then the Communists struck. The Americans were humiliated,
subjected to public trials, and forced out of the mission. Chinese
priests were thrown in jail. The seminary was closed, and the
Chinese Sisters sent home with Red instructions to marry. Bishop
Ford went to death in Canton. Kaying today is a vast prison, where
the Christians still alive look eastward for better days.

12

Wuchow—From the Ground Up

If, about the time when the first Maryknoll missioners went to China, someone had asked concerning that country's most unpromising field for mission work, the answer would have been "Kwangsi Province in general, and the Wuchow area in particular." For among missioners, Kwangsi was a byword for the most arid mission field in all China. "Poor fellow!" a missioner would say to a confrere assigned to Kwangsi. "You'll have to hire a pagan to be your altar boy." The past twenty-five years, however, have seen considerable development agriculturally and commercially, improved communications, good government, an increasing population, all of which favored mission work.

The contrast between Kwangsi Province and adjoining Kwangtung Province, where the Maryknollers first began work, was startling. Kwangtung was a level, well-watered, farm-rich province of intelligent and cultured people. Kwangsi, on the other hand, was a mountainous, roadless, impoverished terrain, of which the main crops were soldiers and bandits. While Kwangtung had 37 million people, Kwangsi numbered hardly six million. The difference was something like that found between the backwoods of Kentucky and the sweet-smelling farmlands of Virginia.

Owing to lack of communications, the Kwangsi people were rugged and freebooting. Practically every village in the region was surrounded by a wall with a watchtower to guard against bandit attack. Many towns had caves and other places of refuge, to which people could flee in time of trouble. Night watchmen patrolled city streets, to the accompaniment of dull beats of wooden drums. The province, with its forested mountains, made an ideal rendezvous for bandits, who could raid neighboring Kwangtung and then retreat into the Kwangsi fastness without much danger of being traced.

As early as 1920, Bishop Ducoeur, of Nanking, invited Maryknoll to take over part of the Kwangsi area under his jurisdiction —particularly the cities of Wuchow and Pingnam and several undeveloped counties. A convert, Father F. X. Farmer, who formerly had been in the region as a Protestant minister prepared a report for the Maryknollers, and in it he called Kwangsi "The Neglected Province," as far as Christianity was concerned. "There are multitudes," wrote Father Farmer, "who have never heard the Gospel. I have preached to thousands who have never heard the name of Jesus; and in all my itinerations, I never met a Catholic priest."

Because Maryknoll was just beginning its mission work in China, the Society could not spare a staff for Kwangsi immediately. Father James Edward Walsh, who was to become Bishop of Kongmoon, took up residence temporarily in Wuchow in 1920, and he was joined by Father Frederick C. Dietz, of Oberlin, Ohio, who was assigned there to study the language. Father Dietz was later to direct the Loting language school, and still later to move to Peking to become a member of China's Catholic Synodal Commission.

In 1925, Father Bernard F. Meyer, of Davenport, Iowa, who had been one of Maryknoll's first four students, was selected as superior of the new territory in Kwangsi. Father Meyer had gone to China in the first departure group and had spent most of his time in the Tungchen mission, where he built up a flourishing Christian community. In 1925, he was in America, raising funds for the South China missions. It was early in 1927 before he could get into Kwangsi and organize the foundations for his new assignment.

It was good that Father Meyer's youth had been spent in a farming region. He was used to seeing the barren soil of winter transform itself and produce autumn's rich harvest. For the task that faced him in Kwangsi had indeed a barren beginning—there were hardly 150 Christians waiting for his arrival and these were the result of a half century of French mission work. The city of Wuchow had not a single Catholic, and for a long time was to hold the unenviable title, "The City of No Conversions." In addition to the spiritual barrenness, there was an intellectual hostility awaiting the new missioners. During that period the young and radical Kuomintang was promoting antiforeign outbursts which called for trade boycott and cancellation of extraterritoriality. Fortunately there was also some good will built up by the charity of Fathers Walsh and Dietz during their sojourn there, and especially by their hospitality to refugees when Wuchow was under siege by Kwangtung troops.

When Father Meyer arrived in the Kwangsi territory, he set up his mission center at Pingnam because there at least he had a nucleus of Christians. However, he realized that the city of Wuchow was the key to the whole area. It was the commercial capital of Kwangsi, and the major port of the province, situated on the West River, a straight run from Hong Kong, some thirty hours away by boat. Despite the fact that the city had no Catholics, Protestant groups had made a good beginning there, and Father Meyer was confident that his own missioners would do equally well once an integrated program was started.

Father Meyer's first report, covering the year 1928, showed considerable progress in his new mission territory. Catholics had increased from the original 150 to 721. Three districts were staffed with eight Maryknoll priests and one Maryknoll Brother. One dispensary, one student hostel, and thirteen village schools were already operating. Another bright note was that 800 catechumens were under instruction, promising a doubling of the Catholic population within a year, and still another was the fact that Wuchow City had twenty-five Catholics.

In 1931, Father Meyer was appointed canonical superior of the Wuchow Mission, which in the previous year had been officially cut off from Kongmoon. Three years later the mission was established as a prefecture, and Father Meyer was named prefect. By that time conversions were averaging better than a thousand a year. Archbishop Mario Zanin, Apostolic Delegate to China, sent a special congratulatory letter to Monsignor Meyer, because the highest average of converts per missioner in South China in 1935 was established by the Wuchow Prefecture. An average of 60 converts was attributed to each priest in the mission.

Like all of South China's Maryknollers, Monsignor Meyer wanted to establish a seminary as quickly as possible. At first he sent his students to Bishop Walsh's seminary in Kongmoon. When he had sufficient seminarians (about thirty-five), he built a seminary at Tanchuk, not far from Pingnam. The spirit of the mountain boys who wanted to become priests was illustrated by one youngster who arrived late one evening at the Tanchuk seminary. He had traveled all the way from Watlam by riding on the back of a bicycle. The journey had taken three days, and the uncomfortable bike-taxi ride had cost the boy $200 Chinese.

The first Wuchow priest was ordained in 1933. The arrival of this priest in Pingnam was the occasion of great rejoicing on the part of the people. Two years later a Chinese Sisters' novitiate was established at Pingnam, under the direction of Maryknoll Sisters. After five years of training, four members of the new community, the Congregation of the Charity of the Sacred Heart, were professed. These were the first Chinese Sisters in the history of Kwangsi Province. The Maryknoll Sisters also conducted a school to train women catechists at Pingnam.

In 1938, an area of 15,000 square miles of the Wuchow territory was taken from the prefecture and set up as the independent Maryknoll mission territory of Kweilin. This was a definite sign of growth. The Wuchow mission at this time was left with 8,000 Catholics and 1,500 catechumens. There were 8 dispensaries operating in the mission in 1938, giving a total 89,609 treatments for the year. The mission staff consisted of 11 Maryknoll priests, 2 Chinese priests, 1 Maryknoll Brother, 3 Maryknoll Sisters, 6 Chinese Sisters, 56 seminarians, and 99 catechists.

Word came from Rome on July 20, 1940, that Wuchow had been elevated to the status of vicariate, and that Father Frederick A. Donaghy, of New Bedford, Massachusetts, had been named the first bishop. He returned to the United States and was consecrated a bishop on September 21, 1940, in St. Mary's Cathedral, Fall River, Massachusetts. Bishop Donaghy took direction of the mission at a critical time. China and Japan were at war, and in a short period America would be in the conflict. Refugees were already entering Kwangsi from the war zones, and mission facilities were being taxed. Early in 1942, three civil prefectures were cut off from the French Nanning mission and attached to Wuchow. The transfer added 750,000 Chinese to the responsibility of Maryknoll.

The war brought many new people into the province and opened new opportunities for conversion, but one of the strange effects was that it also interested many local people in the Church. For example, in Wuchow City, work among the refugees led to conversion of many citizens who had previously been indifferent. Night classes had been set up for the refugees who wanted to study doctrine. City people living near the refugee camp asked if they might be permitted to join the classes. Eight successive classes were held in the two following years, and three fourths of the candidates who persevered and were baptized were regular Wuchow residents. Later when the refugees moved on, the city people stayed and built their own church.

During these early years of the war, Maryknollers were able to help a number of American fliers who made emergency landings in the area. When Lieutenant Mortimer Marks, from Bayonne, New Jersey, was forced down by empty gas tanks over Wuchow, Father Peter A. Reilly, of Roxbury, Massachusetts, and Father Russell Sprinkle, of Middletown, Ohio, hurried to his aid. They took Lieutenant Marks to the mission, and under cover of darkness, aided him in dismantling his P-40 for shipment to an American base. Father Sprinkle hired a junk, helped load the plane aboard, and guided the pilot for three days and nights, back to safety. The travelers stopped at Maryknoll missions along the West River for meals.

"I was amazed to find an American priest in each one of those ports," Lieutenant Marks said later. "On future trips over that country, you can be sure I'll be tipping my wings to all those boys."

But it was not only American planes that came over Wuchow. Japanese bombers and fighters plastered the whole region. One bombing raid in 1943 left hundreds of Chinese dead, and thousands homeless. Bishop Donaghy and his missioners received high praise from Government officials for the relief work they did. One bomb hit next door to the bishop's house, but the missioners ignored their own broken doors and windows and devoted themselves to rescue work. Bishop Donaghy and his priests set up relief stations, gave food and shelter to all Chinese needing them, and also distributed small sums of money to the people who were even worse off.

Another bombing of Wuchow took 1,800 lives and wiped out a third of the city. A few months later, the mission itself was destroyed in an attack. Father Sprinkle was trapped for hours in the ruins, and suffered serious injuries that troubled him for some time thereafter. Despite the danger and their own losses, Bishop Donaghy and his missioners refused to leave the city as long as they were free to carry on their works of charity.

In the last half of 1944, the Japanese began a drive to cut Free China in two. The line of advance was directly on Wuchow. The Wuchow missioners decided to hold out until the last moment, in case the invaders should be stopped. The next news was that Japanese troops had entered Wuchow. A letter arrived in Chung-king from Father John M. McLoughlin, of Elmhurst, New York, saying that, although all at the mission had evacuated ahead of the enemy, the Japanese were hot on their trail because they had given shelter to a local mandarin who had been wounded. Father McLoughlin explained that Christian charity would not allow the missioners to turn the mandarin away, despite the fact that he jeopardized their position by attracting much attention. The next word came from the American consul in Kunming, who announced that five Maryknoll missioners had been captured by the Japanese.

For a long time, no further news was heard of any of the Wuchow group. Maryknoll headquarters never gave up hope that somehow the group had escaped, and that hope was justified when a message finally came through. All the Wuchow Maryknollers were safe and free, deep in the Kwangsi mountains. "Don't worry about us. Just keep us in your prayers," said the message. "We plan to keep busy and out of sight as long as possible."

After the priests of Wuchow had left the city, Bishop Donaghy ordered Father Albert V. Fedders, of Covington, Kentucky, to transfer the Tanchuk seminary to the mountains. In a remote mountain village, the seminary operated during the rest of the war, with six priests and one Brother serving on the staff. The full story of the wandering seminary did not come out until the end of the war. It is an epic worth retelling.

When Father Fedders at Tanchuk had received word of the approach of the Japanese, he hired a boat to take the seminary staff and students farther upriver. The procession that filed onto the boat was reminiscent of Noah's Ark. There were 11 pigs, 47 ducks, 2 guinea pigs, a police dog with 4 puppies, 3 priests and 22 seminarians. This entourage, of course, needed a mountain of baggage, so that also was brought along. The party set off with little speed, confident that they were well ahead of the Japanese troops. Suddenly an advance patrol of Japanese was sighted. Priests and seminarians strained at oars, and a tattered cloth sail was run up to catch any vagrant breeze. A day and a night of hard rowing followed, before the boat reached its destination. The little army of animals and men debarked, loaded down with baggage, and began the thirty-mile hike to their intended refuge. Just before reaching the mountains, the group halted at a Maryknoll mission. There they found eight other missioners, also forced to flee from their stations as the enemy closed in. Seminarians and livestock and Father Fedders continued on up the trail, while ten Maryknollers remained behind like a rear guard.

The next day the missioners sent a Catholic farmer into a town twelve miles away, to find out what was happening. He returned with the information that the Japanese were all over the place. The missioners decided to hold out as long as possible; but the following morning, they were awakened by news that two hundred Japanese soldiers were marching on the village. Without further delay, the Maryknollers hurried from the mission and up the mountain trail. They climbed a steep and rocky path beside a twisting river that tumbled between gorges. Behind them they could hear gun fire, as the enemy took over the little village they had just left. All day the nine priests and one Brother trudged —always climbing up and up. At nightfall they reached the little adobe-walled mission that Father Meyer had built in the hills fifteen years earlier, and there they found the seminary already organized amidst the host of ducks and pigs and dogs.

After some time in the mountain refuge, the priests not connected with the seminary grew restless. There was no telling how long the war would last, and they wanted to get back to active work. Besides, money was running out, and so large a number of persons put a heavy drain on provisions. It was finally decided that four of the missioners would try to reach Free China. Three of them would stay there at work, and one—Father Arthur F. Dempsey, of Peekskill, New York—would attempt to return with funds. The party of four set out early one morning. They could not take to the roads, for fear of meeting Japanese, so they had to use rough mountain trails. For four days they hiked through the mountains; then they spent two days traveling in a boat through rapids. It was the hardest traveling Father Dempsey had done in fifteen years in China.

During part of their journey, the four missioners stayed with the aboriginal Yao people. The Yao men wore long hair twisted and tied on the top of their heads. Few of them had ever seen a white man, and the missioners with long noses, pale faces, light hair and eyes, were the source of much curiosity and amusement. Ordinarily the Yaos resent any intrusion into their domain, and they drive strangers out forcibly. But some Yaos had often gone to the mission at the foot of the mountains to get medicine, and sometimes they had been invited to spend the night at the mission, so they were acquainted with missioners and not hostile to such. For past favors, the Yaos were glad to reciprocate by showing superb hospitality to their Maryknoll visitors.

At last the worn-out group of missioners reached an American air base. Funds for the seminary group were sent to the chaplain there, from the Maryknoll headquarters in Chungking. Father Dempsey prepared to begin the long trek back through the mountains. Then the American Air Force stepped in.

"If you can guide us to the mission," said an officer, "we'll take you over in a new Mitchell bomber, and drop the money at the front gate."

Father Dempsey had been worried about traveling back through the mountain with all the money. The officer offered a perfect solution. The money was wrapped tightly in a cloth package, and then wedged with straw in a bamboo basket. The Mitchell plane took off. Father Dempsey knew the countryside almost as well as he knew his prayers, and in no time the plane was over the whitewashed, mud-walled compound. The crew chief picked up the money basket and began to count aloud. Suddenly he dropped the basket through the open hatch. It landed right in front of the mission door. Father Dempsey recognized Father McLoughlin's red hair as the latter hurried out and scooped up the basket. Mission accomplished, the Mitchell bomber tipped its wings and returned to its base.

After the end of the war, the Maryknollers hurried back to
their posts. Many of the missions had been destroyed; others had
been occupied by the Japanese or by the puppet government that
had been set up; and practically all the missions had been looted,
between the time the Japanese withdrew and the Maryknollers
returned. But it wasn't the ruined condition of the missions that
bothered the Maryknollers most: it was the appalling condition in
which they found the people. The Chinese were clad in rags, impoverished and starving. Men, women, and children were but skin
and bones, suffering from beriberi and from all sorts of skin in-
fections due to malnutrition. Children were afflicted with worms
and dysentery. Many regions had epidemics of small pox and
cholera.

Father Sprinkle, who took over the Pingnam mission, opened a
dispensary. Then he almost had his heart broken by the suffering
that poured through it, and the fact that he possessed so little to
work with. His diary gives a picture of what most of the missioners
were facing:

"There is one case after another of skin diseases of all kinds and
descriptions, most of them infected. In the last two weeks, we
have had three cases of third-degree burns, all infected, one from
fire, two from boiling oil. There has been case after case of children with eyes almost closed from cataracts due to worms; boils
galore; varicose veins that are a mass of infection from knee to
instep; infected ringworms; infected skin ulcers; back aches; stomach aches of every sort; one broken wrist; one appendicitis case;
malaria and cholera all around us. We do not have any bandages,
so we use paper. Most of the medicines were destroyed, and all
of the equipment is missing—such as scissors, scalpels, suture
needles, and so on. Bishop Donaghy has gone to Hong Kong to
beg every penny he can to set up congee kitchens to combat the
starvation that stalks us day and night."

The missioners did heroic work during those terrible days.
Gradually life began returning to normal for the Chinese who
survived, and once again the missioners were able to undertake
the direct work of conversion. Bishop Donaghy even began opening new stations, and into one new region he sent Father Mark A.
Tennien, of Pittsford, Vermont.

When Father Tennien had arrived in China twenty years earlier,
he had been assigned by Father Meyer to open a new mission in

Jungyun. It was a job that almost cost him his life. He met with open hostility and undercover persecution. He was the bearer of a message that was not wanted. Exhausted from his seemingly hopeless task, he fell ill with fever, and was at death's door when a native catechist arrived and nursed him back to health. The catechist's name was Ue Chi Cheung, more familiarly known to the missioners as "Big Six"—a name derived from his size and the fact that he was a sixth son. With the coming of Big Six, Father Tennien's fortunes changed. Slow progress began, and eventually a thriving mission was established.

During the war years, Father Tennien headed the Chungking headquarters for Maryknoll. He did yeoman work in informing the outside world what was going on in China, and his radioed dispatches appeared in papers all over the United States. During those years he also wrote the best-selling book, *Chungking Listening Post*. At war's end, when Father Tennien returned to Wuchow, Bishop Donaghy assigned him to a pioneering task. He was to open up Shumkai—Blue Cloud County—to the church. No priest had ever been there before.

Father Tennien's first step was to send his faithful Big Six into the area to prepare the way. Big Six made friends at Shumkai's city hall, and began giving out medicines to win good will. Then came one of those strange acts of coincidence that so often play a major role in a man's life. Father Tennien was driving his jeep to Shumkai, to begin work. As he turned a bend in the road, not far from his destination, he saw a truck that had gone off the road and plunged over the side of the mountain. He hurried down to the wreck and discovered six injured men. They had been lying there for some time, because no one else had cared to stop—for fear of becoming involved. Father Tennien emptied his jeep of its baggage, loaded the injured men aboard, and took off for the Shumkai hospital. At the hospital he learned that one of the men he had rescued was the popular mandarin of Blue Cloud County.

The fame of the good deed was spread abroad. Immediately officials of the region began to go out of their way to show cooperation. People greeted the missioner with smiles. Big Six's traveling medicine stand was swamped wherever he set it up. The teachers and influential men of Blue Cloud Village held a meeting, and three hundred signed up for baptism. This number quickly mounted to a thousand, and the figure began snowballing through the district. Father Tennien was faced with a problem that he had never expected: he had a mass convert movement on his hands. Five hundred more people in Blue Cloud asked to join the list. In a nearby village, fifteen hundred people sought instruction. The village of Lamteng asked Big Six to come and speak to its eighteen hundred adults, and the response to the talk was enthusiastic. Father Tennien dispatched an urgent appeal for help to Bishop Donaghy. Every available catechist was sent into the region. More missioners were hurried to Shumkai. Chinese priests from Canton were loaned. Chinese Sisters were brought in from Pakhoi.

All over the entire area, instruction went on. The pressure was so great that Father Tennien had to refuse instruction to small villages; his personnel allowed him to accept no group smaller than two hundred. As the convert movement blossomed and grew, a large and beautiful church was erected near Blue Cloud Village. In other villages, Mass was celebrated out of doors until chapels could be erected. The first converts were baptized, and Bishop Donaghy journeyed from Wuchow to administer confirmation. Then an ominous cloud appeared on the horizon. Communist armies moved down from their Russian-protected sanctuary in the north. The converts realized that they might soon be asked to die for the Faith they were joining, but this did not deter them; and catechumens asked for instruction and baptism in even greater numbers. Up until the day that the Communists poured into Blue Cloud and took over the area, the Church was receiving new children.

An unforgettable picture of what the coming of communism meant to the Wuchow Vicariate, was written by a young Cleveland priest, Father Frederick J. Becka, a professor at Wuchow's Holy Family Seminary. This wonderful institution had never closed its doors from the day they had been opened. Flood, famine, and war had raged around it. But always the missioners managed to carry on. Then came the Reds, and this is how Father Becka, who was later hung up by his thumbs and tortured before being expelled from China, describes those last days:

"In our area of South China, the Communists brought suppression of religion to dramatic completion, when they shut down our diocesan seminary for native priests. They tore up the hope of the harvest at its root, and tore up our hearts with it. This is how it happened.

"The caliber of our Chinese seminarians can best be judged by the fact that almost every one of the boys returned to the seminary after a short vacation, on July 1, 1951. And this, despite threats and innuendoes hurled at them by Government representatives and Communist sympathizers in their villages. The faculty was cut down from five to two: Father Laai was rector, and professor of Latin, religion, and Gregorian chant; Mr. Ngaan taught mathematics and Chinese literature. The budget would not permit a larger staff. Each of the seminarians brought rice as part payment for his tuition. That rice came from parents who were living on starvation diets, and heavily oppressed by unfair and ridiculous taxation. But the parents were eager to make any sacrifice so that their boys might become priests.

"The seminarians did nothing but work and pray during the first month. By order of the Reds, the seminary was to be self-supporting. Each and every inch of ground was dug up, hoed, raked, and weeded; every variety of Chinese vegetable was planted. A sty was built to pen in three pigs; two beehives were erected; twenty-three chickens were purchased; rabbit raising was avidly taken up; two of the seminarians learned how to make clothes. The boys smiled despite sunburn, sore backs, and aching muscles. They laughed about their primitive and crowded quarters.

"Three months later the axe fell. The reason for foreclosure, said the Reds, was that the boys had to return home to take part in the division of the fields.

"Father Laai was summoned to the magistrate's office in Pingnam. 'The Government wants to know,' said the magistrate, 'how the seminary is progressing. Are there any foreigners on the faculty? Is Father Laai receiving any foreign funds?'

"Justifiably proud of the seminarians, Father Laai minced no words in praising them. When he finished giving an account of his stewardship, the Government representative smiled as only a Communist can, and said: 'Fine! Now close up the seminary.'"

"That evening Father Laai returned to Tanchuk with the sad news. He spent two hours and a half explaining to the seminarians the Government's decision. 'Though you must return home,' Father said, 'you must never give up the hope of becoming priests.'

"Afterwards he related that telling the boys they must go home was the hardest duty he had ever had to perform.

"In the evening we had a Chinese banquet behind locked doors. After it was over, everyone rose and sang the 'Holy Family Hymn.' The volume and feeling of the musical cadences shattered the rafters.

"I've been told that the Chinese always hide their emotions. And from my short experience of five years among them, I have found this to be true. But such was not the case on the morning when the boys left for home. Not one went out through the main gate with dry eyes.

"Theirs were not the only tears shed that morning. They left, and we have not seen them since. God keep them until the day of our return!"

13

Manchuria—Land of Many Masters

Late in 1925, Father Raymond A. Lane, of Lawrence, Massachusetts, Maryknoll procurator in Hong Kong, received a cablegram from Father James Anthony Walsh, instructing him to proceed north to Mukden, Manchuria, to undertake language study preparatory to opening mission work there. The new territory was in southeast Manchuria, bordering Maryknoll's Korean mission along the Yalu. It was an area about the size of the State of Kentucky, with four million people, some four thousand of whom were Christians. Included in the mission were a few large cities, such as the coal-mining center of Fushun, the port of Dairen, and the border city of Antung.

It was an historic Christian area, because within the confines of the new mission was the Christian village of Ch'a Kou, where the first Catholic foundation in Manchuria had been made in 1841. Practically the entire village was Catholic, and the parish there promised to be a fertile field for vocations. The early French missioners had made rapid progress in Manchuria up to the time of the Boxer Rebellion in 1900, when Christians were dispersed and many churches destroyed.

Manchuria once controlled all of China, for it was the home of the Manchu dynasty that conquered the Chinese. But the Chinese had slowly absorbed their conquerors, and at the time of Father Lane's arrival in Manchuria only a few hundred thousand Manchus were left in the population of 35 million. Sturdy peasants from North China, principally from Shantung Province, were pouring into industrial rich Manchuria at the rate of a million a year. A large number of Japanese immigrants were also coming into the territory since Japan had been ceded the Port Arthur territory by Russia in 1904.

For their first year the Maryknollers lived with Bishop Blois at Mukden, from whose vicariate the new Maryknoll section was to be taken. In February, 1927, the two pioneer Maryknollers, Father Lane, and Father Joseph P. McCormack, of New York City, entered the new territory. Father Lane chose Fushun as the mission center. The city was an industrial and coal-mining capital, the hub for a network of railroads, and the area for the Japanese coal-mining concession. The largest open-pit coal mine in the world was located here. The whole area was a challenge, for while such places as Fushun and Dairen had been modernized, once away from them and the railroad, the region was primitive and lawless.

Father Lane realized immediately that the work in Manchuria fell into two categories. First, there were the Chinese and Manchurian natives and immigrants, and secondly the Japanese. More and more of the latter were entering the territory and Father Lane agreed that they should not be neglected. He assigned Father Leopold H. Tibesar, of Quincy, Illinois, to begin work among them at Dairen, a city with 212,000 inhabitants. The new pastor began organizing a Japanese parish, and building the first Catholic church in the city, under the patronage of the "Star of the Sea."

During that first year, Father Lane also drew up plans for a Fushun central house, and assigned Father J. Leo Davis, of Scranton, Pennsylvania, to start work in Antung. In the following year, Father Lane opened his seminary in Fushun. He reported the event very simply:

"We have twenty boys at Fushun in preparation for the priesthood. Six others will join them after the Chinese New Year, in February. These with four additional students at Mukden bring the number of seminarians to thirty. This is the most important work of the foreign mission apostolate, and needless to say, most of our attention and care will be given to this work. The seminary has not yet been built. The boys are sleeping and studying in the one room which serves for the seminary at present. Imagine twenty of them in a room 20' by 20', and you can appreciate our situation."

In 1930, Father Lane began building his Fushun center. The buildings were to house the seminary, an orphanage, an old folks' home, an industrial school, and a novitiate for a native Sisters' community that he planned. He also hired a house in the Chinese section of Fushun and opened a small hospital with a Catholic Chinese doctor in charge. The first Maryknoll Sisters arrived in Dairen in the spring of 1930, and another group was promised to Fushun for the following year. The outmissions of Fushun were also strengthened during the year.

Typical of these missions was Linkiang, far up the Yalu. Father Joseph A. Sweeney (later to work in South China) was the pastor of this parish. The background to the Linkiang story appeared in a large Catholic paper in far-off Tientsin. The article was written by a Chinese, and there gives a good insight as to how the Oriental mind regarded the work of the early Maryknollers:

SPREAD OF FAITH
IN LINKIANG

LINKIANG: This town is located at the eastern boundary of Leao Ning, in a mountainous and wooded district, where bandits and the lawless element ply their trade. This accounts for its backwardness in the progress of civilization and the lack of evangelization.

The writer, a postal employee, was assigned to this town about two years ago and felt deeply the sadness of his spiritual condition as he was unable to perform his Easter duty. Last year, however, Father Joseph Sweeney of T'ung Hwa, in his great zeal for souls, undertook the tiresome and perilous journey to Linkiang, where he discovered seven or eight Christians in all, and they were somewhat lukewarm Christians, owing to the great distance from church and priest.

Those Christians were greatly benefited and encouraged by the visit of Father Sweeney, and the good work

began to progress again, thanks largely to the zeal of catechist Wong Chin San, whom Father Sweeney sent.

On his second visit this year, Father Sweeney found
a total of more than 200 faithful (including the catechumens) awaiting him, and among them, to his great surprise
and pleasure, were five or six former Protestants. Because
of this increase in the number of Catholics, Father Sweeney
informed the bishop of the need of a chapel, and bought
a piece of land in the town for that purpose.

Father Sweeney has made excellent use of his medical
knowledge, and has a good supply of modern remedies,
which he bestows on all who need them, regardless of
whether they are Catholics or pagans. No one is turned
away without treatment, and the very poor receive some
monetary help. Thus the miseries of the body are relieved, as well as the diseases of the soul. To help the
afflicted, to strengthen the weak, to glorify God, and to
love men, all this is united in one man, a man of excellent
virtue.

How great a blessing for us Catholics to have such
an excellent missioner! What a happiness for our eastern
district is such a welcome star! We are indeed hopeful
that we shall shortly see great progress in the propagation
of the Faith.

For Christmas, 1930, Father Sweeney, Father Francis A. Bridge,
of Midland, Pennsylvania, and Catechist Wong made a remarkable journey to the northernmost boundary of the mission where
they celebrated Mass at Antu. The trip required a month and a
half on the road and was made through a wild forest and mountain region in temperatures that dropped to forty degrees below
zero. It was so cold that even the numerous Changpai Forest
bandits remained indoors. Over some sections of the trail, no
white man had ever passed, and it was an area that had never
seen a priest.

The missioners had to carry their own food—wild pig, venison,
fungus and rice. They spent their nights in crude Chinese inns.
Travel was largely by mule-drawn *pali*, a Manchurian type of sled.
On two occasions while descending steep mountains, the pali
was smashed to splinters. Each time the missioners were able to
roll off into the snow before the crash came, but they had to halt

while a new sled was built on the spot. They reached Antu on December 23, and located several Christians. A small room was rented for the celebration of Mass.

"While the Christians were at prayer," wrote Father Bridge, in a letter to Maryknoll, "a Chinese passing by heard the sound. He listened for a moment in amazement and dawning hope; then hastening to the room, he knocked at the door and entered. He was from south of the Great Wall and had not seen a priest in ten years. The tears of joy of this man alone would have been ample recompense for any hardships of the Changpai trail."

On January 25, 1932, the Sacred Congregation of Propaganda Fide established the Fushun Mission as a prefecture, and a month later Father Lane was named prefect apostolic. The mission at this time had 20 Maryknoll priests, 5 Chinese priests, 2 Maryknoll Brothers, 20 Maryknoll Sisters, 4 Chinese Sisters, 30 aspirants for the priesthood, and an equal number of postulant Sisters. The following year saw the start of work among the Koreans in and around Fushun, and the erection of a new Fushun church.

One of the main projects of 1933 was the establishment of an industrial school to produce "Maryknoll Missionarts." Under skilled teachers, orphan boys and old folks were trained to turn out beautiful wood carvings and needlework. The income from the project was to provide funds for the orphanage and old folks' home. The wood carvers made large and small crucifixes, statues, tabernacles, candlesticks, and book stands. The needlework department produced Gothic and Roman vestments, and other altar requisites. Many of the liturgical objects made at the mission were sold in the United States. Besides bringing in added means for development, the Missionarts trained orphans in jobs that would later enable them to earn their own support.

During this period of development, there was considerable unrest in Manchuria. The Japanese were gradually taking over the country, and were meeting with resistance. Armed bands of robbers stalked the outlying regions, and fanatical patriots objected to the presence of any foreigners. Although the Maryknollers in the area had encountered some bandit gangs and had had some trouble with soldiers, no serious incident developed until one day during the Big Cold—January and February—of 1936. Father J. Clarence Burns, of Toledo, Ohio, was at the Tunghua mission on the morning of February 5, when a man came in to report that an elderly couple five miles distant were dying and wanted a priest.

Father Burns had just gotten out of bed after six days of sickness, but he bundled himself up well, and accompanied by two Chinese of the mission staff set out for the sick people. The group was hardly three miles out of town when it was ambushed by fifteen bandits who had sent the false sick call. One of Father Burns' helpers, Catechist Ch'iu was early left behind because he was an old man and could not keep up. Father Burns and his other assistant, Wu, were hurried off the road into the trackless mountains. Night after night they traveled through waist deep snow, breaking through ice, stumbling over hidden bushes and roots. The party moved only from sunset to dawn in order to escape being seen, and the night-time low temperatures added to misery. At last the party reached a deserted cabin about fifty miles from Tunghua.

There Father Burns lay unconscious for five days and but for the devotion of his helper, Wu, he would have died. Many times during the long nine months of captivity Wu saved the priest. On several occasions Wu could have escaped himself, but he chose to remain with the American. Spring, summer and fall came and passed. The bandits by this time were being hard pressed by soldiers, and they were in flight again. Father Burns' shoes had worn out by this time and he was in misery in the new-fallen snow as he tried to keep up with the bandits. Some wanted to kill him because he was slowing them up.

One day a wild argument took place among the men, and Father Burns heard Wu crying out, "Do not kill the Father—do not kill the Father!" Father Burns felt that death was close. But Wu won the day. The bandit captain came up and said, "Father, it may mean the loss of my head, but I cannot kill you. The soldiers are after us. We have no food. So we go, and the Father can return home. I beg the Father to ask his God to protect me. I, too, do not want to die. I want to go home and see my old mother."

Suddenly, the bandits disappeared over a hilltop. Father Burns' bewilderment and awe was broken by Catechist Wu's exultant shouting, "They are gone, Father! Let's go home!"

For several days the priest and catechist wandered through the mountains and forests seeking a way out, trying to find shelter. At last, cold and starving, they arrived at the gate of a town late at night. The sentry on guard refused to let them enter, fearing a bandit trap. At last the sentry called the commanding officer, and priest and catechist were brought into safety, and returned to Tunghua.

But no such happy ending was in store for Father Jerry Donovan. On October 5, 1937, this young Pittsburgh priest was kneeling at Benediction in the Hopei mission when a man entered the sanctuary and called him out. Once in the sacristy the man drew a gun and ordered the priest to go with him. An unsuspecting altar boy, Francis Liu, entered the sacristy and was also taken prisoner. The priest and altar boy were hurried out into the growing dusk. An alarm was almost immediately given, but no trace of the missioner was found. Two weeks later, Francis Liu stumbled back into the mission; he had been released by the bandits, to deliver their note demanding $50,000 ransom. Francis recounted what had happened.

"They tied us up," he said, "and made us walk quickly. We traveled all that night and the next ten nights, sleeping in the hills in the daytime. Then we came to a lean-to that had a roof but no walls, and there we stayed. We covered ourselves with grass at night to keep out the cold. Father and I also suffered from swollen feet.

"The bandits took Father's trousers and gave him two pairs of cotton trousers in return. They also took his shoes, and gave him a pair of sneakers. They threatened Father with death, but he only said: 'Do as you please. The Church has no money for ransom.' Father was thin and tired when I last saw him, but he was in good spirits.

"He was always in good spirits. We talked a lot during those two weeks, and he was always trying to give me courage. I was afraid—so afraid that, even after I was freed, I trembled for days. Father would smile at me and say: 'Don't worry. There's nothing to be afraid of. They'll let you go home soon. Pray hard.'"

Weeks and months dragged by, but no clue to the missioner's whereabouts was obtained. Then on February 11, 1938, Father Jerry's frozen body was found on a snow-covered mountainside. A piece of rope twisted about his neck told the grim story. The official consular telegram reported as follows:

"Ludden (U.S. Consul General at Mukden) and Father Thomas Quirk of Catholic church report positive identification of the body discovered by the military authorities as that of Gerard Donovan. Difficult to determine exact time of death, but it is believed Father Donovan died one week before the discovery of his remains. Emaciated condition of the scantily clad body indicates extreme hardships suffered during captivity. Body partially eaten by wolves. Military authorities state there are no gunshot wounds and attribute death to strangulation."

The news of Father Donovan's death had many impressive repercussions. In the United States, a student of Fordham University, upon reading the story in a New York City newspaper, immediately caught a train to Maryknoll and asked if he might take Father Jerry's place. In Hopei, across the river from Fushun, a young man, who had been putting off baptism for years because of ridicule from his friends, surprised everyone by asking not only for baptism but also for the privilege of being a pallbearer at Father's funeral.

Another effect of the death was in Fushun. Six years earlier, when the missioners were constructing a chapel, a Manchurian carpenter named Kuan was hired to make a canopy over the altar. He proved to be really talented, and the mission then engaged him to make a carved tabernacle and a crucifix. Father Lane was so impressed with young Kuan's skill, that he kept him on the payroll and the Missionarts project was begun. The master craftsman taught carving to his apprentices, and a market was found for their products. Yet during all that time, Kuan remained a pagan. When Father Donovan's body was found, Monsignor Lane asked Kuan to carve a crucifix for the coffin. As Kuan sat at his bench, fashioning the figure of the crucified Christ, and thinking about the sacrifice of the young Pittsburgh priest, the full significance of the cross of Christ unfolded itself to him for the first time. He asked for baptism.

By an apostolic brief issued at the Vatican on February 13, 1940, the Fushun Mission was erected as a vicariate, and Monsignor Lane was named the first bishop. He was consecrated in his home city of Lawrence, Massachusetts, the following June. The new vicariate had 10,332 Catholics, 2,805 catechumens, 30 Maryknoll priests, 5 native priests, 33 Maryknoll Sisters, 2 Maryknoll Brothers, 51 seminarians, 50 native Sisters (including novices and postulants), and 90 catechists. There were 20 central missions, 9 dispensaries, an orphanage, an old folks' home, an industrial school, a high school, and 9 elementary schools. Missions among the Japanese and Koreans were well developed in Dairen, Fushun, and Antung. Fushun also had two Chinese parishes.

Then came December 8, 1941, and the attack on Pearl Harbor. Bishop Lane and his missioners were carted off to jail. The Sisters were left free a little longer—time enough to send the seminarians and Sister novices home, and to make arrangements for the old folks and the orphans. Bishop Blois, in Mukden, sent some priests to the Fushun area to help out for the duration. The internment of the Maryknollers was to last three years and eight months. Most of the American priests were repatriated on the *Gripsholm* which exchanged American civilian prisoners for Japanese civilians. Bishop Lane chose to remain in Manchuria, however, and Father Edward A. McGurkin of Hartford, Connecticut, volunteered to stay with him. During the time of internment the missioners adapted themselves well. Bishop Blois, of Mukden, supplied the Maryknollers with the necessaries for offering Mass and the Japanese authorities permitted them to do so.

Later on the two American Maryknollers were transferred north to Szupingkai where they remained interned with the priests of the Missions Etrangeres de Quebec. There they also joined another Maryknoller, Father Armand J. Jacques of Windsor, Ontario.

On the Feast of the Assumption of Our Lady, August 15, 1945, news came that the Japanese had surrendered and that a Russian army was marching on the city. The Japanese guards fled and with no one to prevent them, Bishop Lane and the two Maryknoll priests walked to the railway station and boarded a train leaving for Mukden.

They arrived in Mukden to find the city being looted by Russian and Chinese soldiers. The Americans waited in the railroad station for daylight in the hope of being able to get aboard a train for Fushun, thirty miles to the east. They were entertained by a group of Russian soldiers, all young boys, carrying tommy guns. One young Red from the Ukraine did a Cossack dance; another danced and sang to the accompaniment of a guitar he had stolen from a Mukden store; a third sang "Rose Marie" in Russian. It was a time for fraternization between the various allies. Everything was in the spirit of good-fellowship.

Bishop Lane stayed at Fushun until Christmas, and then transferred his residence to Dairen. At Fushun he found that the Russian soldiers had looted the mission, carrying off everything of value. He also learned that one of the Chinese Sisters, to escape the advances of Russian soldiers, had jumped from an upper window in the convent. With her back broken, she had crawled through the mud to some bushes where she hid until the soldiers were gone. She was permanently crippled by her experience.

Just before Christmas, Bishop Lane escorted the native Sisters to Dairen and remained there for the next six months. The State Department arranged for an American ship to pick him up and return him to the United States for the Maryknoll General Chapter that was to be held soon. About the time when Bishop Lane left Manchuria, the Russians, having taken all the loot they wanted, began evacuating and allowing native Communist troops to assume control. Fighting broke out between Chinese Nationalists troops and the Communists, but the latter, well supplied by the Russians, gradually succeeded in getting the upper hand. When they did, the curtain of darkness fell.

Only occasionally since then has the curtain been pierced. Here is a bit from one letter that came through: "Many of the people are already preparing to flee to Tientsin or Peking, to escape the terror. I don't dare think of my family, because I can't do anything for them. I have received no news from them: my poor old father, my brother, my wife, James, Bernadette, Bede—I commend them all to Almighty God. I do not want to flee, and I am not well. Yet with all these sorrows weighing on me, I would rather die or go begging in Tientsin than go through the incredible cruelties of the Communists. Pray for me, dear Father, that God may grant me strength of body and soul."

There was one last crack in the curtain. It came in the form of a letter to Bishop Lane from Michael Pai, a young Catholic professor, who reported the death of his uncle, Father Maurus Pai. The latter was the oldest Chinese priest attached to Maryknoll's Fushun Vicariate. It was a pathetic letter, but also a hopeful one because it demonstrated a faith that Communist guns cannot shoot down. This is what the letter said:

"On the morning of December 9, shortly after breakfast, five armed Communist soldiers entered the house of my uncle, Father Maurus Pai. Without giving any explanation, the soldiers ordered my uncle to accompany them to their headquarters. There, despite the frigid

Manchurian winter, Father was stripped of his clothes and was thrown into an unheated prison.

"After three days, Father Pai was led from prison and brought before the Communist tribunal. There he was charged with spreading the American religion, with hiding arms, and with plotting against the Communists. When Father said his religion was not American, and denied all the charges, he was beaten with whips and dragged back to prison.

"After ten days of this torture, Father was released. The Reds told him that he could not take shelter in the house of anyone. In this way, they hoped that he would die of cold or hunger. However, one of the Christians found him and took him home.

"The Christian tried to persuade Father to flee. He replied: 'Where can I go? Without the order of my bishop, I cannot desert my people.'

"That night, about eleven o'clock, the Communists came to the home of the Christian. Father was again seized. He was again stripped of his clothes, and was led naked through the icy streets to the prison. There he was given a burlap bag to cover himself.

"On Christmas Day, he was led to his church, where the Communist tribunal had assembled. Then he was beaten with sticks and whips until he was unconscious. When he revived, he was taken back to his prison.

"Father Pai was in this cold prison until January 17. On that day, at nine o'clock in the morning, he was called from the cell and, still clad only in the burlap bag, was led before the tribunal.

"Regional Prefect Chao, and a man named Li, head of the local government, read off the charges and asked the Reds how Father should be sentenced. The Reds cried out that he should die. Chao then said: 'This man is already quite old. Perhaps if we beat him, he might be then discharged.'

" 'He is a slave of the Americans!' the Reds shouted.

"The tribunal then passed the sentence of death. On the way, Father knelt on the ground, joined his hands, and began to pray.

" 'Look at him! He is praying,' said his executioners. They laughed and beat him. 'Get up and die!' they cried.

"But Father, on account of his wounds, could not get up, so the soldiers dragged him the remaining distance. When they arrived at the pond, the man in charge ordered Father to kneel. Since he could not, he was shot in the head from behind. When the Reds fired a third time, Father gave up his soul to God.

"Later, the same Christian who had given him shelter was able to cover Father's corpse with a burying mound. The ground was too frozen for digging a grave."

14

Philippines—Tragedy in the Pacific

The only Asiatic nation ever completely converted to Catholicism in modern times is the Philippine Republic, and the 17 million Catholics of the Philippines equal the combined total of all the other Catholic bodies in Asia. Practically the only inhabitants of the islands who are not Christians are the Moslems (Moros) of the south, and the aboriginals who live apart from Filipino customs and life.

The cross was first raised over the Philippine Archipelago four centuries ago (1521), and to Philip II of Spain goes the credit of developing this outpost bastion of Christianity. In the forty years from 1565 to 1605 the remarkable feat without any parallel in history—the conversion of almost an entire people—was accomplished. Great cathedrals were built, and enormous churches erected. Long before Harvard College was founded, Manila had the Catholic university of Santo Tomas, founded in 1611. Almost overnight the Filipinos turned from a state of paganism to that of Christian civilization.

But the Spanish made a great mistake, the same mistake that was to plague their work in Central and South America: they failed to build up a native clergy and hierarchy. Spain ruled for 333 years, yet when the end came in 1898, all five bishops of the islands were Spanish, and the few Filipino priests ordained were solely helpers to the Spaniards and not builders themselves.

Manila's late Archbishop O'Doherty explained the situation clearly: "If the Spanish friars made a mistake in their policy of governing the Filipinos, it was solely in this, that they failed to realize that a day might come when Spanish sovereignty might cease. They neglected the Catholic principle that no Church can rest upon a substantial basis unless it is manned by a native clergy."

When the last shot of the Battle of Manila Bay sounded the death knell of Spanish colonial power, it marked too the withdrawal of the Spanish religious force from the field. The new American conquerors multiplied schools, roads and introduced sanitation and hygiene, but they also brought a subtle and creeping materialism. Many of the new Masonic rulers of the islands had little sympathy for the traditional Faith. It may take a long time to build an edifice, but only a short while to tear it down. The Filipino fought to retain his beliefs, but through the new educational system installed by the Americans he saw his Faith being undermined and broken.

The Holy See expected that the Catholics of America would take care of the problem their own nation had created. In 1920, however, there were only two American secular priests in the islands, although there were thousands of American businessmen and zealous Protestant missionaries. The Holy See began to send European missioners, but their number was small.

At the urgent request of Archbishop Michael J. O'Doherty, of Manila, Maryknoll began work in the islands in 1926. The young Society was hard pressed for personnel because of its commitments in South China, Manchuria and Korea. It was decided, therefore, to concentrate the Philippine work in centers of influence. Father James M. Drought was transferred from China to pioneer the undertaking, and became director of St. Rita's Hall, a hostel for young men students in Manila. The same year saw the first contingent of Maryknoll Sisters arrive in the islands, and during the years to follow they sent a large number of missioners. The Sisters operated St. Paul's hospital, St. Mary's Hall, a student residence for university women, a college, and other schools.

The students were being trained as the future leaders of the Philippines. The Maryknollers worked with these students, strengthening their Catholic life, and finding employment for them after graduation. Many graduates were placed as teachers in both Manila and the Provinces. During the summer vacation period teachers from the Provinces were brought in for special training in catechetical work.

Father Drought, who was the superior at the time, was an especially talented and gifted man. While Director of St. Rita's Hall, he successfully carried on a public apologetic campaign against a Protestant minister who threatened to do much harm to the spiritual welfare of university students. He was of great service to Archbishop O'Doherty in Catholic Action activities, and he also helped to systematize and modernize the tangled finances of the archdiocese. He was one of the principal organizers of the Catholic Students' Conference, and sought to develop a strong Catholic Press in the islands. During this time, Father Drought formed a lifelong friendship with a young Filipino who was to become internationally famous as an editor, winner of the Pulitzer Prize, Foreign Minister of his government, aide to General MacArthur, Ambassador to the United States, and President of the United Nations. This young man was the energetic and brilliant Carlos P. Romulo. It was in such young men that Father Drought saw the hope for the future of the Philippines.

When Father Drought was called home from the Islands to take on more responsible work for the Society, Father John J. Toomey of New Bedford, Massachusetts, replaced him. In October 1928, Father William A. Fletcher, of Fall River, Massachusetts, was assigned to Manila from South China, as secretary to Archbishop O'Doherty, chaplain of St. Mary's Hall, and first director of the Catholic weekly radio program. Father Robert E. Sheridan succeeded Father Toomey as director of St. Rita's Hall. Later, Father Austin Hannon became director and played an important organizational role in the XXXIII International Eucharistic Congress held at Manila in February 1937. The work of the Maryknoll Sisters was expanding rapidly, and by 1930, the Sisters' community had almost half a hundred members in Manila.

Under President Franklin D. Roosevelt, conditions in the Philippines changed for the better. For the first time since the islands had been taken from Spain, a Catholic Governor-General was appointed. Many of the irritating Masonic influences were removed, and the Church took a new lease on life. Father Drought, back at Maryknoll, New York, sought a way to focus attention on the Philippines, and he broached an idea to officials at Notre Dame University. From that consultation, resulted "Philippine Day," held at the University on December 9, 1935, honoring the new Commonwealth of the Philippines which President Roosevelt had established.

The convocation at Notre Dame was presided over by His Eminence, George Cardinal Mundelein, of Chicago. Attending it was President Roosevelt, who received the degree of Doctor of Laws. Likewise honored was Carlos P. Romulo, who at this time headed a chain of newspapers and was Regent of the University of the Philippines. Mr. Romulo was the guest of Maryknoll before the convocation, and with Father Drought composed a memorable speech in which he pointed out the Catholic heritage of his homeland. He declared that Catholicism was much more than a religion of the state. "It is the religion of the people," he said. "And the people, not the State, are sovereign."

In 1941, Maryknoll decided to expand its work in the Philippines and three priests were sent to Cebu. Father Sheridan was made superior of this new group. In the same year a tremendous stride forward was made when authorities at three of the largest secular colleges invited priests to hold religious instructions for Catholic students in their schools. Father J. Russell Hughes, a Maryknoller from New York City, immediately began courses of religious instruction at National University and Lacson College. The Jesuit Fathers took care of Manila Law School. A special "Academic Mass" was inaugurated by Rev. Edward McCarthy of the Columban Fathers, and was celebrated every Sunday at Santa Cruz Church. It was attended by a weekly crowd of 2,000 students. One of the regular speakers was Father William T. Cummings, San Francisco Maryknoller.

Then came that fateful day in December, 1941, when Japanese planes took off from carriers in the Pacific, streaming eastwards to devastate Pearl Harbor and southwards to smash Manila and Corregidor. The Philippines were planned as Japan's first conquest of the war, and to the people of the islands came years of horror and suffering, as Japanese troops landed and fought their way southward to victory.

There are many memories of those heroic and crowded days of early war. But the recollection that is uppermost in the mind of the author of this book is a picture that appeared one morning in papers all over the United States. It was taken during the siege of Bataan, and showed Father William T. Cummings standing before a crude altar offering Mass while the battle raged around him. And this is the way I shall always remember Father Cummings. The air was dense with the smoke of burning forests. The sound of gunfire, the coughing and whine of hurrying military vehicles, lent distraction to the ear. Through the haze, above the din, could be seen and heard Father Cummings as he offered one of his last Masses on earth.

I want to remember him as he stood before the rough, wooden map table that served as his altar; his vestments wrinkled, his khaki pants contrasted against the white of his alb, his heavy soldier boots caked with mud. I want to remember him saying Mass in those strange surroundings as unconcernedly as if he were offering the same Sacrifice at home in the Maryknoll chapel. This is my way, but there are others who remember differently.

Brigadier General Carlos Romulo, aide to General MacArthur, remembers another and earlier Mass on Bataan. It was said on Easter Sunday. When General (then Colonel) Romulo returned to his headquarters after hearing that Mass, he remarked to a fellow officer: "I'd give anything to be back in Manila today. What a great editorial I could write!"

"About what?" asked the officer.

"The sermon I just heard at the field Mass. The chaplain, a Maryknoll priest, Father Cummings, coined a phrase that deserves to ring around the world. He said, 'There are no atheists in foxholes!'"

General Romulo later escaped from Bataan, and Father Cummings' phrase from that Easter battlefield sermon did catch fire and flame around the world.

There are others who remember Father Cummings. There is the boyhood friend who grew up with him in San Francisco, and who likes to remember him as he was in 1926 when he came to Maryknoll—a tall, thin, bespectacled youth, already a major seminarian, full of zeal and fire to help the unfortunate people of the world. Father's sister, Edith, remembers the June day of 1928, when, in the San Francisco Cathedral, Archbishop Hanna ordained the young Maryknoller to the priesthood. It was the happiest day of her life.

There are young priests now who remember Father Cummings as their genial, kindly professor. There are thousands of Catholics who remember him as a speaker in pulpits across our country, pleading for funds to aid Maryknoll's work. A Maryknoll superior remembers the many letters and entreaties he received from Father Cummings, all asking that he be sent to the missions despite a back injury that had kept him in the homeland. This same superior also remembers how Father Bill wore him down, and how in 1940 Father was finally assigned to the Philippine Islands, because it was believed that there his health could withstand the rigors of mission life. An Army colonel remembers the day, just after Pearl Harbor, when Father Cummings entered his office at Army headquarters in Manila.

"Colonel," said the priest, "I want to get into the Army. I don't care whether I get a commission or not. I don't care whether I have a uniform or a place to sleep. But the boys will be needing priests, and I want to help them."

The colonel remembers how he was moved by the priest's sincerity and zeal; how he granted his request and commissioned him a lieutenant.

Nurse Juanita Redmond best remembers Father Cummings for a day in Base Hospital One on Bataan. Despite the markings on the hospital, enemy planes bombed it. The wounded and sick in the building were thrown into a frenzied panic.

"Right in the middle of the bombing," says Miss Redmond, "Father Cummings, the Catholic chaplain, came into our ward.

" 'Boys, that was tough,' he said, 'but let's pray to God they don't come back.'

"He stood there praying, with his hands in the air. He prayed for about five minutes, and then another wave of bombers struck. One bomb fell only a few yards from him, and a piece of it broke his arm and cut his shoulder, but he never stopped praying, and his voice didn't falter.

"It wasn't until the last bomb fell that Father Cummings finished his prayer. Then he turned to another chaplain who had come in, and said: 'All right, partner, take over. I'm wounded.'

"He certainly saved a great many lives that day, because if he had not come in and told the boys to stay by their beds, a good many more would have run out into the open and been machine-gunned."

It is the next morning that an Army doctor remembers. The doctor saw Father Cummings, arm in sling, trudging along the road to the front lines, shortly after dawn. The doctor reprimanded him.

"What are you doing here, Padre? You belong in bed. Get back there right away!" the doctor called out.

Without pausing in his stride, Father Cummings calmly replied: "Doc, there are a lot of men up front far worse off than I am. I'm going up to help them."

There are still some persons who remember the letter that was drawn up that day by the patients and staff of the hospital. Addressed to President Roosevelt, it was a commendation by the men of their chaplain. Whether that letter ever left besieged Bataan, we have no way of knowing.

Then there is the little Army nurse, as Irish as Tipperary, with raven hair and sparkling eye. She remembers especially one evening on Bataan. She was married then, to a young lieutenant. She will never forget Father Cummings as he performed the marriage ceremony in the front lines, under fire.

The list of those who remember is long. There are a pitiful few who recall Father Cummings as he dragged himself along during the Bataan Death March. Sergeant Curtis Jefferson remembers the Maryknoller at Bilibid Prison, where the Death March survivors were taken. There Father Cummings used contacts outside the prison to smuggle in extra food and rations for the prisoners.

"He was always cheerful," said the sergeant. "He was a great morale booster. When he would meet you, he would say, 'Hello, Joe! Things are looking up today.'"

Major Albert Talbot, another chaplain, remembers talking with Father Cummings one day, and next day seeing him put aboard a ship for transfer to a prison in Japan.

Finally, there are those who remember the last days. Captain Sparks was on the same transport. He, too, has memories of the Bataan Padre.

"Father Cummings died like a hero," he said. "He is the priest who got, and deserved the Distinguished Service Cross. He had a fine, strong voice, and at night in the hold of our ship we heard him exhorting the men to keep up their courage, hold on to whatever life they retained.

"Conditions were frightful. We had tropical clothes, and the cold was paralyzing. Men were going insane from starvation. Five spoonfuls of water were given each of us daily. Father Cummings used to give a little talk to the men who were dying. Then one night we failed to hear him speak. We were told that he had died."

A priest from Toledo, Ohio, remembers Father Cummings' death. "I was with him when he died," reports Chaplain John E. Duffy, Colonel, U.S.A. "Right up to the end, he told us to hold on, that we would soon be safe. I remember wondering how a dying man could have such a strong clear voice."

These are the memories, crowding one upon the other. Memories of tired men. Memories of men sick with malaria, dysentery, beriberi. Memories of men with faces pinched from hunger and pain. Memories of smoke and dust, of high heroism, of despair, and of death.

But for myself, I want to remember Father Cummings as he stood before his altar on Bataan—the way the last picture of him was taken and sent to America; the way millions of Americans last saw him. For that was the purpose of his going to Bataan in the first place—to bring Christ to those men.

For the other Maryknollers, the torture of imprisonment was to last much longer. There were 53 Maryknoll Sisters in the Philippines at the outbreak of the war, and some of their experiences during these years were truly hair-raising. Sister Trinita Logue, of New York City, spent nine months in the infamous Santiago Prison, the longest time a western woman ever remained there. Another story of those days concerns the mystery surrounding the strange disappearance of Sister Hyacinth Kunkel, of New York City.

When the Japanese invaded Luzon, Sister Hyacinth was at the Maryknoll Sisters' school at Baguio. The other American Sisters were arrested and taken to a concentration camp. Two other Sisters were left behind with Sister Hyacinth—Sister Una, an Irish national, and Sister Carmencita, a Filipina. This small group remained at Baguio until the Japanese confiscated their house, near Christmas of 1944.

The Sisters sought refuge some miles away at Atab, a remote, mountain village. Because the Maryknoll house was badly bombed and they had nowhere to go, the three Sisters took up residence in some caves.

Towards the end of April, the Sisters heard that American troops had landed on Luzon, and they joined a party of 500 refugees who hoped to get to the American lines. The party of refugees started out, guided by an Igorot who knew the mountain trails. There were quite a few religious in the group and the Maryknoll Sisters were not always together. Suddenly Sister Hyacinth was missed. The line of refugees was searched and questioned. Many people had seen her and talked to her. But there was no trace of her to be found. Later the whole area was searched, and even American soldiers were sent up looking for Sister, but she had vanished as completely as if she never existed.

The priests on Cebu were able to avoid capture for some time. Father Sheridan took to the hills there with Filipino troops. Father William R. McCarthy, of Waterbury, Connecticut, went to Lahung to serve the American Air Force men, and Father Timothy Daley, of Palmer, New York, worked among the Chinese evacuees. But by the last half of 1942, they were all rounded up and interned on Luzon, first at Santo Tomas Internment Camp, and then at Los Banos, where living was so hard that many like Father Russell Hughes, of New York City, although eventually set free, died soon after from the effects.

Freedom came in the form of the Eleventh Airborne Division. Father McCarthy gives us a graphic picture of his rescue:

"The morning of February 23, 1945, began like any other day in camp. The majority of the prisoners began to stir about 5:30. A few minutes before 7:00 we lined up for breakfast. As usual, the Japanese soldiers were taking their setting-up exercises at that hour. New guards were fastening their cartridge belts before replacing the men who had been on duty during the night.

"We heard the roar of nine C-47 airplanes just as the new guards began to leave their quarters. Then we saw the Angels coming down from heaven. The Japanese forgot about their setting-up exercises and ran for their rifles. Bullets whizzed through the straw barracks even before the paratroopers hit the ground. Afterwards we learned that Filipino guerrillas had surrounded the camp during the night, and were ready to open fire at 7:00 a.m.

"Inside the barracks, we all hugged the floor, trying to make ourselves as small a target as possible. Then the shooting stopped, and we heard an American voice shout, 'Cease fire.' An officer ran into our barracks to tell us to be ready to leave in 15 minutes, carrying as few belongings as possible. Later we learned that a battalion had formed a roadblock three miles from the camp to bottle up some 8,000 Japanese troops in the hills. Pursuit planes, P-38's, circled above the Japanese installations to keep the troops occupied and prevent any counterattack.

"Men, women, and children mingled with the American soldiers. Pieces of chocolate, the first candy we had seen for three years, were distributed. And each soldier passed out what seemed to be an endless supply of cigarettes. Shouts of joy, loud chatter and laughter were heard on all sides. 'Where are you from in the States?' was the first question asked by prisoners. I remember one woman asking a sergeant if any of the boys were from Jersey. Without a smile, the sergeant replied: 'We're from Texas. This job is too tough for any guys from Jersey.' His Texas enthusiasm seemed to overlook the fact that the Eleventh Airborne was a unit of valiant men from every section of the country. Whether from Texas or New Jersey, they were a welcome sight.

"Fifty-two armored amphibian trucks had crossed Lake Laguna de Bay with the troops. The dazed prisoners, stunned by the long months in prison and the climax of that morning's events, stumbled toward the trucks. Patients on hospital cots, some bloated from beriberi, others too weak from starvation to walk, were carried to the trucks. Men, women, and children followed, bundles under their arms or dangling from sticks, carrying their scant possessions with them."

With the end of the war, the missioners came out of their internment and concentration camps, to pick up the pieces and start anew. Father McCarthy returned to Cebu and reported almost complete devastation there. The Sisters returned to their wrecked and stripped buildings. They immediately began the task of reconstruction, and their new college in Manila is a model for the rest of the country. Because the immediate postwar years placed a heavy drain on the personnel of the Maryknoll Fathers, the priests formerly assigned to the Philippines were transferred to other posts.

But conditions in the islands were very bad. In 1951, there were only as many priests in the Philippines to care for a population of

20 million as there had been at the time of the Spanish-American War when the population numbered 7 million. There were about 1,500 priests caring for the parishes: an average of one parish priest for every 14,000 people. Nine out of ten Catholics were unable to hear Sunday Mass because of lack of clergy. Only 5% of the island's children were in Catholic schools. It was estimated that 83% of the people died without benefit of the Last Sacraments. Missioners came to the islands from the Jesuit, Columban, Divine Word, Oblate and La Salette Fathers, but many more were needed.

That same year saw Maryknollers being forced out of China, and their expulsion gave Maryknoll sufficient personnel to reconsider work in the Philippines. Acting on the invitation of Bishop Rufino J. Santos, Apostolic Administrator of the Lipa Diocese, Maryknoll accepted six parishes in the south-central part of Luzon. Nine priests were assigned to begin the Lipa work, and later others were added to the group.

Bishop Raymond A. Lane, Maryknoll Superior General, in announcing the resumption of the Filipino work, declared: "When in the past persecution raged in China, the Philippine Islands were the base for many missioners who labored there awaiting the blessed day when they could return to their beloved Chinese people. History repeats itself as our South China Maryknollers join other missionary communities in the Philippines.

"In these days of such widespread hostility toward Westerners in Asia, it is not inconceivable that the day will come when the Catholic millions of the Philippines will supply the vanguard of apostles for missionary work on the Asiatic mainland. Toward this end all the Western world must labor to build up a Filipino clergy that not only will be sufficient for its own islands but will flow out to the non-Christians of the continent of Asia."

15

Oriental Work in the United States

"Unsung, unheralded, and unknown" might be a fitting description of a substantial group of Maryknollers—priests, Brothers and Sisters—whose mission work has kept them confined within the boundaries of the United States, but who nevertheless are rendering as important service to Mother Church as if they were laboring in some remote corner of Africa, Asia, or other foreign region. These are the missioners who work in Hawaii and in Oriental parishes within the confines of the continental United States. Their number is substantial. In Hawaii, for example, there are 14 houses of Maryknoll Fathers with 28 priests and one Brother; and nine convents of Maryknoll Sisters with a total personnel of 144 Sisters. Their work, too, stems from the early days of Maryknoll.

It has often been asked why a foreign-mission society, like Maryknoll, should have sent missioners to the Hawaiian Islands. The answer is simply that, although the islands were evangelized for a century, they were still largely mission territory in a very real sense, with their population composed of native Hawaiians plus Chinese, Japanese, Koreans, Portuguese, and Puerto Ricans. Such a mixture of cultures and languages caused a very real problem, and demanded missioners who could understand the problem. In addition, the main Portuguese families that emigrated to the islands took the attention of the few priests on the islands, thus cutting down the attention that could be given to the other groups.

The first persons to preach Christianity in the Hawaiian Islands were Protestant evangelists from New England. When the Holy See assigned the Congregation of the Sacred Heart to work in the islands, the priests found strong opposition on the part of Anglo-Saxon non-native families, even to the point of persecution. However, by 1850 the Fathers of the Sacred Heart could claim successful penetration of the Hawaiian populace.

By this time, too, many large plantations had been built up. The easy-going Hawaiians saw no point in a life of agricultural drudgery, and as a result, laborers for the sugar-cane and pineapple plantations had to be brought in from Europe and the Orient. This influx of peon labor raised havoc with religious work that the Fathers of the Sacred Heart had established. Many different nationalities were represented, economic conditions among the workers were terrible, and since most of the workers were unmarried males, many serious moral problems were created. All of these conditions made a natural need for an army of missioners.

There were other difficult aspects to the work. The five large islands comprising Hawaii are separated by miles of ocean. Few roads existed on the islands, and the work camps were isolated. This lack of easy communications was additional reason for a large body of missionary personnel. But unfortunately, far too few Catholic priests were sent to Hawaii. Protestant missionaries, numerous and heavily financed, were carrying the day. Even scores of Mormon missionaries were on hand to build up congregations.

All of this non-Catholic activity gave serious concern to the Catholic bishop of Hawaii. He petitioned the Holy See for help, and as a result, in 1927 the first Maryknollers were assigned to Honolulu. Father William S. Kress, of Cleveland, Ohio, was the first Maryknoll superior there, and he was given charge of the Sacred Heart Parish. It was his intention to build upon the youth of the islands, and he immediately began a school and arranged for Maryknoll Sisters to teach in it.

Pioneering the work with Father Kress was Brother Philip Morini, of Amsterdam, New York. An idea of the methods Brother

Philip used to awaken interest in the Church may be acquired from one of his early reports:

"While walking down Manoa Valley one day, I saw in front of a country store, fifteen or twenty young men and boys lolling about aimlessly. I started a conversation with the oldest one and asked what they did for amusement. He shrugged his shoulders in real Hawaiian fashion, and said, 'Nothing to do up here.' I asked if they would be interested in boxing and wrestling, and he replied that they would, but had no one to teach them. To arouse their enthusiasm, we went into an open field across the road, and selected the heaviest fellow of the group to demonstrate a few holds. The crowd by this time had attracted many more, and they roared with laughter at the ease with which the heavy fellow was put down.

"The following Sunday there was only one small boy at the country store. Upon inquiry, I learned that the other fellows did not think I was coming, so they went swimming. We went up to the swimming hole. In a little while they were out and dressed and ready for their athletics, which they practiced under a large tree. Later it was proposed that they come and meet in the church basement once a week. This provided an opportunity to introduce the catechism between and after bouts. After some time, the boys began coming to Mass."

Such approaches and activities helped to build a thriving parish. Today at the Sacred Heart Church there are five priests and one Brother. The pastor is Father George C. Powers of West Lynn, Massachusetts. Attached to the parish is the Maryknoll School, staffed by 38 Sisters, and consisting of an elementary school of 900 students and a high school with 350 pupils.

Besides regular parish work, the islands offered many opportunities for specialized service. Social service work; youth work; institutional work among the lepers, blind, deaf, crippled, delinquent; all of these were but a few of the openings and the Maryknollers took advantage of them all. When Father John M. Coulehan, of Cumberland, Maryland, was honored by the Juvenile Court for his youth work, he caused Judge Martin Pence to look up in surprise when he protested: "I deserve no award for my work with Hawaiian youngsters. I was only trying to perform my priestly duties to the best of my ability."

Another Maryknoller with a big appeal for youngsters is Father

Hubert M. Pospichal, of Elma, Iowa. He served in Korea before coming to the islands, and there picked up the nickname "Pied Piper," because of the way children followed him about. Father Pospichal lost none of his charm when he took up work in Hawaii. His daily Mass is crowded with his friends, he has a waiting-line of altar boys, and his public night prayers are a parish event. Few parish small fry want to go home to bed without Father's nightly blessing. Strangers often wonder what magic Father Pospichal uses. "No magic at all," replied a fellow missioner to one questioner. "The children love Father 'Poss' because he loves them. A long time ago he learned that we get back just what we give."

The clipping from the Hilo daily was terse and to the point. "The past three years have marked a turning point in the distinguished history of the parochial schools on the Big Island," declared the paper. "The 'new deal' in Catholic education here stems from March, 1947, when the Maryknoll mission society was engaged to staff St. Joseph's Parish. The Rev. Thomas V. Kiernan, M.M., was named pastor on March 17 with instructions from Bishop Sweeney to start a new consolidated parish school building program which eventually would include elementary and high schools and new residences for the instructors.

"The elementary school was dedicated on August 29, 1948, and opened for classes on September 13.

"The bishop dedicated the high school on October 9, 1949, although it had already been occupied in part on September 12.

"The high school gymnasium was completed in January, this year."

Father Thomas V. Kiernan, of Cortland, New York, is a man who gets things done, attractively and reasonably. When he was a missioner in Wuchow, China, he built a church that won international attention for its fine architectural style, and was written up in the pages of *Liturgical Arts* magazine. Now, pastor in Hilo on the Big Island that gives the whole group its name of Hawaii, Father Kiernan has developed a parish setup that would be the envy of most mainland pastors. Using modern quonset construction he erected two schools that contain, besides classrooms, a library, clinic, offices, cafeteria, auditorium and recreation rooms. Large, airy, practical, and easy to keep clean, the buildings are a model for island school construction.

Thus goes the work in the islands. In all the Maryknoll parishes and schools excellent progress is being made. But much remains to be done in Hawaii, and many problems of the old days still remain. While about one-third of the population are baptized Catholics, only 25% of these people are practicing Catholics. Much of this neglect is due to mixed marriages through which many are lost to the Faith. Few Japanese have been brought into the Church, partly because they cling to their Buddhism, and partly because of prejudice built up in the old days when the Catholic Church was labeled "the Portuguese Church."

Vocations are still too few. In past years little attention was paid to building up a native clergy. Many bodies of missioners are now working in the islands, but all know that they are but a temporary solution. Since 1941 when Bishop James T. Sweeney was sent from San Francisco to head the Diocese of Honolulu amazing progress has been made. A diocesan preparatory seminary, a large percentage of whose boys are of Japanese extraction, has been established. Religious life on all the islands is on the upswing. Maryknollers feel that within two more generations the island will be self-sufficient both in vocations and material support. Until then, however, there will still be need for mission groups such as Maryknoll to work in the islands if Catholicism is to continue its dramatic march in making Hawaii America's Christian bastion in the Pacific.

Maryknoll's work among the Orientals in the United States began in 1920 when a mission for the Japanese was established in Los Angeles. By the time Father William Kress left in 1927 to pioneer the work in Hawaii, he had built up a strong foundation, giving the Japanese mission tremendous importance in the Japanese colony. The editor of a Japanese newspaper in Los Angeles wrote an editorial piece on racial discrimination which he concluded by saying:

"We Los Angeles Japanese people deeply appreciate the kindness shown our people by the Maryknoll Fathers and Sisters. Sometimes I feel disgusted and angry when some Americans mistreat the Japanese because they are not members of the white race, but when I close my eyes and think of the other types of Americans, such as the Maryknollers whose hearts burn with love, affection and kindness, I find myself so thankful to God and to America, and I am always encouraged to renew my efforts to promote the brotherly love of all the people, especially between Americans and Japanese."

The Los Angeles mission even had international attention. A clipping from the Manchuria Daily News for August 31, 1934, gives a long story on Maryknoll's Los Angeles work, and makes the announcement that the Empress of Japan has donated 2,000 yen to the American mission, following a report from the Japanese consul in Los Angeles, who had stated that his "party visited the school and the home, and they were greatly impressed with the work that is being done." A most favorable impression was created in Japan when Brother Theophane Walsh, of Roxbury, Massachusetts, led his Catholic Boy Scouts on a tour of their ancestral homeland.

The present physical parish was completed in 1939, under the direction of Father Hugh T. Lavery, of Bridgeport, Connecticut, who was to give practically a whole priestly lifetime to the mission. The church, which was dedicated that year to accommodate 500 worshipers, blended Oriental, Italian and California architectural styles. The altar of the church was patterned after an altar in a Maryknoll mission in Japan. The parish plant included, besides the church, a large school, an auditorium, and a rectory. Maryknoll Sisters taught in the school from the time of its foundation.

During these years, there was much prejudice against the Japanese. The Maryknollers took a firm stand in speaking up for the people among whom they worked. They spoke out for the repeal of the Oriental Exclusion Act (passed in 1924) when such frank speech was not appreciated. They fought against the stigmas placed on the Japanese.

When the war came with Japan, the Government, acting with more haste than prudence, arrested the Japanese and loaded them wholesale into concentration camps. Maryknollers protested the injustice, protected Japanese property, and tried to make the violent separation of people from their homes as easy as possible. Twelve Maryknoll priests went into the camps with their charges, who were cut off from the rest of America by barbed wire and patroling sentries. Later in the war Japanese boys, born in this country, were allowed to get out of these camps by enlisting in the army. Despite the harsh treatment they had undergone, they proved that they were ready to die for America. The highest decorated division in the war was a Japanese unit. Gradually Americans became ashamed of the treatment that had been meted out to these citizens.

The wartime work in the camps resulted in many conversions, and much good will for the Church. When the war ended, the Japanese in America sought to pick up the threads of their broken lives. Many of them did not return to California but preferred to settle in the midwest or East, where there was not as strong prejudice as they had experienced in California. Those who did return to Los Angeles found that others had moved into their former homes, and as a result the Japanese were forced to scatter over the city. Los Angeles' "Little Tokyo" is now only a memory.

It took a while for the Japanese Mission to get re-organized following the dislocation and war's end, but today it is thriving once again. Father Lavery was able to announce in 1953 that he possessed a flourishing community of over a thousand Japanese Catholics. He credited the school with building up this nucleus of Christians, pointing out that while only 9% of the children in the school were Catholics, many of the others through their education would be led into the Church. When the school began thirty-five years earlier there were only two Catholics in the parish.

The Los Angeles parish really came of age when the first of its boys was ordained at Maryknoll in 1949. He is Father James S. Tokuhisa, now attached to a Maryknoll Mission in Japan. A second boy from the parish was ordained in 1953, Father Thomas W. Takahashi, and he too is a Maryknoller in Japan. There are other seminarians at Maryknoll from the Los Angeles parish. Some day they too will take the Faith brought to them by Maryknollers to the land of their ancestors. Then the circle will be completed.

Another Maryknoll mission for the Japanese was started in Seattle in 1920. A grade school was begun in 1926 under the direction of Father John C. Murrett of Buffalo, New York, and staffed by Maryknoll Sisters. Progress in Seattle was good, and the early years recorded the conversions of two Buddhist priests, and many influential Japanese. In 1926, there were only 21 Japanese Catholics in Seattle. Five years later there were more than 300.

Like the Japanese of California, Seattle's Japanese were also taken from their homes at the outbreak of war. The priests at the Seattle mission also went to the concentration camps to care for their charges. Again like their California brothers, the Seattle Japanese were willing to demonstrate with their lives that they loved America. A single wartime casualty list contained the names of three boys from the Japanese parish. Two had been killed in Italy, the third wounded. Father Leopold Tibesar, of Quincy, Illinois, their pastor, wrote from the Hunt, Idaho, relocation camp where he was living that the dead boys were "among our best. Both were exemplary in their Christian lives, a powerful influence for good among the younger boys. They had been received in audience by Pope Pius XII just before going into battle."

The Seattle parish never recovered from the blow it received when the war dispersed its parishioners. After the war it was re-opened, but few Japanese returned to their former homes. One of those who did return home, Mrs. Theresa Matsudaira, mother of twelve children, was chosen in 1951 as "Catholic Mother of the Year"—a great honor for a woman born in Japan to be so singled out from America's 28 million Catholics. Since other racial groups had occupied the area, it was felt that the Seattle work was no longer in Maryknoll's missionary pattern. In 1954, Maryknoll withdrew from the parish, and it was turned over to the Seattle Archdiocese.

Maryknoll is also responsible for two Chinese parishes in the United States. In 1946, Father Martin J. Burke, of Brooklyn, New York, began work among the Chinese in Chicago. A veteran of many years in South China, Father Burke had returned to this country in 1942 for special work among Chinese Americans. During the war he was decorated by the Chinese government with the Order of the Dragon for his efforts in behalf of the Chinese in the United States. He was transferred to Hawaii as superior of all Maryknollers there in 1949, and was succeeded as pastor of St. Therese Mission in Chicago by Father Michael J. McKiernan, of Pomeroy, Washington.

The second Maryknoll parish among the Chinese was accepted in 1949 in New York's Chinatown at the Transfiguration Church on Mott Street. For many years the Salesian Fathers had done excellent work here. Father James F. Smith, of Norwalk, Connecticut, was the first pastor. When he left to become regional superior of Maryknollers in Hong Kong, Formosa and the Philippines, Father John M. McLoughlin, of Elmhurst, New York, took charge of the parish. Maryknoll Sisters teach in the Transfiguration school.

16

Kweilin—Land of Gingerbread Mountains

Did you know that China once had a Catholic emperor? It happened this way. In the seventeenth century the Ming dynasty ruled China. The country had two capitals—the Northern Capital at Peking, and the Southern Capital at Kweilin. When the Manchus poured down from the north they conquered Peking, and the Mings there were overthrown and put to death. The next Ming in line of succession was in Kweilin, and his name was Yungli. When he was proclaimed emperor, the Manchus came after him. Many members of Yungli's family had been converted to Christianity—his mother, Helena; his wife, Anne; and his son, Constantine. They had all been instructed and baptized by the Jesuits who had so much success in China among the upper classes of this period. After sixteen years of pursuit, the Manchus finally caught up with Yungli and his family. The emperor was strangled. The next day Constantine, who had succeeded to the throne upon the death of his father, was also executed. Thus it happened that for the space of one day, a Catholic was the last ruler of the Ming dynasty, and Kweilin was his home.

Kweilin was the most beautiful city in all of South China. Because of its importance as the Southern Capital it has many monuments and historical connections. The area about the city is broken by an unusual type of limestone mountains, which rise suddenly like gigantic pagodas watching over the former home of China's rulers. These bizarre, strangely formed obelisks give the region the air of another world, far different from the rest of Kwangsi Province, to which Kweilin belongs.

Even the people around Kweilin are different from those found in Wuchow, farther south. The language heard as one walks about the streets is Mandarin, and there are a friendliness and a culture not found in other parts of Kwangsi. Also near Kweilin live some of the aboriginal Yao people—one race that the Chinese civilization did not engulf and assimilate.

On October 6, 1932, the first two Maryknollers arrived in Kweilin. They were Fathers John Romaniello, of New Rochelle, New York, and Arthur C. Lacroix, of Newton, Massachusetts. They had gone up to Kweilin from Wuchow at the request of Bishop Albouy, of Nanning, who lacked priests to care for the region. The following year the area, which included about a dozen counties in the northern part of Kwangsi, was officially and formally added to the Wuchow Mission. At that time, Catholics in the region were few; but five years later (February 15, 1938) sufficient progress had been made for the Holy See to take the area from Wuchow and set it up as an independent prefecture. Father—who then became Monsignor—Romaniello was named the prefect.

The story of any mission is the story of the men who work in it. To tell the story of Kweilin a few quick portraits of some of its missioners will be given. These men are ordinary Americans, possessed of an idealism that led them halfway across the world to labor for others who lacked their opportunities, both materially and spiritually. They came to China in troubled times, and lived practically their whole mission lives surrounded by war and turbulence. They had no particular desire to become heroes, but circumstances demanded the heroic, and they rose to meet the challenge. They sought only to be priests, and so they opened their catechumenates, began their novitiate for Chinese Sisters, and spread their Christian influence far over the Kweilin countryside. But the times demanded more of them, and they were ready to give whatever was asked.

As the war in China hammered its way up the Yangtze Valley, Kweilin seemed far removed from the fighting, but it was only a matter of months before Japanese bombs were screaming down on the Southern Capital. The Chinese from the coastal cities moved inland, and Kweilin became a goal for refugees. The normal city population of 80,000 swelled to 100,000, then 200,000, then 400,000, and continued to grow. Factories, universities, governmental offices, and refugee camps sprang up all over the area. Kweilin became a strategic air center, second city in size and importance in all of Free China.

Monsignor Romaniello was far from being static. His Catholic parish in Kweilin was growing rapidly, and the influx of refugees gave him new opportunities for service. The dispensary at the mission was busy from dawn to dusk, with hundreds standing in line for medical treatment. The mission opened a rice station to feed the hungry, provided overnight shelter for the homeless, and gave presents of money and clothing to the most needy. All of this activity was continued during the frequent bombings, for Kweilin was attacked from the air on an average of once every two weeks during the entire war. The mission itself had suffered much bomb damage, and the missioners had replaced the broken windowpanes with pages from *The Saturday Evening Post*. Every time the sirens screamed warning of a raid, all the missioners and people would head for the nearest limestone cave of the many that surrounded the city. Monsignor would remain behind to lock doors. Sometimes he cut the time too close, and with enemy planes roaring overhead, New Rochelle's gift to China could be seen sprinting down the deserted streets to a place of safety.

Finally, in one raid the mission itself was reduced to an ugly pile of rubble. The people watched sadly as Monsignor Romaniello gathered his few possessions from the wreckage, and started for the waterfront.

"He is going home," said the Chinese.

When the Monsignor reached the waterfront, he entered into negotiations with a boat owner. Finally he walked onto a large houseboat.

"This is home," he announced to the watching Chinese. And from that houseboat mission, he continued directing his rice line and dispensary. In a single year the dispensary gave 188,000 treatments.

Few people in Kweilin were unacquainted with the big smile and cheery greeting of the chubby, round-faced Italian-American Maryknoller. His unquenchable good spirits were the perfect tonic for the Chinese who were suffering so many trials. No problem was too big or too small for Monsignor Romaniello's attention. His mission was the gathering place for people of every social class and from all over China. He would have lunch with a man like John Wu, the distinguished international jurist who helped to draft the Chinese Constitution and headed the Supreme Court, and who became a Catholic during the Japanese occupation of Shanghai. An hour later he would be solving a problem of some destitute refugee family from Shantung, or Hong Kong or any part of China.

Kweilin became the base for the famous "Flying Tigers"—Americans who were fighting the invading Japanese long before their homeland had entered the war. These intrepid young men became his close friends, and Monsignor could be seen regularly pedaling his bike out to their base to say Mass. Later, when the American Air Force was near Kweilin, Catholics and non-Catholics made the mission a gathering place. Monsignor kept a pot of coffee always simmering for his guests. One American became lost when looking for the mission one day, and tried to get directions from a young boy who knew no English. Finally in desperation the flyer made the sign of the cross. A big smile broke out on the boy's face. He made the sign of the cross in return, and led the flyer to Monsignor Romaniello.

On another occasion a couple of flyers had to make a hurried exit from a damaged plane. After parachuting safely, they found themselves surrounded by countryfolk. Knowing that, if they could reach a Maryknoll mission, they would be brought to safety, one flyer pulled a rosary out of his pocket. The bystanders looked at the rosary. One Chinese pulled a rosary from his pocket. Then, before taking the flyers to the mission, the Chinese delivered an impromptu speech to the crowd on how "we Catholics are winning the war."

Monsignor Romaniello instructed his missioners throughout the territory to assist any American flyer in trouble. Father Joseph W. Regan, of Fairhaven, Massachusetts, guided eight different flyers to safety. Another Maryknoller—Father Francis X. Keelan, of Waverly, Massachusetts—made two trips of two hundred miles each to take flyers to the American base near Kweilin. Other Mary-knollers acted as part-time chaplains at American bases.

When the Japanese troops began to move on Kweilin, Monsignor and two of his priests decided to remain as long as possible to aid the refugees. "We shall go out on bicycles if the area is invaded," he wrote to Maryknoll headquarters. "If the Japanese come in the north gate, we will go out the south. It is as simple as that."

And that was the way it was done. As advance guards of the Japanese entered the city and began their work of destruction, the prefect and his two priests escaped through an unguarded gate. The few belongings they had time to gather were strapped to their bicycles. They made their way to the airfield and evacuation.

Not many days after the end of the war, Monsignor Romaniello was back in Kweilin. An American officer drove him from the airfield to town. The place was a shambles, and hardly a building was intact. As the missioner and his friend walked down the narrow alley that led to the mission, the officer spoke up.

"Monsignor," he joked, "you walk first. If a mine goes off under your feet, you'll surely go to heaven. I'm not so sure about myself, and besides, I have a family in America."

Characteristically, Monsignor Romaniello stepped in the lead and hurried down the alley. There was work to be done. Kweilin needed rebuilding. Mines or no mines, the people of Kweilin would soon be returning to their homes, and he intended to be ready to greet them.

The missioners went back, and reconstruction was commenced in the midst of great poverty and disease. Those first few years after the war were hectic ones. But at last life began to take on a few of the normal aspects, and the Kweilin work was enlarged. Father Lacroix was assigned to a town called Hsingan, an agricultural village lying in a bowl-shaped valley north of Kweilin. A canal built two centuries before Christ supplied the area with plenty of water, and as a result farming was more prosperous than in other parts of the prefecture.

Hsingan had no Catholics. Father Lacroix rented a shop, and struggled along for six months. He had three dozen Catholics when he was transferred to relief work in Canton. Father Armand J. Jacques, of Windsor, Ontario, a veteran from Maryknoll's Manchurian mission, became the new pastor. He went from village to village, trying to break the ice. He borrowed two catechists from another mission, and opened a dispensary. A sizable group was organized to study the doctrine. Then along came one of the catechists who had worked for Father Jacques in Manchuria. He was put to work. Three Manchurian Catholic refugees dropped in to see their old pastor and were signed on as catechists. Then, Teresa, a Fu Jen university trained girl, a leader in Catholic Action at the University, showed up from Manchuria. Before long Father Jacques had 24 catechists traveling the countryside.

Within a year, Father Jacques had 600 baptized Christians, and 800 catechumens studying the doctrine in eleven villages around Hsingan. The whole countryside was opened to the Faith, and Father Jacques had to rule that only those villages could receive instruction where a majority of the people signed up as desirous of baptism. On Father Jacques' desk at the end of that first year were lists of names from thirty villages awaiting instruction. Over a hundred additional villages had expressed a desire to study but had to be put off because of lack of teachers. Father Jacques estimated that the Hsingan mission would grow at the rate of 3,000 converts a year.

"Why do you want to study the doctrine? The Communists may be here soon," Father Jacques asked each village's applicants.

The words varied in the answers but the meaning was always the same. "We want the eternal happiness that the Church teaches. We do not know what the future will bring; but if we are baptized, we shall have no reason to fear."

Another area where tremendous postwar progress was made was Chuanhsien—a bustling little city, almost on the Kwangsi-Hunan border. During the war most of the inhabitants had fled the city. After the Japanese evacuated, the people returned to their ruined homes. They were struggling to rebuild when Father Edwin J. McCabe, of Providence, Rhode Island, arrived to live among them and care for a mission field almost as big as his home state. He found pitiful conditions: houses in ruins; farm tools destroyed; livestock and work animals killed for food; 70,000 people dead during the war; the region's survivors suffering from cholera, malaria, dysentery, and worms.

Father McCabe's first task was to care for homeless children— one crop in which Chuanhsien had a surplus. He organized the Foundling Association, as a system more practical than an orphanage. Abandoned infants were taken into foster homes, and the mission supplied powdered milk and clothing for their care. Of the sixty infants, mostly girls, that were left at the mission and soon placed in foster homes, only four were still requiring aid in 1950.

When Father Wenceslaus F. Knotek, of Racine, Wisconsin, came to assist Father McCabe, the two missioners turned their attention to the many homeless boys roaming the area. The boys' ages ranged from ten to fourteen years, and their parents had been killed during the war. Father McCabe visited some Government officials and persuaded them to lend him some buildings. Then he and his assistant went about the streets looking for homeless boys, and telling them that the Catholic mission would provide a home for them. Beds, clothing, and food were begged from relief agencies, or purchased with funds sent by friends in America. The Chuanhsien Boystown soon had 110 citizens.

About this time, Father McCabe, who had spent the difficult war years taking care of thousands of refugees, was ordered home on furlough. His successor as pastor was Father Lloyd I. Glass, of Cresco, Iowa, who is built like a wrestler and has an infectious good humor that draws people to him. Father Glass had been in the Kweilin mission territory since 1935. He soon began building up legends by his stamina on mission trips and his outstanding ability for mastering the tongue-twisting Mandarin language.

During the war Father Glass had been sent up to neighboring Hunan Province to protect the property of Italian missioners who had been interned. He moved into the region, cleared the missions of the officials who were occupying them, built up a lot of good will that helped the Italians to get released after a few months, and then returned to his own work in Kweilin. He became very popular among the American airmen; and when the war ended and he went home on furlough, he made the trip in style as guest of General Patrick Hurley, in the latter's personal plane. After a year at home, he went back to China to give Father McCabe a breather.

The wartime contacts of Father Glass helped him in his new work. Former members of the Flying Tigers sent him their poker winnings to keep Boystown open. Many a soldier who served in the Kweilin area contributed to the work. Father Glass arranged for the orphan boys to get three years of industrial training after they finished the eight years of schooling at Boystown. During the first two years, 480 boys were taken into the home, given food, shelter, and training in a trade.

The missioners did not confine themselves to the Boystown work alone. When they learned that Chuanhsien was subject to periodic floods that ruined crops and washed away precious topsoil, Father Knotek drew up plans for a dam to protect the village, and asked the people to co-operate in the project. The missioner directed the construction of the clay-and-rock dam; the villagers did the work; and the mission provided them with relief rice while the building went on. After the dam was finished, Father Knotek made the villagers responsible for its upkeep, and trained them in the method of opening the sluices and controlling the flood water. Thus an evil that had lasted for centuries came to an end through the work of the Catholic mission.

Father Howard C. Geselbracht, of Chicago, Illinois, was brought into Chuanhsien to open a dispensary. He also traveled about from village to village, carrying six types of commonly used medicines, and treating the sick. Vaccinations were given to Christians and catechumens, and to any non-Christians who asked for them.

To combat the high rate of interest on loans (300% for a three-month period), Father Glass set up a rice bank, limiting membership to Catholic families. In a village of fifty families, for example, the mission would buy 5,000 pounds of rice, loaning each family 100 pounds. Interest was 30% for the first year, and slightly higher for the second and third. By the end of the third year, the mission would get back its original investment, but an equal amount remained in the co-operative to start the process over again, and this time the people themselves shared in the interest payments.

All of these projects bore fruit. Starting from nothing in 1947, the Chuanhsien mission had three thousand Christians by 1950, with eight hundred candidates under instruction for baptism. No relief assistance was given to catechumens, so the mission could not be accused of making "rice Christians." If a catechumen or his family became so desperately poor that he must be helped, the aid was given only on the condition that he withdraw from the catechumenate. Besides studying Christian doctrine, every catechumen had to take a course in the Thousand Character Classic, designed to overcome illiteracy. Finally, Father Glass started the Legion of Mary among his Catholics, to create an *esprit de corps*

THE MEANING OF MARYKNOLL

that would make all Christians grow stronger in their Faith, and would bring in new Christians.

During the recent years before the enslavement by Communist hordes began, the Legion of Mary was being formed all over China. One of the most ardent promoters of the Legion was Father McCabe, back from furlough in America. It is significant that the Reds manifested great hatred towards the Legion, a hatred that few people in America can understand. Bishops, priests, Brothers, and Sisters have been expelled from China because they were connected with the Legion. At one time, twenty-seven Catholic young men and young women, of good families in Shanghai, were banished to nameless prisons because they would not denounce the Legion.

The influence of these Legionaries is illustrated by the case of Margaret Mary Wong, who lived in a Maryknoll mission in South China. Margaret Mary was converted in 1950, when the Reds were beginning their persecution. She became a member and an officer in the Legion, and one day she was arrested by the police. Proudly Margaret Mary acknowledged that she was a Legionary; and time and again, through a period of several hours, she flatly refused to sign a statement against the Legion.

Unknown to Margaret Mary, a German doctor, veteran of World War II, stood nearby that day and was impressed by the Chinese girl's performance. Months later when he reached Hong Kong, he described the scene to a Maryknoll Sister.

"Sister," he related, "I have a background of lifelong prejudice against the Catholic Church; but on that day, I was filled with admiration and respect for the spiritual institution that could inspire such a demonstration of devoted courage. I am convinced that the Catholic Church is the only force today that can really fight communism, for communism can be crushed only by the spirit that filled the frail, little frame of Margaret Mary Wong."

It is not too difficult to understand why the organization-conscious Chinese Reds, drilled by the Russians not to concern themselves greatly about individuals but to seek out and destroy every idea and every piece of social machinery that can interfere with the completeness of the Communist victory, marked the Legion of Mary for special attack. For an illustration of their anti-Legion technique, we have the story of our Maryknoll confrere, Father Albert V. Fedders, of Covington, Kentucky, director of the Legion of Mary in the adjacent Diocese of Wuchow.

"For fifteen months," reports Father Fedders, "I was imprisoned by the Reds in the Church sacristy of Taaiwan. The crime I had committed—so they often told me—was establishing the Legion of Mary."

When the Reds arrested Father Fedders, there was one single matter of interest—the Legion of Mary. For fifteen months, the "attack" on the Legion continued. Its members were questioned all day and long into the night.

"The Security Police," explains Father Fedders "forced the members of the Legion to turn over their rosaries, medals, and Legion prayer cards. Members couldn't plead that their beads had been broken or discarded; they were made to hunt up the pieces and turn them in. They couldn't excuse themselves for having thrown away the prayer card; out they must go and find it. One lad explained that he had tossed his into a rubbish heap. Soon I saw him bring it back, crumpled, smeared, tattered. That soiled piece of paper was 'evidence' against the Legion."

This rabid energy of the Reds to track down everything connected with the Legion puzzled the Legionaries.

"The Legion! That's all they harp on! What did we do in the Legion, but pray, work to help the priest, and propagate the Faith?"

And of course that is precisely the explanation of the interest of the Reds. Here, they concluded, is the hard core of the Catholic elite, the never-say-die's, who will take Christianity underground.

Another thriving parish of Kweilin during those last days was in Laipo, an early mission where Christians were being made slowly. Then in the last two years under the Nationalists, and the first under the Communists, fifteen hundred new Christians were baptized. Father Regan, pastor of Laipo, attributes much of the success to three zealous Chinese Sisters, trained by the mission for its own native Sisterhood. Father Regan described their work in a report to Maryknoll, after the Reds had forced him out of China. He wrote:

"We sent the Sisters out to open classes of instruction. Ordinarily the Sisters began each class; and when it was going fairly well, they turned it over to a woman catechist. They then went on to open a class in another village. They returned from time to time to each village, to check on progress; and they were always on hand during the last week before baptism, to put the final touches on the catechist's work.

"Because the Sisters were usually running two or three classes at one time, they were kept busy hurrying back and forth from one village to the other. I often marveled at how they could remember the names of so many people.

"Mission work was not easy during the first year of the Communist regime. The countryside was filled with bandits and guerrillas, and a great deal of fighting was going on. Once a Sister found herself in the midst of a pitched battle. She had to spend the night with a family in the hills, and put on secular clothes in order to return to her class the next morning. Many times the Sisters were threatened by the Reds, and ridiculed for teaching religion and for working with Americans. The Sisters replied that they were working for God, and they quietly kept on with their apostolate.

"For the last few months before we left Laipo, the Sisters had a very difficult time. The Reds made them take off their habits and put on secular clothes. The Reds forbade them to go to Mass or to talk to a priest. A great deal of pressure was applied to induce them to complain about the foreign priests and to tell the priests' faults. Many times they were grilled and threatened by the Reds, but never did they say a word against any priest.

"One of the saddest experiences of my life was the day I gave the Sisters their last Holy Communion. The Reds were forcing me out of China. The Sisters were staying. They were going back to their families to live as laywomen. They left and we left at the same time: we for America; they for a life of slavery under communism. They tried to be cheerful. 'Don't worry about us,' the Chinese Sisters said, 'but pray for us.'"

It is believed that Kweilin was the most rapidly growing mission in China when the Reds struck. All over the prefecture unusual progress was being made. In the final year before the Communists came, there were stationed in Kweilin 26 Maryknoll priests, 1 Chinese priest, 6 Maryknoll Sisters, 27 Chinese Sisters, 25 seminarians, and 55 catechists. The 9 mission dispensaries gave 274,250 treatments in that last year. There is no telling how far the work would have gone had it been left unhampered. What God's plans are for Kweilin, we may never know. It is certain, however, that the Reds will not have the ultimate triumph.

17

Calvary in China

One by one, the Maryknollers were driven out of Kweilin. One by one, they were arrested and deported. Old Christians were left without their pastors. New Christians were left without guides and instructors to lead them. At last the day came in 1952 when only one Maryknoller remained in this formerly active mission. He was Father Robert W. Greene, of Jasper, Indiana. After he, too, was expelled, he recounted his experiences in a best-selling book, *Calvary in China*. No summary narrative of a third person could capture the pathos and terror of the experience Father Greene endured. He must tell the story himself, so here is his description of those terrible days under the Reds:

"I'm still a bit baffled by the sudden turn of events that changed my position as a 'criminal condemned to be beheaded' to be a free man once again. When I arrived in Hong Kong last April 20, I had not seen another priest for fifty-three weeks.

"For the first four months of 1952, I was held in solitary confinement. On April 3, soldiers took me from my own room and marched me to the church. There in a little storeroom off the sacristy, my belt, rosary beads, pins, and loose articles were taken away. That night the inquisition began. It was eight days and nights of ceaseless harping on my guilt as an 'American spy,' that preceded a mob trial in the town of Tungan, China.

"That trial was on Easter Sunday, and lasted from nine in the morning until almost four in the afternoon. I was sentenced to be beheaded. This sentence was later commuted to expulsion from China.

"Before I was taken from Tungan, under guard, I had a chance to visit the mission. It was the last and biggest worry I had. I had preserved the Blessed Sacrament in the house—something I needed very much in those endless days when I was in solitary confinement. As soon as we got inside the house, I pointed to the place where I had hidden the little ciborium. They finally brought it out, and in a flash I had the Host in my mouth.

"The Communists yelled as soon as I closed my lips on the Blessed Sacrament. But I lifted some unconsecrated hosts for them to see, and said, 'When we pray we do this.' Their cries to spit it out stopped when they fingered the wafers.

"Later, soldiers escorted me on the trip to Hong Kong. I was paraded through the streets of Pinglo, Laipo, and Kweilin, amid cries of 'American devil!' I can still hear voices in the night, shouting this.

"Right up to the time I was brought to the border, I still thought that they intended to kill me. But the guards finally released me in front of the barbed wire barrier on the China-Hong Kong border. I stepped across the border into a free land.

"I had been in Tungan for over five years. I was stationed there with Father Gregory Gilmartin, of Waterbury, Connecticut, and Father Irwin Nugent, of Dorchester, Massachusetts, when the Communists 'liberated' the area. For a time mission work went on as usual, but it was not many months later when the Catholics began to be searched as they came to church. Then the Reds 'advised' the mission help to leave. The political commissar of that district boasted to the cook that they had a noose around the mission and would draw it tighter and tighter.

"After October, 1950, our house at the mission became our jail. The Reds would not permit us to leave the premises or to talk with our Christians. On April 9, 1951, Father Gregory Gilmartin was told to pack his baggage, as he was to leave within the hour. Three days later the Reds announced that Father Irwin

Nugent was also to leave. Both priests had no idea of their destination when they left, but imagined that they would be put into
a concentration camp at Kweilin. I later learned that they were expelled.

"After they were gone, I saw no other foreigner. From January
of 1952 until my actual arrest on April 3, I did not speak a word
to anyone, except in response to repeated periods of interrogation
by the Communist officials. The people were forbidden by the
Reds to speak to me or to have anything to do with me.

"During that time no news came in from the outside, and I
didn't know if America was at war or not. In my house there was
always a guard. The Communists kept telling me that I would
soon be able to leave China. Meanwhile they questioned me re-
peatedly about the guns with which the mission had been provided
during the Sino-Japanese War, for its own protection and against
my wishes. For a time I thought that this was the only charge
they had against me.

"During those months I lived in two rooms; all the other rooms
and buildings at the mission were sealed. There was nothing but
the two empty rooms, and to walk up and down, up and down.
Three times a week I was allowed to visit the nearby village to buy
what I was to cook for myself. It was my tough fortune never to
have learned how to cook. All told, I lived on rice and eggs for
fifty-three weeks.

"The people had been warned and threatened by the Reds not
to talk to, or recognize, the 'imperialist.' The older people just
turned away when they saw me coming, but the youngsters picked
up fruit skins and rocks to throw at me as they cursed the Americans.

"During that time I found it hard to get money. Sometimes the
Reds permitted me to obtain it from another priest 35 miles
away. The messenger I employed would use the money to buy
goods, and then pay me when he had sold them on his return.
Only at my 'People's Trial' did I find out that this messenger was
a Nationalist guerrilla—for then I was charged with giving money
to guerrillas, on this account.

"Even water was hard to get, because the Red soldiers had put
a lock on the well cover. And there was always red tape involved
in getting approval for opening the well. In April, 1951, the Communists came to search the mission. They found a brass badge with

'U.S.' stamped on it. They also found a toy medal that had been given to me by a child at one time. They also took an ordination photo of mine. These they removed as evidence. Later the Reds produced a composite picture, with the U.S. placed on my pocket and the medal a little lower down. For them this photo was proof that I was a spy.

"Fifteen soldiers and a high-ranking Red official came to my quarters with this picture on April 3, 1952. The official said that he was my judge and had come to try me.

"He paid no attention as I tried to explain, but said, 'You are not a priest at all. We have checked up on you.' The soldiers stood me up against a wall; one of them trained a tommy gun on me. I tried to say some prayers. But all they did was to take a lot of pictures and accuse me of being a spy and giving out news.

"The Red official told me that if I signed a confession to the effect that I was an American spy they'd be merciful and let me go. I replied that I was a priest and therefore could not tell lies. I said that I had never done anything against their government.

"I was grilled, with four guards holding me erect at bayonet point, until about one o'clock the next morning. Whenever one set of guards got tired, another group relieved them. But still the interrogation went on. Witnesses made statements that twisted innocent actions of mine into incriminating evidence.

"This grilling continued for eight days, with only one day's break. Under their persistent inquiries, I got so rocky that I had the worst headache I had ever felt—right down into the jawbones. At night after the interrogations were over, the guards shone bright lights into my cell.

"During the interrogation periods, the Reds bound my arms tightly by a tourniquet through the elbows, with the rope running behind me to put on pressure. They gave me the treatment when I said they were twisting my answers.

"During the interrogations I was living on the borderline all the time. I prayed that I would not lose my mind. The tourniquet they applied to my arms was at least something definite. It was pain. But it was what they did to my mind. They administered a brutal, brain-scraping, psychological third degree to achieve a personality-splitting terror that left my mind reeling. I prayed that I wouldn't deny my Faith. I'd read of persecutions before and I'd always figured it was a case of either denying the Faith or not. But the way the Reds do it, it isn't that simple. Their persecution is so subtle that some Catholics were duped by it and convinced that they were being good Catholics.

"I awoke with a start one night about an hour after I had been released from an eight-hour interrogation, to the realization that I had signed a confession admitting that I had offered a guerrilla $150 to kill a guard before the gate of the mission, and had paid $60 because the guerrilla had only wounded the soldier. Actually that soldier cut his own hand while chopping wood.

"When the next interrogation began I started off the interminable hours by denying all that I had signed the night before. I was again tied with ropes that held my arms in a painful position. After the interrogation had proceeded for a couple of hours, I had the sensation of seeing all this as a detached third person without relation to myself. I had to keep repeating my own name to hold onto reality. When I refused to sign another statement, the Reds gloated that they already had my 'first confession' so that it really didn't matter.

"At the first private 'trial' that took place on Palm Sunday, the Reds brought three guerrilla leaders and my cook as witnesses. It was difficult to realize the change in my cook after his four months in prison. We had always gotten on well, and he had been faithful and loyal. The Communists arrested him sometime after they had forced him to leave my employ. At the private trial, he told lie after lie, 'proving' that I had broken every one of the Ten Commandments so I couldn't have been a priest. I was an American spy.

"The guerrillas alleged that I had been their leader, that I had met them on various occasions, and had supplied them with money and medicine. I did not know any of them. They had been rounded up months earlier, and were 'confessing' to save their own heads. After the private trial, the Reds interrogated me almost continually until it was time for the public trial on Easter Sunday. This was held in a large auditorium. I was placed on the stage, between four soldiers, and made to keep my head bowed. Over four thousand people jammed the hall. The witnesses came on one by one.

"They accused me of waking the help at four o'clock in the morning. They accused me of 'sins' against the Fourth Commandment; they said that I had not obeyed my mother's wish to come home. My cook claimed he had seen the letter where such a wish was expressed—but he never let on at the trial that he didn't know a word of English.

"Each accusation was followed by the shouting of slogans by the Red in charge. After each shout, the audience screamed, 'Kill him! Kill him!' Before the trial was over, I was unable to hear a word they were saying. I felt my jaws sag lower and lower, and wondered if I could utter a sound. But they never gave me a chance to talk. It was only after I had been brought back to prison after the trial—which lasted over six hours—that I learned that I was to be beheaded. The guards asked me if I had understood the sentence.

"The following morning, however, the same judge explained that the sentence had been changed to expulsion. One of the reasons for the new decision was the fact that my brother was a mere laborer, one of the 'common people.'

"The thing that impressed me most and that I'd like to impress on our people, is that what the Communists hate most is Mary. A Russian general flung the challenge squarely at me: 'You say you're the chosen of God. Well, we're the picked troops of Satan. We'll see who wins.'

"When the Communists commuted my sentence from death to expulsion, they told me: 'Don't think you're getting away with anything. We've gotten what we wanted out of your trial. We've destroyed the Church in this district. We've proved that Mao is greater and kind and merciful in letting a criminal like you live. You're not going to get away anyway, because we're going to take over America in ten years.'

"Ten years ago I wouldn't have believed it, if anyone had told me that Tungan would go Communist. But it happened. I saw my parishioners shot in front of the church, as I watched helplessly from the window of the room where I was held prisoner. I'd hear the Reds coming, beating drums and waving banners. Then I'd see my people led into the churchyard. They'd be shot in the back of the head, their faces blown off, people I knew. I saw heads hanging from poles in my village. That's communism.

"I used to read about priests and Sisters being persecuted. But I never thought I'd see it happen. Now I know we didn't pray enough for them. The Blessed Mother got me out; but the Chinese priests and Sisters are still there, and they're suffering."

18

Kyoto—The Banners Are Flying

On the Feast of Mary's Assumption, 1549, that intrepid visionary, Saint Francis Xavier, stepped from a Chinese junk to the shore of southern Japan. He was the first Christian missioner ever to set foot in that mysterious and feudal land, and the only two Christian Japanese in the entire nation were the companions who had come with him from the far-off Indies. Xavier had studied the situation well. He concluded that, for the Japanese, Christianity must come from the top down, and so he set off to reach the people of influence at the capital city, sacred Kyoto.

Francis Xavier was to endure many trials and heartaches, before he should leave Japan to go unknowingly to his death on Sancian Island. But when, after twenty-seven months, he did go, he left behind in the land of the samurai a nucleus of five thousand Christians. More missioners arrived—Jesuits and Franciscans—and within fifty years from the day Xavier set foot in Japan, the Island Empire had three hundred thousand Catholics. Then the persecutions began—death-dealing persecutions with some of the most terrible tortures ever devised by mind of man. Wave after wave of oppression beat against the Catholic Church. In the year 1637, alone, some thirty-seven thousand Christians were put to the sword at Nagasaki. Foreigners were excluded from the country, and the rulers agreed that Christianity no longer existed in Japan.

Two and a half centuries passed. Generation after generation of Japanese grew up and died. At last came the day in 1854, when Admiral Perry led his seven warships into Yedo Bay and, under the threatening guns of his men-of-war, opened Japan to the West. The French missioner, Father Petitjean, landed in Japan several years later to act as chaplain at the French consulate in Nagasaki. He was the first Catholic priest in the city since the terrible days of persecution.

Then, on the Feast of Saint Patrick in 1865, a small group of Japanese men and women stopped to gaze up at the little cross that Father Petitjean had erected on top of the tiny church he had built—the Church of the Twenty-six Martyrs of Japan. The priest saw the group stop, and hastened to invite the gazers into his church, so that they might view the interior and he might have the opportunity of putting in a word for Christianity. The Japanese entered, but they were wary.

"Have you a shrine here to the Lady Virgin?" one asked. Father Petitjean led them to his statue of the Blessed Mother.

"Was it the Teacher-King who sent you here?" inquired another man.

"I have been sent here by the Holy Father in Rome," replied the priest.

"Have you no children?" came the query.

"I am a spiritual father," Father Petitjean answered. "A priest in my religion is forbidden to have children."

There was a pause as the Japanese talked among themselves. Then a woman spoke up: "The hearts of all here are the same as yours. At Urakami nearly all have hearts like ours."

The news went speeding around the world. After the empire had been more than two centuries without priests, fifty thousand Catholics existed in Japan. The prophetic words of Francis Xavier, writing in 1552 to his superior, Ignatius Loyola, were recalled: "The Japanese people is the only one which seems to me likely to maintain unshaken the Christian Faith, if once it has embraced it."

But peace did not come yet, for Christianity was still proscribed. A new persecution of six years' duration broke out. Catholics who refused to forswear their Faith were torn from their homes and imprisoned. Before the Japanese Government called a halt and allowed freedom of worship in 1873, more than two thousand Japanese Catholics had died from ill treatment. However, once peace was made, French missioners hurried to Japan, and the Church began a steady growth.

The year 1933 saw the first Maryknollers depart for Japan, to begin language studies under the direction of Archbishop Chambon, preparatory to taking over a mission field. Arrangements for the field were worked out during 1934; and early in 1935, Father Patrick J. Byrne, of Washington, D.C., who had pioneered the mission in Korea, left Maryknoll to take up his duties as superior of the new Kyoto Mission—the historic territory that so occupied the mind and hopes of the Jesuit, Xavier.

When Maryknoll was assigned to Japan, Kyoto was a city of a million people. Over the centuries, it had continued to hold title to being the cultural capital of the Japanese Empire. Seven universities were located in Kyoto. It was the center for painting and sculpture; and in it were produced the finest tapestries and silk work, the best lacquerware and porcelain. Kyoto was also the center for Japan's leading religious sects.

"That noble borough of Brooklyn is credited with some 130 Catholic churches," Father Byrne reported. "How the loyal citizen of Kyoto must sniff in disdain, when he compares this paltry number with his own phenomenal total of 1,818 temples. Shiga County, in our territory, is still the most deeply religious district of all Japan, with temples and shrines to the number of 5,954, and an even greater number of resident Buddhist and Shinto priests."

The only Catholic church of the mission was in the city of Kyoto. It was a sturdy building, forty years old, and not too far from the center of the city; and naturally enough, it was named after Kyoto's apostle, Saint Francis Xavier. Before the persecutions, the Kyoto area had been the site of a flourishing Catholic compound, which included a church, a middle school, a Brothers' novitiate, and a seminary. By 1935, nothing remained of that once-prosperous Christian center but its corrupted name, *Daius*—the Japanese had transliterated the word from the Latin *Deus* meaning "God." The mission had about a thousand Christians, and received a "bonus" from the Osaka Diocese from which it had been split—two Japanese priests. One of them, an old man, was to die shortly after a very saintly life. The other, young and vigorous, Father Paul Furuya, was destined to become the first Japanese Bishop of Kyoto.

The mission work in Kyoto was slow and difficult. An average of four converts a year per priest was considered good. Father Byrne saw no easy course, and he began laying foundations in works of education and charity that he hoped would one day bear fruit. In 1937 he began work on a tuberculosis hospital, the first such institution in an area where many Japanese were afflicted with the disease. In that same year the Kyoto Mission was erected as a prefecture; and as its prefect, Father Byrne was once again elevated to the rank of Monsignor.

In 1940, because of the delicate political situation existing between Japan and the United States, Monsignor Byrne presented his resignation to the Holy See. Father Paul Furuya was named Apostolic Administrator for the prefecture. In 1940, too, the Kyoto Mission counted 1,865 Catholics in a population of two million. There were 13 Maryknoll priests in Kyoto, 3 Japanese priests, 1 Maryknoll Brother, 4 Maryknoll Sisters, 11 Japanese Sisters, and 6 catechists. The tuberculosis hospital had 43 patients; the mission's 4 schools educated 264 pupils; and converts during the year totaled 112. At this time, 9 districts were staffed.

After the outbreak of war, the Maryknoll work came to a standstill. All the priests, with the exception of Father Byrne, were interned. He was restricted, but allowed to live in his own house during the war years. Four Maryknoll Sisters, also, were left free. During those years the Japanese priests made two hundred converts, but the total number of Christians was cut by deaths and by departures to other localities.

When the Japanese Government finally announced that it would surrender to the American forces, Father Byrne came out of his enforced retirement and spoke over the national radio. There was great fear among the people concerning what the Americans would do when they should land on the home island. Father Byrne assured the Japanese that the Americans were not coming for revenge, that there would be no wholesale slaughter and no unjust arrests. His speech did much to insure a peaceful occupation by American troops. During the critical first days of Allied control, he worked closely with General MacArthur, whose respect and approval he won.

The Maryknollers returning to Kyoto and other parts of Japan after the war, found conditions of great poverty and suffering. The immediate task was one of relief. When Father Leo J. Steinbach, of Chariton, Iowa, arrived in Kyoto in 1946, after eleven years as a missioner in Korea and four years as a chaplain in Japanese relocation camps in the western United States, he found a city without hope. To the thousands of poor people, the future held only poverty, starvation, disease. Because of transportation breakdowns and black markets, the prices of food were rapidly climbing out of reach of average families.

Eager to take advantage of the chaotic conditions, the Communists organized parades and demonstrations in Kyoto's streets. In thousands of public speeches, they promised food, clothing, jobs, and homes to everyone.

Father Steinbach, however, lost no time on speeches. Using his own limited resources, he purchased ten tons of California rice to give to the poor. He offered his overcoat to an ill-clad man he met on a street of Kyoto. He gave his last blanket to a poverty-stricken family during winter, saying "Your need is greater than mine." He asked friends in America for personal gifts of clothing, and the friends responded generously.

But the priest realized that a permanent organization was needed for systematic aid to the poor. With the help of twelve young men from the Maryknoll parish in Kyoto, he formed a St. Vincent de Paul Society. The group became professional beggars for the sake of charity. From farmers they begged food; from merchants, donations; from the wealthy, clothing; and from all, they begged prayers.

Every Saturday, twelve hundred people stood in line outside St. Francis Xavier Church in Kyoto. The poor and the crippled, Buddhist and Shintoist, pagan and Christian, Protestant and Catholic, each received a family-sized basket of food. And often Father Steinbach had an extra package, a pair of shoes or a bundle of clothes, for the children.

The efforts of this American priest to feed the poor attracted national attention in Japan. Groups from other cities visited Kyoto to study his methods. Such major newspapers as Kyoto's

Miyako Shumbun and the Tokyo *Mainichi*, featured the story of his work. Local and national government officials, church groups, and American authorities praised his amazing achievements. But the most moving tribute came from an elderly Japanese grandmother, barely able to carry her basket of food, who told him:

"The Communists promised us food; you gave it to us."

Only two American jeeps had ever visited the small Japanese village of Ujidawara, near Kyoto. The first carried tax men, sent to collect the yearly assessments from the people. The second carried policemen, sent to search the village for concealed weapons. The people of Ujidawara thereafter were suspicious of all jeeps, and many were fearful the morning they saw a third one entering the village.

The driver of that third jeep was Father Steinbach. The villagers looked in surprise at this tall, thin man with a broad smile and an unruly head of curly hair. Father Steinbach announced that he had brought with him motion pictures and colored slide films to be shown in the village.

When the people recovered from the shock of seeing a jeep which brought good news, they flocked around him. Through their mayor, they even invited Father Steinbach to return. Thereafter he traveled to Ujidawara every Tuesday evening in his jeep to hold classes in religious instructions for adults and children.

Father Steinbach, however, gives others credit for the success of his work. He claims that charity soon becomes contagious, and cites as proof a few of the groups which have helped him. The restaurant guild of Kyoto supplied cooks to prepare warm meals for the Saturday crowds. Five doctors volunteered to operate a clinic for the poor on evenings and week ends. A group of barbers provided the St. Vincent de Paul Society with tickets for distribution to the poor, each ticket entitling the holder to a free haircut. Numerous shopkeepers contributed money or clothing. In one year more than 60,000 farmers in the Kyoto area donated food. In fact, in some months, the farmers donated more food than the poor were able to carry home.

"Whenever that happened," said Father Steinbach, "we gave the perishable food to orphanages or hospitals, and held the remainder until the following week when another group of 1,200 poor families paid us a visit."

Nor did Father Steinbach limit his work to Kyoto. He also distributed clothing to the needy in villages, each bundle prepared so that every member of a family received at least one garment. Some 200 villages were aided by gifts of clothing, some donated by friends of Father Steinbach in America and the rest contributed by grateful Japanese families who have been helped by the St. Vincent de Paul Society.

Another major project started by the Iowa Maryknoller was a mobile dispensary, which made regular visits to some 200 communities without resident doctors in the Kyoto area. For those who need further treatment, Father Steinbach arranged transportation to the clinic operated by the St. Vincent de Paul Society, or to one of the hospitals in Kyoto.

In addition to his extensive charitable activities among the poor, Father Steinbach traveled to the country each evening to teach religion classes in small villages like Ujidawara. He and a group of volunteer catechists from the Maryknoll parish provided doctrine instructions for some fifteen hundred people in twenty nearby villages. And requests to start new classes continually reached Father Steinbach, the majority from villages that contributed generously to his appeals for food and clothing.

Most of the requests echo the sentiments of the mayor who, watching Father Steinbach and his helpers load a truck of food to take to Kyoto, told one of the St. Vincent de Paul workers: "Here is a man who thinks only of helping others. He lives to the fullest his teaching that all men are brothers. We should like to learn about his religion."

Father Steinbach gives his own formula for success in a carefully thought-out statement of mission methods. He reports:

"We know that Communists have made great strides throughout the world in recent years. They do not spend much money on property or buildings; rather, they concentrate on training leaders, distributing vast amounts of literature, printing all kinds of posters, providing their agents with loud-speakers and with transportation, to enable them to spread their teaching.

"If Communists have won many to their way of thinking by such means, why should not Catholics use similar tactics? Why cannot each diocese, vicariate, or prefecture apostolic, in Japan buy a truck, or at least rent one for a day or two at a time, install a loud-speaker, and do some widespread campaigning for Christ? A phonograph could be taken along on each trip, and concerts could be followed with talks on the things we have been sent by God to tell the people. Literature, especially small leaflets, could be distributed after the talk. Later the truck could move on to another place.

"Sometimes, when the truck is parked by the wayside, farmers who are working in the fields can be taught the essentials of Christianity. It is hard for various reasons to get these people together for public lectures in a hall. As a rule, they work early and late, and the only available hall is often far from their homes. When they get home after their day's work, it is usually dark, and they must get their supper. On the other hand, music and a talk made available to them during their working hours, provide them with diversion and an occasion for a brief rest.

"Most farmers work in groups. By going out to them in the way suggested, we may well be able to give them topics of conversation that will not only be welcome, but profitable as well. If we succeed in planting only a few seeds in their hearts, we may look to God to give them the grace that will bring them to lecture halls or to regular instructions later.

"This type of propaganda does not entail any great outlay of money. Trucks as well as loud-speakers may be rented for moderate prices, for a week at a time. Our Catholic young men are usually anxious to take part in work of this sort. We must remember that, when Christ sent out His Apostles, He did not tell them to buy property or to build churches, but to preach and teach.

"During the first three centuries of Christian history, not many churches were built—much building was impossible—but there was a great deal of preaching and teaching. Most of the money collected was used for charitable purposes. We know definitely that this was true in the case of Saint Paul. We must remember, too, that after many people had been converted in any one locality, they themselves saw to it that they had some place in which to meet. When churches were built, the Christians provided the funds.

"Our condition in Japan today is similar in many ways to the conditions that prevailed in the early Church. We do have opportunities to teach, but our funds are not sufficient for much building. Property is expensive, and it is not only difficult to build, but most of the churches we have built are not really permanent, even though they were expensive.

"In the Kyoto area, we are now working in twenty separate places and find that we can use the village halls for catechetical instruction as well as for Mass, free of charge. We have found that, when a number of people have been converted in any one village, the people themselves start looking for property on which to build a church. The children busy themselves not only with reciting the Rosary for the purpose of getting their own church, but also with saving their pennies to help.

"It is quite necessary under all circumstances to stress the word 'Catholic.' We have observed how the name of this or that candidate for election was dinned into the ears of the people, along with slogans that had been adopted by the various political parties. For us, the name to be stressed is 'Catholic.' We, too, should have slogans. By way of concrete suggestions, we submit the following: 'We are all children of God.' 'God is our Creator.' 'Love the one true God above all things.' 'Let us love our neighbor as ourselves.' A few slogans of this kind, repeated constantly, will certainly sink in. For the Japanese are now living in a religious vacuum. Though they perform various Buddhist or Shinto ceremonies, they know very little about their own religion.

"Obviously, the missioner cannot do all the work himself. It is not hard, however, to find in any one of our parishes young men who will be glad to co-operate, if we provide them with the tools. Happily, slide projectors, movies, leaflets are available. We can also provide song and prayer cards. Medals, holy cards, and perhaps some hard candy, should be available as prizes for the children.

"We have often found that, by addressing ourselves especially to children, we can start work in villages that have not a single Catholic. And we have also found that the children repeat what they hear, with the result that not a few adults are attracted and come for religious instructions later.

"After teaching the children for awhile, it is good to recite several decades of the Rosary with them. Far-reaching results can be attained if a special and well-chosen intention is announced for each decade. One decade can be offered for the sick people of the village; another, for the mothers and fathers; a third, for the teachers, the old folks, or all those who have died in the village.

"When the children go home, their parents are sure to ask them why they prayed. If the children answer that they prayed for their parents, for the sick, the aged and the deceased, they cannot fail to make a good impression on the other members of the family. Sometimes we have time to vist the sick ourselves and to bring them a few little gifts.

"All the work done by our twenty young teachers is on a voluntary basis. It is done in their spare time in the evenings. Striking is the fact that they themselves are now looking for more volunteers. This is necessary because we have lost several from our original group of workers: they went off to the seminary to study for the priesthood, so that they could spend their whole lives in working for souls. At least three found their vocation in this way, and several others are now planning to enter the seminary. Though this kind of night work is not easy, a number of our young helpers were not satisfied to spend only one night a week on the road. They started catechism classes in their own homes, inviting the children of the neighborhood to attend.

"The new Constitution of Japan gives us full liberty for teaching and preaching. We are under obligation to make full use of that freedom. Sowing the seed is our task. Our main purpose is not to perform a tremendous number of baptisms in the immediate future, but to implant Christian ideas in the minds of as many non-Christians as possible. If we do that in this, our day, God Himself will see to it that many souls will be baptized in His own good time. The Japanese people want to know about Christianity. It is high time to do some real campaigning for Christ."

In 1953, overwork broke down Father Steinbach's health, and he was summoned home to America for rest and recuperation. He returned to Japan early in 1954 to rejoin the other Maryknollers who were working in the pattern he had set. Father James F. Hyatt, of Seattle, Washington, is a man cut from the same cloth as Father Steinbach. His Catholic Center in Kyoto is radiating the brightness of Christianity throughout the whole region. Father George J. Hirschboeck, of Milwaukee, Wisconsin, is also using the social action of the Gospels to make Christ known along the principles established by the Vincent de Paul work.

19

Building with Japan

Another interesting development in Kyoto has been the work of Father John C. Murrett, of Buffalo, New York. When he returned to Kyoto in 1946, Father Byrne asked him if he would teach at the Imperial University in that city. Father Murrett agreed and moved out to the University grounds, where he was given a small house to live in. During an early class, shortly afterwards, he noted that one of his students was unusually pale and thin, and seemed ready to faint. Upon inquiry, the priest learned that the boy was the second oldest of eight children; the father of the family was unemployed; there wasn't enough food at home for all, and the little children had to be fed first. The interview ended with the decision that the undernourished student should live at Father Murrett's house and share the priest's rations. In September, the second starving student was brought home to the little house. The two boys were good company for the priest, who helped them with their lessons and personal problems. By the end of the year, they had both become Catholics.

Then one night—a cold, snowy night of January, 1948—a fire broke out at Sanko College. Three dormitories burned to the ground, and fifty students were left homeless. Within a few hours, the population of Father Murrett's little cottage had risen to thirteen students in addition to the priest and an old woman who served as housekeeper and cook. The cottage was jammed to the rafters. But by the time the first year's anniversary of the fire rolled around, three more students had been added to the group. How Father Murrett managed to fit them all in, was a great mystery, but his generosity found a way.

In 1952, Father Murrett returned to America for a brief vacation, and wrote out a long report of his work. An extract follows:

"Today eighteen boys are living in the cottage built for two, and a waiting list of forty more stands knocking at the door of my heart. Six years have passed, and of the thirty-two students who have lived with me, most have been baptized and have engaged in some definite work of Catholic Action. Three have been presidents of the Legion of Mary groups, many others are active in Vincent de Paul work, three have taken up work among the deaf and dumb, five have gone to the seminary, and three others are now in the United States on scholarships."

Here is a magnificent record of what one priest can do in training leaders for the new Japan. Father Murrett today is dreaming of a student hostel he wishes to build in order to be able to enlarge his work. But so far, the twenty thousand dollars he needs has been lacking. He is confident, however, that some day he will get it. Then he and the students will move to a new home, and he will have more boys than ever.

The Kyoto group are not the only Maryknollers working in Japan. Another group began working out of Tokyo in the postwar years. Father Michael J. McKillop, of Brooklyn, New York, acted as Catholic representative and one of the original organizers of LARA (Licensed Agencies for Relief in Asia), which was set up by SCAP (Supreme Command Allied Powers) as the approved private relief agency in Japan. Later he was replaced by Father Harold J. Felsecker, of Milwaukee, Wisconsin. This work took the missioners all over the Islands and the charity they were able to distribute in those days kept many thousands of Japanese alive.

Father Leopold H. Tibesar, of Quincy, Illinois, was assigned to work with the National Catholic Committee of Japan, an organization of the Japanese hierarchy patterned after our own National Catholic Welfare Conference. He became director of

Catholic Charities (Caritas), and assistant director of the Social Action Section, as well as Secretary General of the National Committee. In Tokyo, as a local project, the Archbishop started a Catholic Club, and Father Tibesar was placed in charge. The club obtained space on the seventh floor of the Mitsukoshi Department Store in the Ginza District, and a Catholic chapel was opened. It was equivalent to Macy's renting out its top floor as a Catholic church—only the Tokyo space was given rent free. Many conversions were made in this unique Catholic "parish," and a 1952 report states that over four thousand Japanese took catechetical instructions there. The department-store church also sent three boys to the major seminary; a number to the minor seminary; one youth to become a Brother; and several girls are postulants for the Sisterhoods.

The Kyoto Mission, also, was rejoicing in the year 1950, because in that single year eight young Japanese left the mission for the seminary. Their number represented a 100% increase over all the previous years of work in Kyoto. One of the seminarians was Michael Tokugawa, descendant of Tokugawa Ieyasu, the rabid persecutor of the Church, who began his suppression in 1614. The Tokugawa family ruled Japan from 1603 to 1867. Michael Tokugawa's father was a baron, and Michael might have inherited the title if he had not gone to the seminary. Another of the seminarians who left in 1950 is Michael Hachijo, a handsome and intelligent young man, who also belonged to the nobility. He is the son of Viscount Takamasa Hachijo.

Another interesting project conducted by a Maryknoller in Japan is the work done by Father William A. Kaschmitter, of Cottonwood, Idaho, who founded and became the director of *Tosei* (Eastern Star) News Service. Father Kaschmitter had formerly directed *Lumen* News Service in China, an organization founded by Maryknoll's Father Frederick C. Dietz, of Oberlin, Ohio. The news service furnishes the Catholic position to Japan's press, and sends Catholic news of Japan out to the entire world. Father Kaschmitter's work has played an important role in the fight against the materialism that some Americans tried to impose on Japan, particularly in regard to artificial means to control Japan's growing population.

All of this Maryknoll activity has played an important part in the growth of the Church in Japan. Today the Kyoto mission field has a flourishing Christianity that augurs well for the years ahead. The postwar growth of the Church there has been phenomenal. Twenty-one parishes now exist in the Kyoto Diocese. The Redemptorist, Marist, and Viatorian Fathers are working side by side with the Maryknollers. Sisters of various nationalities work in the diocese. In addition to the Maryknoll Sisters who pioneered in the area, two other American communities of women—the School Sisters of Notre Dame and the Sisters of St. Joseph of Carondelet —are also busy with hospital and school work. The diocese has nine girls' schools, and two boys' schools, and some Dominicans from Chicago are initiating university work. There are also two hospitals, two day nurseries, and an orphanage.

In 1951, Monsignor Paul Furuya was consecrated bishop of the Kyoto Diocese, in an impressive ceremony attended by members of the hierarchy and missioners from all parts of the country. He was also made an honorary member of Maryknoll. Bishop Furuya had worked hand in hand with the Maryknollers from the time they entered the Kyoto territory, and he held the respect and admiration of all his priests. During the war he was given a hard time by the military government of Japan, whose members suspected him of being a spy, and he was held for a month in prison because of his connection with Maryknollers.

Bishop Furuya's parents were devoted Christians of the Osaka Diocese, and his father served as catechist to the venerable Father Fage in Osaka. During the war when Kobe was bombed, neither Mr. nor Mrs. Furuya would desert the old priest. After the fire caused by the bombing was brought under control, survivors searching the ruins of the Kobe church found the remains of Father Fage and Mr. and Mrs. Furuya. The three had died kneeling before the shrine of the Blessed Virgin. This was the heroic stock from which Kyoto's first native bishop came.

This is also the same type of stock on which the church is being built in today's Kyoto. Men and women who will work for their Faith, and if need be, die for it. Father Edmund T. Shambaris, of Waterbury, Connecticut, recently sent to Maryknoll headquarters in America the story of a group of recent converts who were building a new Christian village on top of a remote mountain. The story was one that was written in the tradition of our own great American pioneers. Because it shows the kind of new Christians who are building the new Japan, it is reproduced here:

"But, Father, we're not like the ordinary Japanese," protested Nakamura-san. "We work twice as hard as the ordinary Japanese."

This bit of boasting sounded very much like a loud blowing of one's horn and should, I thought, have been said with tongue in cheek. To work twice as hard as the ordinary Japanese farmer, would be a considerable feat. So I put on a "doubting Thomas" look and asked to be shown the evidence. I was.

Heiwa-mura is a pioneer village. In these days of sky-scrapers and paved roads and TV, it is hard to even imagine a pioneer establishment outside of a Hollywood movie set. But tucked away in the mountains north of Kyoto, on the top of Mt. Tai San Ji, stands the quiet, hidden village of Heiwa-mura. "Peace" is what it would be called in English—"Peace Village."

After a long, steady climb, the traveler suddenly, and almost without any warning, emerges on the top of the mountain, and there drinks in a panorama that would make any travelogue narrator go into ecstasies. Standing there, one finds it easy to feel that the people of the mountaintop live close to God.

One might expect to find a desolate hermitage in this mountain fastness. Instead, on the plateau summit the climber sees a small, cleared settlement of about twenty tiny houses, clustering together. There, indeed, is a refuge from clutter and confusion—a refuge literally carved from the wilderness.

It all began five years ago, although the dreaming and planning go back much further.

Morita and Nakamura had been buddies for years, visiting one another and frequently discussing the future—which they saw only in rosy colors. Those were the days of dreams. But they were also the days of Japan's imperialism. Morita and Nakamura were caught up in a machine for which they had no liking—the machine of war. They, along with millions of other young men, were called into military service. They were parted to serve overseas.

Morita and Nakamura did not meet again until years later, after the war had been fought and lost. Their paths crossed in Kyoto, where one worked in a bakery and the other in a bicycle shop. The war was over but not the dreams. Japan was building a new nation. Why couldn't they build a new world for themselves and their families?

The two friends heard that the Government was giving out parcels of abandoned or uninhabited land to returned veterans, as part of a rehabilitation program. Instantly they knew what they wanted to do. Years earlier, they had rambled through the hills and mountains around Kyoto, and they had always been attracted to the mountaintop of Tai San Ji. There was the place to build a new world! But would the Government give them the land?

After many trips to Government bureaus and the unraveling of miles of red tape, the two friends finally held a paper that made the top of Tai San Ji theirs. But one condition was attached: in a specified number of years, they must have a definite amount of land under cultivation. The job was too much for two to do alone, so they looked around for additional partners. Few men were interested in such a difficult and backbreaking venture. But in time Morita and Nakamura found fourteen pioneer spirits like themselves.

To establish a village and make farm land from a remote mountain fastness is a challenging undertaking. It is even more formidable and discouraging when the job must be done "on a shoestring." The start was not propitious. Sun, wind, rain, and wild animals worked against the pioneers. The untamed soil did not respond to plowing. Instead of top grass, matted vegetation with roots a foot deep had to be removed; the patient workers cut it into squares and lifted it out, piece by piece.

About this time, in the town of Aoyagi where they had gone for supplies, Morita and Nakamura met Father Clement Boesflug. The veterans were immediately attracted to the priest. They had rejected Buddhism years earlier, because it did not answer the problems of life. They listened to the American missioner, and then asked that instructors in religion be sent to the mountaintop.

After working from the crack of dawn, the pioneers would stumble into catechism class at eight or nine o'clock at night. Some fell asleep from fatigue, others stayed until the early hours of morning, asking questions. This went on until the workers and their families had finished their studies and were baptized.

Father Boesflug helped those new Christians in every way he could. Through friends, he procured supplies such as cement, nails, tiles, food, and so on. In return the converts built their own chapel in the center of the new village.

The big project now is a waterworks. For five years the villagers have hauled water by buckets from the bottom of the mountain.

They figure that in about a year they will have water flowing through the long trench they have dug. Electricity will follow as soon as the water is flowing.

The last time I was in Peace Village, Nakamura asked, "Where shall we put the electric outlets in the chapel?"

Yes, things are looking up in Heiwa-mura.

In late 1953, Maryknoll accepted an invitation from Bishop Benedict Tomizawa to staff a mission territory in his Diocese of Sapporo, on Hokkaido—Japan's northernmost island. The Diocese of Sapporo covers all Hokkaido and has a total population of almost four and a half million people. The area entrusted to Maryknoll included the civil districts of Iburi and Hidaka, and the southern portion of Sorachi, including the town of Iwamizawa. Bishop Tomizawa was an old friend of Maryknoll because he was a native of Kyoto City, and had worked with the Maryknollers from 1946 until his consecration and appointment to Sapporo in 1953.

Maryknollers began work in this new area in 1954. Part of their territory contained the last 15,000 members of the Ainu race, a Caucasian people whose origins are obscure. Some anthropologists claim that these legendary non-Asiatics came from European Russia, and that when they were separated by successive waves of invaders in pre-Biblical times, a large band moved east across Siberia to settle in the island where the remnants now live. The Ainus still cling to their ancestral customs, but as a race they are dying out because through intermarriage they are being absorbed into the Japanese family.

With the acceptance of the new work on Hokkaido, Maryknoll was indicating that operations in Japan had returned to normal. The postwar reconstruction period had ended. What the future holds for the Japanese people, is something no man can foretell. However, the people of Japan know that, in their hours of need, they can always count on the missioners. A recent example of this basis for trust was given during one terrible flood, which struck in the Kyoto area last year.

It was the late summer of 1953. All the day long, heavy black clouds had been gathering over Kyoto, threatening rain. About nine o'clock in the evening, after hearing confessions, Father James F. Habenicht, of St. Louis, left his mission to go to a home in his parish where the block Rosary was being said. On the way the skies let loose, and he was drenched before he reached his destination. The rain had slackened off by the time he started home. But around midnight, the deluge began again, and continued for hours. Rain beat down so loudly in Kyoto City that it awoke Father Thomas J. Prendergast (hometown, Utica, New York), who had a hard time getting back to sleep.

In the little mountainside village of Wazuka, the people listened to the pounding rain in fear and trepidation. Only a short time before their village had been hit by a flood. On that occasion those villagers who had ventured outside their doors had been carried away by the swirling waters, and many had perished. Under the new threat, the people huddled in their homes, fearful that angry waters would again invade their village.

The rain continued to fall in seemingly solid sheets. Hour after hour it poured down. Streams became swollen and spread their banks. The reservoir behind Wazuka filled to capacity and began flowing over. Towards dawn the dam of the reservoir yielded to the tons of pressure behind it—first a trickle through a small fissure, then a roaring wall of water bursting its bounds.

Down on Wazuka surged the flood. Through the village it swept, ripping houses from foundations, washing all before it over the mountainside. Of the hundred-odd inhabitants of Wazuka, only a half dozen escaped with their lives.

Down upon the lowlands rushed the angry waters, boiling and tossing with debris and human bodies. Into the hamlet of Ide roared the avalanche. The sounds of collapsing houses and the screams of the drowning rent the early morning air.

Father James S. Tokuhisa, a Maryknoller from Los Angeles, had left the Aodani parish by jeep early that morning to say Mass in Kawanishi. Approaching Ide he noticed the terrifying height of the water. He was shocked to see houses collapsed, and people struggling in the rushing muddy waters.

Father Tokuhisa immediately went into action. He was so excited and so busy that he has no idea how many bodies, alive and dead he pulled from the waters. He was the first outsider on the scene, and he made trip after trip, loading his jeep with survivors and the dead. Twice he crossed a bridge that threatened momentarily to collapse into the river. When the bridge did collapse just after he crossed it for the second time, and when he saw the pile of bodies growing higher, he knew that more help was needed.

He then contacted the head of the Kyoto diocese, Bishop Paul Furuya. The latter immediately called Father Hirschboeck, and appointed him relief director with headquarters at the Catholic Center in Kyoto. Father Hirschboeck got word to all the Kyoto parishes and almost within minutes help was on its way to the stricken area. Maryknoll Fathers Witte, Mooney, Karlovecius, and Eggleston, and Marist Fathers Marsden, Glynn, and Hill, led bands of workers into the doomed area. The Maryknoll Sisters rushed out to give aid and consolation.

Father Tokuhisa got in touch with the National Safety Force in Kyoto, calling for workers, trucks, and boats. "I was muddy and bloody," he recalls, "and so excited, that I scolded everyone— policemen, firemen, reserve army, doctors, and town officials. They seemed to be acting in slow motion."

Within twelve hours of getting word of the disaster, Father Hirschboeck had twelve truckloads of relief supplies moving into the stricken area. Food, clothing, towels, soap, bedding, and kerosene were delivered there. All these goods had been donated by the Catholics of Kyoto. At eight o'clock that night, with the immediate rescue work under control, Father Tokuhisa finally celebrated his Mass that had been scheduled for fifteen hours earlier.

But the work of the missioners did not end with that night. There was still the gigantic need for relief and rehabilitation. People, stunned by the sudden tragedy to their villages, were unable to help themselves. Officials counted 350 dead and missing, 433 injured, and 504 houses completely destroyed.

Young Catholics from Kyoto joined with Catholics from Fushimi and Kawanishi, to carry in vital supplies needed by the survivors. A truck brought them as close to the scene as possible. Then with packs of goods and tools strapped to their backs, the relief squads hiked through the devastation for two and a half hours. The people around Wazuka greeted their helpers with tears. The supplies the squads brought were exactly what were needed. The only other supplies that had arrived had been flown in by helicopter and were not nearly enough.

The sights that met the relief teams were heart-rending. Rough-hewn coffins were piled up waiting for burial. Village streets were lost under five feet of sand and rocks that had been carried down by the waters. Dead bodies were continually being found, some as far away as Osaka. On one spot on the mountain, rescuers saw the Jin-tan medicine factory. Half of it had been knifed off by the flood, and the remainder hung precariously over a cliff that the torrent had created. Everywhere, destruction and misery abounded.

Day after day the individual parishes of Kyoto sent out crews of young people. One group built a new house, another shoveled mud (sometimes four feet deep) from houses yet standing, still other groups passed out vitamins and food. Father Tokuhisa set up a barber shop and gave free haircuts, as expertly as he had done when a student in Maryknoll Seminary. Catholic Boy Scouts were on hand to act as guides for relief groups newly arriving. Sodality women kept a laundry going, around the clock.

The only opposition came from Communists. They had poured into the area several days after the flood, and were waving red banners and shouting propaganda all over the place. In the Ide village office, they completely covered one wall with pictures of Lenin, Stalin, and Malenkov. They urged the villagers to revolt against the Government that had "allowed" such a disaster to happen. When they gave help, they asked the recipients to join the Communist Party. But the people were not fooled. Some villages asked the Communists to leave since they did not seem to be interested in doing any practical relief work.

Two weeks after the flood, when life was returning to more normal patterns, Father Tokuhisa organized a day of prayers for the victims. A Solemn Requiem Mass was celebrated on the school grounds at Ide. Catholics from Kyoto, Nara, and Aodani were on hand to swell the singing, as were many of the bereaved families.

After Mass the visiting Catholics remained for more relief work. By day's end they had cleaned six more houses of mud and debris, built one temporary house, and put galvanized tin roofing on three other houses.

The police department at Ide visited Father Tokuhisa and told him that the members wanted to give him a decoration for the part he and others had played in saving 170 lives at Ide on the morning of the flood. Father Tokuhisa thanked the police, but declined the award.

"I told the police representative," Father Tokuhisa reported, "that it was my duty to save souls and lives. A man shouldn't get an award for only doing his duty."

20

The End of an Era

With the foundation of the Kyoto Mission, Maryknoll was fast approaching the end of an era. The man who, under God, was responsible for the growth of the Society that only twenty-five years earlier had been but an idea was Father James Anthony Walsh. When he had come on the scene, foreign missions were a nebulous subject thought of in terms of cannibals and wild men of Borneo. Few Americans had ever seen a missioner, and those few who had, thought of him as a foreigner speaking broken English and surrounded by a strange un-American romanticism.

Father Walsh had changed all that within a generation. He had made the missions a part of ordinary American life. He had brought a dream into reality, setting it firmly on its course. After the early death of his cofounder, Father Price, he had to carry the burden alone. True, he had raised up helpers, but he was the captain of the ship, responsible for its operation and the direction of its course. He was possessed by an ideal, but not obsessed by it to the exclusion of everything else. He was truly Catholic and everything that concerned the Church Universal was of interest to him.

Bishop James Edward Walsh, one of his first students, gave this picture of him: "When one considers the multiplicity of the 'other things' that made up his life this marked priestliness of the cofounder is all the more revealed as a basic, permanent part of him. It had to be. Busy executive is a mild term to describe his assignment. He was the initiator, promoter, organizer and administrator, both on the practical and spiritual plane of a work which was at once brand new, wholly unknown, capable of great development by its nature, and very anxious to grow and to grow quickly by its inner urge; and he was all these things at a time when help was scarce, helpers few. Meanwhile he was also Superior of the Seminary and of the whole Society. Thus he had to be a business man, a literary man, an executive officer, a household manager, a family father, a spiritual shaper and leader, and something of a peerer into the future, all at the same time. Many a priest finds himself combining some or all of these activities in some moderate measure—or trying to—on occasion. But there was at least a threefold marvel in the way in which he combined them, in the dexterity with which he met their varied, constant demands. In his case: (1) Each separate function was carried out in what might be called extravagant measure, in full and absorbing degree; (2) each function was carried out with notable success; and (3) he remained the eminently priestly priest at every moment through it all."

Father James Anthony Walsh had pioneered the way for mission America. But once the way was shown, he did not expect his spiritual sons to sit back. He wrote to members of the Society:

"It may seem to some of you that Maryknoll has come to the end of its pioneer days. Actually, our work has just begun. When one mission field is sufficiently tilled to leave it to the labors of native workers, the Maryknollers will pass on to break new ground in other fields. It is not probable that our portion will ever be other than the hard, inspiring lot of a pioneer. There should be no dimming of the freshness of our vision of the Master's vineyard."

He was a great man for working things out in detail, and putting his planning on paper. He drew up, for the students at Maryknoll, a five-point exposition that would make their vocation clearer to them and also afford them a means to offer to relatives a logical basis for the work they had chosen to do. These five points were:

1) The Catholic Church, by very name, is universal and should contain all nations.

2) The peoples of pagan lands are living in a darkness and misery of error, and there is a crying need to bring them the light of truth.

3) No time is more acceptable for this task than the present when pagan people are confused, disillusioned, unhappy—and are unable to sustain this burden because they are not fortified with the love of Christ.

4) The sacrifices of self-exiled American youths who become missioners will arouse extra vocations for the work of Christ in our own land and will bring increased blessings and graces from God upon the Church in the United States.

5) American Catholics must be taught to change their attitude in regard to the financial and spiritual backing that they are obliged to give to the mission effort.

It was this careful attention to detail that led Father Walsh to build his Society on strong foundations. His motto was "Seek first the Kingdom of God." He felt sure that if he did this, God would take care of everything. This was the reason that led him into such a rapid mission expansion: Kongmoon, Wuchow, Kaying Kweilin, Korea, Manchuria, Japan, Hong Kong, Hawaii, and the Philippines. It was the same spirit that carried him through the depression years beginning with the Wall Street collapse in 1929. During these years, he expanded Maryknoll's work in supreme confidence that God would not let him down.

"I never worry," he told a close friend. "I believe that we are doing God's work, and that if we do our part, He will do the rest."

In 1931, Father Walsh made what was to be his last mission journey. He was pleased to see how well his men were established. He was also equally pleased to see the large number of men working in the mission world from other mission societies of the United States.

"We of Maryknoll do not wish to be exclusive," he wrote his priests. "I strongly urge you to treat other missionary societies not as rivals, but as co-operators. It would indeed be unfortunate if, because Maryknoll has the exclusive name of CATHOLIC FOREIGN MISSION SOCIETY OF AMERICA, we should think we have a monopoly.

"From our earliest days we have possessed a tradition of working together closely with other societies and Catholic organizations. We worked with the Fathers of the Divine Word in promoting the Catholic Students' Mission Crusade. When the Irish Maynooth Mission of St. Columban wished to establish an American branch, we did everything in our power to facilitate this work. We must not think merely of Maryknoll's vocation, but of our country's and of the world's as well."

One day a prominent Italian Cardinal, who later told the story to some Maryknollers, was having a private audience with Pope Pius XI. During the discussion of ecclesiastical matters the Cardinal proposed that Father Walsh be raised to the episcopacy.

"For what reason?" asked the Holy Father.

"He founded Maryknoll," replied the Cardinal.

The Holy Father waved his hand in a negative gesture. "It is not our custom to raise priests to the episcopacy because they are founders of societies," he said. "What has Father Walsh done for God and the Church?"

"Father Walsh is the man," answered the Cardinal, "who single handed gave the idea of the importance of foreign missions to the Church in the United States, and who promoted the idea to the point that most Catholics in America have some knowledge of, and interest in the universal Church."

"Since this is so," decided the Holy Father, "we will examine the case."

On the night of April 24, 1933, Father Walsh was having dinner with a close Boston friend, Father James F. Kelly, at the latter's parish in Jamaica Plain. The friendship went back to seminary days, and Father Kelly had been very helpful in the foundation of Maryknoll and in overcoming early growing pains. The two cronies had just finished dinner when the doorbell rang, and the Maryknoll Council entered. One look at their gloomy faces and Father Walsh imagined the worst. Something terrible must have happened to bring his assistants hundreds of miles to locate him in person.

Father Patrick J. Byrne (of Japan and Korea fame), who was a Council member at the time, acted as spokesman of the group. He seemed to be struggling to get the words out.

"Father General," he said, "we have just received advice from

Rome. It seems we have been making a mistake, a very grave mistake."

Father Byrne paused, as if the calamity was so serious that he could not go on. Father Walsh did not know what to make of the situation. Never before had his assistants pursued him from New York to Boston. He prepared himself for what was to come.

"The mistake," continued Father Byrne, "is that we are calling you Father General, whereas, Your Excellency, it should be Bishop General."

Thus did the news come to Bishop-elect Walsh. It was official approval of his work from the Holy See. All Maryknoll rejoiced at the honor, and a flood of congratulations came in from friends all over the world. "The American Church is proud of Bishop Walsh," declared the Hartford *Transcript*. "The historic honor of the episcopate has never been more worthily bestowed." The *Catholic News*, of New York, stated: "Maryknoll is Father Walsh; Father Walsh is Maryknoll. The task he accomplished was mighty, the anxieties have been indescribable, the labors unending, the results blessed."

Bishop Walsh was consecrated in Rome, on June 29, 1933, twenty-two years to the day after he had been commissioned for the task of founding his Society. Cardinal Fumasoni-Biondi, Prefect of the Sacred Congregation of Propaganda, was the consecrator. Archbishop John T. McNicholas, of Cincinnati, and Bishop John J. Dunn, of New York, represented the American hierarchy and acted as co-consecrators. For his episcopal motto, Bishop Walsh chose three words that had so often been applied to the development of Maryknoll: *Primum regnum Dei*. They were taken from Christ's words as quoted in the gospel of St. Luke: "Seek ye *first the kingdom of God* and his justice: and all these things shall be added unto you."

Two days after the consecration, Bishop Walsh had a private audience with Pope Pius XI in the latter's study at the Vatican. The Holy Father presented Bishop Walsh with a pectoral cross, and "as a mark of special esteem" added a beautiful cameo ring. Then turning to the little group present, the Pope spoke with great ardor and enthusiasm concerning the work of Bishop Walsh and Maryknoll.

Bishop Walsh returned to Maryknoll to get back to work. He

was hardly home when he received word that two close friends who had been at the consecration had suddenly died. One was his co-consecrator, Bishop Dunn, and the other was the Sulpician, Father Joseph Bruneau. Both friends were regarded by Maryknollers as their own, since both had been close to the Society, before and after its formal foundation. One by one, the links with the early days were beginning to disappear. Even Bishop Walsh was showing signs of ill health. Ever since the consecration, his vitality seemed to be lessening.

"It is better to wear out than to rust out," Bishop Walsh had said frequently. Although his life's many labors had left him with a great weariness, he refused to slow down. There were departure ceremonies, ordinations, talks, and his regular duties as Superior General. In 1934, he began to plan another mission trip to the Orient, but his doctors forbade it. They sent him for a rest to Europe, and later to Florida. He started out from this latter place to visit Maryknoll houses in the West, but had to be carried off the train to a hospital in Jacksonville.

In April, 1935, he was back at Maryknoll and took part in the Holy Week ceremonies. In June he ordained sixteen seminarians in the Maryknoll chapel, but could hardly finish the ceremony because of weakness. He also presided over the Departure Ceremony that year. But he could not deceive himself or others. He had not long to live. When Monsignor Francis X. Ford, of Kaying, was nominated bishop and wrote to the Superior General asking if the latter would consecrate him at Maryknoll, prudence might have ruled out such a trying and long ceremony. But Bishop Walsh was still the father of Maryknoll; indeed, after his own consecration he continuously refused to allow Maryknollers to call him anything but Father General. He replied to Bishop-elect Ford that nothing would give him greater pleasure than to act as the consecrator.

The ceremony took place on September 21, and from somewhere Bishop Walsh summoned strength for the ordeal. In fact, he seemed to grow stronger as the consecration Mass progressed. But it was to be his last public appearance. On December 5, 1935, he celebrated his last Mass. After that date, he no longer had strength. He was anointed on December 8, but he clung to life. On Christmas he heard the seminarians outside his room singing carols, and his own beautiful hymn, "Only a Veil."

He had written this hymn as a curate in Boston, after a visit to a dying woman who was going blind. The woman had a great devotion to the Blessed Sacrament, and although she was losing her physical sight, Father Walsh felt she was on the point of at last seeing behind the veil of bread. When he returned to the rectory, he could not help jotting down the following lines, and later setting them to music.

> Only a veil between me and Thee,
> Jesus, my Lord!
> A veil of bread it appears to me,
> Yet seemeth such, that I may not see
> Jesus, my God.
>
> Lift not the veil between me and Thee,
> Jesus, my Lord!
> These eyes of earth can never see
> The glory of Thy Divinity,
> Jesus, my God.
>
> Keep then the veil between me and Thee,
> Jesus, my Lord!
> Some day 'twill fall when my soul is free
> To gaze on Thee for eternity,
> Jesus, my God.

The weeks and months passed. Confined to his bed, Bishop Walsh could only offer his sufferings and prayers for the work of Maryknoll. This he did gladly. The beads of his rosary were continually slipping through his fingers. Spring came to Maryknoll and the air was heavy with blossoms and freshness. But Maryknoll's Father General was growing progressively weaker. His lungs were congested, and a growth within his right lung was crowding out life. Holy week came, and his suffering was intense. His racking cough was an agony to all who heard it. On Easter Sunday pneumonia set in.

Father John J. Considine, of New Bedford, Massachusetts, who was one of Bishop Walsh's Assistants General, kept notes of those last days. Here is his account of them.

April 11:   Naturally, Father General has been able to participate in none of the ceremonies this week. He seems to suffer great pain from this very deprivation since he has great love for ceremonies. I recall one Holy Saturday in the old chapel in Rosary House when the sun suddenly came out as Father General was about to intone the *Gloria,* and how he sent one of the seminarians to push back the curtain so that the rays might stream in on the altar.

April 12:   Father General had a miserable day today. I feel that the sound of his distressful choking cough will haunt me for a long time. Both in my room above and in the office below it can be heard now almost any time of the day. This morning the altar was set for Easter Mass in his room, but at the last minute he told the Sisters to transfer everything to his chapel. I realized how disappointed he would be through the day at the reflection that he was not able to witness Mass, so I walked to his bed with the vestments on and asked, "Why won't you let us have Mass here? We won't mind however much you may cough during it." Apparently this was the assurance he wanted and he agreed immediately. He believed he would be giving too much disturbance to the others present.

April 13:   Father General continued in great distress, though he felt well enough late in the afternoon to request Sister Mary Rachel to read a portion of his Easter mail. He was able to give an indication of what reply should be sent to each writer. She had hardly left the room when he sounded the bell and called her back. "You have forgotten several things," he remarked, and mentioned a number of messages and spiritual bouquets. She replied that they were all noted. "But you have forgotten to acknowledge the bunny that came from the convent." A fine example of his attention to little things throughout his life. I dropped in this evening, mentioning that I had come only to say howdy, that I had nothing special to say. He thanked me and said he was very sorry he was not able to talk. He was huddled over on his side in extreme misery, both from the unpleasant taste, and from the unpleasant odor of the dregs, which was exuding from his lungs.

April 14:   I arrived at Father General's quarters this morning at seven and found Father Drought already there. He met me in the sacristy and remarked that the Superior's condition was very grave. "In fact," he said, "he is dying." It was a bit of a shock, since he had been so gravely ill so frequently that we had come to take his crises almost as a matter of course. Naturally it was clear that they could not occur many more times, since each attack left him weaker than the previous one.

I said Mass in the chapel, and Father Drought signaled to me to try to give Father General Holy Communion. I gave him about a sixth of a Host. After Mass I went in to him, and it was clear that he was in grave sufferings. His whole face was livid, while his eyes were glassy and bulging. He would throw his arms back desperately and cry, "God!" every few moments, varying occasionally with, "Jesus, Mary, Joseph." I stayed awhile in the chapel and went back the second time, and tried to help him, but to no avail. As I placed my hand on his forehead, he said, "Absolution. Absolution." I gave him absolution.

I went to the office immediately after breakfast and made preparations for the announcement of his death. At ten o'clock Father Drought telephoned, suggesting that I come up and ask any of the other priests whom I found to come likewise, since Father General was near the end. I arrived just as the line of priests was proceeding into his room, each giving absolution as he passed the bed. The lividness and distention of a few hours earlier were gone. He held a sitting posture, and small portions of exudate continued to come from his mouth. He was limp and white and apparently in a coma. Mother Mary Joseph sat at his left and was very composed. As she noted the death rattle she remarked quietly, "That is the end." Death came at 10:26. There was no great struggle.

Thus did James Anthony Walsh, pioneer, apostle, and founder of Maryknoll, go home. His last recorded words were, "Jesus, Mary, Joseph." To the service of the Holy Family he had given his life; they were his last thoughts in death.

"Sunset Hill, we suspect," wrote one of his spiritual sons that evening, "experiences a deep satisfaction tonight. Almost a quarter of a century ago it made the acquaintance of one who, despite many absences, became intimately linked with this gentle eminence behind Ossining which lifts its lovely head high above the Hudson Valley. Tonight he is not absent.

"And tonight it is evident that he will go away no more. But the wind seems a little plaintive, the swaying trees a bit fretful; there is a touch of melancholy in nature's family. With the joy of possession there seems present as well the pain of loss. He is here, and yet he is here no longer.

"For repose and sleep are but death's mirages; the reality is otherwise. Sunset Hill holds the body of Maryknoll's founder but his soul is with God."

The funeral was held in St. Patrick's Cathedral on Friday. The New York papers called it the most significant funeral since the death of Cardinal Farley. The gigantic church was packed with priests, monsignors, bishops and archbishops. Archbishop (now Cardinal) Edward A. Mooney celebrated the Mass. Archbishop McNicholas delivered a superb eulogy that said all, a eulogy that brought pain to his own voice and tears to his own cheeks; for he was speaking not only of a great churchman, but also of a close friend. Then the procession wound its way back to Sunset Hill, and Archbishop John G. Murray, of St. Paul, gave the last blessing as the earthly remains of Bishop Walsh were put to rest beneath the shadow of the great crucifix of his own God's Acre. He who had come here so often to pray for his dead sons and daughters was now made one with them.

Shortly before he died, Bishop Walsh had written letters to all Maryknollers, giving his last thoughts, counsels and wishes. These were now made public. Because a compilation shows so well the nature of the man who wrote it, this last testament, as it were, follows here:

My beloved Maryknollers,

I make no distinction among you, since we are all missioners. Whether our daily tasks are in the homeland or on the field, we are of one heart and one mind—pledged to the converting of the world, with special interest in the people entrusted to our care by Rome.

The sands are going down in the glass, and my days are evidently numbered. I write in the expectation of my departure, with God's grace, for the life that changes not.

It has been my privilege—a rare one for a cofounder—to see the work of Maryknoll developed to a promising maturity. I thank God for the bountiful Providence which from the beginning has been so strikingly manifest.

I am far from thinking that our development is perfect. No one has been more conscious of weakness than I, who for all these years have been at the head of our Society. I have often lamented my own shortcomings and my limitations. All I can say for myself is that I have tried to be the willing instrument of God, who has urged me forward, leaving to me the duty of watching that I should not trip.

You, my beloved Maryknollers, have been my comfort, my pride and my joy. I am fully aware that while much credit has been given to me, because of my position in the Society, my work would have been a failure without the help you have so generously given me. I am especially grateful to you because you have borne with my limitations. God certainly uses the weak for His divine purposes. But after all, our work is His work, and you will make no mistake if you look to Him for guidance. All that He seeks from you is generosity and ready willingness to use the opportunities—or to meet the difficulties—which inevitably present themselves.

There are many counsels and admonitions I would leave with you, but above all else, take care that your work for Maryknoll brings you closer to Christ and increases your desire to seek His will in all things—be it life or death! Let Him be your tower of strength! Cultivate reliance on His Divine Providence! "I can do all things in Him Who strengthens me."

To work for Christ is a greater privilege. To labor with Him, and in Him and through Him, mindful always that we are His willing instruments, is the assurance of our success, spiritual especially, and often material. Learn to be familiar with Christ as an elder Brother. Speak to Him as if His presence were visible, and, in the silence of the tabernacle, or in your own room—listen!!!

Let His humility and that of our Blessed Lady and St. Joseph mark your lives!—I cannot urge you too strongly to be humble. The self-opinionated person accomplishes little and is a disturbing influence. Try to see the other person's point of view, and remember that arguments, unless sincerely employed to get at the truth, are of little or no use.

Throughout your life as Maryknollers, whatever your capacity may be, respect your Superiors. They may not always measure up to your ideal, but they represent God from Whom all authority comes.

Be generous, self-forgetting and patient—then your life as happy, holy and successful missioners will be assured.

I have often urged you to appreciate what is good in societies others than ours. Keep up this spirit, but watch closely that loyalty shall be a shining virtue in your life—loyalty to the Society, to your Superiors, and to one another. That all may be one in Christ, is my prayer.

The spirit of Maryknoll is often praised—at times much overestimated. But we who hear the word kindly, while regretting that we do not reach the ideal, may yet be heartened as we are humbled.

You, dear Maryknollers, have the future of our Society in your keeping. That future will be secure if you remain humble, with childlike faith serving God and others for God, from the simple motive of love. PRIMUM REGNUM DEI! I have no fear for the future if Maryknollers, in all their actions and discussions, will forget self and keep in mind the will and glory of God.

May each of you persevere in your holy vocation, and fight courageously to the end against worldliness and the powers of darkness! My wish is that you remain simple, generous, cheerful and selfless, loving God and His saints with a strong personal affection, as little children love good parents. May God keep you faithful to the highest ideals of those who would follow Christ!

I leave you with the affection of a father for his children, my one regret being that I could not know each of you individually as I would. I pray that, through the marvelous workings of Christ's Mystical Body, I may remain united with each of you and that you may recognize me as your father and friend until that day when, by God's grace, we all meet in heaven for a wondrous reunion of the Maryknoll family.

But now I leave you to our Heavenly Father; to Christ, our Mission Leader; to the Holy Ghost, our light and strength; and to the loving Mother of us all, Mary, most humble, Queen of Heaven.

Adieu, Maryknoll! A *Dieu!* To God! In His Hands thou art secure, and under the protecting favors of her who mothered the Saviour of men, all will be well with thee!

Keep me in filial remembrance, and know that if God finds me worthy, I will be your helper until we meet merrily in heaven.

Affectionately in Christ,
James Anthony Walsh

With Bishop Walsh's death the first era of Maryknoll history had come to an end. A new day was now to begin. It would be a beautiful day, a day of accomplishments, but still a different day, the first time in its history that Maryknoll was without its founder and director. He had burned his ideas and ideals into his followers. He had anticipated the end, and prepared for others to take over. He knew that they would carry on the work. And the confidence that the father placed in his sons was not misplaced.

When the twenty-fifth anniversary of the Society came in June, Maryknollers all over the world were looking toward Hong Kong where the General Chapter of Maryknoll was to convene the following month and elect a new Superior General. The Chapter opened on July 16, and after the formalities were disposed of, ballots were cast and Bishop James Edward Walsh, of Kongmoon, was chosen to head the young Society. Bishop Walsh, no relation

to his predecessor, had been one of the original group of students
to enter Maryknoll, and a member of the original mission band.
He had been appointed to lead the China work after the death of
Father Price, and now he was asked to take over the Society
operations, after the death of the other cofounder. He arrived at
the home Knoll in September and quietly moved into his job.

Bishop James Edward Walsh was to govern Maryknoll for the
next ten years, and under his capable administration the Society
was to expand and undergo a period of tremendous growth in
both personnel and missions. When at Maryknoll in 1946, Bishop
Raymond A. Lane, of Manchuria, was elected at the Third General
Chapter to succeed him, Bishop Walsh returned to China to imi-
tate and direct in Shanghai an organization of the Chinese hierarchy similar to the National Catholic Welfare Conference in
the United States. A prolific writer, he was to author many books
during this period, and to compose all of the editorials appearing
in *The Field Afar*. Even after his return to China, he was to
continue this editorial work. When Bishop Walsh was elected
Superior General in 1936, he delivered a speech of acceptance to
the Chapter delegates. During this talk, he gave an inspired and
beautiful tribute to the meaning of Maryknoll. This is what he
said:

> Maryknoll, blessed word that carries our hopes and fears and in-
> spires all our love;
>
> Maryknoll, garden of God that inspired and nourished and brought
> to fruition in our unworthy selves that holy vocation which is
> dearer to us than human life;
>
> Maryknoll, ardent reaper in the fields white for the harvest, that is
> pouring out, and ever will pour out, its full resources and its own
> life blood to achieve its divine purpose of saving the souls of
> men;
>
> Maryknoll, fount of zeal, concept sprung from the loving depths of
> the Sacred Heart of Jesus thirsting for souls on His Cross;
>
> Maryknoll, name that is already blessed on earth and known in
> heaven, we rededicate ourselves to the full realization of your
> glorious ideal.

By the time Bishop Lane took direction of the Society in 1946,
Maryknoll had weathered two severe storms. The first had come

when Bishop James Anthony Walsh died, and the second during the violent upheaval of World War II. Bishop Lane was to be faced with his own problems, particularly the persecution of the missions and missioners by the Communists. Under Bishop Lane's direction additional mission expansion took place, and a large scale building program for new training accommodations was inaugurated in the United States. In point of time, and particularly when viewed in the light of the history of the Church, Maryknoll is still an infant. Yet under its first three Superiors General, Maryknoll has been privileged to make valuable contributions to the peoples it served, and to make more full the body of the Church.

James Anthony Walsh had placed his mark on his Society and upon his priests. That mark was God's own command to seek first the kingdom of God. As long as Maryknoll continues to pursue this course, neither war nor persecution can stay its work of mercy.

21

Bolivia—High and Low

"You must be from the United States," said eight-year-old Fernando, the first time he saw Father Joseph J. O'Neill, of St. Albans, New York.

"How did you guess that?" asked Father O'Neill.

"Because all men from the United States have big feet and big voices, and walk in a big hurry."

"And do you make friends with them?" inquired the priest.

"Only with the ones that have big smiles," quickly replied Fernando.

Maryknollers with big smiles and in a big hurry moved into Latin America when war with Japan cut off the Far Eastern mission fields. On February 11, 1942, the Sacred Congregation of Propaganda assigned Maryknoll an area in northern Bolivia known as the Pando Vicariate. Two months later, April 5, Archbishop (now Cardinal) Francis J. Spellman, of New York, presided at a special Departure Ceremony in which Father Alonso E. Escalante, of New York, Father Raymond J. Bonner, of South Ardmore, Pennsylvania, and Father Thomas J. Danehy, of Manitowoc, Wisconsin, were assigned to pioneer the new Latin American work. A month later they were sending reports back to Maryknoll from the region of the Amazon headwaters.

Bolivia, they explained, is a land of rugged mountains and steaming jungles, one of the most difficult mission countries to be found anywhere. Although 99% of the people are Catholic in name, actually less than 25% of the people practice their Faith. The main reason for this is the lack of priests, because among 3½ million Bolivians, there are only about 400 priests—approximately one for every 8,750 persons, compared to the one priest for every 650 Catholics in the United States. Bolivia is twice the size of Texas with less than half the population of that state. Nine out of every ten Bolivians have Indian blood, and 85% are illiterate.

The Maryknoll mission of the Pando Vicariate is located in the Amazon lowlands. Without roads or railroads, the area is undeveloped, and the many tributaries of the Amazon flowing through the region are the only means of getting around. The jungle is a paradise for wild life, but a problem to the missioner. The alligator, which the natives call cayman, dwells in all the rivers, and grows as long as sixteen feet. Giant anacondas or boa constrictors coil up like huge fire hoses in the swampy forests. Jaguars, wild pigs, and many other forms of animal life roam the area. Also found in the rivers are the piranas—small fish, traveling in schools, that can rip the flesh off a human body in a matter of minutes.

The largest town in the vicariate is Riberalta, and it was chosen as the mission center. In many respects, it reminded the first missioners of a frontier town in the United States before the turn of the century. Its sidewalks (when such exist) are boards running along each side of grass-covered streets.

"Even in the Twentieth Century, this vast jungle area remains in much the same state as it was created by the hand of God," declared one early report. "Some savages still roam the jungle with bow and arrow, and not too long ago murdered a priest passing through the region. The entire area would be overlooked by modern man if it were not for the rubber and Brazil nut trees. The men, women and children who collect the rubber and nuts live far in the jungle. These people have been without priests for so long that they have almost forgotten the practice of their religion."

The first three missioners set to work organizing the Riberalta mission and preparing for the large group that was to be sent down from Maryknoll that fall. On January 18, 1943, Father Escalante was appointed vicar apostolic, and was consecrated a bishop at the Shrine of Our Lady of Guadalupe, in Mexico City, Mexico, on May 9. Bishop Escalante had been born in Mexico, but his family had been forced to flee to the United States during the persecution. He had become an American citizen, and had entered Maryknoll. After his consecration, the new bishop hurried back to his mission to be on hand to welcome the first contingent of Maryknoll Sisters, coming to set up a school and hospital in the Riberalta parish.

One of the early mission centers staffed by the Maryknollers was the forest settlement called Cavinas, far up the Beni River. Here live the Cavin Indian tribe. When Father Ambrose C. Graham, of New York City, arrived, the village was in a tumble-down condition. The natives were suffering from malaria, anemia, worms, and a host of tropical diseases. Father set to work to remedy the situation, and later Father Gordon N. Fritz, of Newport, Minnesota, and Father Joseph A. Hahn, of Whitestone, New York, arrived to help in the task. The Padres' first move was to halt the inroads of the jungle by clearing the land. Then new houses were put up, and the decrepit huts destroyed.

A community store was opened by the mission where the Indians could buy the goods they needed at reasonable prices. The Indians had previously sold their rubber to some of the large companies operating along the river, and the missioners organized a cooperative, taking the rubber to Riberalta where it was sold for a higher price. Several small industries were set up. All profits from the Cavinas ventures were used for the people—building new houses, buying tools, and financing an occasional fiesta.

The missioners also had to act as doctors and nurses. They treated everything from malaria to snake bites. Although a dispensary was open at appointed hours, they were on twenty-four-hour call because the jungle has a way of creating emergencies. They even had to care for the Cavinas animals, and Father Graham once dosed a horse bitten by a snake by pouring kerosene (the only thing available at the time) down the animal's throat. In seconds the beast was up on his feet and running around as if it were in training for the Kentucky Derby.

The Indians have very poor memories, and are slow to learn. When the mission was building the first houses, Indians carried mud and sand by handfuls. Father Fritz showed them that they could do better with boxes. They were like children with new toys and they didn't seem to be able to fill the boxes fast enough. Yet when the Padre returned an hour later, they had forgotten the boxes and were carrying the dirt in both hands again. Father built wheelbarrows for the job, demonstrating to the workers how much sand could then be moved. The Indians' eyes shone. They started running back and forth with the empty wheelbarrows. Carefully, the Padre explained the purpose of the wheelbarrows, and after a half hour the Indians caught on and began carrying dirt in the vehicles. The next morning when Father showed up on the job some Indians were bringing dirt in their fists, and others were pushing empty wheelbarrows around aimlessly. It took days before the lesson of the wheelbarrows stayed with the Indians.

Life is never dull at Cavinas. One night Father Fritz was sitting in his house reading his breviary when he heard cries coming from the village. An Indian rushed in to tell him that a *tigre*—a jaguar —was loose in the village and at that moment was in the Padre's pigpen. Father Fritz hastily grabbed his gun and started out the door, only to find the angry cat coming to meet him. He shot the beast when it was only four feet away.

"It was a small tiger," reported Father Fritz in his diary to Maryknoll headquarters, "only about six feet long. We were glad to get him because of the many animals he had been killing. The Indians skinned and roasted the beast and had a feast on him next day. The dish looked good, but I stuck to pork since the tiger had killed one of my pigs but had himself met death before he could escape with his dinner."

One of the main projects Bishop Escalante organized was a public health program. Practically everyone in the region had malaria, almost 100% suffered from verminosis, tuberculosis was rampant, and in certain areas over 90% of the people had amoebic dysentery. The heart of the medical program was (and is) the small, modern hospital built during the war by the American Government and turned over to the Bolivian Government as a gift to the Bolivian people. The mission agreed to operate the hospital under contract, and Bishop Escalante brought in Maryknoll Sisters to staff it. Attached to the hospital are an out patient department and a pharmacy. The Sisters also began a visiting-nurse program, which takes care of the sick right in their homes.

The second part of the program was put into operation as soon as the hospital was functioning. All school children were vaccinated

against smallpox. A routine health examination was given every
child every six months. People with communicable diseases were
isolated. All patients coming to the hospital were examined for malaria and parasites. The third part of the program was health education. Weekly classes in health were introduced in the Riberalta
school. Hospital and dispensary patients received training in
cleanliness and personal hygiene. The Sisters also began teaching
mothers the proper care of their children.

The public health program has been very successful, and Bolivian officials have called the Riberalta hospital, "the best hospital
in Bolivia." The most recent annual report from Riberalta shows
that the hospital had 430 admissions in the year; the dispensary
gave 43,873 treatments; and 6,349 home visits were made. Health
conditions, particularly in the Riberalta area, have been consid-
erably improved.

In 1949 Bishop Escalante left Bolivia to undertake the establishment of the Mexican Foreign Mission Seminary, an institution organized by the Mexican Hierarchy and patterned after Maryknoll.
A number of Maryknollers were also assigned to assist him in this
project. Father Danehy, one of the pioneer Maryknollers, was appointed Apostolic Administrator of the Pando Vicariate to supervise the affairs of the mission. In 1953 Monsignor Danehy was
named a bishop and he was consecrated in his home town of
Manitowoc, Wisconsin, April 22, 1953.

The new bishop had traveled all over his vicariate and several
times had close calls from death while journeying about the region.
On one occasion, when he was still a monsignor, he and Father
Fritz went to La Paz for supplies for the Cavinas mission. They
bought the things needed, loaded the supplies aboard a C-54 cargo
plane, and took off from the high Andean airport of La Paz for
Rurrenabaque at the headwaters of the Beni River. As the plane
came in for a landing on the rough jungle airport, a wheel locked
and the big ship plowed into a series of ditches at the end of the
field, ripping off a wing and crumpling the undercarriage. Fortunately neither Monsignor Danehy nor Father Fritz was hurt in the
crash; and the plane did not catch fire, so the cargo was saved.

It was another day before all the cargo could be salvaged from
the wreckage by Father Fritz, and Monsignor spent the time buying a pair of big dugout canoes. Then while Father Fritz lashed the
canoes together with rope and vines, Monsignor hired the town's

only tractor and began hauling the supplies to the river. The canoes weighed about two tons each, unloaded, and the main power
for moving them downriver was to come from the current, but an
outboard motor was to give the extra power for steering. The next
morning the two missioners set out on the five hundred mile trip to
Cavinas. Everything started well. They skillfully passed through
the twenty miles of logs and rapids that form the first part of the
river. At nightfall, they stopped the outboard motor, cooked in the
canoes, ate their supper, and lay down to sleep while the canoes
drifted peacefully along.

About two o'clock in the morning a bump awoke the sleepers.
They were in a nest of logs and directly in front of them a huge log
stood upright in the river. The water roared as it split around the
obstacle. Seconds later the canoes crashed into the log, the colli-
sion forcing the canoes to almost stand on end. Cargo and missioners were thrown into the river. Father Fritz grabbed for some
boxes floating by.

"Let them alone," Monsignor Danehy shouted. "Get the canoes
or we'll never get out of here."

By this time the canoes had slipped off the log and were slowly
sinking. It was a considerable struggle for the two men to get the
heavy craft to shore, but they finally beached the canoes. Then the
missioners tried to locate any cargo that might be around. They
found a brief case containing matches and a flashlight, and got a
fire going. They stood shivering over the fire, trying to dry out,
while some wild jungle animal paced back and forth on the bank
above them until morning.

By daylight the two travelers managed to rescue a few more
items. They had the canoes, the motor, and gasoline. Food, cooking utensils, clothing and personal possessions were all gone. With
one small salvaged tin they began bailing the canoes; and when
the job was done, the two priests took off again. Late in the afternoon they came to a little hut, and were able to buy some food.
They then went on until nightfall. Having learned from experience, Monsignor Danehy and Father Fritz decided not to travel
that night. But their caution did them little good. During the night
the river went down—a common occurrence in the jungle—and
morning found the canoes high and dry on a mudbank. Hours were
spent digging a channel to get the craft afloat. That afternoon a
submerged log knocked the motor off the canoe. Although the

motor was rescued, the rest of the day was needed for cleaning and drying it. That night they lay down to sleep without supper while swarms of mosquitoes attacked them.

The fourth day found their bad luck continuing. A strong wind kept them from moving until late in the afternoon. Then the pump on the motor went out of commission. For a day and a half, with little food to give them strength, they paddled the heavy canoes. Finally Monsignor Danehy rigged up a Rube Goldberg contraption that permitted the motor to run as long as he or Father Fritz poured water into it; thus they chugged along until they became stranded on another sandbar. The sixth and last day was not too bad. The missioners sighted the Cavinas landing far ahead, about noon. Just then they hit the worst submerged log of the trip, and completely smashed the motor. Under the hot midday sun, they had to paddle the last hour and a half. In midafternoon they arrived at the mission looking like barbarians—sunburned, dirty, unshaven, and clothed in tattered garments.

Bishop Danehy had another approach to death in 1952. He was traveling upriver to Cavinas with Bishop Raymond A. Lane, Maryknoll's Superior General, who was making a mission visitation. They were traveling on the mission launch, *Innisfail*, and Brother Gonzaga Chilutti of Philadelphia, Pennsylvania, was acting as pilot and skipper. On the evening of the Feast of Our Lady of Lourdes (February 11), Father Bonner was at the wheel, while Bishop Lane and Monsignor Danehy were sitting in the bow of the boat, enjoying the evening breeze. Brother Gonzaga came up and called the bishop's attention to the lovely sunset, and then went away a few feet to sit at the engine pit and watch the motor, because the muddy Beni River water was causing pump trouble. As he sat there, he was reciting the Rosary.

Suddenly there was a loud crash—and glass showered over the heads of Bishop Lane and Monsignor Danehy. Their first thought was that there had been an explosion, but on looking up, they saw the branches of a tree over the pilot house. It was an immense ambaibo tree, at least a hundred feet high. The flood water of the river had loosened its roots, and without warning it had silently crashed down on the boat. The tree had fallen on Brother Gonzaga, and if it had come down a second earlier would have crushed Bishop Lane and Monsignor Danehy. The tree had apparently struck Brother on the back of the head and neck, knocking him into the engine pit. His back was broken and he was unconscious. He died shortly after, and was buried at a mission station along the river. The launch was a complete wreck. As only four feet separated Bishop Lane, Monsignor Danehy, Father Bonner and Brother Gonzaga, anyone of them, or all of them could have easily been killed. For His own reason God chose Brother Gonzaga.

Bishop Lane in writing about the incident remarked that he could not help remembering the same date of some years earlier. He had been praying in his garden at Fushun, Manchuria, that news would come about kidnaped Father Jerry Donovan, when he was called to the telephone to be advised that Father's body had been found. That day had also been the Feast of Our Lady of Lourdes. Brother Gonzaga, who had led a very holy and devoted life, had often stated many times that he wanted to die on a feast of the Blessed Mother. He was devoted to the mission and the people, but ill health was about to force him back to the United States. Bishop Lane has said that as Brother sat praying that night, he might well have been asking God to arrange things so that he would never have to leave Bolivia. The falling tree could well have been God's answer.

After Bishop Lane completed his visitation of the Bolivian mission, he announced a six-point plan for Christian living, designed to stem communism and build a vigorous Christianity. The six points of the program were: Leadership, Worship, Education, Health and Welfare, Mass Communications, Catholic Social Action.

Many of the Bolivian mission stations in the Pando Vicariate are models for other Maryknoll projects. The San Jose Parish near Riberalta maintains a primary school, an orphanage, a carpentry shop, and recreational facilities. This parish built a 300-foot bridge over an arroyo that floods every rainy season and cuts San Jose off from the main pueblo of Riberalta. Cachuela Esperanza Parish operates a primary school, aids in village sanitation, and provides housing for the poor. At Conquista there are a primary school, an adult-education program, and a health education program taught by Maryknoll Sisters.

Some of the forty-five Maryknoll priests, Brothers, and Sisters in the area spend days and weeks upon the rivers, visiting the scattered settlements, and thus they staff a mobile parish. Some of the diaries of the first Maryknollers in the region read like the journals of the pioneers who explored our own United States. Those missioners took 1,000-mile trips in canoes. Father Fritz, Father Graham, and Father J. Gerard Grondin made such long journeys, and wrote back to Maryknoll about their experiences, with the nonchalance of someone reporting a week-end jaunt by subway to Coney Island. Father Graham moved through the jungle without guides or worries. He once traveled by horse from Cavinas to Riberalta, sleeping in the jungle at night alongside a fire to keep jaguars away, and often hacking his way with a machete during the daytime.

Conditions have improved since then, and now missioners travel in small launches, or at least in canoes with outboard motors. Father Lawrence J. Burns, of Wakefield, Massachusetts, and Father Walter J. Valladon, of Oakland, California, are continually moving up and down the jungle river for the purpose of visiting remote settlements, baptizing, offering Mass, passing out medicine and other help. They travel over unexplored streams, stop at unmapped settlements, talk to Indians whose bodies are painted and whose noses are pierced with fishbones. Months at a time, the two missioners are away from their fellow priests, from decent food and comfortable beds. They endure the sun, the heat, the rain, and the insects. And when they do finally get back to home base for a rest, they are anxious to be off again. They know that hidden along the jungle rivers are souls—and it was for those souls that they left the comforts of America, and for those souls no trial of body or spirit is too great.

Maryknoll's work in Bolivia, however, is not confined to the jungle lowlands. Priests and Sisters are to be found in different parts of that varied country. The jungle mission is the Maryknoller's own vicariate; elsewhere they work in Bolivian Dioceses. Twenty-one Maryknoll priests, one Maryknoll Brother, and five Maryknoll Sisters are to be found in the Bolivian Dioceses,—an entirely different world from the jungle mission. The vast plateau of Bolivia's altiplano has a mean altitude of 12,000 feet above sea level. There live three quarters of the population of Bolivia— Aymara and Quechua Indians, who cultivate the rocky soil or work in highland tin mines.

Parish work in the highlands is far different from that in the jungle, or that in the United States. The Maryknoll parish in Calacala (near Cochabamba) is set in this Indian world. Some twelve thousand people live in this parish, which has now built up a flourishing Catholic life and has one of the most modern schools in all Bolivia. This school, incidentally, is the first parochial school in Bolivia. A former pastor of the parish, Father Charles A. Brown, of New York City, described the routine of Calacala parish life in a report to Maryknoll. He wrote:

"Last Sunday, just before the 8:30 Mass, a young fellow arrived at my house with two horses and asked me to visit a sick woman. It was too late to go immediately, so I said the Mass, and at 9:05 we galloped away. The woman was dying in childbirth. I heard her confession, took the information for the marriage to the man with whom she had been living for twenty years, married them, gave her Holy Communion, and anointed her. Four sacraments within thirty minutes!

"A baby across the street was seriously ill. I hurried over and baptized him. Then I galloped back for the 10 o'clock Mass—which started at 11:07. Later in the afternoon, while off on another sick call, I heard that the woman who had received the four sacraments that morning had died."

The highland missioners are often called upon to protect the Indians' rights. Father John J. Lawler, a native of New Bedford, Massachusetts, who founded the Calacala parish, received word that some fifty Indian families had been told by the landowner to leave their homes. Under the feudal system long in vogue, the Indians receive a plot of land and, in return, work four days a week for the landowner and give him a share of their own harvest and flock increase. When the land is sold, the Indians are transferred with it. The particular dispute arose when the Indians asked an increase in their wages from five and a half to six cents a day. The landowner cut off water from the Indians to force them to move. Father Lawler consulted a lawyer and found out that although legally the owner was not obliged to give a raise, he could not force the Indians off the land. At a three-hour meeting, the missioner persuaded the landowner to allow the Indians to remain on their land, and to grant them the desired raise and other benefits.

On another occasion, when whooping cough broke out among the Indians, Father Lawler got in touch with the American Medical Commission, arranged for them to vaccinate the children of the area, and then put on a big drive to persuade the people of the necessity of vaccination. Whooping cough is usually fatal in Bolivia, when accompanied by malnutrition, but the missioner's efforts halted the epidemic in Calacala.

In addition to the altiplano and highland parishes, Maryknoll has parishes in the lowlands. These center about the city of Santa Cruz, an old colonial foundation that, before the coming of the airplane, was largely cut off from the rest of the world. An example of this type of parish is the one at Cotoca, which embraces about a thousand square miles of rural farmland. About 11,000 people live in the parish. When the Maryknollers first arrived in the parish only six people made their Easter duty, and not a boy from the parish had gone to the seminary for almost two centuries.

Now parish life is thriving, several boys have gone to the seminary, and a number of girls are preparing to become Sisters. A group of native Sisters are working in the parish, and practically all of the school children have made their First Communion. The parish dispensary is busy in the fight against malnutrition, worms, malaria and conjunctivitis. A home economics course is sponsored by the parish, and the priests work hand in hand with the Inter-American Agricultural Service in an attempt to improve the economy of the region.

Father James W. Fitzgerald, of North Cambridge, Massachusetts, who is stationed in Cotoca, describes life there in these terms: "The life of a missioner is essentially a restless one . . . Down here, time is not only suspected, but it is held in high disrepute. Deliberateness, slowness, comfort, and silence reign. This tempo is a difficult hurdle for the average missioner, who feels the pressure of time upon the Church. She must establish a functioning, self-supporting, native Church, and then move on. But the missioner must adopt Saint Paul's mission methods of patience and understanding."

22

Peru—Reaching for the Sky

White crosses dotted the side of the precipitous mountain road, as the little patched up truck steamed its way through the Andes at an altitude of almost 16,000 feet above sea level.

"Juan, who is responsible for these shrines?"

The young Quechua driver smiled at the missioner and answered: "They are no shrines, Padre. Each cross marks the spot of a fatal accident. Here a truck toppled over the mountainside. There a man slipped after drinking too much *pisco*."

For the first time the Maryknoller understood the sign pasted on the cracked windshield: "Riders forbidden to sleep while truck is in motion."

It was on such a mountain pass as this that Father Thomas J. Carey, of Newark, New Jersey, was crushed to death when the truck he was riding skidded over the edge and toppled, end over end, down the mountain. It was on such a mountain pass, too, that Father Joseph P. Meaney, of Arlington, Massachusetts, was found near death from pneumonia. It was an Indian who saw Father Meaney laying there unconscious. The Indian passing by the Puno mission happened to mention to one of the priests what he had seen—"a dead white man lying by the road up the mountain."

Father John A. Waldie, of New York City, hurried to the scene, and recognized his one-time rector. He brought the sick priest into Puno where he was nursed back to health, and told his story. Father Meaney, pastor of Ayapata, had fallen sick. When he realized the seriousness of his illness he had mounted a horse and tried to get over the mountains into Puno. But crossing the pass he had blacked out, fallen off the horse, and would have certainly died in the cold bleakness but for the chance remark of the Indian.

These few indications of the nature of the terrain in Maryknoll's sky-high mission in Puno, Peru, give an accurate picture of conditions under which the missioners are working. Puno lies in the southern part of Peru, on the shores of Lake Titicaca, the highest navigable lake in the world. The area is rocky and barren, and only the sturdy llamas and timid vicunas nibbling at the sparse altiplano grass really feel at home. This is the region of the Aymara and Quechua Indians—the men wearing bright ponchos and woolen head coverings shaped much like a football helmet; the women dressed in derbies or pancake hats and multicolored petticoats that make them appear like pinwheels of color. The area was once the haunt of the mighty Incas, that advanced and warlike race that conquered western South America from Ecuador to Chile, and that fell before a handful of Spanish adventurers who came seeking gold and souls.

The first Maryknollers were assigned to Puno in 1942. They arrived in the city that gives the province its name, took over the direction of the city's only parish, opened a school, and laid the foundations for a seminary. Some Maryknollers spread out over the altiplano to staff churches, long deserted. The region suffered from a dearth of priests, and beautiful colonial churches where once a vital Catholic life had flourished were closed and decaying. Father Francis X. Lyons, of Philadelphia, one of the early missioners, relates an incident that happened to him and that dramatically brought home the great need of priests in the Andean highlands.

"There was a dusty vocational placard hanging on the sacristy wall. It read: 'In the United States, one priest for every six hundred Catholics; in Peru, one priest for every thirteen thousand souls.'

"It caught my eye that morning, as it did every morning while I was unvesting. I was studying the drawing of a chalice raised in benediction over the upturned faces of a great crowd, when I heard a noise behind me. An Indian had come in.

"Since he was chewing coca, I really smelled his presence before I saw him. I laid the vestments on the scarred dressing table in the dingy sacristy and turned toward the visitor. When I bowed, he dropped on one knee, and before I was aware of his intention, he kissed my hand.

" '*Tatai*,' (which means 'Father' in his language) was all he said, so I asked how I could serve him.

"The Indian stood there shyly for a moment, grasping his woolen cap in his gnarled and twisted hands. His body, clothed in home-spun trousers and jacket, was bent slightly from years of heavy work. His calloused feet shifted nervously in their thonged sandals.

" 'A baby, *Tatai*,' he said.

" 'To be baptized?'

" 'Yes, *Tatai*.'

" 'Is it very sick?' I asked.

" 'Very sick, *Tatai*. It rests at the church entrance.'

"I took off the other Mass vestments, put on the surplice and stole for baptism, and followed the man down the long, dark nave of the church to the baptismal font. When he had picked up the little bundle of blankets from the corner near the door, I opened the ritual.

" 'What do you ask from the Church of God?' I inquired in Latin, and then continued with the ceremony. Reaching out to make the sign of the cross on the baby's forehead, I removed the blankets from the tiny face.

"The baby was dead. It had been for days.

"I put the blanket back over the face, and said as gently as I could: 'The baby is dead. I can do nothing.'

"The Indian's face fell. His body began to shake silently, and I knew he was crying in a quiet, suppressed way. Slowly he sank to the wooden flooring and laid the baby at his side. Then he grasped me around the knees.

" '*Tatai*,' he begged, 'baptize the baby!'

"I looked down at his tear-wet face, and explained as best I could: I would baptize a live baby—yes; a dead baby—no. I also pointed out, so that his sorrow might not be repeated for another child, the fact that, if it is certain a baby is going to die and no priest is near, any lay person can perform the baptism.

"Apparently the Indian was not listening, for when I finished he said, 'But *Tatai*, a dead baby baptized must surely be better than a dead baby not baptized!'

"He would not be consoled. When he saw that there was nothing I could do, he picked up the lifeless bundle and shuffled out into the sunlight, tears still in his eyes. Through the doorway, I watched him go, wondering how many days he had walked with his sad little burden, seeking a priest.

"I thought, too, how inadequate was that vocational poster that I had seen in the sacristy. If only it could show how great is the need of these Indians—how terrible the disappointment and heart-break of such a one as the man who had come with his dead child —it would be far more convincing than it is with cold impersonal statistics."

It was in encounters such as this that the Americans began to realize the scope of their work. Father Vincent A. Cunningham, of Scranton, Pennsylvania, had an experience somewhat similar to that of Father Lyons, but fortunately his ended more happily. He was called into the sacristy of the parish church in Puno to baptize a sick baby. He did so, and after the ceremony asked the parents where they came from. They gave him the name of a village eighty miles away, which was part of the Puno parish. Father Cunningham mentioned later that he knew the parish was large, but that its size had never struck him so forcibly as when he learned that Indians had had to walk 160 miles to have a sick child baptized.

Almost immediately after they arrived in Peru, the Maryknollers accepted parishes hidden in the mountains, and there they lived cut off from most of the rest of the world. Those were difficult parishes, with little in the way of modern convenience. One of them is set in a deep valley—so deep that the sun reaches the floor of the valley only a few moments each day. To get to other parishes, the missioners had to travel over perilous mountain trails, crossing 16,000-foot heights where a sudden snowstorm could mean disaster. The daily life of one of these missioners is described by Father Meaney, who almost met death alone in the mountains, as mentioned earlier in this chapter. Here are some pages from his diary, in which he writes about himself in the third person, referring to himself as "the pastor":

"MONDAY. This afternoon, *cachapari*, or 'returning of the crosses,' took place. For the Feast of the Holy Cross, it is customary to bring down to the church all the crosses that top the various mountain peaks about the village. Inspiring sights are these crosses dominating the countryside, some of them on peaks two thousand feet above the village.

"These crosses remain in the church for the feast and the four days following it. They are repaired, if necessary, and repainted. For *cachapari*, selected groups of Indians carry the crosses to the mountaintops. On each brink, the procession halts, and the pastor blesses the cross; then the Indians gather around to kiss it before it is restored to its place.

"TUESDAY. When preparations were being made for Mass, it was discovered that the chalice had been forgotten. That meant a return to the parish house and the cancellation of a trip to Ollache until another day. It turned out that the error was providential. If the pastor had not remained in the village, he would not have received a call from a young man who reported that his father had been thrown from a horse and was in a serious condition. With his pockets full of bandages and medical supplies, the pastor set out at once.

"The injured man was a horrible sight. He had been catapulted over the horse's head and had landed, forehead down, on a rock. The frontal bone had been smashed in; there was a large, gaping wound in the forehead; the face was swollen to twice its normal size and was bathed in blood. The man had been carried to the village and had been lying for several hours where the pastor found him. No one had dared attempt to dress his wounds, and he was suffering intense pain. The pastor rushed back to the mission house for some instruments and medicine. It took over two hours to get the patient cleaned up and made comfortable.

"Hardly had the pastor finished with this man, when a call came from an elderly woman who was at death's door. Since the Blessed Sacrament was not reserved because of the pastor's intended visit to Ollache, it was necessary to celebrate Mass again, and Viaticum was given to the injured man as well as to the old lady.

"THURSDAY. The wife of the sacristan was reported sick this morning. The pastor went to see her. She was lying on the ground, in a little shack about five feet long, three feet wide, and five feet high, which the poor sacristan had taken for his home when he had been evicted from the temporary school building several weeks ago. The shack was beside the temporary school. The poor woman might have well been lying out in the road. And she had pneumonia!

"Shocked at what he saw, the pastor went immediately to the temporary school and ordered the teacher and the pupils out of one of the two rooms. Without delay, all obeyed and took their benches with them. The pastor went out in the fields and cut down some dry weeds, and carried them in to make a bed for the poor woman. The weeds were covered with sheepskins, and then the woman was carried in. The pastor had taken his medicine kit with him on this trip, and was able to do something on the spot.

"MONDAY. The pastor had received a special invitation to take breakfast this morning at the house of Doña Felicitas. It was somewhat unusual for a breakfast! There was chicken soup, with legs—claws and all—thrown in. There were a large dish of potatoes, more chicken, and several ears of the corn for which Ollache is renowned. There was coffee, too, as black as shoes. After breakfast Doña Felicitas brought out the rest of the chicken and more ears of corn. These she wrapped in newspapers for the Padre, lest he suffer from hunger on the ride back to Macusani.

"TUESDAY. Many weeks ago, the Indians had been urged to re-thatch the roof of the church. Those who had come in from a considerable distance for Mass on Sunday had brought their bundles of straw with them, and they remained in the pueblo over night. Others, who live nearer the pueblo, returned home yesterday and came in today with their bundles. The ceremony of thatching the church roof (and well it might be called a ceremony) began Monday night.

"Each village had sent in a group of four musicians. These men had reed instruments, and one of them had a small drum which he beat with a single stick incessantly. Each group circled the church and then remained in the vicinity of the church all night. It was difficult to sleep, as the music that is played for the thatching is something special. About nine o'clock this morning, work began. Each village has its own section of roof, and there is no trespassing.

"First, the old straw was rolled off, and then the new straw was laid on. For this, there were between two and three hundred men on the roof. Down on the ground there were as many more, and an equal number of women helpers. There were hundreds of onlookers, who really were relief squads.

"The whole affair was quite thoroughly organized. There were groups who made straw rope for other groups of women. These made up bundles small enough to be handled easily by the men on the roof. After tying the bundles, the women passed them on to men, who ran the bundles up to the thatchers on a rigging like a breeches buoy.

"These riggings were decorated with little flags, and some had cowbells attached. The bells added to all the clatter and chatter and helped to create a holiday atmosphere. All the workers were happy, glad to be doing something in a big way for Father's house. This thatching wasn't work: it was a privilege!"

The experiences of Father Meaney are typical of those of all missioners caring for mountain parishes. From these home stations, the missioners journeyed out to other villages, some of which had never been visited by a priest in the people's memories. Father Donald C. Cleary, of Newark, New Jersey described one such trip for the readers of the Maryknoll magazine. The experiences he recounted are worth another telling:

"The valley of Tambopata, on the eastern slope of the Andes, is along one of the routes to that vast jungle land known as the Peruvian selva. It is less than three thousand feet above sea level, and while still mountainous, boasts a hot climate and heavy vegetation. Among its many precious woods is the prized tree from which quinine is made. Less fortunately, this valley has, also, many sorts of reptiles and insects, including the malaria-bearing mosquito.

"Tambopata lies at the end of a rough trail, a two-day journey on foot or muleback from Sandia. In over five years, the place had been visited only once by a priest. I arrived in the valley, hot and weary, one day in June, to find a large part of the community prostrate with malaria.

"Every house had at least one person sick of the disease, and in some homes entire families lay ill. It was the first time in many years that the disease had become epidemic, and the Indians were full of fear. They told me that many persons had died, and that many more had fled the district, abandoning homes and crops. Some of the sick, seeking relief from the burning torment of fever, had flung themselves into the icy mountain stream that flowed through the valley, and had died of shock.

"I set up headquarters in one of the abandoned homes and gave quinine injections until my supply was exhausted. I also heard confessions and anointed the stricken who were in danger of death. It was a time of great physical suffering, but also of great grace. Over thirty Indians died, but not one of them without the last Rites of the Church, or in the case of the children, without Baptism. Couples who had been living together for years were married, and others reconciled. Many persons turned from sinful ways, and returned to God's grace.

"At last the epidemic waned, and I decided to go to another village, called Pilco, in which there might be a few isolated cases of malaria. The news of my coming preceded me, and on arrival I was welcomed and taken to the bedside of the only sick person in the village. This was a young man, about twenty-five years of age. He was tall and muscular, but showed, in sunken cheeks and glassy stare, the ravages of the disease. I did what I could for him, but there was little hope of recovery. I inquired about his spiritual condition, and explained to him the need of drawing close to his Creator.

"The sick man was unmarried, but was living with a young woman who was the mother of his two children. I begged and argued and prayed, but he remained firm in his refusal to receive the sacraments. He insisted that he was young and strong, and that he would soon get well. As it was then late in the day, I gave him a crucifix. Asking him to pray, I left for the quarters prepared for me.

"The next day, after celebrating Mass, I returned to the dying Indian's bedside and remained with him all day. I explained his condition—pleaded with him—prayed. He grew weaker and weaker, but still refused to amend his life. Conscious to the end, he refused to pray or to ask God's pardon for any offenses he had committed. Finally, he died unrepentant. As I left the house, fatigued from the long vigil and disheartened by my failure, I thought that in heaven, too, there must be mourning for the one who did not do penance."

The experience of the American missioners soon convinced them that the task of bringing the mountain people back to their Faith was a gigantic one, and it could be solved only by building up a vigorous native clergy. The policy of the mission was established with this in mind, and the first and foremost task was to be the finding and training of native vocations. A five-point plan was drawn up and put to work:

1) A *campaign among the people based on Puno's need for*

priests. Every type of publicity was used to make known this need. Posters were printed in the United States, sent to Puno, and distributed throughout the diocese. Maryknollers were assigned to travel through the region to talk in schools on the need for priests, and on seminary life and training. The people of the region were invited to visit the seminary. The first effort discovered thirty-four vocations, and proved that the vocations were there.

2) *Centralized parochial schools.* The Puno missioners were convinced that the parochial school was the key to developing vocations and building up Catholic life. Parochial schools were planned for the two language groups (Quechua and Aymara) found in Puno. In these schools vocations would be nourished; and other boys and girls would be trained so that, later on, they would form solid Christian families from which vocations might come.

3) A *good minor seminary.* Maryknollers, under the direction of the bishop of Puno, built a new minor seminary and designed a training schedule geared towards the future lives of the students as mountain priests. Emphasis was placed on the development of leadership and initiative. The seminarians would also share in the responsibility of running the summer camp that was conducted on the Pacific Ocean each summer for the poor boys of Puno.

4) A *good major seminary.* It was found that Puno would not support a major seminary but it is hoped that Maryknoll will be able to cooperate with the Archbishop of Cuzco in staffing a regional seminary in Cuzco, Peru.

5) *Field training and supervision of the newly ordained.* It had formerly been the custom to send a newly ordained National priest to an abandoned parish, where he had many problems and little financial assistance. Fresh from the seminary, lacking experience and missing companionship, he was in danger of losing the *esprit de corps* so necessary in a zealous clergy. It was part of the plan to put each newly ordained priest with an experienced priest for a period of at least two years. During this time the new priest would be trained with care in every detail of running a parish and winning souls to Christ. He would be impressed with the necessity of always having a neat appearance, and of keeping records in detail. When these priests would come to Puno City for a rest, a special house would be there to welcome them into its homelike atmosphere. This section of the plan has been applied to the first two priests ordained in 1952, and has proved most satisfactory.

This campaign to provide priests for Puno has paid dividends all along the line. In the city of Puno, itself, there are three separate operations. The first project carried on by Maryknollers is the city's only parish, San Juan. About 20,000 people take part in the life of the parish, both in Puno and on the outskirts of the town. Besides the regular religious activities of any parish, special projects are carried on at San Juan.

A weekly newspaper, *The Voice of San Juan,* is published and used in connection with the parish's literacy drive. It is estimated that two hundred people annually receive literacy training through the work of the project. The parish recently established a home economics school—a sort of high school of domestic arts offering courses in home making, dressmaking, cooking and child care. Twenty-three girls were enrolled the first year, and the number is growing. The parish operates a small dispensary to serve the very poor. The San Juan parish also takes care of some outlying Indian villages. In one of these, a model farm is in the planning stage. New fertilizers and a new type of potato seed have already been demonstrated on the parish farm in Ichu, and the parish was responsible for the building of a road into this remote village, so that trucks and jeeps could get in. The parish also has a library and ample recreational facilities. A newly constructed auditorium serves for basketball and other games; plays and dances likewise take place there.

It is difficult to assay the complete success of the San Juan work. When the first Maryknollers arrived at the Puno parish, they were unwelcomed and unwanted. There was, in fact, an attempt to drive them out, and their house was stoned. However, now they are the most respected men in Puno, and no civic activity is deemed a success unless the San Juan priests have a share in it. When the Maryknollers took over the parish, few men came to church. Now the male population of Puno forms the backbone of the parish.

The second Puno activity is the *Colegio San Ambrosio,* which has been called the "Notre Dame of Peru." The name comes from the fact that the trophy room of the school is lined with gold and silver cups, banners, and medals, won as prizes in sports programs in which San Ambrosio successfully defeated schools three and four times its own size. San Ambrosio is actually two schools: one with five primary grades, and a second with five secondary grades. Some

250 boys are being trained at San Ambrosio to become leaders of the highlands.

The third Puno project, which is the pride and joy of all the priests, is the Seminary San Ambrosio. It was established in 1944 and now occupies a new, modern, block-long building. About 180 boys have entered this minor seminary since it was first opened, and another few years will see a steady stream of its graduates taking their places in developing the Catholicity of the highland diocese. The seminary should develop the Indians into excellent leaders, since leadership depends upon training and personal qualifications, not upon race or background.

Maryknollers are now working in other sections of Peru besides the Puno mountain district. At the base of beautiful Mount Misti lies the sun-drenched city of Arequipa, known as The White City because of the volcanic rock out of which most of its buildings have been erected. Here in the second largest city of Peru, Maryknoll has its language school, where the newly assigned Maryknollers come to study the ins and outs of Spanish. On weekends the priests go out into the city and neighboring villages to say Mass for people who otherwise would be deprived of the Holy Sacrifice. The Americans have friends all over the city, and are a fine influence for good. An Arequipa parish is also staffed by Maryknoll.

From Arequipa, north over blinding and arid desert-land, the traveler comes to Lima, City of Kings and Saints, Peru's capital. Lima is one of the most beautiful of all cities in the western world, and certainly the most historic. Here, the Spanish conquistadors built their capital. Through Lima there literally passed a king's ransom in gold and precious stones. In Lima lived four great saints, a claim no other city in the western hemisphere can make. These four saints were Saint Rose of Lima, Saint Turibius, Saint Francis Solano and Blessed Martin de Porres. It is strange to many North Americans that after centuries Lima had never erected a parish named for Saint Rose of Lima. But that was the case until Father John J. Lawler, of New Bedford, Massachusetts, was transferred from his flourishing parish in Cochabamba, Bolivia, to begin a new parish named after the New World's first woman saint.

In 1951 Father Lawler was sent down to Lima; presented with a tract of land, 10,000 souls, $115.25; and told to start a new parish. The results accomplished by the diminutive, red-headed priest have caused something of a revolution in the thinking of the people of the Peruvian capital.

Father Lawler had one other asset after he arrived in Lima. That was the assistance of a truly Catholic and dynamic woman, Senorita Maria Rosario Araoz. This lady had been personally responsible for persuading ecclesiastical authorities to start the new parish. It was she who obtained the land. The $115.25 that had been turned over to Father Lawler was money she had collected. When Father Lawler was unable to find a place to live, Senorita Araoz moved out of her home, into rented rooms, and turned her house over to the priest, for use as a rectory.

Father Lawler immediately moved into the churchless parish. Mass was said on Sundays in the patio of a Japanese school. Soon the missioner added a second Mass—then a third. Packed crowds attended the Holy Sacrifice, despite the fact that the people had to stand and kneel on the cement of an open patio. After a survey of the new parish, the Maryknoller drew up plans for an entire parochial project. These plans called for: (1) church to seat 600; (2) rectory for four priests; (3) convent for 15 Sisters; (4) primary school for 700 children; (5) school auditorium to seat 350; (6) land for a secondary school when needed.

Because there was a complete lack of educational facilities in the area served by the parish, Father Lawler decided to build the parochial school first. When he proposed his plan to the Lima authorities, it was not warmly received. There were no parochial schools in Lima; and because religion is taught in public schools, the authorities believed that parish funds should not be used for a school. Father Lawler, however, is a very persuasive man. He pointed out, as reasons for a school, the fact that a parish is only as strong as the people in it, and that Catholic education is necessary to influence the whole school life. Permission was granted. Nine months later, the Cardinal Archbishop of Lima publicly stated, at the dedication of Father Lawler's school, that he hoped every new parish in his archdiocese would start with a parochial school.

After permission to begin the school was secured, Father Lawler turned to the problem of raising funds. First, he went to see the Minister of Education, to ask for a grant. The Minister was cordial, and promised $3,300 for Father Lawler's building fund.

Next, he made a survey of his parish. He learned that 55% of his people are poor; 43% are middle class; and only 2% are fairly well-to-do. He divided the parish into blocks; wrote a personal letter to each family; and had block captains deliver them. Monthly donations began coming in. Then the pastor sponsored a series of affairs. A bazaar, a concert by the National Symphony Orchestra, a dinner party at a chicken farm, and a play by the American Colony Theater Group, brought in funds.

Meanwhile, Father Lawler signed contracts for building the first section of the parochial school. Maryknoll Sisters arrived to teach in the school, which accepts both boys and girls—an innovation in Latin America. The school is self-supporting. Father Lawler then began work on the auditorium. That now serves as a temporary church, allowing the congregation to be indoors. Then he built the rectory, but turned it over to the Sisters until their convent should be ready.

Besides building Lima's first parochial school, and having the first parish named after the city's great Saint Rose, Father Lawler has a number of other firsts to his credit. His parish had the first evening Mass offered in Lima under the new Papal regulations. He is said to be the first red-headed pastor the city ever had. But his most important first came in 1953, when the parish's first candidate for the priesthood left for the seminary. Father Lawler has done a tremendous job in Lima in building this parish in large part on funds collected locally. His continued success comes from hard work, and from never missing an opportunity to help his people.

Thus the work in Peru progresses. In 1953 there were 22 Maryknoll priests busy in Peru, 3 Maryknoll Sisters, 1 Maryknoll Brother; and working with the Maryknollers, were 7 Peruvian Sisters and 29 Peruvian lay teachers. The work in Peru has given a countless number of people the chance to receive the Sacraments; has restored the Faith in areas where it was being forgotten; has trained new leaders, educating children and adults; has improved family life and raised the moral tone in areas where the priests work; has provided charitable assistance that has kept people alive and held families together. All of these things, like all the work of Maryknoll, have been made possible by generous-hearted Americans who give literal interpretation to Christ's command to help all men.

23

Chile—A World in Miniature

Chile is a small representation of the whole Western world. The country is approximately as long as the United States is wide, and about as wide as Long Island is long. In the north is a burning tropical desert, rich in nitrates and copper, boasting areas where rainfall has never been recorded. Moving south, the traveler comes to the rich central valley with its farms and vineyards where live most of the people of the country. Next is the lake district, a region of wild fjords and beautiful forests that annually harvest bumper crops of tourists, timber, and wool. Finally, the traveler reaches the mist-shrouded land of Tierra del Fuego extending into the region of the polar ice cap. Thus in the length of Chile every sort of climate is encountered.

But travel in Chile is not only horizontal. To leave the country landwise one must go up and down. Along the eastern boundary runs a natural barrier—the wall of rock and ice known as the Andes. In Chile the traveler finds the highest spot in the Western Hemisphere, the snow-shrouded peak of Aconcagua. From almost any part of the country one can get a view of the Andes.

In other ways, Chile is like a small representation of the world.

Although the country has Indians in its population, these people of the Araucanian tribe are a definite minority, and are confined to the southern lake region below Temuco. Chile's population is largely made up of European stock: Irish, English, Italian, Spanish, and German predominating. The nation is one of the most advanced countries in Latin America, and is a leader in the field of progressive social legislation. Many social laws were enacted in Chile, long before the United States put similar laws into effect.

The first Maryknollers for Chile were assigned in 1942. As in other parts of Latin America, they found the main religious problem to be a lack of priestly vocations. The cause for the scarcity of priests was in part the economy of the country, which kept a large mass of the people landless and poor, and in part the lack of Christian family life. Only a third of Chilean marriages were witnessed by a priest, and it is impossible to expect vocations to flourish from such unions. The Maryknollers quickly came to the conclusion that their task in Chile was to strengthen family life, and that their main effort should be devoted to establishing parish schools.

The work of Father Vincent M. Cowan, of Oakland, California, gives a good example of what has been done in this regard. Father Cowan was assigned to the parish of Portezuelo, which covers an area almost the size of the State of Rhode Island, and which is inhabited by about twelve thousand people who make their living by farming. With no money, or teachers, and with only confidence in God, Father Cowan decided to open three schools in different sections of his parish.

In Portezuelo he began a school next to the church; and by writing letters to many parts of the world he found some Teaching Sisters of Saint Francis who would come and staff the school. Some of these Sisters were from Pittsburgh; others were refugees from Czechoslovakia. The school began with three grades, and then added one each year. The effects of the school were almost immediately felt. Attendance at Sunday Mass improved, and people began taking an active part in parish life. During the first year the Sisters were in Portezuelo, three girls from the parish entered the convent, and today they are professed Sisters. In 1950, the parish's first candidate for the priesthood went to the seminary. The following year, a parish boy joined the Jesuits.

The second school was built in the center of a long-abandoned part of the parish, seldom visited by any priest. A hundred chil-

dren appeared for the first enrollment. The third school was built
in another neglected section of the parish. Over 130 boys and girls
entered during the first week. Although he had planned only three
schools, Father Cowan soon had requests from other parts of his
parish to put up schools. He was offered land and some building
supplies. He tried to refuse because of lack of money, but finally
yielded and opened two more schools.

Father Francis A. McKay, of San Francisco, was assigned to help
out in the Portezuelo parish when Father Cowan was away on vacation. In 1954, Father McKay wrote an article for the Maryknoll
magazine, in which he described a visit to one of these country
schools that his fellow-Californian had begun. The article gives a
good insight into the way Father Cowan attracted helpers of high
quality, and also into what is being done in this once-neglected
part of Chile. Father McKay wrote:

"This widely scattered parish has five schools, mostly hidden in
the mountains. The school we were going to visit is in an area
called Contero. If you have no objection to riding a jeep for two
hours over bumpy roads that keep the vehicle at all sorts of weird
angles, and if you don't mind riding a horse for another hour, over
mountains and through rivers, then you are disposed for a visit to
Contero.

"When you get to your destination, you will find little there. A
few houses, and a school that still needs windows, doors, and floor.
You may be disappointed after the rugged trip, but don't go away
until you have visited inside the school.

"There are seventy-five youngsters in that school, most of them
poorly clothed. They sit at makeshift desks, listening in silence to
the young, energetic teacher. She is the type of young woman
found on our college campuses in the United States. You wonder
what led her into the mountains, away from family and friends,
away from small comforts she had been used to and which she still
could have. You realize, as you watch, that the words, 'sacrifice for
others for the love of God,' have practical meaning.

"The Contero school is only one of five such undertakings in a
single parish in Chile. The young teacher there is only one of
several young women who have made big sacrifices for the love of
God. With such dedication, Maryknoll's work in Chile cannot but
succeed.

"The co-operation of these 'angels of the mountains' is very definitely an answer to a tremendous problem in our efforts to do successful mission work in Chile. We missioners came here because this wonderful Catholic country lacks priests to minister to the spiritual and educational needs of the people. These 'angels of the mountains' have proved that the Catholic laity of Chile want to help us to solve the problem. By their actions, they have proved that they are not only willing to look to us for leadership, but also willing to serve when and where they can.

"When we finally left the little hamlet of Contero, I carried away with me a very valuable lesson. It took a young schoolteacher and seventy-five youngsters to teach me that windows and doors are of little importance to a real school. The teacher had not left her home to teach in a streamlined palace of brick and wood. She could have stayed in Santiago or one of the other big cities, if that had been all she desired. Instead, in primitive surroundings, the 'angel of the mountains' was giving these youngsters the very thing for which I dedicated my own life; namely a knowledge and love of God."

Father Cowan's energies, directed at building up a strong Catholic family life from which would come vocations, were not confined solely to his schools. He also formed the men of his parish into a Catholic Action group that would devote each Thursday as a day of prayer for vocations. The idea was enthusiastically adopted. The men come to church for early Mass and Communion before going to work on Thursday. They dedicate their labor of the day to the parish intention. All day the Blessed Sacrament is exposed, and children and women gather in groups to pray for vocations. In the evening the men return for Rosary, a short sermon, and Benediction. Before Father Cowan's arrival in Portezuelo, no one could remember any case of a boy or girl going off to study for the religious life. Four years after the missioner had opened his schools and begun his campaign for vocations, twelve youngsters had gone away to become priests, Sisters, or Brothers.

The pattern adopted by Father Cowan is the same one used in varying ways by other missioners. In Chillan, Father Frederick P. Walker, of Boston, began a parochial school and brought in Maryknoll Sisters to teach. He also offered vocational training in sewing and carpentry, and established an adult-education and literacy program. In Renaico, Father Francis J. Mulligan, of Jersey City, conducts a school with 650 pupils enrolled. In Cholchol, Father P.

Martin Dunne, of New York City, has a school and also offers
training in home economics and manual arts. Father Joseph C.
Cappel, of Norwood, Ohio, has two schools in his Curepto parish
—one in the country, and one in town. In Panquehue, Father
Stephen P. Foody, of New York City, has a primary school, teaches
in six public schools, has a night school, conducts a literacy program, and provides vocational training. In Talca, Father Jerome P.
Garvey, of San Francisco, has a parish school, and is ready to start
an adult-education and literacy program and also courses in mechanics and carpentry. Father Thomas F. McDermott, of Worcester, Massachusetts, built a model primary school in Galverino,
and brought in Maryknoll Sisters to staff it.

Thus throughout a number of dioceses in central Chile, Maryknollers have begun schools so that youngsters can be taught
the fundamentals of their Faith. The Americans look to the next
generation, when these boys and girls of today will be adults who
will build up the parish spirit and a truly Catholic family life. From
this new generation will come the priests, Brothers, and Sisters so
badly needed in Chile.

One of the most interesting of the Maryknoll parishes in Chile
is in a slum section of Santiago, known as Buzeta. About twelve
thousand people live in this parish, but when the Maryknollers first
went there in 1943, only a handful of parishioners attended church.
The people were uninstructed, and most were so poor that they
were ashamed to be seen in church with the rags that they had to
wear for clothing. The average family income was about $350 a
year, when work was available in a nearby tannery and slaughter-
house. Conditions called for a complete plan of Catholic social
action, and the Maryknollers fell to with a will.

Today the pastor of Buzeta—Father Richard J. Smith, of Collins, New York—reports a vigorous parish life that has raised the
moral standards of the whole area. Almost five hundred children
are enrolled in the parish school. A goodly number of adults take
English classes in the parish night school, in the hopes of getting
better jobs. The parish dispensary is busy, and the Government has
accepted the use of one of the parish buildings to operate a clinic
for mothers. A home-economics course teaches first-aid and nursing, in addition to the usual subjects. A summer camp takes the
poor children away from the slums for a vacation at the beach.
Three parish sports clubs provide wholesome recreation. About

thirty very poor families receive food and other weekly aid from the project, and about 400 children each year are supplied with clothes and shoes.

One of the main successes of the Santiago parish has been its Credit Union which has a membership of about three hundred. The Credit Union has awakened the poor to the realization that by uniting their efforts they can help themselves economically. The Credit Union is now planning a housing project for the area.

The work of the Maryknollers in Chile attracted much favorable comment. During a visit to Washington, the dynamic Bishop of Talca, Most Reverend Manuel Larrain, gave high praise to the American priests working in his country. Bishop Larrain, one of Latin America's most progressive ecclesiastical leaders, referred to the Maryknollers in an interview, saying: "Their apostolate is inspired by a sincere comprehension of our problems and constitutes one of the best foundations for fraternal relations between our people and those of the United States." *El Diario Illustrado*, one of Santiago's leading papers, described the Maryknollers as "young, ardent soldiers of Christ who daily visit the sick, the aged, the children . . . always full of the good humor that is characteristic of them . . . No obstacle or complication deters these men of God."

Much of this praise was caused by two special works carried on in Chile—a Boystown in Talca, and an agricultural school in Molina—which received wide publicity and thus became better known than the parish work. Both of these operations have great influence.

Molina is a placid little town lying in the heart of Chile's most productive farming district. Just north of the school directed by Maryknollers is the famous Casa Blanca winery, the largest vineyard in Chile, and also the largest family owned vineyard in the world. Directly opposite the school is Chile's largest apple orchard, which sends tons of apples to the United States every winter. But even more important are the many *fundos*, or large farming estates, found in the region.

Set in California-like scenery and climate, separated from each other by stately rows of poplar and eucalyptus trees, and ranging up to three thousand acres in size, the *fundos* produce grapes, miscellaneous fruits, wheat, corn, sunflowers (to be pressed for oil); in fact, crops of every type. These tremedous farms are the backbone of the Chilean agricultural economy. They are the source of livelihood for hundreds of thousands of people, who live and work on the *fundos* in conditions much like those of the European serfs. It was to help these workers that Maryknoll undertook the direction of an agricultural-industrial school in Molina. The school was opened in 1947, under the direction of Father James F. McNiff, of Peabody, Massachusetts.

Previously there had been little opportunity for children of poor, rural families, to get a Catholic education. Moreover the missioners believed that, if farming boys could be given a strong technical and moral training, they would be a Christian leaven in their communities upon returning home, would be able to gain a better living, and would gradually raise farm productivity and effectiveness. A large number of *fundo* operators were enthusiastic over the plan. For, while Chile has some reactionary landowners who would keep their workers as poorly paid and housed as possible, most of the plantation and vineyard operators realize that it is to their own advantage to better their workers' lot. But the problem of how to effect the betterment is not a simple or easy one.

"Our people lack a spirit of work," a Chilean *fundo* owner, who is also a member of the Chamber of Deputies, wrote to Father William J. Coleman, of Shelby, Ohio, present director of the school. "It is your task to instill this spirit in those whom you train."

Don Jorge Sanchez, a neighboring *fundo* owner who has supported the Molina school generously, complains that too many workers do not care to think. He illustrates this by telling of an employee who was taught to drive a tractor. Each morning the man would take the tractor to some distant part of the farm. Often after working for a few minutes the tractor would run out of gasoline. Then hours would be lost while the driver would hike back to the farmhouse to get more. It never occurred to the driver to check the gas before starting out.

Another progressive *fundo* owner near Molina decided to tear down the dark, dirt-floored huts in which his workers lived together with their pigs and chickens. He moved the families into tents, and razed the huts. Then he built airy houses, provided with windows and wooden floors. The workers were moved into the new homes and were forbidden to take their animals in with them. The *fundo* owner went off to his central house in Santiago. It was some months before he returned to his Molina *fundo*. Then he was horrified at what he saw. The families had brought their pigs and chickens into the new houses. They had ripped up the wooden floors for firewood. Some families had even made adobe blocks to close up the windows. The owner threw up his hands in despair and decided to make no further efforts to raise living standards of his workers.

Such were some of the problems the new agricultural school had to face. The working families had to be persuaded to send their sons to the school. And *fundo* operators had to be persuaded to help support the boys who came from such great distances that they were obliged to live at the school. To begin to solve the problems, Father McNiff took to the road. His dust-stained cassock soon became a familiar sight. Gradually the number of students was built up. Professors and other teachers were found and hired. Then Father McNiff began a task that took up most of his time—the task of raising funds to keep the project going. Father traveled through much of Chile, asking for help; and he importuned friends in his homeland.

Today the school is crowded to capacity, with 118 boarding students and 55 day students. There are another 60 youngsters in the first and second years of primary grades, which are conducted as an embryonic parochial school, because the school chapel serves as parish church for the area. Besides three Maryknoll priests and one Brother, the school staff includes these Chilean laymen: two professors, two teachers for carpentry and mechanics, and two prefects. In addition, the head of the national agricultural school at Romeral serves as a part-time professor. There are also two young women teachers in the primary parochial school adjoining.

Besides attending to their duties at the school, the priests take care of the local parish and a number of outstations. Father Walter J. Sandman, of San Francisco, says Mass each Sunday for the Casa Blanca workers. Father Coleman goes by jeep to Pichingal, where a new chapel is in the planning state; and then on to Buena Paz, where a beautiful little chapel, built by Father Foody, nestles at the foot of the towering Andean cordillera. These outstations take care of farming people, and from each are drawn many boys for the agricultural school.

The plan of studies at the school is very practical. Subjects taught include general agriculture, stock raising, gardening, arboriculture of fruit trees, beekeeping, carpentry, metal working, mechanical and electrical agriculture, farm bookkeeping and so on.

The school's animal life began with twenty-five chickens; today there are over a thousand. The students have, also, bees, rabbits, and cattle to practice with. Because of the smallness of the land, the cattle are kept on the farm of a neighbor. At this writing, Don Jorge Sanchez, of the Fundo of Saint Anthony the Worker (most of these large farms are dedicated to some particular saint), is searching central Chile to find six good milking cows. These cattle will be used in teaching, and will also provide more milk for the students.

Don Jorge serves on the board of directors of our school, and he has come to its assistance on many occasions. Two years ago he persuaded his uncle to donate 44 beds to the dormitory. Last year he represented the school in Santiago and was able to get a Government subsidy for it.

One of the big needs of the school is more land. Right now every square foot of the acreage belonging to the school is being used. A recent purchase of neighboring land has relieved some pressure, but the Fathers have many plans for expansion. The school has a large garden area, which serves as practice fields for the students, as well as a provider of food. There are orchards containing many different kinds of fruit trees. And, of course, the ever-present grapevines are found, for this area of Chile is largely dependent on the grape for its livelihood.

Finally, the school has shops for carpentry, metalwork, and other projects. The metal shop possesses a large forge, and the boys are taught how to make farm repairs, build buckets, and perform other acts useful in their later life. The carpenter shop has turned out some excellent work for many of the Maryknoll parishes in Chile, and thus is able to be partly self sufficient. The students, under the direction of an expert carpenter, have produced altars, kneeling benches, schoolroom furniture, and Christmas toys. Their work is skillful and beautiful. Unfortunately, the carpenter shop suffered a serious loss lately, when a thief broke in and stole many of the best tools.

The same thief made off with nine pairs of football shoes. It was the night before the football game with the school's big rival, the Romeral school. Romeral won the game by a score of 3-2, but the Molina boys were seriously handicapped by being forced to play shoe-less. Chilean football is actually soccer.

Father Coleman has many plans for developing the school even further. Recently he traded his own jeep to get a tractor for the school. The enterprise and devotion are there. It's only a little thing like money that is holding the project back.

A few years ago a Chilean priest was walking down one of the streets of Talca, not too far from Molina. As he rounded a corner he collided with a laborer, who glared at the priest, and then without warning spit in the cleric's face.

"Dirty, money-grabbing priest!" the man shouted. "You should be in a cage!"

Today that workingman is one of the strongest supporters of the Church. The change that came over him was due to the activity of two men: the energetic head of the Talca diocese, Bishop Larrain, and Father James Manning, of Richmond Hill, New York. It was Bishop Larrain who recognized conditions in his diocese and realized that the Communists were making strong inroads among the working class. He decided to do something about it, and asked Maryknoll to assist him. In 1944, Father Manning arrived.

Bishop Larrain placed Father Manning in charge of a social work aimed at helping Talca's poorer classes, who for years had been victims of social injustice. The beginnings were very humble. A house was found in the poor district and opened as the Institute of Leo XIII. A clinic, a carpenter shop, and a night school were set up. The school offered instruction in mechanics, electricity, radio, mathematics, Spanish, and religion. Father Manning walked about the streets, stopping on corners to chat with workmen and invite them to the Institute. Gradually, the men began coming to the Institute, and before long the program was in full swing. The little house was soon so crowded that larger quarters were needed, and Bishop Larrain turned over an abandoned monastery to the Institute. This was a large, sprawling building with plenty of space. Additional classes were begun, for the wives of the workers and then for their children. A recreational program was started offering sports, games, motion pictures, and dances. Before long the workers' attitude towards the Church was entirely changed.

Father Dominic J. Morrissette, of Winslow, Maine, who assisted Father Manning during this early period, reported: "Ninety-five per cent of our students were Communists or Communist sympathizers when they came to us. But so far, all who completed courses have become good Catholics. They learned that the Church is really interested in them, and one result of this knowledge is that the class bitterness and hatred arising from ignorance are eliminated."

One cold night Father Manning found a boy huddled in his doorway. He took the shivering lad into his house, because only a few days earlier he had heard that two young and homeless bootblacks had died of exposure. Without knowing it, Father Manning that night started a new work—*Los Hombres del Mañana.* The Men of Tomorrow. From that humble beginning, his Boystown grew to today's sixty-five citizens. The boys are given a home at the Institute, and go to school outside.

"We try to make this place like a real home," Father Manning says, "not like an institution. Some of the boys here have been sent to us by the police and the courts, but this is not a reform school. All we are trying to do is provide a Christian atmosphere in which youngsters can grow up normally."

Another Talca project operated by Father Manning is that of the camps conducted each summer at the seashore. Two camps are run, one for boys and one for girls. Besides the citizens of Boystown, some 250 of Talca's poor children are taken out of the slums for a month's vacation. In addition to the vacation, each youngster gets new clothes.

"There used to be a lot of bickering between organizations here in Talca," Father Manning reports, "but it seems that they all have a common interest in children. Our Boystown has awakened the people to the problem of poor and abandoned children. It has also joined people of all classes and faiths to work for a common cause. People respect the Church because they see that we not only preach, but try to practice our beliefs."

Thus goes the work in Chile. Father Arthur F. Allie, of Two Rivers, Wisconsin, is the present Maryknoll Superior in Chile. He has 31 Maryknoll priests working under him, plus 3 Maryknoll Brothers, 14 Maryknoll Sisters, and 25 other Sisters. Maryknoll's 16 parishes have 15 boys in Chilean seminaries. The Maryknollers operate 16 schools, employ 31 teachers and 36 catechists, operate 7 dispensaries, and administer to a Catholic population of 112,000 souls.

Although these statistics may look good, there is still a tremendous amount of work to be done in Chile. Four out of five Catholics are still without proper religious care. Seven out of nine children get no religious instruction. Father Thomas S. Walsh, Vicar General of Maryknoll, who pioneered work in Temuco, Maryknoll's southernmost parish in Chile, paints a picture that is far from bright and points out the need for increased Catholic activity, if other groups are not to win Chile. He writes:

"In view of the high level of distinction that the Chilean people have achieved in so many fields, one naturally looks to the Church and asks whether it has kept pace with the intellectual and industrial advance the country has made. Though one is impressed with what the Church is and with what the Church has accomplished in Chile, one is more impressed with what the Church might accomplish. Great opportunities are opening up to the Church in Chile, and the problem is to devise ways and means of making the best use of them.

"Fortunately, God has favored the Church in Chile with a hierarchy that is apostolic, zealous, and forward-looking. The hierarchy has developed one of the best Catholic Action organizations in Latin America. Catholic Action has done much to itensify Catholic life, to instruct the ignorant, and to bring the lukewarm back to the regular practice of their Faith. But the great handicap of the Church in Chile, as in practically all countries of Latin America, is the lack of priests. Although the bishops are able and apostolic, and have the auxiliary arm of a zealous Catholic Action, they are unable to provide adequately for the ordinary needs of their people. They simply do not have enough priests to make it possible for their people to assist at Mass regularly and to receive the sacraments. Much less are the bishops in a position to supply the priests needed to enable the Church to go ahead and make progress.

"Meanwhile, two very powerful forces are at work against the Church, and those forces are expending enormous resources in an effort to fill the vacuum left by the Church. Those forces are communism and Protestantism. For over twenty years the Communists, with unlimited economic resources at their command, have labored with vast energy. But the Communists have not been alone in recognizing the decisive and strategic position that Chile occupies in South America: the Protestants, too, have been quick to see that, if they establish themselves in Chile, they will be able to build themselves into a force of real weight and influence for all of the Latin-American republics.

"Consequently, the Protestants are working mightily in Chile. In Temuco alone, a city of only 50,000 people, there are sixty-seven Protestant missionaries from the United States, and there are hundreds more up and down the country. And though the Protestants have achieved a less spectacular success than have the Communists, it would be foolish to deceive ourselves with the idea that they are accomplishing nothing. They are quite definitely going ahead. It is highly probable that, in another ten or fifteen years, they will be a force of very great influence in this country.

"Not until the Chilean hierarchy has a much larger number of priests at its command, will it be in a position either to combat effectively the forces that are working against the Church, or to make use of the many exciting opportunities that are opening up. In the long run, the Church in Chile will have to recruit its clergy from within the country; but meanwhile—the Church must look to other countries for help. Today no country is in a better position to lend a helping hand to the Church in Chile than is the United States."

24

Guatemala—The Sun Shines Bright

Maria Vicente was twelve years old when she died—a pretty, black-haired, smiling child. Her death made little difference to the world. Twelve-year-old children die every day. The sad part of Maria's story is that she need not have died if her father had had but ten dollars.

A death in Maria's family started the chain of events. Vicente, her father, had to borrow ten dollars to pay for the funeral. To repay this debt, Vicente had to leave his home in the Cuchumatanes Mountains of Guatemala, and go down to the coastal lowlands, to work in a banana finca. Maria went along to cook her father's tortillas. Seventy-five percent of the mountain people who go to the coast return home with either malaria or tuberculosis. Maria was no exception—she brought home both diseases. For a little while, the mountain air seemed to help her. Then her liver became infected, and she died.

Maria's story is the story of thousands of Indians of Guatemala. It is a story that few non-Indians know, and even fewer care about. But there is one man who heard Maria's story and resolved that it should not be repeated. He is Father Edmund McClear, an energetic, athletic missioner from Royal Oak, Michigan.

Some time ago, as part of its educational motion-picture program, Maryknoll decided to tell the story of the work Father McClear has performed in the mountains of Guatemala. At first it was planned to build the film around the death of Maria Vicente, but that idea was soon dropped because her passing only began Father McClear's story. The producers did, however, cling to the idea of telling events through the eyes of a native, and that is how the motion-picture, *The Story of Juan Mateo*, came into being. Millions of Americans have seen the film on television, here in the United States.

The world of Juan Mateo lies deep inside the Cuchumatanes Mountains. It can be reached only by horseback or foot, over precipitous trails that consume long hours. It is far off the Guatemalan tourist circuit, and therefore its inhabitants are unspoiled, living in the ancient manner of their ancestors. The locale of the story is a backward, dirty little town, set 8,000 feet up in the Cuchumatanes, and named Soloma, which means "The Tree by the Lagoon." The tree and the lagoon have long since disappeared, along with any glory that Soloma might have had. The original parish church collapsed during an earthquake about a century ago, burying hundreds of Indians in its ruins. The successor to that church was ready to collapse, too, and Father McClear was busy making repairs on it when we arrived.

Father McClear's territory contained 40,000 people, a typical Guatemalan parish. It included four towns (San Juan, San Mateo, Santa Eulalia, and Barrillos), each having seven to twelve *aldeas*, or Indian villages. With the exception of a few ladinos (people of mixed blood), the inhabitants are pure Indians. It is impossible to visit villages in the area without climbing or descending mountains. Because of the altitude, physical exertion is very tiring. Despite this, Father McClear had to make eight-and-nine-hour sick calls on horseback.

The mission center at Huehuetenango (pronounced Waywaytenango) is the gateway to Soloma and the Indian world of the Cuchumatanes. The traveler leaves Huehuetenango in the morning and, by car or bus, climbs up to the 12,000-foot pass that opens into the mountains. There the road ends, and one must take to horse or foot. The next hours are spent in vertical travel through a wilderness. Finally the traveler emerges on the top of a moutain and sees, almost a mile straight below, a broad valley.

The inexperienced horseman will prefer to make this descent by foot. At the bottom he remounts, and then rides through the town of San Juan Ixcoy, where occurred one of the last, big Indian uprisings, during which every non-Indian but one was put to death.

The traveler rides the length of the valley; climbs another mountain; and drops down into a second valley, in the center of which is Soloma. Our first view of Soloma was at dusk, through a heavy curtain of mist. There is seldom a day on which clouds do not cover the town. They begin to descend about three in the afternoon, and do not lift until nine or ten o'clock the next morning. Because of its altitude, the town is cold when there is no sunshine. Although we were in the tropics, we found ice in the fountain in the morning.

After a survey of Soloma and its surrounding *aldeas*, and a talk with Father McClear, we decided to tell our story through the eyes of a twelve-year-old Indian boy. A script was outlined, based on Father McClear's experiences and work and on the lives of the picturesque mountain people. Next, we began to look for the characters in the picture. We found Juan Mateo without difficulty. Or perhaps it might be better to say that he found us.

We walked out of the mission one morning and saw a number of boys playing a game on several gigantic beams that the Indians had brought in for reparing the church. Each of the boys had a piece of pine resin. One boy would slap a piece down on the beam, and then the others would take turns throwing their own pieces at the first one. If a boy hit the first piece and made his own stick to it, then the original thrower was retired. The boy who captured all the bits of resin won the game. One player—dressed in the traditional loose, brown, slip-over jacket—immediately attracted our attention. He had a big, infectious grin, was very boyish in his actions, and made quick, intelligent movements.

"Who is he?" I asked Father McClear.

"Juan Mateo," answered the missioner. "He lives on the other side of the mountains. He wants to be a priest, but I'm having a little trouble with his father."

We talked to the boy and asked about his family, and so on. Then we selected him on the spot for the lead in the film. Later we met his father, mother, and two sisters. Without any hesitation, we decided to use the whole family and tell as much of its story as possible.

Juan Mateo is a descendant of the early Mayan Indians. He belongs to the Mam tribe. Many centuries before the coming of the white man to the Western Hemisphere, Juan's ancestors moved south from Mexico, looking for new land in which to plant corn. They would settle for awhile, and when that area was worked out, they would move on. Corn was the center of the Mayan economy, just as it is the life of the mountain people today. Wherever the Mayas settled, they built great monuments and cities in honor of the gods they worshiped. The area around Soloma is a treasure house of unexcavated ruins. Father McClear has always had the hope of unearthing and restoring some of the sites, but the pressure of daily work does not leave the necessary time.

The script for the film wrote itself. Our part was simply to tell what happened in the village and to Juan Mateo's own family. Through the eyes of the boy, the viewer of the film sees the arrival of the missioner, his reception by the people, the hostility of Juan Mateo's father, and the work of the missioner in his attempt to win the good will of the mountain Indians in order to help them.

The people of Soloma are poor. The average family gets about $56 in cash income a year, and this sum is for the work of father, mother, and children combined. The people live largely on a diet of tortillas, eggs, and the twenty-seven kinds of herbs they gather on the mountain slopes. They eat meat about once a week. They grow corn for their tortillas, and they keep a few chickens and pigs. The better-off among the Indians have sheep; an occasional farmer owns a mule or horse, which he uses to carry supplies for a daily wage of about forty cents.

The health of the Indians, as long as they remain in the mountains, is fairly good. They suffer from minor complaints, particularly from bad teeth. The most dreaded disease for adults is pneumonia; for children, the most common is worms. There is considerable eye trouble in the area. There are a number of serious accidents, caused by using the machete. Widespread and constant are malaria and tuberculosis, brought back by workers from the coast.

Father McClear's work in the highlands of the Soloma region was twofold: spiritual and physical. He was meeting with considerable success, largely because of hard work. His day began at six in the morning and ended at ten at night. During that time he and his three, full-time catechists were kept busy. The catechist Mateo, and his son, Andres, went to the various villages to prepare the adults for the Sacrament of Matrimony, which had been neglected during long years, and the children for their First Communion. The missioner built on the principle of the family. A two-week course in doctrine was given a man and woman before they were married. The catechists lived right in the *aldea* during this time. Usually a number of couples were under instruction at once. They were married in a joint ceremony. Brides and grooms were given little mementos to wear: the grooms received Holy Year pins, on each of which was engraved a picture of the Holy Father; the brides were given buttons commemorating the Guatemala Eucharistic Congress. Father McClear had picked up surplus supplies of these pins and buttons in Guatemala City. His parishioners were very proud of them, and the wearers created a new social class in Soloma.

Baptisms also kept the Padre busy. He averaged about three thousand baptisms a year. On some *fiestas* he recorded as many as four hundred baptisms in a single day. Sick calls were always breaking up his schedule. When a mountain Indian dies, the survivors want the blessings of the Church, and the tolling of the church bells as the funeral party proceeds to the cemetery. Shortly after his arrival, Father McClear announced that the bells would not be tolled for the deceased unless the priest had been notified as soon as the person became ill. Now even a headache will bring a summons for the priest. This exaggerated concern caused many false alarms, and added many extra hours in the saddle. But Father McClear believed that reaching the many people who would otherwise die without a priest was well worth the instances of wasted effort.

In the field of social charity Father McClear devoted considerable time. He had a clinic that was open every day. He treated all sorts of sundry ills, and conducted a dental business that could be the envy of many an American dentist. For the price of two eggs (which help pay for the novocain), Father McClear would pull a troublesome tooth. During the first year of his dental clinic, he kept track of the number of teeth pulled, by putting the extractions in a large jar. At the end of that year, he had more than seven hundred teeth. After that he merely pulled the teeth without keeping count.

One of the most memorable things that this writer saw in Soloma was the group of people, all of whom were once blind, who now go about their tasks, with their sight restored. In his first days there, Father McClear had found a large number of Indians suffering from a virulent form of cataracts. The sufferers were blind and useless. The priest discussed the situation with a world-famous specialist in Guatemala City, and the doctor told him how to make a simple test that would show whether an operation might restore the sight. The doctor offered to operate, free of charge, on any Indian Father McClear would send to him. With the help of some friends in Guatemala City, a little house was rented. There the missioner sent his sick and blind. One by one, they received treatment; and one by one, they returned home, cured.

Another type of long-range work was equally impressive. Father McClear opened an industrial school to train the mountain women, and help them to earn some cash for emergencies such as the one that cost Maria Vicente's life. He bought wool from the Indians; paid other Indians to clean and spin it; and then, at the school, had it woven into beautiful rugs. Each rug contains three thousand hand knots per square foot. The nap is about an inch in length. The rugs will last a lifetime. Many were sold to the tourist trade in Guatemala. The missioner also started the women weaving place mats and coasters out of straw braid. Recently the school received an order from the Marshall Field store in Chicago, for some of those items. In the realm of agriculture, Father McClear introduced a new wheat and a better fertilizer. He operated an experimental farm that set an example for the Indian men.

All of these things entered into the story of Juan Mateo. But there was another element, an intangible that had to be told. The Indians have a fierce pride in their ancestry. Except for the small minority who desert the Indian way of life, the native people look down on the whites and object to their presence. It is true that the Indians have experienced many injustices at the hands of whites. They have been pushed off their land, forced into servitude, denied any rights, and taken advantage of, time and time again. It is a rare white or ladino who ventures to travel the region unarmed. Having journeyed through the area with non-Indians, and having seen the hostile glances and gestures, I understand why the whites distrust the Indians. But the whites fail to realize that the fault lies not with the Indians, but with themselves.

The only exception to this hostility is the missioner. Once an Indian catches sight of the clerical collar, his scowl becomes a smile. Father McClear, while traveling, wore a red-checked shirt with his clerical collar showing inside it. The Indians sighted that red shirt miles away, and ran down from steep corn fields or hillside pastures, to greet their Padre and have their heads touched in blessing.

Juan Mateo tells the situation clearly in the film, when he says: "Those who love the Indians are loved by him in return. Those who despise the Indian are likewise despised." This is the underlying theme of the film. It is a conflict that is solved only after Juan Mateo's father sends the boy off to the City of the Dead, as a punishment for having associated with the white missioner.

The City of the Dead is really Zaculeu, whose celebrated Mam pyramids and temples have been restored. It was at Zaculeu that the Indians fought their last great battle against the invading conquistadors, and it was there that their native civilization perished. Today Zaculeu stands as a reminder to the Indians of the glory that was once their own. Yet at Zaculeu Juan Mateo learns that greatness is not merely in the refinement of knowledge and skill. He realizes that, while his ancestors knew the sciences of astronomy and mathematics, and also were able to design and erect tremendous buildings, they had moral shortcomings. Zaculeu was built by slave labor; and in the very temple that nearly costs the boy his own life, human sacrifices had been offered.

"My ancestors were great," Juan Mateo concludes, "but they lacked the love and kindness that Padre Edmundo teaches."

Thus Juan Mateo and Raymundo, his father, learn that a man can be proud of his people's past without excusing its faults or wishing to be back in it.

Because the film was to be shown in schools throughout the United States, it was decided that, for educational purposes, a glimpse of the story of Guatemala should be given. Guatemala is not only the Indian highlands. It is the big centers like Guatemala City, where life has all the pleasant conveniences of our modern world. It is the Atlantic and Pacific coastal regions.

Guatemala is also Antigua, once the capital for all of Central America. Antigua—of which the original name was "Very Noble and Very Loyal City of Saint James of the Knights of Goathemala"—prospered and became famous long before the founding of the first English colonies in the new world. Antigua was the center of the great religious orders, whose members went into all parts of Central America to teach the Indians about Christ. At the height of its development, in 1773, Antigua had fifty-seven churches, eighteen convents, a university, eight colleges, five hospitals, and an orphan asylum.

But Antigua also had two evil genii. They are called "Water" and "Fire"—two towering volcanoes that hang over the city. In 1541, earthquakes cracked the sides of the volcano called Water, and a tremendous lake in the cone of the mountain was released, completely wiping out Antigua. In 1773, the volcano called Fire began acting up and, together with a series of earthquakes, destroyed the second Antigua. The capital was then moved to the newly founded Guatemala City, and Antigua was left in ruins—the most impressive monument of colonial grandeur that exists in the New World.

All these places play a part in the film. And through the magic eye of the camera, we visit each.

The actual making of the film was a lark for Juan Mateo, his family, and his friends. They were merely re-creating their everyday lives. Of course, there were certain compensations. Juan Mateo and his father had their first ride in an automobile, when we took them down to Zaculeu. They had an even bigger thrill when they went to Guatemala City, via their first airplane ride. To these simple Indians, who were used to trudging long hours, and even days, to visit friends or to make a pilgrimage to some shrine, the magic of the white man's transportation was almost unbelievable.

It was decided to put an optimistic ending in the picture, even though in real life Juan Mateo's father refused to let him go to Guatemala City to study for the priesthood. The film ends with Juan Mateo entering the Indian school in the capital, to prepare to become a leader of his people. Since we returned home, word has come that Juan Mateo's father has changed his mind, and Juan Mateo will soon be studying in the seminary in Guatemala City.

The Soloma area, where the film was made, was once a center for pagan spirit worship, and has received much attention from anthropologists. The near-by town of Santa Eulalia was given over to idolatry, and the celebrated author, Oliver LaFarge, once lived there investigating pagan practices. It is a tribute to Father McClear that the town is today a flourishing Catholic center. Mass is now said there every Sunday by Father Daniel J. McLeod, of Quincy, Massachusetts. Father McClear described one of his first visits to Santa Eulalia in this manner:

"The cave near the pueblo of Santa Eulalia in Guatemala, is taboo to strangers, and all kinds of weird tales are told about what happens to those who enter without knowing the proper password. 'Tis said in these parts that one woman who entered the cave several years ago lost her mind completely upon leaving. Others say that flashlight batteries mysteriously fail within the slippery, dirty passages.

"This cave was once the home of Jolom Conop, an idol worshiped by an Indian religious cult. Oliver LaFarge has written about both the cave and the cult, in his celebrated book on the Indians of Santa Eulalia. I made up my mind that I would investigate the taboos of the cave.

"I engaged two local men as guides. One was Juarez Diego, a sly old fox mentioned by LaFarge. The other, a younger man, was more pliable. At the edge of the ravine near the cave, Juarez, fearing possible sanctions from the tribe, made an excuse and disappeared. The younger guide and I made the steep descent, and at the base I asked where the cave was.

"'It might be behind that bush up there,' he said, pointing to a bush about forty feet above our heads. Behind the bush was a small opening into the mountain—so small, in fact, that I had to get down on my hands and knees to enter.

"Inside, it was pitch black until I turned on my flashlight. Then I could discern logs with notches cut into their sides. Those crude steps were very slippery, but I managed to reach the bottom, where I found a rather large cavern. A small stream was tinkling through one corner, and off to the right was a passageway. The Indians claim that the cavern runs through the mountain and ends under the Catholic church, about a quarter mile away. I set out to see where the passage led.

"Down a little farther was a shelf of rock, strewn with the remnants of burnt copal, used to pay homage to Jolom Conop. Beyond that were more ladders and more caverns. Finally, by getting down on hands and knees and squeezing between two big rocks, I entered the last cave. No doubt, at one time Jolom Conop lived there, but now the cave contains nothing but stalactites, and also tons of black soot from ages of burning wood heavy with copal.

"Not all my time in Santa Eulalia was spent in exploring the habitat of Jolom Conop. Instead of the resentment I had expected, the Indians proved to be the most responsive group I have met since coming to Guatemala. Between three and four hundred came each day and spent the whole morning listening to doctrine. They loved the Catholic religion, once it had been explained to them. Their own crude religion is a relentless burden with very little compensation offered: endless prayers and burning of copal, rain or shine.

"During the afternoon I was kept busy preparing about a hundred children for First Communion. In between doctrine classes, I tried to straighten out about forty marriages.

"The nights in Santa Eulalia offered a special challenge. I soon learned that I had moved in on a family of rats. Any resentment they may have felt was compensated for by the fact that I generously, if not willingly, shared my food with them. They waited until I had doused my Coleman lamp, and then descended on the table to tidy up any crumbs I had left.

"I stayed two weeks in Santa Eulalia, with most pleasant results. I've promised the Indians a weekly visit from now on. There's promise of a big harvest in that village, despite Jolom Conop."

Father McClear no longer works in Santa Eulalia and the other mountain pueblos he once attended. Mission policy calls for changing missioners around. He is now located farther back in the mountains, on the Mexican border. He has thirty thousand other Indians to care for, and his work among them will undoubtedly bear the same fruit as that in Soloma. Father Paul J. Sommer, of West Roxbury, Massachusetts, is the new pastor of Soloma, and he is carrying on the work begun by his predecessor and is making developments of his own.

Father Sommer had previously labored in Jacaltenango, a remote village set in fairyland scenery deep in the mountains. When Father Sommer arrived in Jacaltenango, this area of 20,000 Indians was the Mecca for all the pagan worshipers of the province. Six chemanes, or witch doctors, conducted their business there and clients came from far away. The new pastor found only primitive living conditions amid widespread poverty (the annual family income averages about forty dollars) and disease.

Father Sommer literally rolled up his sleeves and went to work. By dint of much perspiration and prayer, he built a model mission. The witch doctors went out of business, and the church became the center of village life. The health conditions of the area improved due to the priest's dispensary work, his instructions in personal hygiene, and his vaccination program to control communicable diseases. He showed the Indians how to get more income by co-operative marketing, and how to protect their eroding land by reforestation.

People who knew Jacaltenango before Father Sommer arrived were amazed at the changes he wrought. The once decaying church building became fresh and new looking under its re-thatched roof and coat of whitewash. But more important every Sunday Mass was crowded. On First Fridays there was a tremendous turnout with hundreds receiving Communion. Fiestas were no longer marked by carousing and drunkenness. The backbone of the parish were the men; they were the ones who crowded the Communion rail on Sundays, who led the processions, and who gave the whole tone to parish life. Typically, Father Sommer assigns credit for the success in Jacaltenango to a zealous Guatemalan priest who had once worked in the village, years before. Undoubtedly, that priest did do much to prepare the way. But it was due to Father Sommer's own efforts and those of his assistants, that Jacaltenango became the flourishing parish that it is today.

Maryknollers began work in the Province of Huehuetenango in 1943. Father Arthur F. Allie, of Two Rivers, Wisconsin, and Father Clarence J. Witte, of Richmond, Indiana, were the first missioners to arrive in the area, and they set up headquarters in the city of Huehuetenango ("Place of the Old People"). The parishes of the province were among the oldest in the Western Hemisphere. In the near-by town of Chiantla, records go back to 1619 and attest to the fact that the parish was there even before that time. All the parishes, except one, had been founded before the United States existed.

The Chiantla parish is one of the most interesting and famous of all Guatemalan parishes, and it is a place of pilgrimage because it has a shrine to the Silver Virgin, to whom many miracles have been attributed. This statue of the Virgin is a large wooden image completely covered with robes of silver. It was placed in the church by one of the early conquistadors, who had discovered a silver mine near-by, and it quickly became an object of devotion to the Indians, who in a singular way loved the Blessed Mother of God.

Why do Maryknollers go to Latin American countries which are already Catholic? Although the Faith has been in Latin America since the time of the conquistadors, for many generations the people have suffered in practicing their Faith because of lack of priests. It is to fill this need that Maryknollers go there.

Maryknoll's original seminary (below) is home for the Maryknoll Brothers. Typical of these devoted men is Brother Damien Walsh, of West Virginia, who repaired machinery at Maryknoll (opposite), and is now in Africa.

Bishop James Edward Walsh was one of the first Maryknoll students. He went to China in the first group, became Bishop of Kongmoon, second Superior General.

After being freed from a Japanese internment camp, Bishop Raymond A. Lane was elected third Superior General. He formerly was bishop in Fushun, Manchuria.

Mother Mary Joseph was a teacher at Smith College before joining Maryknoll's founders in promoting the mission movement. She is foundress of the Sisters.

Mother Mary Columba is the present head of the Maryknoll Sisters. This community of devoted women has over a thousand members and is in Asia, Africa, Latin America.

Kentucky reaches to Chile as Father Edward Brophy strolls with friends.

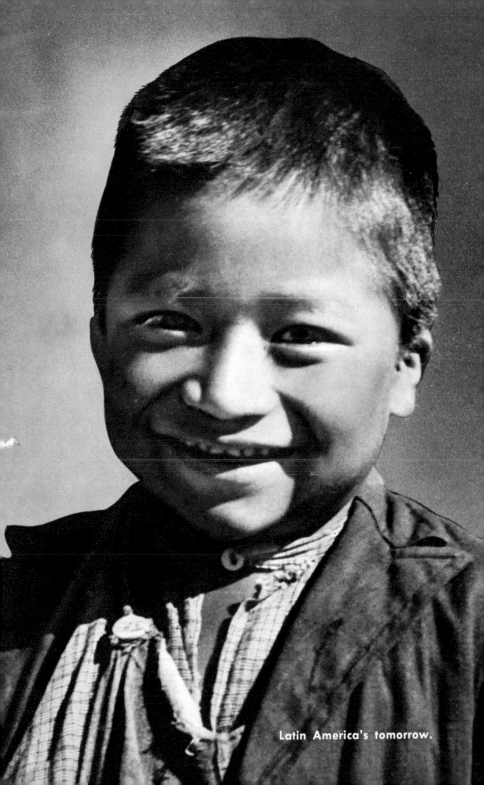

Latin America's tomorrow.

Maryknoll, besides training missioners in the United States, helps also to reach America's Orientals. Father John Toomey, of New Bedford, is off to the ice-cream store with some Chicago Chinatown parishioners

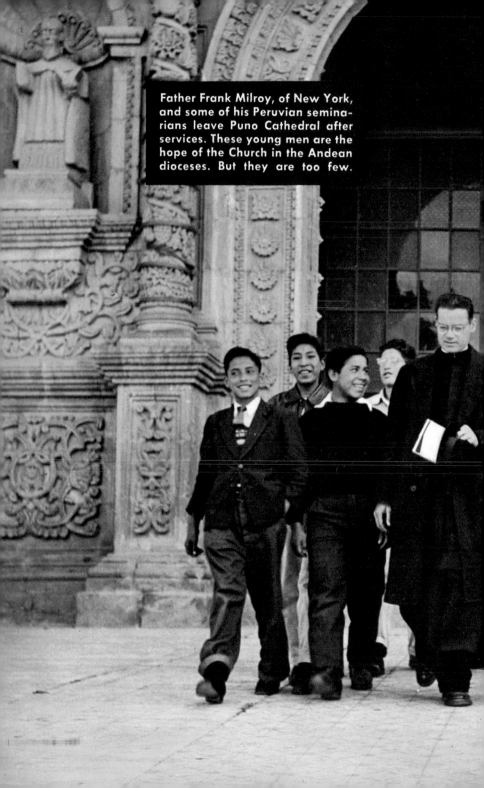

Father Frank Milroy, of New York, and some of his Peruvian seminarians leave Puno Cathedral after services. These young men are the hope of the Church in the Andean dioceses. But they are too few.

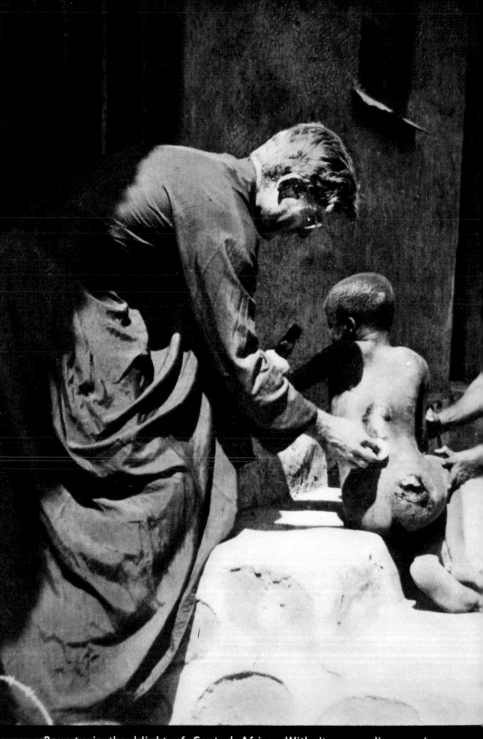

Poverty is the blight of Central Africa. With it come disease, ignorance and immorality. Maryknollers such as Father Joseph Brannigan, of New York City, (above) labor in two large mission areas of Tanganyika.

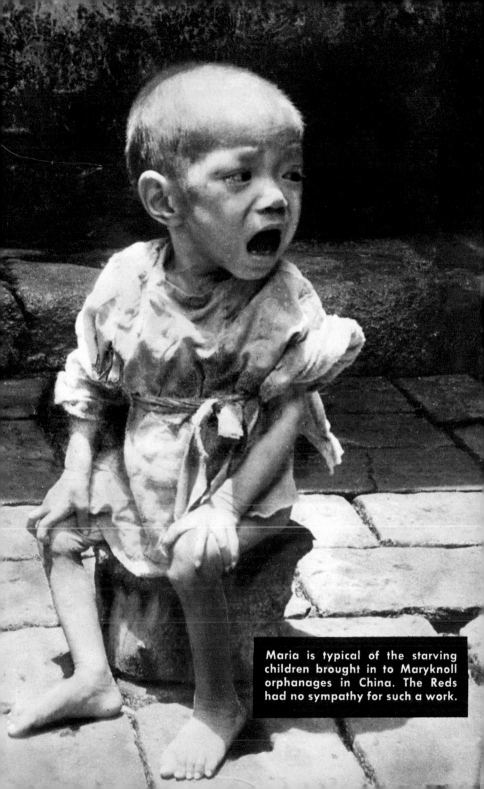

Maria is typical of the starving children brought in to Maryknoll orphanages in China. The Reds had no sympathy for such a work.

Children are children the world over. They are enthralled by a story in Hawaii. They love a puppy in Africa (left). Maryknollers win young hearts to tell them of the God who made all men equal, who became Man for love of all men, and who died on a Cross to prove that love. To preach the good news of our redemption is the main task of every missioner.

"Welcome to Maryknoll," says Father Arthur Kiernan, rector of Glen Ellyn seminary, to these newly arriving future missioners.

Father Thomas Prendergast, of Utica, N. Y., has his own way to make friends in Japan.

"These letters from home keep the mission going," says Father Edward Walsh, a native of Portland, Me.

Over the years this devotion to the Chiantla Virgin grew, and to-day it spreads beyond the borders of Guatemala. Father George L. Krock, of Cleveland, Ohio, is pastor of the Chiantla parish, and has written many interesting reports about the Silver Virgin and the fiestas held in her honor. Here is part of one such report:

"We have two big fiestas each year, here at our Chiantla mission in Guatemala. For more than three and a half centuries, great bands of pilgrims have made their way to this mountain village for the two feasts in honor of the Virgin of Chiantla. From all parts of Guatemala, from Mexico, San Salvador, and Nicaragua, they come on foot, on horse or in bus. One feast takes place in February for Candlemas; the other, in September, honors the Nativity of Our Lady.

"Providing food and entertainment for the large crowds has made each celebration a combination fiesta and fair. Both fiestas last eight days. Local windows have been busy for months making candles, baskets, and cakes. Traveling merchants come a few days early, and set up their tents and shelters of willow branches. Indians from Momostenango bring great piles of handwoven blankets. From Quezaltenango, the Indian women carry huge sacks of rusks and roasted peanuts; the cloth merchants have stacks of weaving for skirts, and bolts of cloth in bright colors.

"The quiet Indians from Quiche have their handmade silver chains and quaint silver crosses. Others have baskets of carved-wood saints. The pottery sellers cover half an acre with their wares. From Totonicapan come the little chests, painted red over yellow. One plaza is full of hundreds of horses for sale. In short, goods of every type are on display. The whole village is filled with booths and milling crowds.

"It is a slow process to make your way to the church, and you pass the stands of candle hawkers crying their wares. Everybody buys candles on the way to church: one for themselves, and one for each of the family who could not come. The church is packed, and as you inch your way in, you feel the heat and smell the clouds of smoke rising from hundreds of candles. The people stand or kneel on the floor to say their prayers, and they pray until their candles are reduced to blobs of melted wax.

"The pews have been removed from the church, and the floor is covered with two inches of sand to protect it against melted wax. The people make their way slowly to the front of the church, toward the little door that leads to the gallery around the sanctuary, and into the chamber of the Silver Virgin. The journey must be made on the knees. Pilgrims surge forward from dawn to dusk, packed closely together, singing hymns and praying. It's a touching sight. Most of the people carry bouquets of flowers—lilies, spikenard, carnations—to be presented to the Virgin, and each person has a big candle to be left at her feet.

"Inside the chamber you see a sight that brings a lump to your throat. Five yards before reaching the statue of the miraculous Virgin, each pilgrim starts waving to Our Lady to get her attention, eager to have his turn to rest a moment before her, to kiss her hand and the foot of the Christ Child she holds, and to touch to weary eyes the cross hanging from her rosary. The pilgrim leaves his flowers on the mounting pile, and slowly backs away on his knees, saying good-bye.

"People who have not seen the Virgin for a long time weep. The sick and the old, who may never have a chance to make another pilgrimage, shed bitter tears. Continuously from the body of the church comes the swell of singing: 'O Mary, Mother Mine.' Hour after hour, day after day, for the eight days of the fiesta it is thus.

"In Chiantla, for feasts of Our Lady, we have the old Spanish privilege of saying Mass in blue vestments. What a sight it makes! The church is a yellow glow of twinkling candles. Incense rises from the flower-banked altar. The tabernacle, the priests, and the altar boys are all decked in Mary's blue. The church is filled with Indians from the different pueblos, each wearing his group's distinctive local costume.

"On days of the fiestas we perform hundreds of baptisms and hear hundreds of confessions. We bless candles and holy pictures. The Indians bring their seed corn to have it blessed and sprinkled with holy water.

"Before they leave, people from the various towns come in groups to make their *despidida*, or leave-taking, as an act of courtesy to the Virgin. Then they back away, singing and waving their farewells before the statue of the Mother of God."

In 1953, Father John F. Lenahan, of Mahanoy Plane, Pennsylvania, now Maryknoll Superior of the whole mission in Guatemala, reported on the progress made in that mission field by ten years of Maryknoll work there. The American missioners in 1953 were caring for a Catholic population of 190,000 people. The mission staff included 22 Maryknoll priests, a Maryknoll Brother, 5 Belgian Sisters, and 175 native catechists. Yearly baptisms ran close to 12,000, and yearly Communions approximated 300,000. Parishes numbered 8; outstations totaled 206; and together they contained 40 churches and 49 chapels. Father Lenahan pointed out that the region's main need was like the need elsewhere in Latin America, namely, for more priests.

From the central parishes, the Maryknollers were conducting ten dispensaries, four recreational programs, two schools, a kindergarten, a farming co-operative, and various other social projects. Three of the Maryknoll parishes furnish farmers with new wheat and corn seed; another parish introduced new techniques of vegetable raising. One parish built a model home to acquaint the people with improved housing. All of the parishes support a house in Guatemala City, where the poor from the rural areas reside while awaiting free hospital services and medical attention.

"Outside of giving the mountain Indian the opportunity to practice his religion," Father Lenahan declared, "the work of our missioners in Guatemala has taught the people an appreciation of their dignity as human beings. All of our parishes report a definite, moral, social and economic improvement in the lives of the people. Recently a trained nurse, Mary P. van Eijk, came to work with us to supervise our clinics. There is still much to be done, and there are many more things we should like to do. It is our prayer that the future will make these projects realities. These ten years have been happy ones for all of us."

25

Africa—Land of Promise

On March 11, 1946, Maryknoll accepted from the Sacred Congregation of *Propanganda Fide* the responsibility for a new mission field in Tanganyika, Africa. Bordering Kenya and the Serengeti Plains, Africa's historic big-game country, the new field was in the care of the White Fathers, who would continue in charge until the Maryknollers knew enough of the native language and customs to assume full responsibility. Within a few months, four Maryknollers were assigned to the new venture. They were Fathers William J. Collins, of Boston, Massachusetts; Albert E. Good, of Cambridge, Massachusetts; Louis I. Bayless, of San Jose, California; and Joseph E. Brannigan, of New York City. Three years later the White Fathers began withdrawing from the area and on June 20, 1950, the Maryknoll Mission was made into a prefecture. Some months later, Monsignor J. Gerard Grondin, of Westbrook, Maine, was appointed the first prefect apostolic.

The above facts are the bare bones of the skeleton history of Maryknoll's initiation of mission work in Africa. They give nothing of the feel of the whole land and people. Father Collins, who was the first superior in Africa, sent back a report on the area shortly after the Maryknollers began work. Here are some of the highlights of that report:

"How should you like a good heaping spoonful of Kikulia for breakfast? Or perhaps you'd perfer some Dholuo for dinner? If not, we'll serve you Kikwaya for supper. The fact is, whether you like it or not, if you come to Musoma you'll get all three, and more besides, for breakfast, dinner, and supper. For these are our languages, and just at present very little else exists in all the world for us.

"Father Brannigan is studying Kikulia, in order to care for one tribe that speaks that language. Father Good is studying Dholuo, language of a people from the Nile Basin who are settled in these parts. Father Bayless and I are plunged into Kikwaya. Above and beyond these local tongues is Kiswahili, the lingua franca of East Africa, prescribed by the British for the schools. We are not at all as dismayed as this Babel might indicate. In fact, we are quite delighted with all that we have found here.

"Let me introduce you to some of the names we shall be using in our tales of the future. The area in which we find ourselves is called the Musoma Mission. It is on the shore of Lake Victoria, and it runs along the border between Tanganyika and Kenya. Down through the middle flows the Mara River, which makes a convenient division of the territory into North Mara and South Mara.

"Father Good and Father Brannigan have crossed the river and are settled at the principal station of North Mara, Kowak. In North Mara there are 95,000 inhabitants, and 5,000 of these are Catholics. The Kowak chapel is a streamlined creation of mud, topped with a grass roof. There are a number of mission schools, both at the center and throughout the bush. The Luo tribe lives around Kowak, while the Bakurias are an entirely different unit, to the east. Father Brannigan is studying at Kowak; but once he becomes able to express himself in the native tongue, he will pack off to his adopted people, setting himself up at Tarime.

"Father Bayless and I are in South Mara, at Nyegina. Our station is older. Here the White Fathers have raised up one of their celebrated structures of brick baked on the spot in kilns that the Fathers set up specially for the job. There are three good mission schools at Nyegina, with 500 youngsters. South Mara counts also a score of bush schools conducted by catechists.

"The population of South Mara is 111,000, of whom 3,000 are Catholics. Thus we Maryknollers are to be in charge of some 206,000 souls, of whom 8,000 are Catholics.

"What about the future? We see three particular tasks ahead for ourselves: first, the opening of five new missions; secondly, the establishment of a considerable number of new schools; thirdly, the setting up of dispensaries and of a hospital if possible."

It is interesting to note Father Collins' remark on the language problem. Similar comments were to come from all the missioners in Tanganyika. A letter from Father Arthur H. Wille, of Watsonville, California, to a friend at Maryknoll, carried this same theme. "I am going with Father Bratton to build a new mission at Kinesi," he wrote. "This will be our first mission among the Basumbiti tribe. A single native is called Msumbiti. The language is called Kisumbiti."

African personal names were just as confusing. Brother Damien Walsh, of Wheeling, West Virginia, was introduced to a young African child. "Brother Damien," said the child's parent, "this is Damien Brother."

Following the local custom of naming children for some aspect of a timely event, the parents had chosen "Brother" because, on the day the infant was born the first missionary Brother had entered that part of Africa. The "Damien" was the boy's baptismal name.

Father Good tried to set the whole problem of names straight in an article he wrote for the Maryknoll magazine. This is the way he told his story:

"The wife of Okech had just given birth to a son. With the sound of the infant's cries ringing in his ears, Okech stood before the door of his mud hut, here in Tanganyika, debating the name his heir should bear. At that moment an automobile carrying officials of the Government drove past. Okech watched the motor car disappear in a cloud of dust. Then he re-entered his hut.

" 'We will name the child Motokar,' he said simply.

"In such a manner, names are chosen for infants here in Luoland—a practice not unlike that used by our own American Indians. It is common procedure among American Indians to name their offspring after the first thing that the father sees, following his child's birth. Each Luo child is similarly named from circumstances accompanying its birth. Such a name becomes the civil name. Of course, if the child is later baptized, it is given the name of some saint.

"Not all children are named after objects or places. Superstition sometimes is the deciding factor. If, for example, Okech's family had suffered a recent death, it is quite possible that the new child would have been given the dead person's name. The reason for this practice is that the family of the deceased hope such a choice will appease the departed spirit and induce it to cause no harm to the relatives it has left behind.

"Most children, however, are named after some thing or event connected with the birth. This leads to names that to our ears are quite odd. I know youngsters who bear such appellations as *Kongo*, *Nedge*, and *Lorrie*. If these names were in our language, they would be Beer, Airplane and Truck. The first child was born during the beer-making season; the second had the fortune to have an airplane pass overhead at the time of his birth; and the third was born near a truck. Okech followed this practice in naming his child after a motor car.

"Sometimes Luo children are named after natural phenomena. Thus, a child born during a rainstorm might be named *Okoth*, or Rain; one born at night is invariably called *Otieno*—Night. The parents of Okech gave their child his name because he was born during a period of famine, the Luo word for famine being *okech*.

"Less commonly, children are named after some great personage. Many a grown man in this region bears the name of the famous chief Kargosa, who ruled about thirty years ago. Some children are named after animals. Thus, if a child should be born at the instant a near-by hyena cries out, the child would be called *Ondiek*—the name meaning Hyena. Special characteristics of the birth are perpetuated in names. A neighbor's lad is called *Okuku* —Easy Birth.

"A movement is under way to inaugurate a three-name system, similar to that used by the Romans. (For example, Marcus Tullius Cicero.) Here, the system would use the person's given name, family name, and tribe name. The difficulty is that, while Luos know their given names and the names of the tribes to which they belong, they have no concept of a family name. Each person here

is like Melchisedech of Biblical fame—without a family, without a
past."

The language problem presented the main stumbling block for
the Maryknoll missioners. There were twelve different tribal languages in the mission and only one or two of them had been committed to paper. To master the others, required long hours of hard
work with tutors, during which the missioners were obliged to write
their own grammars and dictionaries. Within the short life of the
mission, Maryknollers have tackled six of the twelve tribal tongues,
and are preparing to move in on the remainder.

An example of how this was done can be found in the
experiences of Father Delbert W. Robinson, of Canton, Ohio.
Father Robinson was assigned to work among the Bangoreme
tribe, which has no written language. He had no grammar and no
dictionary with which to start, and he could find no one to help
him. Then he met a boy who knew a little Kingoreme, the language of the Bangoreme tribe. When this source of knowledge
dried up, Father Robinson spent his days walking among the
people, picking up a word here and there. Gradually he put his
notes in order, and began trying to speak with the natives.

"The Padri knows Kingoreme very well!" said a native, after
listening patiently to the priest one day. "The trouble is that no
one understands his Kingoreme yet."

But hard work eventually bore fruit. Today as Father Robinson
travels in his mission, the people no longer say: "We are very stu-
pid. We cannot understand you."

In addition to his conquest of the spoken language, this missioner has a carefully composed outline of grammar and the mak-
ings of a large dictionary. The men who come after Father Robinson will be able to stand on his shoulders. With the language
learned, Father Robinson was at last ready for work. He opened
a mission at Iramba with somewhat surprising results.

"The effect of the new mission on the Bangoreme tribe has
been astonishing," he reported. "It's something like what happens
when a sleepy village in America is suddenly chosen for the site of
a factory. Overnight the people wake out of their lethargy, to be
swept up in a whirlwind of activity. Such a U.S. town grows by
leaps and bounds as people arrive, seeking employment. Hotels,
restaurants, theaters, churches—all spring up like mushrooms,
before the surprised residents have stretched their limbs and wiped

sleep from their eyes. Their village has become a boom town, bustling with activities.

"The inauguration of the Iramba mission has caused a boom that has been heard in all corners of the Ngoreme kingdom. The Bangoreme tribe, though living in the bush, are energetic and progressive people. Their kingdom borders the mighty Serengeti Plains and the lands inhabited by the much-feared Masai tribe. The Bangoreme are quick to perceive the material advantages that the foreigners' civilization has to offer. They have a sharp sense of values. The new mission means jobs; it means a school; it means a church for those among them who have already experienced God's grace.

"Every day we see more and more natives moving into the neighborhood of the mission, securing new lands, erecting new homes, and seeking jobs. These people want to be in on the ground floor, to receive the advantages and opportunities the mission will have to offer. So much moving and construction is going on that there is a shortage of sisal poles for building, grass for roofs, and trees for support.

"Many of the people who are moving into the neighborhood are non-Christians. Something like fifty per cent of them have begun to study the doctrine. Many of these are studying because they are caught by the general enthusiasm of their neighbors. We encourage them. Desire to worship and serve the true God will be the motive, once Christ's Gospel and graces have a chance to work on the souls of these people for whom Christ died.

"What is the Padri doing in the midst of this boom? He is bringing Christ into the homes of the Bangoreme for the first time. A church hasn't been built yet: but High Mass is sung every Sunday, within mud walls and under a grass roof. An average of about 80 Christians assist at Mass on Sunday, and about as many confess and receive Communion. They are hearing the Gospel for the first time in their own language and they listen with eager attention to the instruction that follows. An Offertory collection is taken up, and all who are able give their mites."

Many people picture Africa as a land of hot and dense jungles. Actually most of the continent is open. The Maryknoll territory in Tanganyika is mainly a plain of rocky soil, with little vegetation and hardly any trees. Although it is in the equatorial region, the area is actually cool because it is a plateau about a mile high.

The once-abundant game is now dwindling, and while zebras, hartebeests and gazelles are seen, lions and hippos are becoming rare sights.

"Actually, African insects cause more suffering and are a greater threat to health and life than the big game," says Father Thomas N. Quirk, of Portsmouth, New Hampshire. "Insects are everywhere, while animals try to keep out of man's way. Of all the insects, ants are the most troublesome, especially the safari or traveling ants."

According to Father Quirk, the safari ants are recognized as leaders in their own world. They build for themselves skyscrapers twelve to fourteen feet high. They march to battle in two columns, about fifteen feet apart. They depend upon force of numbers and ferocious attack for success. In their search for food they will attack animals and houses. The only things that can divert their march are DDT, kerosene, or warm ashes.

"Once I accidentally stepped into a column of safari ants," Father Quirk recounts. "In less than ten seconds, my legs were covered with them. They waited for a signal from their leader, and then all bit me at once. The larger ones inflict severe and painful wounds. Many old African hands tell of fleeing for their lives from safari ants. I believe them."

But it is not with big game that the diaries and reports from Africa are concerned, nor even with insects and snakes. The main subject is the African people and it is easy to understand how those simple children of God catch hold of the hearts of the missioners. Blessed with little of this world's goods, the native Africans have a great dignity and are capable of enormous sacrifices for their new-found Faith. There are many stories about beatings and persecutions inflicted on those natives who embrace Christianity.

One of these stories concerns the Queen of Sherati. Her name is Adogo, and she was the third wife of Nyatega, the King of Sherati. Because she was the favorite wife, custom made her the Queen. But she was royal by her own right.

"Adogo was beautiful to behold, graceful, charming, and very happy," says Father Good, who knows her. "She ruled the royal household smoothly and tactfully. She made everyone around her happy. She knew many languages. She was, indeed, an ornament of the King's court."

One day in the market, Adogo heard Franciscus, the Catholic catechist, teaching the mysteries of Christ. The message touched the soul of Adogo and for two years she came to listen to Franciscus teach. Finally she asked for baptism, but the Fathers at the mission told her she was not ready. For several years, Adogo continued to ask to be baptized and each time she was put off. All the other people who had studied with her had been baptized. The thought made her very sad and she decided to go to the mission center at Kowak to learn the reason for her refusal. After walking twenty-eight miles to Kowak, she met one of the missioners.

"Father," Adogo said, "all who have studied with Franciscus, the catechist, have been baptized. All except one—the Queen of Sherati. I believe, Father, that I have not been baptized because I am not the first wife of Nyatega, the King of Sherati."

"That is true," answered the priest.

"Then I will leave the King," replied Adogo. "I will no longer be Queen of Sherati."

So Adogo took up residence with an old Catholic woman who lived near the mission. Every day she went to pray at the mission. When Nyatega learned where his third wife was, he became full of rage and rushed to Kowak to drag her back to his court. But Adogo hid so that Nyatega could not find her.

"Never, never will I live as third wife!" she declared.

In the eyes of the people of Sherati, Adogo remained their Queen. Had not Nyatega paid a dowry of cows to her father? Had not the King celebrated the marriage feast with her? Therefore, she should return home to Sherati. These were the opinions of the people. But the Fathers at the mission did not agree. They had watched Adogo at prayer, and knew that she was sincere in her desire to become a Christian. So at last they baptized her and gave her a new name, Magdalena.

Near the Kowak mission lived a young man named Sylvanus, who, also, was a Catholic. Sylvanus admired the beauty of the former Queen of Sherati, and he fell in love with her. He wished to marry her, but the elders and chiefs of his tribe forbade the marriage because they were afraid of Nyatega. The father of Sylvanus, however, approached Nyatega. To his surprise, he learned that the King was willing to give up his favorite wife, provided he would receive as many cows as he had paid for her. Sylvanus drove twenty cows to Sherati and the bargain was sealed. Thus Sylvanus and Magdalena were finally married at the little Kowak church.

"Sunday after Sunday," says Father Good, "Sylvanus and Magdalena, and their little family, attend Mass and devotions in our mission church. There the former Queen of Sherati bows in humble homage to the King of kings."

Of all the people in the Tanganyika mission, the most primitive and colorful are those of the Bakuria tribe. Father Brannigan pioneered work among those people, and when he returned home on furlough, Father Joseph A. Reinhart, of Stratford, Ontario, took charge of the parish. He wrote a long report on his work for friends in Canada. The report gives a good account of mission work in that region of Africa, of the conditions under which it must be performed, and of the people for whom the missioner labors. Here are some highlights from the report:

"Some days seem to be full of work and trouble and suffering. I'll never forget my first safari to a distant mission station. I rode ten miles on the motorcycle and then left it at a village and began walking. It was near noon by then and the heat of the sun made me feel like a piece of steak being broiled over charcoal. Soon it began to rain and I was drenched before I arrived at the mission station. After an hour of examining catechumens, in a hut whose grass roof had been blown off, I started back.

"Trying to jump over a swollen river, I missed and had a dunking. When I got to the village, I could not start the motorcycle. I was cold and hungry and so tired that I felt like going to sleep right there in the rain. Finally I got the motor started—and found that the light didn't work. I followed the road as best I could and then I saw a welcome sight: the pastor's jeep. Its taillight guided me home. I should have loved to luxuriate in a hot shower at the end of that day, but we don't have a shower at the mission.

"When I came to Africa, in 1950, I was assigned to the Rosana mission. As far as climate goes, it is the coldest of our missions in Africa. My work is among the Bakuria people, who live in the environs of Rosana. The mission is built on a 5,000-foot-high escarpment. It commands a wonderful view of the sweeping plain below, where lie the native huts and the cultivated fields of vegetables and grains.

"Rosana has two rainy seasons, and when rain falls, it is almost impossible to keep clean if one does much traveling. The soil is the deep red type, very adhesive. Anyone who is particular about neatness should stay away from Rosana in the rainy seasons. We appreciate the rain, though, because it is the source of our water supply. Aluminum roofs channel the precious liquid into four large tanks. We use 'oceans' of water for building purposes, and the water in the tanks saves many a trip to the Mara River.

"The Bakurias are one of the most colorful tribes in this part of Africa. They are a pastoral and agricultural people, living on lands that once were fertile but that have deteriorated through erosion and excess grazing. Few Bakurias can read and write; most of them have seldom, if ever, spoken to a white man. They used to war continuously with the nomadic Masai tribe, famous for cattle-and-wife-stealing tactics. Near the mission can be seen the many stone fortifications into which women and cattle were herded during raids. The Bakurias, having had contact with a lawless tribe, have become famous as the greatest cattle rustlers in all East Africa. This section ranks fourth in criminal cases, most of which are cattle stealing charges.

"Everyday Bakuria dress varies. Some are decked out in a pair of earrings. Old men throw a blanket over one shoulder, toga style. Some of the younger fellows wear khaki shorts and shirts, even shoes and stockings. But the boys and girls who shepherd the flocks and herds wear hardly anything. Old women wear blankets. Younger women drape pieces of cloth over their bodies, sarong style. Dresses are saved for extra-special occasions. Costume jewelry for the Bakuria women consists of brass bands around the arms and legs; these are put on when the girls are young. The Christians often remove these bands, revealing muscles like those of Popeye. Many Bakuria women wear beauty marks on the face and chest, proof of painful tattooing with a reed when the victims were young. Bakuria women also weigh themselves down with many necklaces of multicolored beads and other charms.

"A favorite form of ornamentation is the pierced ear lobe. Most Bakuria girls have their ears pierced when they are small. Inserted into the openings are small wooden blocks. The size of these blocks increases with the years and so does the size of the ear lobes, until the owner is satisfied with the length. Some let their long ears dangle in the breeze. Others prefer to adorn their ears with large brass coils. The old men wear brass earrings, too; only with them the adornment is a sign of age and maturity.

"It is at a dance that we see the Bakurias dressed in their best. The purpose of the afternoon dance is for young blades to find wives who are good at cooking and at cultivating gardens. Evening dances take place after the circumcision rites, when boys and girls become grownups, eligible for marriage.

"A young Bakuria on his way to a dance wears a fancy animal hide around his body. His face is painted with yellow, red and blue pigments. The crowning touch is a showy headdress. A Bakuria lass wears a red leather skirt in two pieces, reaching below the knees in the back and to the middle of the thighs in the front. She may have as many as twenty necklaces around her neck. A colored strap encircles her head, and another is tucked under the tip of her chin.

"The girls cover their bodies with animal fat. When they dance in the hot sun (what an odor!) they really shine as they hop up and down. The dancers form in two lines, facing each other, and jump in time with the beat of the drum. This continues for hours; there seems to be no end to their endurance. The boys pound the ground with their heavy sandals, while the girls take more delicate steps, similar to those of a boxer skipping rope.

"How do we missioners train our Bakurias for baptism? Usually it starts with a six-month course in the prayers given by a catechist in one of the outstations. This is followed by six months' study of the small catechism. The last six months are spent near the central mission where the candidates study the big catechism. We prefer to have them near the mission for the last six months, because that gives them a chance to meet the Christians and attend daily Mass and devotions. By way of teaching converts to support the Church, we have them do two hours of manual labor for the mission every day during their final period of study. Our prospective Christians get a stiff test before being admitted to baptism, and most of them pass.

"When this mission was first opened, there were few Christians. Now we have over a thousand."

When Maryknoll arrived in the Musoma Mission in 1946, there were 8,234 Christians; 1,018 catechumens; 2 mission stations and

2 schools. The 1953 report, sent to Maryknoll by Monsignor Grondin, showed the progress that had been made in seven years. At that time the Musoma Prefecture had 14,759 Christians; 4,332 catechumens; 36 grade schools with 2,370 students; and 2 dispensaries. That year a native priest was ordained, and there were 29 seminarians. The Maryknoll Sisters had set up a native novitiate and 14 girls were training to become Sisters. The mission staff numbered 26 Maryknoll priests, 3 Maryknoll Brothers, and 10 Maryknoll Sisters. By 1954 the Musoma Mission was sufficiently established to permit Maryknoll to begin negotiations to take over an adjoining territory of equal size in the Maswa-Shinyanga region.

But more important than statistics was the attitude of the natives towards their missioners. An experience of Father John M. Schiff, of New York City, demonstrated this. Father Schiff rode into a native village on his motorcycle, and noticed all the children running away to hide. But when the motorcycle stopped, the youngsters recognized Father Schiff and ran out to greet him.

"Why did you run away?" asked Father Schiff. "Are you afraid of me?"

"Oh, no!" exclaimed one of the boys. "We ran because we thought you were a white man."

"Well, don't you think I am a white man now?" inquired the puzzled New Yorker.

"No, you're not a white man," explained the African boy. "You're a priest."

26

Formosa—Earthquake Island

Father Michael J. O'Connor, of New York City, has developed his own personal seismograph on Formosa. He merely watches the water in a washbasin. If it splashes more than six feet away during a tremor, then he hurries outdoors. The Maryknoll mission on Formosa sits plumb astride the earthquake belt running from Japan to the Philippines. Although most of the shocks are weak and sectional, they still average one a day. The last big earthquake was in 1935, when three thousand people in the area were killed. But on one single day recently, Father O'Connor counted forty-seven separate quakes.

Formosa is an island, about a hundred miles off the coast of Red China. It is slightly larger than the State of Maryland, and contains close to nine million people. Portuguese mariners, who discovered the island for the occidental world, named it *Ilha Formosa*, or Beautiful Island. The natives call it *Taiwan*, or Terraced Bay. Blessed with good climate and rich soil the island produces vast quantities of rice, tea, fruit and vegetables. Its forests are luxuriant with cedar, teak, ebony and camphor trees. Some areas get heavy rain. Keelung has a yearly average of 219 rainy days a year, during which about 200 inches of rain fall.

Many years ago, during the Ching dynasty, the Chinese emperor sent a very wise magistrate to rule over the aboriginal tribes who inhabited the mountains of Formosa. The name of this man was Woo Feng. In a short time after his arrival on the island, he gained the confidence of the aborigines, and he made considerable improvement in their way of life. In one thing alone, however, Woo Feng was unsuccessful. He was unable to persuade the tribes to end their custom of head-hunting.

Eventually Woo Feng announced that he would allow the people one final killing for their sacrifices, and after that there would be no more. He also warned them that, after this killing, there would be misery and war in the land. He described this last victim, telling where the man could be captured and what clothes he would be wearing. On the day foretold, the head-hunters found their victim on the path the magistrate had described, and dressed exactly as had been foretold. They killed the captive. Only after they had chopped the victim's head off, did they realize that the murdered man was their beloved magistrate! Misery and war followed; but because of the great sacrifice of the magistrate, the tribes stopped their head-hunting. Years later the aborigines erected a temple in Woo Feng's honor.

Today some descendants of those aboriginal head-hunters live in the territory that is the Maryknoll Mission. They keep to the old ways (minus head-hunting), preserving their own traditions and customs. Father Armand Jacques has made himself the apostle of the tribes within the Maryknoll area and has special permission from the government to enter the closed mountain reserve where they live.

Long a prey for Japanese pirates, Formosa became part of China in 1683. After that country's defeat in the Sino-Japanese War, in 1895, the island was ceded to Japan. The Japanese developed the economy of the island and turned it into one of the great granaries in the Far East. Battered by American bombers in World War II, the island came under Chinese control following the surrender of Japan. When the Nationalist Government fled the mainland Reds, their exiled leaders set up headquarters on Formosa, where they rule today. The island is a great prize, and the Communists would like to get control of it.

In 1950, with missioners being forced out of China by the Reds, the Holy See asked Maryknoll to send a contingent to Formosa as soon as possible, to take charge of a mission area in the region of Taichung. Almost immediately assignments were made to the island, and the first group of American missioners began work there. On the day of August 11, 1950, the territory assigned to Maryknoll was made a prefecture, and shortly after that Monsignor William F. Kupfer, of Flushing, New York, was named prefect. The new mission is about thirty miles long and sixty miles wide. It contains some already established missions, and a number of Chinese priests.

Monsignor Kupfer set up his headquarters in the city of Taichung, a modern bustling city of 200,000 people. The church is centrally located in one of the busiest parts of the city. There are a number of other religious establishments in Taichung. Four Sisters of Providence, from Terre Haute, Indiana, run a boarding school for girls; these Sisters had been expelled from China, and had brought with them their Chinese Sisters of Providence. Another refugee native community, Sisters of the Immaculate Heart of the Virgin Mary, are also in Taichung.

"Maryknoll's mission field on Formosa is most promising," wrote Father O'Connor shortly after his arrival. "There is much work to be done but the Catholics in our mission are good, thanks to our Spanish Dominican predecessors and their fifty years of labor. Still vast areas of the mission are yet untouched by priestly work. But the foundation is solid and the future bright."

Father O'Connor was assigned to the most southerly mission, at Tienchung to be curate to Father James T. Manning, of New Rochelle, New York. There were four outstations attached to the mission and one of them was a village whose entire population was Catholic. The mission also had some refugee Hungarian Sisters working in it.

The missioners at Tienchung found themselves living in a goiter-ridden area. One out of every five women, and one out of every fifteen men, suffered from advanced cases of "big throat" disease. The missioners set out to determine the cause. They examined the diet of the people and learned that, although the Formosans were eating fish, the fish came from homemade, freshwater ponds lacking iodine. One of the Hungarian Sisters, Sister Alena, is a trained nurse, and with her help, preventive measures were devised.

Word was spread throughout the area that the "Lord of Heaven mission" was preparing to give free treatment to persons afflicted with the "big throat" disease. Medicine would be given out on Tuesdays at the mission. The first week, 250 people showed up, the next week 500, and quickly the number increased to 4,000. The crowd became so great that another "goiter day" was established for Thursdays at the Kholiengkha outmission.

Early on Tuesday morning large caldrons of water are set boiling in the mission at Tienchung. Powdered milk, furnished by the War Relief Services of the National Catholic Welfare Conference in the United States, is then mixed with the water. By seven o'clock the distribution starts and it goes on all day. A record is kept for each person. Into a cupful of warm milk, the goiter medicine, purchased by the mission, is put; the dosage is two drops the first week, four the second, eight the third, and ten from then on.

By ten o'clock the mission yard is jammed. The people are formed into a long, twisting line. Most of the crowd are women and girls, but there are also children and a sprinkling of men. It is not a pleasant sight because the goiters are ugly masses of flesh, some hanging almost to the waist. The Sisters and lay helpers give out the medicine, while Fathers Manning and O'Connor walk up and down the lines, greeting and chatting with the people.

"The Catholic Church is very kind," some people say.

"See, Father, it is getting smaller," others tell the missioner, pointing to their necks.

The mission had printed a small two-page leaflet, which is given out to new-comers. It takes its title from a Chinese proverb: *When You Drink Water, Think of Its Source.* The leaflet tells that the goiter medicine is not from any government or relief agency, but from the Catholic people in America. It explains that the medicine is given to the people of Formosa, not because the missioners are rich, but because they are following the example of Christ in helping the poor and the needy.

The anti-goiter campaign is already meeting with success. Small goiters have disappeared, and the larger ones have decreased. The main problem is one of preventive medicine—a difficult idea to get across to people not yet afflicted. But the Fathers have spread the word throughout the area that, if a person doesn't want to get a goiter, she or he would be wise to come to the mission for medicine to prevent the disease. Six missions are now carrying on the campaign.

"We have no idea when 'Operation Goiter' will end," says Father Manning. "Every week from three to five hundred more come. But there must be some limit to goiter cases in this area!"

That the work of the missioners is appreciated, there can be no doubt. The printer who made up the leaflets explaining the source of the medicine, was one of the non-Christians who were deeply impressed.

When delivering the finished job, the printer told Father Manning: "I cannot charge you for this work. A religion that is as charitable as yours, is a good religion. I am interested in it. When can I start to study the doctrine?"

The most recent statistics for the Taichung Prefecture show a Catholic population of 5,687, with 1,185 catechumens ready for baptism. This is an almost infinitesimal part of the area's total population of 1,700,000. However, eight parishes have been established, and the personnel of the mission is growing quickly. There are 20 Maryknoll Fathers in active work, 7 Chinese priests, 1 Viatorian Father preparing the way for a middle school, 7 Providence Sisters, 4 Sisters of Mercy from Hungary, 12 Chinese Providence Sisters, and 42 Chinese Sacred Heart of Mary Sisters. Of special interest is the presence within the territory of a group of 19 Jesuit scholars engaged in one of the major linguistic projects under way in Asia today. With expert care these men, representing some ten different nationalities, are compiling a polyglot dictionary, in reality a series of many dictionaries. As basic technique they are employing the Wade system of Romanization and thus far their series includes Chinese-French; Chinese-Spanish; Chinese-English; Chinese-Hungarian; Chinese-Latin and will add others to the list. In late 1953, the first contingent of Maryknoll Sisters reached Formosa. With this large body of personnel, Monsignor Kupfer hopes to see the mission work make rapid progress.

"The greatest single need for the progress of Catholicism in Taiwan is the Catholic school," says Monsignor. "On the entire island, there is but one Catholic high school. The most important item on Taichung's agenda is the opening of two Catholic high schools—one for boys and one for girls. We have purchased land

and have drawn up plans for new schools. After Communism shall have failed, our Taichung-trained Catholics will be able to help the Church on the mainland get back on its feet."

That's the way all the Maryknollers in Formosa look at their work. It is not a stopgap while the Reds control China. It is the building of a bastion of Christianity, from which some day an army of religious and lay missioners will pour back into the mother country, to rebuild the Christian edifice that the Reds have undermined.

Meanwhile, Maryknollers spend themselves generously to relieve the distress that the migration from the mainland has brought to Formosa. A notable contributor is Father Francis O'Neill, Maryknoller from Providence, Rhode Island, who is Formosan representative of Catholic America's War Relief Services. His headquarters are in Taipeh, the capital of the island.

Despite the great host of souls in the Taichung territory, Maryknoll has accepted an additional mission in the Archdiocese of Taipeh with headquarters at Miaoli, fifty miles below Taipeh City, capital of Formosa. Some seventy per cent of the Taiwanese speak the difficult Chinese Hoklo dialect, prevalent in southern Fukien Province, off the coast of which Formosa is located. The remaining thirty per cent speak the Hakka dialect which has its origin in northern Kwangtung Province. Maryknollers under Bishop Ford worked among the Hakka people who lived in great part within Bishop Ford's Diocese of Kaying.

Now Maryknoll priests and Sisters of Kaying, under the leadership of Father Charles P. Hilbert, are among the Hakka people who are strong in the neighborhood of Miaoli.

Other missioners from a Maryknoll field on the mainland are several fine young Chinese priests who made their start in the Maryknoll preparatory seminary in Fushun, Manchuria, and finished their training at the major seminary conducted by the Irish Jesuits in Hong Kong. For these priests, Mandarin is their native tongue but they have learned Hoklo and are zealously operating city missions among the Taiwanese.

"My quarters are hopelessly small," remarked one of these priests, Father Paul Yang, when a Maryknoller visited him recently. "The crowd every evening just can't fit in here."

This seems to be the big story out of Taiwan: our modest quarters are bursting at the seams.

27

Hong Kong—Doorstep of the Dragon

A little ribbon of steel and wood is the solitary link between the free world and Eurasian communism. This lone connection is the Man Kam To railroad bridge, which spans the border between the British Crown Colony of Hong Kong and Red China. Trains no longer rumble across the short bridge, but over its rough surface stumble the refugees from tyranny to drink deep draughts of freedom's clean air.

The British colony that has become so important a strategic outpost to the free world consists of two parts. There is the permanent British territory of thirty-five square miles, ceded to Great Britain by China in 1841 and 1860, and there are New Territories of 355 square miles leased to Great Britain in 1898 for a period of ninety-nine years. Contrary to popular belief, there actually is no city of Hong Kong. The beautiful metropolis of 750,000 people, often referred to by that name, is really Victoria, the capital of the colony, located on Hong Kong Island. Across the harbor is Kowloon, second city of the colony, and beyond that are twenty-two more miles of British-controlled territory before the China border is reached.

When the British took over Hong Kong, it was a desolate, rocky place with seemingly little future. Today it is crowded, rich, and one of the most important centers of trade in the world. The founder of the Chinese Republic, Dr. Sun Yat-sen, told Hong Kong students that he acquired his revolutionary and modern ideas when walking through the busy streets of the colony. He compared Hong Kong with his birthplace only fifty miles away— one bustling with activity, the other sleepy and antiquated.

"I began to wonder," declared the Chinese leader, "how the English could transform the barren rock of Hong Kong within seventy or eighty years, while China in four thousand years had no place like Hong Kong."

Maryknoll's connection with Hong Kong chronologically falls into three parts: before war, during war and after war. Hong Kong was the entry point for the first Maryknollers assigned to China. It was the place where Father Price died and was buried. On All Saints' Day (November 1), 1920, Fathers Walsh, Dietz and Cairns offered the first Mass in the newly established Maryknoll procure in Kowloon. Father Cairns was then assigned to take charge of the house as procurator. The following year the first group of Maryknoll Sisters arrived to begin work in the colony, and the prewar story of Maryknoll in Hong Kong is largely theirs.

The Sisters opened a convent and kindergarten. They established an industrial school in which Chinese women and girls made silk cassocks and liturgical vestments. They began the Holy Spirit School for Chinese girls, and for a time conducted a novitiate to train native Sisters for the Kongmoon and Kaying missions. Their work quickly expanded, and soon there was a large body of Sisters busy in the colony. In 1935, the Maryknoll Fathers erected a building at Stanley, eleven miles from Victoria, to serve as a language school, rest house and procure. From that time on, there were a substantial number of priests and Brothers in residence, the majority of them preparing to begin mission work on the Chinese mainland.

On December 7, 1941, Father John C. Troesch, of Springfield, Illinois, procurator in Hong Kong, drove into town from Stanley to pick up eight young Maryknollers, recently ordained and arriving from the United States for language studies. The Clipper plane landed on schedule, and the new missioners were taken to Stanley for a big welcome by the twelve Maryknoll priests and five Maryknoll Brothers resident there. The next morning the young missioners received the startling news that the Clipper had been bombed and sunk during a sneak Japanese attack on the colony.

The outbreak of war threw Hong Kong into confusion. The Japanese forces poured over the Chinese border and fought their way down the Kowloon peninsula. The Maryknollers knew that they were trapped on the island, but tried to keep their lives as normal as possible. Father Bernard F. Meyer began Chinese classes for the newcomers, and their recital of Chinese tones was punctuated by the booms of British cannon. For days the battle went on. Kowloon fell. Next the Japanese landed on Hong Kong itself and began to fight their way out towards Stanley. Machine guns, mortars, rifles and cannon exploded round the missioners, day and night. Some of the priests went out to bring spiritual aid to wounded and dying British and Canadian soldiers. Benjamin Proulx, a young Canadian soldier, who later escaped, met one of those priests and told the world about it in a syndicated article.

"I had just left headquarters," he related, "when the air-raid alarm sounded and Japanese planes came over for about the tenth time that morning. I started looking around for a place to duck when I noticed one of the Maryknoll Missionary Fathers sitting under a tree. Most of the branches had been blown off by bomb fragments, and it was more like a burnt wooden stake than a tree. But the Maryknoll Father was sitting there calmly and smiling at me.

"He crooked his finger and I went over and sat down beside him. 'Would you like to receive Holy Communion?' he asked.

"I am a Catholic and since the Japanese attacked I had not had a chance to go to confession or receive Communion. I knelt and made my confession. There were Japanese bombs heaving the ground beneath us, but his voice was calm and steady as he murmured the words of absolution. Then he drew from his pocket a small metal container, which contained the Host, and gave me Holy Communion. Then we sat in silence under the tree and watched the planes wheeling high above us.

"That was the way the Maryknoll Fathers were all through the siege of Hong Kong. They were utterly oblivious of danger. They cared for the wounded. They gave the Last Sacraments to the dying. They gave counsel and hope and life again to men whose wives and children were hostages to the Japanese. They consoled and helped women who had gone half out of their minds because of the things they had seen and been through. All the terror and violence of the Japanese could not make them leave their work. I suppose that was why the Japanese might hate them so much. When you are dealing out death and horror, you expect to see men cringe. The Maryknoll Fathers did not cringe."

The Japanese reached the Maryknoll rest house and language school at about dawn on Christmas Day. Some of the Fathers were celebrating Mass when the invaders came and began smashing in windows for entrance. Father Meyer, just getting ready for Mass, left the chapel, went downstairs and unlocked the door. The Japanese rushed at him with their bayonets—but, to their amazement, he stood there calmly, telling them in Cantonese not to commit any rash act. He told them that they were in a religious house (they thought it was a barrack), and that the only soldiers present were three wounded men in the corridor.

"We owe a lot of credit and a big debt of gratitude to Father Meyer," reported Father Troesch later. "If it were not for his bravery, the Japanese in their fury might have bayoneted us all."

The soldiers rounded up the missioners and confined them to a downstairs room. Then the Japanese began to loot the house in very thorough fashion. Late on Christmas afternoon, the priests were marched out of the house and down the hill. The Japanese were bayoneting British soldiers and the priests believed that their turn would come next. Some Japanese officers argued about the prisoners, finally deciding not to kill the missioners then. At last they were taken to a small garage and locked in. The priests had nothing to eat all Christmas Day and the day following. On December 27, they were given some siege biscuits and water by their captors.

On December 29, the missioners were allowed to return to their looted and wrecked center house. They remained there until they were taken to an internment camp on January 21. In the camp the priests found the Maryknoll Sisters from Kowloon. The camp was full of British and American civilians, and life there was very difficult. Some of the priests and Sisters were repatriated in a prisoner exchange, after six months in the camp; and two months later Bishop Valtorta, of Hong Kong, was able to get the other priests and Sisters released into his custody. At the end of the year, the Japanese ordered the missioners out of the colony to the neutral Portuguese colony at Macao. Eventually most of them reached Free China.

Two of the Maryknollers—Father Meyer and Father Donald L. Hessler—volunteered to remain in the internment camp to care for the civilians. The priests did tremendous work during the dark days that followed. Father Meyer was always able to find some food for sick people. He showed the internees how to plant gardens to increase their meager rations. He developed a method of getting salt from the sea, and persuaded the prisoners to supplement their diets with grasses and weeds, which would give vitamins. In addition, the two priests set up an active Catholic life in the camp.

After the war, the internees drew up a testimonial praising the two priests. "There are few among us," declared the long document, "who do not have good reason to be thankful to Fathers Meyer and Hessler. The absolute sacrifice and selflessness of these two priests was a shining example to all of us." When all the prisoners were freed, Fathers Meyer and Hessler left the camp to set up relief work for the poor and homeless in Hong Kong. These two dynamic and apostolic men could not be idle in the face of need.

With the end of the war, Hong Kong again became the gateway of the Orient. The Maryknoll Language School was cleaned and refurnished. Again missioners passed through Hong Kong, this time on the way to resuming apostolic work in China. The terrible days of internment were soon forgotten. Then suddenly the men who had crossed the Man Kam To bridge with jaunty and confident steps began streaming back as shrunken and broken men. The Communist tyranny had come to China.

In the twelve months of 1951 a total of 1,374 priests and Sisters were forced out of China. The number was scarcely less the following year as 1,115 missioners were uprooted from their work and expelled across the Man Kam To bridge, many under armed guard, after being imprisoned and sentenced by "Peoples' Courts." The Maryknoll Language School opened its doors to welcome expelled missioners of all nationalities who had no residence in Hong Kong, and the tales of Communist persecution and brutality were told there in the babel of many tongues.

Father Thomas J. Bauer, a Brooklyn Maryknoller who edited the China Missionary Bulletin and represented the NCWC News

Service in Hong Kong, interviewed these priests, Brothers and Sisters, and sent out the stories that made the world realize that the Chinese Communist government was embarked on a program to eliminate the Catholic Church. All Catholic news of China was transmitted by Father Bauer to the correspondents of the UP, AP, Reuters, Agency France and other news services in Hong Kong. When Father Bauer's health failed at the end of 1952, Father Mark Tennien, himself an expelled missioner, took over the task.

With the expelled missioners came long lines of native refugees. Thousands upon thousands of them poured out of China into the freedom of Hong Kong until at last almost two million of them crowded every available bit of space in the already well-populated colony.

The Maryknollers who were expelled from China were immediately reassigned. Some of them went to Formosa, some to the Philippines, a few to Japan. At the invitation of Monsignor Riganti, the then administrator of the diocese of Hong Kong, and with the encouragement of Archbishop Riberi, Apostolic Internuncio to China, a group of Maryknoll priests undertook refugee work in Hong Kong. The chapter that these latter have written is one of the finest in Maryknoll's long story of help to the world's suffering poor. Under the leadership of Maryknoll's Regional Superior at the time, Father Thomas J. Malone, of the Bronx, New York, and of Father William P. Mulcahy, of Framingham, Massachusetts, the Hong Kong Maryknollers have won the respect and admiration of British officials and international relief organizations.

Father Paul J. Duchesne, of Cohoes, New York, is the director of the Catholic Central Bureau's Welfare Committee in Hong Kong and is official representative for the War Relief Services of the National Catholic Welfare Conference in the United States. He had previously done relief work in Canton. Because the duties of this Maryknoller take him to all parts of the colony, he had a better-than-average insight into conditions and needs than most people in Hong Kong. According to Father Duchesne, Hong Kong has the densest refugee population per square mile in the world.

"Of the almost two million people who have fled to the asylum of Hong Kong from the tyranny of Red China," reported Father Duchesne in 1953, "perhaps one half have ways to eke out a living. Three hundred thousand can be considered well off. Three hundred thousand are crowded, ten and more to a room six feet wide, that compel sleep to be taken in shifts. Ten thousand refugees, including whole families, are sleeping on the streets, in alleys, in doorways and on roofs of buildings."

"In none of these refugee settlements are the people beggars," points out Father Mulcahy. "They aren't interested merely in financial handouts. As they say, such aid solves no problem at all. They want a small home and some type of work, anything that will bring in even a little money every month, so they can hold up their heads."

Father Duchesne's Welfare Committee provides all manner of assistance to the refugees. For an impoverished family it may purchase a coffin so that the survivors can bury a dead relative; for another, it may provide seed grain; for another, it finds food, or a little money to pay for medicine. In his 1953 report, he noted that during the preceding year he had distributed 3,517 bales of clothing and the equivalent of $15,000 in medicine. He works in close cooperation with Hong Kong's five Catholic hospitals and ten Catholic dispensaries; he aids five Catholic orphanages and an old folks' home. In another aspect of the Welfare Committee's work, he arranges for a priest to be on hand each day at the Chinese-Hong Kong border to meet expelled missioners, escorting them to one or another residence in the colony.

Recently, Father Duchesne visited sixty refugee families living at the city dump and scavenging through refuse. Groups of families have their specialties: some collect rags; others, bones or twine, or paper. The rags are sorted and baled to be sold for paper manufacture. Bones are ground into fertilizer. Broken bits of plastic are melted and made into buttons. Tinfoil and empty toothpaste tubes are melted into lead.

"Here are men who fled tyranny," says the Maryknoller. "They do not sit and wait for someone to feed them. They do not beg or ask pity. They are trying to make their own way. The only requests they had was for someone to come and vaccinate their children, and that some day a school be built nearby so that their children might have the opportunity for education. We are taking care of both requests."

Father Duchesne pointed out that Hong Kong's population has been more than doubled since the refugees came, and that naturally every facility of the colony is taxed. At least fifty thousand children are deprived of schooling because of lack of schools. The colony's tuberculosis hospital has five hundred beds, but at least five thousand persons die of the affliction yearly. These are but a few of the problems that the missioners in Hong Kong are facing.

When a fire broke out in one of the wretched refugee settlements and many people were left homeless, Sisters Imelda and Mark opened the big Maryknoll School building to the refugees, and gave them food, milk and clothing. But the Sisters did not stop there; they decided to get new homes for the people. They talked their plan over with Father Duchesne, persuaded the Government to turn over two parcels of land, begged money from everyone they knew (and many they didn't), obtained building materials at cost, and set the refugees to building. When the project was completed, seventy-one duplex cottages were up. Each has a cement foundation, sand-brick walls, and an asbestos roof. Each building is designed to take care of two families, totaling ten persons. Each family has a large bedroom, a kitchen and bathing facilities. The cost for one family comes to $375, and the cottage is given outright to the family. The only condition is that the family be destitute.

The *Hong Kong Standard* applauded the work of the Sisters, pointing out that the Government had been unable to solve the problem, and declaring: "The Roman Catholic Welfare Committee, without any fanfare, has successfully erected good, livable houses cheaply. . . . Vast possibilities have been opened up by this excellent pioneering in cheap housing, and the Urban Council should take a lead from the Catholics and apply their techniques to the task."

Father John F. Curran, of Butte, Montana, went a step farther. He built a model house to show the refugees what could be done. The house was constructed of quarry stone from nearby hills, and was plastered inside and out. The wood for doors and windows was of native camphor. The floor was cement, and the roof was asbestos. The finished house measured twelve by seventeen feet and cost $125 in American currency. The main items of expense were $35 for labor, and $30 for roofing. Father Curran then proposed a plan of cooperative building to aid them in erecting similar homes for themselves. Mr. J. Wakefield, the Resettlement Officer of the Hong Kong Social Service Bureau, enthusiastically supported the project and offered to have the hillside site terraced. Twenty masons were hired to cut granite blocks. The refugees in family groups supplied the labor to dig the foundations, carry the stone, mix cement and help the masons. Mr. Joseph Li, a Hong Kong Chinese, contributed $10,000 Hong Kong currency to begin the project.

Earlier, when Father Curran had crossed the border to freedom in Hong Kong in 1952, he was a sad man. He felt that the Reds had put an end to his mission work among the Chinese. But as events turned out, the change was not in work, but in change of locale. His new assignment was to start a mission in the Ngau T'au Kok hills.

"When I first looked down the valley that is my mission," he recalls, "I saw scattered the pitiful shacks of my refugee people. I noticed more than one hut built of old, five-gallon gasoline cans. Every inch of space in the shacks was used—as many as ten people to a room. In one place I saw a series of mud piles. I learned that some refugees had constructed homes out of mud bricks, without using any mortar. The first heavy rainfall collapsed them completely."

There were nearly three hundred huts in the valley, holding over a thousand people, with only fifteen Catholics in the entire group. Father Curran rented a one-room hut to live in. His first chapel was a shack. He wandered through the area making the acquaintance of the people, and was shocked by their poverty. He looked for some way to help the people to earn their living. When Father learned that a worker could earn a day's rice by making rattan goods, he engaged a teacher and soon had a group of refugees weaving baskets. More recently one refugee was given a metal-working shop, employing five others. The shop obtained a contract from a Hong Kong restaurant to make pewter dishes. Other refugees were helped to establish small businesses.

Father Curran then built a modern brick school to hold five hundred children. The school was blessed early in 1953, and named in honor of Pope Pius XII, Father of Refugees and Pope of the Missions. Through the help of the Chinese Catholic Club, doctors and nurses volunteered medical aid, and Father Duchesne provided medicines.

"Thus 1954 finds us well established in our little parish across the Jordan River," reported Father Curran. "Our congregation has grown and we have several hundred non-Christians under instruction. We are still doing what we can to help the refugees, while aiding them to help themselves."

Father Howard D. Trube, of New York City, was assigned to the refugee area of Tung Tao Tsuen, where about seventy-eight thousand people live. He first resided on a second floor, over a shop where he opened a library and reading room. Gradually he began spreading his influence by finding jobs for the poor, sending the sick to the hospital and buying them medicine. Father Trube organized a weaving and embroidery cooperative with over 100 members. Funds were begged and borrowed to build the factory and purchase the machinery. Its products have been seen by religious goods stores on Barclay Street, New York, and orders have been given for quantities of the woven materials. Then he built a small house that eventually would become a hostel for the deaf and dumb. A catechist was hired to teach the catechumens, and later the Maryknoll Sisters sent two of their number to help teach the women. On December 8, 1952, Bishop Bianchi, of Hong Kong, visited the refugee camp to confirm seventy new Catholics.

Father Trube's next project was a school. Cardinal Spellman sent a $6,000 gift for the building, and a subsidy for it was sent from Maryknoll headquarters in America. Brother Albert Staubli designed a chapel-school-library combination building. On a visit to Hong Kong Cardinal Spellman set a small marble plaque in the school in memory of Bishop Ford, whose name was given to the school. Then a clinic was opened, and volunteer doctors and nurses came out from the city to give medical help. Thus in the space of a year, Father Trube had built up a flourishing and substantial mission. When Cardinal Spellman revisited the completed plant a year later, he left another gift of $54,000 to construct nine such additional centers among the refugees.

Father Peter A. Reilly, of Roxbury, Massachusetts, began among the refugees by renting the second floor in the only two story building towering over the makeshift houses of some 20,000 refugees in Kaulungtsai. A free clinic provided by British ladies, all registered nurses, distribution of clothing, milk powder, assistance of unemployed, instruction classes keep Father Reilly occupied. Over one hundred were baptized by the end of 1953 and Father Reilly still crowds them into his upper story chapel.

"What a difference a few months make!" says Father Stephen B.

Edmonds, of Cambridge, Massachusetts. "When I was assigned to work among the refugees, I made daily trips from the Maryknoll house at Stanley to Chaaiwan. On first entering the area, I was none too kindly greeted. Even the children shied away from me. But now, as I go about my work among the refugees, I find a wonderful spirit of friendliness to greet me. The children follow me all about, and the adults give me friendly smiles and nods."

Father Edmonds' simple statment does not tell of the hard work he had, building up the thriving parish he now directs in Chaaiwan. When Father Edmonds first came to the area he found five thousand refugees crowded into nine hundred huts. They were all very poor, and striving in every way to eke out a subsistence living. Father Edmonds set up a rattan-weaving factory for the men, and the Maryknoll Sisters hired the women to make embroidery goods. Free medical care is given to the sick; and Father Edmonds helps the poor with money, old clothes, blankets and shelter.

The fifteen hundred children of the settlement were a problem. Father Edmonds went into conference with Government officials and was given a large tract of land. Brother Albert drew up the plans, and under the direction of Sister Mary Imelda, the school building was commenced. Meanwhile the Sisters conducted school in a temporary, barrack-like building. When, later in 1953, the school was dedicated and opened, Hong Kong officials praised Brother Albert and the Sisters for their excellent work in putting up a substantial and beautiful building at a fraction of the cost needed for erecting other Hong Kong schools.

Father Edmonds also built an imposing stone recreation center on land donated by the Government. The center contains rooms for games, a lecture hall and a library. Through the lectures many converts were made. Today the parish has a strong Legion of Mary group, and Sunday Mass is celebrated for standing-room crowds. Father reports that putting Christ into the Chaaiwan camp is a tremendous task with almost unlimited possibilities. He looks forward to a big harvest of souls in the coming years.

The Maryknoll missions in Hong Kong aided more than 25,000 refugees during their first year of operation. Today the missioners operate 4 dispensaries, 3 schools, 2 co-operatives, a dental clinic and an employment office. During 1953, one mission alone gave regular unemployment relief to 235 families, provided rent for 78 other families, and distributed clothing to 9,867 persons. Dispensary treatments in a single year amounted to 26,000.

Dr. Howard A. Rusk, international relief and health authority, writing in The New York Times, gave a description of a visit to the Hong Kong refugee settlements. He said in part:

"The Maryknoll Fathers, long one of the leading missionary orders in China, have started a series of housing developments in which permanent granite-block houses are being erected at a cost as low as $140 a family unit. The developments have one lavatory house for each hundred families, and a central water tap where the rationed water is available four hours a day. The houses are being built on hillsides made available by the Government, and, since these must be terraced, the underlying granite is available on the spot.

"Each development has a church that serves as a community center, a school and a small dispensary. Last Sunday, when this writer visited such a dispensary in clinic hours, a team of five physicians headed by one of Hong Kong's leading pediatricians saw more than one hundred sick children. All of the doctors had given up their one free day to help in this free clinic, which was organized and directed by the pediatrician's wife."

It is the children who particularly touch the heart of the missioner. Father Duchesne, who knows the refugee youngsters very well, paints a sad portrait when he writes:

"Who are they? What have they done? Why are they sad? They are the children of China's refugees now crowding Hong Kong. They are the children who run the hills. They play with pebbles; they amuse themselves by gathering firewood. A shiny cigarette wrapper or an empty pillbox fills them with joy. Real toys are not for them. Little girls will hold candy in their grimy hands for an hour, the longer to savor the pleasure of eating it.

"Their faces are pinched—cracked by the winds. Heads are cropped with dull razors, or the hair is long and scraggly. Hardly a head is free from boils, pink eyes, or running ears. Sad eyes are used to tears. Sunken cheeks and toothless gums betray the lack of vitamins. Distended stomachs tell of worms. Swollen feet announce beriberi.

"For a party to which we were told that 135 of these children had been invited, that number of padded garments, oranges, and

apples were prepared. Before the distribution got under way, several hundred children had their hands out. Children appeared
from behind boulders and came up over the hills in swarms.

"The refugee children never have any of the good things to eat
and seldom have enough of any kind of food. Seldom is there
candy or cake—never ice cream—yet they love to eat sweets as
do all children. Actually, they are always hungry.

"For them there is no school, no church, no movies. They have
no roller skates, no shoes, no radio, no music. Their 'homes' are
little tarpaper and tin huts on the mountains, in the valleys, in
tunnels. These homes have no electricity or running water—a telephone is a mystery. These homes have no windows. The floor is
dirt, which turns to mud when rain falls. Four bricks are all that
is needed to make a stove; an old stool serves as a table. The ten-
ants sleep on boards. The children's bare toes have never known
the delightful pleasure of reveling in the fuzz of a carpet. They
never smile; they run from strangers. They can't bring home a
stray puppy dog because they could not feed it—there are no scraps
from the tables in their homes.

"In not even the remotest sense, may these unfortunate children
be said to suffer because their plight is their own fault. And usually
it is not the fault of their mothers and fathers."

This is the sentiment that all the missioners in Hong Kong
bring to their tasks. The ambassadors of Christianity are not,
however, the only ones working among the refugees. Hong Kong's
Communists come among them appealing for support. When a
fire destroyed some shacks in one refugee camp, the Reds showed
up and passed out some relief.

"But the Chinese who have come here from the mainland,"
says Father Trube, "cannot be bought so cheaply. They went
through such propaganda methods before, and know too well
the actual outcome when the Reds gain control. These refugees
are here because of an ideal. They sacrificed everything they owned
to flee from tyranny. That's why they are so deserving of the help
of men of the free world."

28

The Maryknoll Brothers

"Will there be a place for me in your new Society?" a young Catholic working man asked Father James Anthony Walsh back in 1912 when he heard of the founding of Maryknoll. "I know I have no vocation to the priesthood, but I would like to serve God in some way."

Father Walsh assured his questioner that there would be a place for him in a group of Brothers then being formed. Thus the Foreign Mission Brothers of Saint Michael came into being and received the first members even before students arrived at the newly created Maryknoll. Ever since that day, the contribution made by such loyal Catholic men to the work of Maryknoll is beyond measure. For it is the Brothers of Maryknoll who keep things running smoothly in the various Maryknoll seminaries, colleges, houses of studies, and procures in the United States and in similar establishments on the foreign mission fields of the Orient, Latin America, and Africa.

They do the clerical work in the offices; buy the food and other supplies; take care of the painting, carpentering, and building repairs; do the electrical work in the various houses; look after the grounds, vineyards, gardens and farms, and feed the livestock. In the missions they also teach English and science, conduct trade schools and dispensaries, supervise the construction of buildings. No matter what the work, there is a Maryknoll Brother to do it.

For nearly a quarter of a century, Brother William Neary, of Pittsfield, Massachusetts, has been working quietly and efficiently in mission countries of the Orient. The results of his specialized efforts are apparent in both Korea and Japan, where he has constructed more than a hundred buildings of various types. Churches built by Brother William have won high praise from veteran missioners, both as models of good taste and as examples of excellent workmanship. In 1953, Maurice Lavanoux, managing editor of *Liturgical Arts* magazine, visited Japan to study religious art and architecture in that country. From a professional point of view, Mr. Lavanoux was impressed by the work of three men, whom he praised in these words:

"I would urge all those in charge of building operations in Japan to sponsor the work of such architects as Fathers Charles Freuler, C.M., and Antonin Raymond . . . and Brother William Neary, of Maryknoll, whom I met in Kyoto and who guided me on several memorable expeditions . . ."

Mr. Lavanoux speaks with no little authority. He is secretary of the Liturgical Arts Society, whose purpose is to devise ways and means for improving the standards of taste, craftsmanship, and liturgical correctness current in the practice of Catholic art in the United States.

Brother William was born in North Adams, Massachusetts, on November 11, 1902. He attended St. Joseph's School in Pittsfield and was graduated from Berkshire Business College as an accountant. By the time he entered Maryknoll, in 1923, he already was a skilled carpenter. When he later took up architecture, he practically became a one-man mission construction crew. In the years since he left on his first overseas assignment, to North Korea in 1926, Brother William has put up practically every needed type of mission structure. His eighteen rectories, seventeen chapels and fifteen churches became the focal points of mission stations. In addition, he has built at least eleven houses, six convents, five meeting halls, five small schools, three combination churches-rectories, two sanatoriums, two central houses, one large school and miscellaneous smaller buildings.

Brother William was twenty-three when he was assigned to Maryknoll's Korean mission. Buildings were so urgently needed that he had to skip the customary year of language study and start immediately to work. Yet he used every spare moment to study the language, and his contact with the workingmen gave him plenty of practice. In a short time, he was chattering away in the complicated language with almost the same finesse as a native. Fellow missioners say that, despite his crowded schedule, he always found time to help the poor. Quietly, he would bring a poor family food and clothing, and almost seemed embarrassed when one of his fellow missioners noticed his charity.

"One of my first jobs in Korea," Brother recalls, "was remodeling some old Korean homes. They were nothing more than shacks, in an abandoned silver-mining area. That winter I lived in a shack covered only by tarpaper, while working on a new house for a missioner. It rained nearly every day. I was walking, working, and sleeping under an umbrella. Perhaps the final outcome of the job was an evidence of my feelings at the time. Missioners dubbed that particular job the classical Irishman's nightmare."

Another incident he likes to recall happened at Saiho, in the mid-thirties when a certain high priestess of a devil-worshiping cult leveled vile threats at Brother when she learned that he was going to build a small church there. On the building site was an ancient oak tree, before which the high priestess regularly conducted ceremonies. She personally assured Brother that devils would burn to the ground any building constructed there. Brother William went methodically ahead and finished the job. Later the high priestess retired from the locality. For reasons never explained, the oak tree withered and died as soon as Mass was celebrated for the first time in the new church.

"Funny thing about the oak-tree episode," chuckled Brother. "The son of the high priestess came into the Church. Guess the old girl herself went back to the minor leagues."

When World War II forced an end to mission building, Brother William returned to the United States, but not to be unemployed. There was plenty of building to be done around the various Maryknoll houses and Brother William was the man to do it. At the end of the war he was sent to Japan to start construction work needed because of the rapid growth of the Church there. It was his adaptation of Japanese construction that attracted the attention of the editor of Liturgical Arts, and won favorable comment.

"I guess I had my share of consolations," Brother William reflects. "I always got a lift, returning to places where I'd done some building. I'd look at the people in the churches worshiping God, and I'd remember how, just a year or so earlier they had used an old shack for a church."

After the war a large number of servicemen came to Maryknoll to be Brothers, and since that time, the stream of vocations from the armed forces has been steady. This is in part due to the age limit for entrance (21-30), which is the time most young men finish their military service. Like all Maryknollers, the Brothers are representatives of all parts of America, and of all groups. Some had held commissions in the armed forces. Others had gone to college or had come to Maryknoll directly from farm or factory. They are mature young men, who have chosen a life of sacrifice after prayerful thought and decision.

Entrance day is near September 29, the feast of Saint Michael the Archangel, patron of the Maryknoll Brothers. The Brother-candidate is known as a postulant, and this period may last from six months to a year, depending upon the time of entrance. At the completion of the postulancy, the candidates enter a year of novitiate training. The Brothers' Novitiate is located in Brookline, Massachusetts. Here he lives a life of prayer and work. Here he is invested with the cassock and cincture and receives a religious name. At the end of the novitiate year, he takes an oath of stability and obedience to Maryknoll and is given an assignment.

The Brothers work in Maryknoll houses in the United States and abroad. The tasks that they perform are very valuable to the Society. Brother Daniel Doherty, of Dorchester, Massachusetts, graduated from Harvard University and was a professional chemist. He came to Maryknoll in 1924 and for many years taught chemistry to the seminarians. Because of his special abilities, however, in 1936 he secured a B.S. in Library Science and is currently in library work. Brother Felix Fournier, of Brooklyn, entered Maryknoll in 1938. Assigned to the Guatemala mission, he has done wonderful work in helping to keep the various missions running smoothly, and in aiding the Indians to more prosperous agriculture. In Africa, Brothers Damien Walsh, of Wheeling, West Virginia, and Fidelis Deichelbohrer, of Wyandotte, Michigan, are supervising a large-scale building program of Maryknoll's new mission there.

Brother Kevin Grimley, of New York City, and Brother Frederick Steinbach have supervised Maryknoll farms for many years, and have saved the Society thousands of dollars in food bills. Brother Francis Wempe, of Cumberland, Maryland, has been with Maryknoll since 1924. In China he performed outstanding dispensary work, and played a large part in the preparation of a standard Cantonese-English dictionary. Brother Clement Hansan, of St. Mary's, Kansas, has been the right-hand man of missioners in Japan for many years.

Elsewhere in this book, many Brothers have been metioned for the contributions they have made to mission work. One of them is Brother Albert Staubli, who worked in Kongmoon and now in Hong Kong. Bishop James Edward Walsh, formerly Brother's superior in Kongmoon, penned a tribute to this valuable mission worker which is worth repeating. Bishop Walsh wrote:

"He arrived in China in 1921 with an equipment that might have been thought modest. He had youth, sinewy strength, a Maryknoll vocation, a knowledge of the wheelwright trade, a skill with tools, and a sense of humor. Most of these assets he had brought from his native Switzerland a few short years previously. He had tarried in America just long enough to pick up the mission vocation and a knowledge of English. It never took him long to learn anything, he mastered the elements of the new vocation and the new language quickly and well.

"The South China missions were new and embryonic, but they were getting ready for some expansion and development. A modest building program was in order, if the mission gains and advances were to be consolidated and made permanent. A practical builder was needed. The young Swiss wheelwright had become Brother Albert. He was ready. Off he went.

"That was twenty-five years ago. Today the wheelwright is known throughout the South China missions as architect, engineer, contractor, builder, mechanic, carpenter, woodcarver, artist, Chinese linguist, Oriental psychologist, and general trouble shooter par excellence. Any one of these attainments plus the spirit of the mission vocation would suffice to make a missioner. The combination makes a sort of mission army rolled into one man, and it makes that man a very useful person to have around.

"Brother Albert made a good start in China—perhaps the best possible start for a missioner—by opening his heart to the Chinese people and keeping his eyes open at the same time. His was not a blind championship of everything his new friends did; it was rather a discriminating understanding of their good qualities in spite of what they did. In those days the mission work was no rougher and tougher than it is today—perhaps even less so—but it was more difficult to perform because of the inexperience of the missioners. They were learning—and the Chinese around them were helping them to learn with every trick in the native repertoire.

"The Chinese are the best people on earth in all the essentials of natural character, but they are also the world's masters for shrewd wisdom in practical affairs. They are seldom without an axe to grind, although it is not often visible to the naked eye. Their devious, oblique methods of approaching a totally hidden objective reach a height that can only be called art. When the objective turned out to be something innocent and good, Brother Albert was confirmed in his fondness for the people. In cases where the objective was not so good, Brother Albert appreciated the cleverness of the method—as one artist with another. He understood the people and got on well with them from the beginning.

"Nobody who ever saw the Loting chapel will need to be convinced either of the beauty of the Oriental style in its own right, or of its suitability for Catholic missions in China. One of the first mission buildings designed and erected by Brother Albert, this little gem of Chinese architecture remains one of the loveliest of all his many productions. The designing was the easy part of the assignment. The hard part was the supervision of the construction, with the constant cajoling, brow-beating, and mollifying of the native workmen, which it entailed. He already had the vocabulary to wax eloquent on building problems. Even at this early date, he used to read his meditation in Chinese written characters every morning, and his proficiency in the language grew apace. By the time this project was finished, all the workmen were his friends, and he had taught wood carving to several of the carpenters as a specialty to improve their livelihood. Some of the workmen were later converted. In many ways the little Loting chapel was a model building operation.

"Calls for the mission builder began to pour in and Brother Albert's life became a rush from one task to another. He was

limited only by his inability to be in two places at once. He repaired the Sunchong chapel; went through the Communist up-
rising and built the Kongmoon chapel with Communist strikers
as his workmen at the same time; designed and built the Kongmoon seminary, the Toishan hospital, the chief buildings of the
Gate of Heaven leper asylum; helped the Sisters in the construction of the beautiful Maryknoll Convent School in Hong Kong;
and worked on other jobs too numerous to mention, here and
there in the missions. Meanwhile he was learning a lot about
China and was making himself completely at home in that land.
He was unconsciously preparing for harder jobs in harder conditions.

"Pearl Harbor day found Brother Albert moving around the
missions, a few steps ahead of the raiding and occupying Japanese
military. He had some close calls—but God had work for him to do
and kept him out of harm's way. During the first period of the war,
he erected the new Taipat mission plant and helped Father Constantine Burns with some construction work at Wanfau. Brother
Albert belonged to the mission staff of the Kongmoon Vicariate,
and he had carried out most of his building operations in that
territory, but it was always understood that he was ready and happy
to take on any building problems anywhere in the South China
Missions.

"In 1944 he went to Wuchow to assist Bishop Donaghy in some
important construction, which was to round out the central mission
plant. That work proved a race against time. Japanese soldiers had
already taken Kweilin and flooded over the northern half of Kwangsi Province, making Wuchow a sort of enclave in an area of occupation. Meanwhile more Japanese were making their leisurely
way up the West River from the southeast, with Wuchow as their
obvious objective. The occupation of the city was only a matter of
time, depending on the plans or whims of the invaders. In those
days most of the city people departed, for pastures new and green
in hills far away, while it was still possible to do so. Those who remained were heartened to find Bishop Donaghy, Father Reilly,
and Brother Albert working on the new mission structure with
every appearance of serene confidence in the future. The work
was timed nicely. The day before the occupation force arrived,
Brother Albert saw to the finishing touches, paid off the workmen,
and departed, under the bishop's orders, to join Father Mc-

Laughlin and Father Fedders in the mountain mission of Topong.

"Another job had been completed. But nobody was destined to profit by it for the moment, as Bishop Donaghy and Father Reilly were obliged at the same time to vacate the city and seek refuge in a little village to the north. The newly built mission property was perforce left to the mercies of war and warriors, until better times should materialize.

"The Topong saga is one that will be long remembered in Maryknoll annals. With a global war surging all around them and local bandits adding to the gaiety, Father McLaughlin, Father Fedders, and Brother Albert settled down to maintain their tiny mountain mission against the world. Cut off from Bishop Donaghy, who was isolated in a still more dangerous pocket, and bereft of all supplies and outside help, they transferred the native seminary to this out-of-the-way place, maintained it there, kept up the local mission work and kept themselves alive, without a break in continuity, until peace was declared. It was not a time or a place to build, yet Brother Albert found the means to carry out some much-needed repairs and to make the bulging quarters ship-shape.

"After that he looked around for the most urgent work and decided it lay in the commissary department. How to keep alive was truly the real problem in the situation. 'Suppose I take the job of feeding the family,' he suggested. He was elected on the spot.

"Brother Albert proved to be a cross between a procurator and a magician. He started raising pigs, chickens, and garden produce immediately. He carefully salvaged seeds and grew continuous crops of vegetables throughout the whole period. His chickens thrived until a pest invaded the neighborhood; then, when some of his own flock got the disease, he fed them a few sulfa pills he had saved for an emergency, and the flock was cured overnight. This is a good use of modern medical science when life depends on a few eggs and an occasional chicken. The livestock and garden produce eliminated the serious danger of starvation that had threatened the completely isolated mission.

"He undertook, one day, to protect the mission from an imminent raid of local bandits. 'I'm glad I did not have to use the Mauser,' he remarked, 'because I do not know how the thing works.'

"Either mission work makes men resourceful, or else God picks men of resource and sends them into mission work. Or perhaps both conditions are true. At any rate, in South China there are many missioners who would welcome the companionship of Maryknoll's young Swiss wheelwright—who is no longer young and is much more than a wheelwright—whenever they find themselves in a tight spot."

Today, Brother Albert is carrying on in Hong Kong, and the school and parish buildings he has erected there are of beautiful and enduring construction as is his faith which has led him to devote his life to God. The work of most of the Brothers goes unsung and unheralded. Only eternity will tell of the tremendous good accomplished by these men who lead a hidden life. Like Saint Joseph, the Brother remains in the background. His consolation comes in knowing that his life of prayer and sacrifice leads to the salvation of souls he has never seen, as well as his own salvation. The successful Maryknoll priest must be a spiritual man, but the successful Maryknoll Brother is a spiritual giant.

29

The Maryknoll Sisters

In late December, 1906, a tall, handsome young woman walked through the crowds of Union Park Street, in Boston, to a ramshackle, crooked old building with sagging-shuttered windows and an uninviting, paint-peeled door. With some trepidation, she rang the bell, crossed the uneven threshold and entered a little hall. She mounted the rubber-treaded stairs. At the top she faced the door that led to the office of Father James Anthony Walsh, Boston's Director of the Society for the Propagation of the Faith. Little knowing the lifelong import of what she did, Mary Josephine Rogers turned the old-fashioned doorknob and went in.

Father Walsh's office was a small room, indeed, but also a charming one. There were bright hangings on the walls, splotches of color against the whiteness. There were piles of magazines, pictures, posters, papers of all sorts. The files were neat but plainly bulging. A globe on the shelf and pictures of bearded missioners everywhere showed the world-wide character of the work done in that little office. In a corner, stood a four-foot statue of Saint Francis Xavier, raising aloft his missioner's crucifix. In the midst of it all was Father Walsh. On his desk were the galley proofs for the first issue of *The Field Afar,* due to make its bow to the public on January 1, 1907. He had been poring over them when the visitor entered.

It was their first meeting although they had corresponded for several months. Miss Rogers was a teacher at Smith College, in Northampton, Massachusetts. The students at Smith were mostly Protestant girls, and interest in church work ran high. There were Bible-study clubs, Sunday-school clubs and ever so many mission clubs studying the work of Protestant missionaries in all parts of the world.

A zealous Protestant teacher, Miss Hanscom, had first broached the idea of a religious club for the Catholic girls. "And Mary Rogers is the person to head it!" she had affirmed. Mary Rogers chose to make her organization a mission club. She had always had a particular interest in Asia. Her uncle was a sea captain and his house was a treasure trove of oriental oddities. He had a Chinese cook who told stories about Chinese people that made her eyes sparkle and her heart glow with genuine love for their souls.

Miss Rogers came from an active Catholic family. Fairly well-to-do, they had spearheaded many Catholic movements. It was her grandfather, Patrick Rogers, who had organized resistance to the Know-Nothing Movement years before.

Faced with the prospect of conducting a mission club, Miss Rogers had found it well-nigh impossible to get material. However, her confessor had directed her to Father Walsh as Director of the Society for the Propagation of the Faith, and she had written to him. The answer was quick, spontaneous, helpful—characteristic of the vigorous mind which went all out in the effort to make Boston conscious of Catholic foreign missions. Father Walsh had sent pictures, letters, and literature. He was only too glad to help her.

Later, when Miss Rogers was at home on the Christmas vacation, she made the historic visit to the Propagation office. Her main purpose was to ask if Father Walsh would be able to go to Northampton soon, and talk to the students. The request was readily granted. Then Miss Rogers looked at the stacks of pictures, the piles of magazines, the wire baskets of letters. She asked a fatal question: "Do you need help, Father? Perhaps I can spend some time during this vacation here."

When she went out of that office, Miss Rogers carried in her arms several envelopes of pictures. They were to be soaked in water, gently peeled off from the cardboard backing, dried flat and returned to Father Walsh for filing. That night, the Rogers' bathtub was full of bearded missioners, slant-eyed waifs, impressive pagodas and strangely habited Sisters. Mary Rogers had started working for the missions.

Soon her group of Smith College Catholics was working with her. The girls translated the letters of foreign missioners; they saved their spending money. Miss Rogers spent her entire vacation helping Father Walsh. The next year she took a position as teacher in the Boston public schools. From then on, her every minute of spare time, winter and summer, went into the work with Father Walsh on *The Field Afar*. She translated letters and articles, wrote stories and worked on the editing of the magazine. She cleared out and began rearranging the files, throwing out photographs or putting them into good condition. Father Walsh had scrapbooks on every mission country, filled with clippings and pictures. These were kept in order, ready with information at a moment's notice.

There were others who helped too. Nora Shea was Father Walsh's secretary, who worked with heart and soul. Mary Dwyer had a mimeographing machine; she did not go to the office, but Father Walsh sent her the work and she returned the completed papers. Victoria Larmour, one of the Smith College group, was in Connecticut then; she sent writings and translations. Mary Louise Wholean, a Wellesley graduate, offered her services. Sarah Sullivan, an excellent secretary, came to *The Field Afar* offices two or three days a week for several months at the end of 1911. These young women worked as individuals, however. Indeed, few of them knew each other.

Most of them were praying hard when, in 1911, Father Walsh and Father Price left Boston for Rome to obtain approval for their hoped-for Foreign Mission Society. There was rejoicing when the news came that, on June 29th, His Holiness Pius X had commissioned the two American priests to begin their seminary. In September the Society was established with its first students at Hawthorne, N.Y.

On January 5, 1912, the first three of the women's group arrived to do secretarial and other office work. They took the old Tulph house. In those days in Hawthorne, there were no street numbers; everybody in town knew the Tulph house. Gradually, the others of the first six Maryknoll Sisters arrived. Mary Rogers came in February to see how the first few were settled; then she came again for most of the summer vacation. She came permanently in September, 1912, when she could resign her teaching post. She arrived just four days after the last of a series of cooks, in a huff at being asked to live in such a desolate place, had departed leaving the priests breakfastless. Mary Rogers volunteered to step into the breach. She was an excellent cook; indeed, it was a sort of hobby with her. In the end, although they had had no such intention at first, the secretaries undertook to staff the kitchen as well as the offices.

That same September, the whole infant organization moved to Sunset Hill in Ossining—known ever since as "Maryknoll." Miss Rogers had presented herself as the prospective buyer of the estate. She had posed as a wealthy young woman from Boston who wished to buy a country residence near New York, because as explained in an earlier chapter, it was feared that the owner might not wish to sell to a Catholic organization. She was accompanied by her chauffeur, a modest, retiring man, who was known in other circles as Father James A. Walsh. A linen duster covered his Roman collar. Miss Rogers played her part well, but she made one bad slip. "Do you intend to build, Miss Rogers?" the owner asked. "Yes," she answered. "What type of architecture do you prefer?" he asked. "Byzantine," she replied. But the slip passed unnoticed.

Miss Rogers agreed to buy the property. That night, in the kitchen of the Tulph house at Hawthorne, she sold it to the Catholic Foreign Mission Society of America, in the person of Father James A. Walsh, for the sum of one dollar. He passed the dollar over the kitchen table; "Maryknoll" existed.

Once at Sunset Hill, the first six Maryknoll Sisters established themselves at St. Teresa's, the farmhouse on the property. They were known then as "Teresians," for both Father Walsh and Mary Rogers had tremendous enthusiasm for the great Spanish Carmelite. Her spirit vivified the five other young women who had cast in their lot with a venture that everybody, except those concerned with it, seemed to believe was doomed to sudden failure.

They were: Sarah Sullivan, who for twelve years had been secretary to the Dean of Harvard's Medical School, who took the name Sister Mary Teresa; Nora Shea, Father Walsh's faithful secretary, who was to be known as Sister Mary Theophane; Margaret Shea, a young girl from Melrose, Massachusetts, who was Sister Mary Gemma; Mary L. Wholean, Sister Xavier in those early days, who died in 1917 before she could see much expansion in the work; and Mary Dwyer, who had come with the original group but did not stay.

From then on, the story of the Maryknoll Sisters has been one of expansion and development. Others came to join them; some stayed and some left after a taste of their rugged life. But the group slowly grew. In 1914, they were constituted a "Pious Society of Women" at the request of Cardinal Farley. On February 12, 1920, when there were forty Teresians to hear the glad news, Bishop Dunn, Auxiliary Bishop of New York, telephoned that Rome had authorized Cardinal Hayes to erect them as a religious congregation. A Dominican Sister from the Sinsinawa congregation arrived in 1917, to instruct the neophytes in the religious life. She was Sister Mary Ruth. In 1919, she was succeeded by Sister Mary Fidelia. Both are gratefully remembered by Maryknoll Sisters as their mentors in the ways of Dominican living. The new Sisters were to be Third Order Dominicans. They took the title, Foreign Mission Sisters of St. Dominic.

In all this time, the women of Maryknoll scrubbed and cooked and sewed. They sent out *The Field Afar* each month to a growing list of subscribers. They issued appeals, letters and literature. Some of them wrote stories or serious articles. Some talked to schools and women's clubs whenever opportunities arose. There was no discrimination of tasks; everyone turned her full energy to whatever work was at hand to be done. They were without public vows, without immediate hope of ever going on the mission field. But they all worked to spread a knowledge of missions and a love for them throughout America. The simple generous spirit of Mary Rogers, known by then as Sister Mary Joseph, pervaded the whole congregation.

Even in those early days, visitors at Maryknoll noted an atmosphere of warm friendliness that animated the Sisters. It was not the rigid formalism sometimes met with in religious, nor yet the individualism that is inconsistent with community life. It has since come to be known as "the Maryknoll spirit." Mother Mary Joseph herself has written of it.

"We have tried from the beginning to cultivate a spirit which is extremely difficult and which for a long time might have been misunderstood even by those who were nearest to us, and that is, the retention of our own natural dispositions, the retention of our own individuality, having in mind, of course, that all of these things should be corrected where radically wrong, and all of it supernaturalized.

"I say that it is a most difficult spirit that we could have chosen for ourselves. After all, it is not so difficult to settle upon a particular type which you would wish your Sisters to resemble, marking out certain observances, certain posture, and you could cut every Sister according to a pattern, or rather, you could pour her into a mold and have her turn out marked with the outlines desired. That is not difficult where we have, or hope to have, in Sisters, docility, obedience and a perfect willingness to be plastic in the hands of their superiors.

"But for us, that sort of development will hardly do. We are reaching out for souls. We expect to go out and live amongst those who will be suspicious of us, who will not like us, who will respect us only when we have proven our virtue, our sincerity and our usefulness to them. Why, then, should they come to us? For no reason at all excepting for what they can get from us. Therefore, it is necessary that we should go forward, should seek those lost sheep of the fold and bring them home.

"And for this we need all our individuality, all our generosity, all our graciousness and sweetness and simplicity, all our powers of gentle persuasiveness—in fact, all of the things which God has given us to use. Each one of us, in her own work, with her own particular little sweetness or attractiveness, is to be used by God as a particular tool to do particular work and to save particular souls.

"That explains our spirit—an attempt to keep our individuality, casting out what is objectionable in it, finding what is good and beautiful in it and supernaturalizing all this, using it, not for ourselves, not for any honor or distinction, not that it may win for us a place in the mission field, but utterly regardless of station or opportunities, only with the thought that it will be used for God's honor and glory and as He wishes it to be used . . ."

The first branch budded in 1918, when Sister Mary Theophane took a group to Clarks Summit, Pa., near Scranton, to help at the Venard Apostolic College.

In April, 1920, Mother Mary Joseph announced that Bishop

Cantwell, of Los Angeles, had asked for Sisters to staff a home and school for the Japanese. In those days, California seemed an immense distance away. Here was a chance to work among Orientals in a land of palm trees and other tropical oddities. "The Missions" —that dream of all the busy secretaries—was coming very close. A month later, the situation was repeated, this time by Bishop O'Dea, of Seattle, where many Japanese had settled. He wished the Sisters to open an orphanage.

Sisters went out on both these projects. In Los Angeles, at 425 South Boyle Avenue, the Maryknoll Home for Japanese children began and later there was a school on Hewitt Street. In Seattle, likewise, an orphanage was opened; later, in 1926, the Maryknoll School for Japanese children and still later on, in 1938, a Day Nursery started.

Things happened fast. Just a year after the Pacific Coast missions began, the first foreign mission assignments were made. Sister Mary Paul was to head a band of six Sisters going to Hong Kong. On November 3, 1921, they set foot in China, the land of which they had read and thought and dreamed for many years. The Maryknoll Fathers had preceded them by some three years. It was good to see again these eager young men whom they had known as students in Maryknoll's farmhouse.

The Sisters started missions in the interior the very next year, when a refuge for abandoned babies was opened in Yeungkong, in the Kongmoon Vicariate. Another such creche started in 1924, at Loting in the same vicariate. It was these Sisters who once were captured on a junk, and held by river bandits for several days.

As the Maryknoll Fathers assumed responsibility for various mission territories in China, they requested Sisters. Thus, in 1933, a group of Maryknoll Sisters went to Kaying to continue training some native Sisters who had begun their religious life in Hong Kong. In 1935, others went to Wuchow and in 1938, more went to Kweilin.

In all of these sections, native novitiates were started, among other works. To build up a native Church is one of the prime tasks of the missioner. In 1926, the first aspirants from the Kongmoon area went to Hong Kong to begin training. In 1931, they returned to Kongmoon with Sisters Mary Lawrence and Mary Patricia and set up the Immaculate Heart Novitiate. There were twenty-eight professed Sisters in this congregation at the time that Communists took over the government of China. They staffed eight missions and conducted a high school in Kongmoon. Nurses and teachers, they were well-educated Chinese women.

Similarly, Chinese communities came into being in the other sections. In Kaying, under Bishop Ford, Sister Mary Marcelline trained the Sister Catechists of Our Lady; in Wuchow, Bishop Donaghy commissioned Sister Moira to train the Sisters of the Sacred Heart; and in Kweilin, Sister Rose Victor was in charge of another group, called Missionary Catechists of the Blessed Virgin Mary.

The effect of these years of training is evident now, when foreign Sisters are all expelled from China. The native Sisters, in lay clothes, can do much for their Catholic people. Some have evacuated to Macao, where they are able to continue their studies. Two Maryknoll Sisters are with them there.

Medical work also flourished in China. Sister-nurses conducted dispensaries in Wuchow, Kweilin, Laipo, Yeungkong, Loting and other places. Two Sister-doctors, Sister Antonia Maria and Sister Maria Corazon, were at work in the China field. In 1947, Sacred Heart Hospital was opened. It was not large, but it took care of some 888 clinic patients a month and thirty-six in-patients at Toishan, in the Kongmoon Vicariate. Here the Sisters could train native nurses in modern techniques. In this way, some of the Chinese Sisters became proficient nurses.

Perhaps most significant of all was the work done by the Sisters in Kaying, Bishop Ford's diocese. He believed that missionary Sisters should be used in direct evangelization of women. That is, they would live, two by two, in small houses in the villages, coming as close as possible to the Chinese way of life. Instructing prospective converts, encouraging new Christians, and serving as a liaison between the shy Chinese women and the priest, they would best serve their missionary vocation. There were seven such "small houses" of two Sisters each, when trouble began with the Communists in 1950.

While all this development was going on in China proper, the work in Hong Kong was also increased. Maryknoll Convent School in the Kowloon section of the city, begun in 1925, grew by leaps and bounds. In 1936, the big building, that housed the school, the industrial section and the convent, was opened on Waterloo Road. It is also a regional center for Sisters coming from the interior of the country. This is one of the landmarks in Kowloon. Situated near the airport, the Maryknoll school building serves as a guide for planes coming into Hong Kong. Besides the school for approximately 800 girls, classes are held for 110 refugee children who come from shanties and caves in the dry hills behind the big building.

On the island of Hong Kong itself is another Maryknoll School for 242 Chinese girls of well-to-do families. These will be future leaders in the colony; they are being trained to Christian principles even though many are from pagan families. An apostolate among girls of this type is a long-sighted mission work.

The years of World War II were turbulent ones for China, naturally. In Hong Kong, the Sisters were immediately interned. After several months of this, some were repatriated to the States; others made their way to American-held territory. The end of the war found the Sisters scattered as far as India, Macao, Chungking. A few of the missions were not occupied by the Japanese at all, although there were many raids. As soon as peace came, the Sisters returned to their mission stations.

When Communists took over the government of China in 1949, refugees began pouring into Hong Kong. More than a million of them lived in huts and shacks, in caves and in the streets of the British colony. The Sisters began relief work immediately. A terrible fire in November, 1950, destroyed thousands of these wretched dwellings. Fire victims lived in the big Maryknoll Convent School building for weeks until houses could be found for them. Out of this experience grew the housing project that has provided clean fire-proof cottages for thousands of refugees. Welfare centers, elementary schools, chapels and clinics are set up in various refugee villages in Hong Kong now. The Sisters work with the Maryknoll Fathers and the Catholic Welfare Organization in these centers.

In the meantime the Sisters in interior missions were suffering Communist persecution. All of them were imprisoned or placed under house arrest for periods varying from a few months to almost two years. During all of 1951 and 1952, they were crossing the border in groups of two or three, exhausted by their experiences.

Three years after the first departure for China—that is, in 1924 —six Sisters arrived at Pyongyang, Korea. An old folks' home and a dispensary were soon opened. Sister Mary Mercy, the first Mary-

knoll Sister-doctor, operated a clinic at Shingishu. A native novitiate, an industrial school and catechetical work were flourishing in
four cities. Then, at the outbreak of World War II, all the American Sisters were interned and later repatriated to the United States.

Only one of the Maryknoll group remained. She was Sister
Mary Agneta, a native Korean, who had been assistant novice
Mistress in the native novitiate at Pyongyang. She stayed through
the war years and was caught by the sudden influx of Russians in
1945, as they overran Manchuria and northern Korea. For the next
five years, it was only by devious means that news of Sister Agneta
reached the Motherhouse in New York. But this news told of her
splendid work in encouraging and training her native Sisters. She
completed their training just in time for the Korean war. Hunted
by the Communists, she went from place to place for many
months. Eventually, she was captured and carried off in an oxcart
over rough, village roads. No one has heard of her since; the pre-
sumption is that Sister Mary Agneta was executed.

In December, 1949, another beachhead was made on Korea.
Three Maryknoll Sisters started a dispensary in Pusan, near the
southern tip of the peninsula. They were unable to get in touch
with Sister M. Agneta behind the Iron Curtain in the north of the
country. The dispensary had hardly started when hostilities broke
out in June, 1950. The Sisters were evacuated to Japan, but in
March, 1951, they were the first civilian women permitted to return
to Korea.

Setting up a dispensary, they were soon swamped by the pitiable
refugees who crowded into the city. Sister Mercy and her Sisters did
and still do heroic work; clinical treatments mounted until there
are now more than 2,000 a day. Reinforcements have been rushed
there; at present, the staff numbers nineteen Sisters, of which three
are doctors, and the others are nurses, pharmacists, medical techni-
cians and catechists. The clinic at Pusan has been termed "the
largest charity hospital in the world." Recently the millionth patient was recorded.

30

Valiant Women

In the early part of 1926, a group of Sisters was forming in Manila, in preparation for opening a Normal College at Malabon, about ten miles north of the city. The need for Catholic-trained teachers in the Philippines was acute. Archbishop O'Doherty had rebuilt a large monastery in Malabon and offered it for this purpose. By July of 1926, twelve Sisters had arrived and were ready to begin the work.

The Sisters' work in the Philippines has been educational for the most part. In 1936, the Normal School was moved to Manila and became Maryknoll College. The large building it now occupies is reputed to be the longest building in the Philippines. A total of 1,056 students attend from the kindergarten up to college work. In 1929, the Sisters built a convent in Baguio, high in the mountains of northern Luzon. A primary school was soon started, using the American curriculum, to serve as a preparation for children who were to go to the States for their higher education. After World War II, this was changed and the Baguio school now follows the Philippine curriculum.

The Baguio convent developed as a prime catechetical center.

Situated on the very edge of the city, it is surrounded by the huts of the Igorot tribesmen. These people were noted as headhunters in the early days of the American occupation of the Philippines. They are still classified as semi-civilized. But through the zeal of Sister Mary Constance and Sister Mary Fidelis, who spent many years among them, almost five hundred Igorots have become Catholics and form a staunch group ready to sacrifice much for their Faith.

When the normal school moved in 1936 to Manila, a primary school was continued at Malabon, renamed St. James Academy by Archbishop O'Doherty in honor of Maryknoll's cofounder, Bishop James A. Walsh, who had died in April of that year. This school, too, has grown rapidly. A high school was begun in 1941. Both primary and high-school students number 1,200 at present. In 1938, a school was begun in Lucena, in what is now Quezon Province, some sixty miles southeast of Manila. Students here, too, have reached the thousand mark, in primary and high schools.

The Lipa School, about 40 miles south of Manila, is a post-war development. Opened in 1950, it now enrolls 750 students. The latest venture is on the island of Mindanao, southernmost of the Philippine group—an island which was never Christianized by the Spanish. The inhabitants are, for the most part, Mohammedan or pagan. Four Sisters went there in June, 1952, to supervise a school of some 575 children at Jimenez, a Catholic town under the care of the Irish Columban Fathers.

The effort has been made in all these schools to use native teachers where possible. Graduates of Maryknoll College in Manila are trained in modern teaching techniques. These, so to speak, permit the mission Sisters to multiply themselves. In this way, a few Sisters are stationed at Malabon with eighteen lay teachers to care for the 1,200 pupils. In all these Philippine missions, a vigorous program of catechetical work is carried out among public school children and those unfortunate waifs who cannot afford any education at all. Each school enlists the zeal of its students to take the Faith to children less fortunate than themselves. The Sisters hope to kindle the mission flame in every heart in their care. In addition, during the summer months, the Sisters go out to the villages and, living in small nipa huts, they instruct the adults and prepare children for Holy Communion.

Medical work began early in the Philippine story. St. Paul's

Hospital, in the crowded Intramuros section of the city, was staffed in 1927. This hospital ministered to the poorest of the city through St. Jude's Patronage, which supplied food, clothing and housing, as well as medical care to those in need. St. Paul's soon acquired a reputation for nursing excellence. A nursing school was begun and had more than sixty students in 1941. The building was remodeled to accommodate 125 beds.

St. Paul's Hospital was completely destroyed in World War II. Not a stone was left upon a stone, and high grass now grows over what was once the populous Intramuros section of Manila. Many of the Maryknoll Sisters formerly at St. Paul's have been absorbed by St. Joseph's Hospital in Manapla, Occidental Negros. This hospital cares for sugar workers on the island of Negros, which is the great "sugar bowl" of the Philippines.

At St. Mary's Hall in Manila, the Sisters staffed a hostel for university students. This, too, was one of the early enterprises; the Sisters began it in 1927. There, students who came to Manila from "the provinces" (as the rest of the country is called) could find a home and Sisters' care.

The years 1942–1945 were years of suffering for the Sisters in the Philippines,—years which have since borne marvelous fruit. For three and a half years, the Sisters were interned, first in one place and then in another, ending up in the Los Banos Camp, on the southern shore of Laguna de Bay. The Regional Superior, Sister Mary Trinita, and Sister Mary Brigida were thrust into torture rooms of Santiago prison in 1944. Sister Brigida was released after four months, but Sister Trinita endured more than nine months. In the end, she was taken to her Sisters at Los Banos Camp, released as unaccountably as she had been imprisoned. The whole group was rescued in dramatic fashion in February, 1945, in a commando raid by American paratroopers. Some thirty of the Sisters, ill and worn out from starvation and poor living quarters, returned to the States. The stronger ones remained in the Philippines to help rebuild the missions.

The Philippines has been rich in vocations to the missioner's life. Fifteen Maryknoll Sisters were born and brought up in these islands. Some of them are stationed in other countries, doing mission work in Hawaii, Korea, Panama, Nicaragua and Japan.

It was in 1927 that Mother Mary Joseph broke ground once more in a new field—Hawaii. Six Sisters left for the island paradise

in the summer of 1927. The first objective was to staff a school in
the Punahou section of Honolulu. The Maryknoll Fathers had recently assumed charge of Sacred Heart Parish. American Catholics
were clamoring for a school staffed by American Sisters. They
envisioned a rather exclusive school for white children; it was quite
a surprise for them to find Chinese, Koreans, Hawaiians, Portuguese, Japanese seated alongside their own American children. But
the group blended nicely in time, just as the many different races
in Hawaii have grown to form a homogeneous whole. There are
now 1,236 pupils in Maryknoll School in the Punahou district of
Honolulu.

The work in Hawaii has been mainly educational. The Belgian
Sacred Heart Fathers also requested Sisters for their parishes. The
same day that the Punahou school opened, four Sisters went to
Kaneohe, a small village on the other side of Oahu Island. The
next year another group crossed to Maui Island to start a school. In
1929 and again in 1931, new schools began—in Kalihi, a poor
section of Honolulu near the docks, and in Waikiki, a famous
beach. In 1944, another school was established in the sugar cane
fields of Oahu. All of these are parochial schools, to which come
the children of many different races. In their early days in Hawaii,
the Sisters undertook, also, to manage the Maui Home for children.
This welfare agency has given a home to many hundreds of children in the quarter century since.

In 1943, the Diocese of Honolulu began two new projects,—a
professional Social Service bureau, and catechetical work organized
on a diocesan basis. A nucleus of Maryknoll Sisters, trained social
service workers, formed the staff of Catholic charities. They were
under the leadership of Sister Victoria Francis, who, before entering the Maryknoll community, had had many years with both
Catholic and civic agencies in the United States and had organized
the Casework Services of the New York State Division of Parole,
supervising the work of some sixty men caseworkers. The Catholic
Social Service of Honolulu soon attained a position of respect
among the welfare agencies of the city.

Two Maryknoll Sisters were assigned to work with the Confrater-
nity of Christian Doctrine in the city. They organized some hundred secular teachers, giving them instruction in catechetical work
and supervising their classes.

In March of 1930, the first Maryknoll Sisters arrived in Manchuria, under the leadership of Sister Mary Eunice. They started work in Dairen, setting up a school. In a few years, other missions were opened, notably at Fushun, where a native novitiate was begun, an industrial school set up, a dispensary started, and an orphanage established. In those days Manchuria was controlled by the Japanese. It was necessary to establish separate houses for Chinese work and Japanese work. In both Dairen and Fushun, this was done. The Dairen school attracted a large number of White Russian children, whose families had fled from Communist Russia.

Work in small villages many miles away, necessitated the opening of convents in Antung and Tunghua. In 1942, all the American Sisters were repatriated. Only five Maryknollers remained—three of them were Japanese, one was a Korean and one a German national. These bravely carried on with the school work. Later, when the Russians swooped down over Dairen, the five were unable to get out of the city. Their memoirs of those days are full of stories of remarkable interest in the Faith, of days and nights of instructing converts and of minute-to-minute living in fear of the Russian soldiers.

In 1946, a group of Sisters went from the United States to Fushun, only ten hours by rail from Dairen. But they were unable to get in touch with the beleaguered Sisters. This group had to evacuate Fushun a few months afterwards. They returned again in the autumn of 1947, but once more had to flee the Reds in December. The Dairen group was able to escape late in 1947. Thus closed the Maryknoll Sisters' missions in Manchuria.

While all these missions were being established halfway around the world, the number of Sisters at Maryknoll was growing so fast that they overflowed every available house on the property. The major Seminary had been built; the priests and students lived in it. This left for the Sisters two houses, a barn, a carriage house, and a dormitory at the top of the *Field Afar* building which had been built near the road. The Sisters lived here, there and everywhere on the compound. In addition, they had bought a piece of property just across the road from the Seminary; the property included a large, hilltop house, which soon was crowded to capacity.

Small wonder, then, that Mother Mary Joseph laid plans for a Motherhouse adequate to care for her growing flock. In 1932, the new building stood in all its majesty, not yet finished, but occupi-

able. On March 1st, 1932, occurred a memorable event—Moving
Day. The seminarians were given a "free day" and helped to move
furniture over. From the houses and barns and dormitory and
carriage house, the Sisters carried lighter items into the new Motherhouse. As they laid their tired bodies to rest that night, they knew
that a new phase of their congregation's life had started.

Every country on earth, it seemed, was asking for Maryknoll Sisters to staff schools. The demand for teachers far exceeded the supply. Therefore, in 1931, the Maryknoll Teachers College was established under the deanship of Sister Mary de Paul. This College, a
member of Catholic and secular educational associations, educates
only Maryknoll Sisters. The curriculum is adapted to train these
Sisters for work in foreign fields under conditions very different
from those in the United States. Starting with only four Sister-pu-
pils, it now numbers more than one hundred.

In October, 1932, a special house was opened at Maryknoll.
Ten Sisters, with Sister Mary Magdalen as superior, began the
Maryknoll Cloister, a powerhouse of prayer and penance earning
graces for all missioners everywhere. There are now eighteen Sisters
there, dedicated to the contemplative life, and following the Rule
of the Third Order of Dominicans, adapted to a cloistered life.

A pioneer group of Maryknoll Sisters went to Kyoto, Japan, in
1937. Misfortune dogged their steps in one form or another. First,
their convent burned to the ground. Then the sanatorium they
were to staff was never completed. It was, furthermore, difficult to
work in the Japan of those days. Suspicion and investigation were
part of every foreigner's life.

In 1939, however, two Sisters went to Tokyo to lay the foundations for a native novitiate. Their group of candidates was just beginning to be formed when World War II broke out. All Maryknoll Sisters were repatriated except one, a Japanese national. She
was able to join the group left in Dairen, Manchuria.

The Sisters returned to Japan in 1947. The work of conversions
progressed apace. Beginning with a convent at Tsu, in the Kyoto
diocese, they soon had convents at Otsu and Hikone, as well as
two convents in Kyoto itself. For the most part, these are houses of
two Sisters each engaged in parish work, instructing converts and
visiting hospitals and homes. In Kyoto, however, a work was begun
to help poor women earn a livelihood, and also to help revive the
home weaving industries of Kyoto. Vestments are made with the

exquisite Japanese silks and sewed by the women. Several conversions have resulted from this work.

Latin American mission fields profited when World War II forced a suspension of work in the Orient. In 1943, following the Maryknoll Fathers, Sisters went to Bolivia, where they staffed schools and a hospital. Sister Mary Mercy, M.D., established at first a small dispensary at Riberalta, center of the rubber producing lands of Bolivia. This dispensary later grew into the hospital mentioned earlier. A second dispensary is also maintained at Guayaramerin, some seventy-five miles away. Through the years it has brought a decided improvement in the health of the people.

Every few months, too, a Sister-doctor or Sister-nurse, together with a catechist, journeys up the wide jungle rivers, staying for several weeks at a time in some isolated village where neither doctor or nurse has been for as long as three years. Here they treat the sick and instruct young and old in the principles of the Catholic Faith which most of the people profess but hardly know.

In the mountain district of Bolivia, where the Quechua Indian women wear their tall, white hats and the Aymara tribe women are replete in multi-colored derbies, is another Maryknoll parochial school. It was often said that such a school could not succeed— that in South America it was impossible to educate rich and poor, Indian and white, in the same classroom. But these differences soon iron out and youngsters learn that God is Father to all of us.

In the same year, 1943, work began in Panama, where many English speaking Negroes had immigrated from Jamaica in the hope of finding work in the Panama Canal project. The American Vincentian Fathers were commissioned to care for those Negroes spiritually. They asked for Sisters to educate the Negro children; thus was born St. Vincent's School. The roster lists almost as many Spanish-speaking children as Jamaican Negroes. In the depths of the slum district of Panama City, the school, with 250 children, is a beacon light to those poor people who are reaching towards the better things of life, both material and spiritual.

One of the social problems in Panama results from the fact that many working mothers must let their children run wild during the day. To help in this situation, the Sisters have opened three kindergartens in various sections of the city. Also, they conduct religion classes for older children and even take part in a radio program for teen-agers. Study clubs, choirs, dramatics, bring the Sisters into contact with hundreds of young people. Regular visits to hospitals and to the Palo Seco Leper Colony round out their full schedule.

On Christmas Eve, 1944, a plane swooped down on the gold-mining town of Siuna, Nicaragua. From it stepped four Maryknoll Sisters, who were warmly welcomed by Bishop Niedhammer, of the American Capuchins. Through the mountains they had leveled a short road leading to the school where the Sisters were to teach; this was called *Bulevar Maryknoll.*

The Siuna school has been of immense value to the whole district. Formerly the town was sodden in its poverty. Filled with single men who had come to work in the gold mine, steeped in ignorance and vice, the place was a byword for all that is unwholesome. Working with the Capuchin Fathers, the Sisters soon earned for their school a fine reputation. Now people who wish to give their children a good education are applying for positions in the mine at Siuna. This lifts the general tone of the village. About three hundred children, many of whom tramp for miles over the mountain roads, are taught the "three R's" as well as manual trades, home-making, music and best of all, religion.

During summers—if one can speak of summer where it is always torrid—the Sisters journey by muleback, river boat and airplane, to areas where there are no Sisters stationed. Two by two, they live in native houses and spend six weeks in giving a thorough course in Christian doctrine for young and old.

During all these years, through storms and fair weather, Mother Mary Joseph had stayed at the helm, at first by appointment and then by election at the General Chapters. She was "Mother," and nobody could quite imagine the congregation under any but her leadership. However, in the General Chapter of 1946, she retired, with the title of Mother Foundress. Sister Mary Columba, who had been a councilor for 20 years, was elected Mother General. From that time on, Mother Mary Joseph has devoted herself mainly to fostering the spirit and family solidarity of her Sisters.

The Motherhouse had been built to accommodate two hundred and fifty Sisters—a fantastic figure it seemed then. But in no time, the building was full; then it was crowded; and before long additional housing was urgently needed. In 1946, Bethany Convent was opened for aged and infirm Sisters. In 1947, a novitiate house was bought at Valley Park, eighteen miles from St. Louis, Missouri.

In 1948, a group of sixty Sisters moved to Crichton House, about five miles from Maryknoll. With the postwar increase of candidates for the community, the Motherhouse, still remained inadequate for both professed and novices. Consequently, in 1953, a third novitiate house was established, this time at Topsfield, Massachusetts.

Two new missions in widely separated parts of the world were begun in 1948. The first got off to a start in September, when three Sisters landed on a tiny island in the South Pacific. It was Koror, one of the Palau group, now known as the Western Carolines. This is part of what is probably the world's wettest vicariate—about two million square miles of water, dotted with tiny atolls and islands. The American Jesuits had just assumed responsibility for the vicariate after World War II. Previous to that time, the islands had been a Japanese mandate. Spanish Jesuits had worked there then; and the people on the islands they had been able to reach were strongly Catholic, but the others were primitively pagan.

The Sisters settled on their island. It was six miles long and half a mile wide. Almost immediately they began classes and tried to pick up the language from conversation, for there are no written grammars for it. A Quonset hut was secured for a school building and children are brought from many other islands to spend the school year there. In 1950, three other Sisters went to Likiep, in the Marshall Islands, some 2,000 miles away but still in the same vicariate. In early 1953, a third group began work on Yap which is closer to Koror.

These three schools are among the most isolated of our missions. Not only are the distances between them great, but transportation is almost unknown. No industries or raw materials tempt commercial planes or ships to enter this vast watery region. As a consequence, the Sisters must be almost entirely self-sufficient. Mail comes about once a month and then at the caprice of government planes routed there on some business of the Department of the Interior, which has charge of the islands. During the long vacation, the Sisters go to other islands in their vicinity, staying for some weeks to instruct the children and prepare them for First Communion.

In December of 1948, a group of Maryknoll Sisters departed for Kowak, in Tanganyika, British East Africa. The first four Sisters included teachers and a nurse. A dispensary and school were projected. Almost from the beginning, the foundation for a native novitiate was laid. More nurses and more teachers were added each year. After five years of preparation, the first native novice received her habit in 1953. In the meantime, another mission was begun, at Nyegina, near the southern shore of Lake Victoria. A dispensary is there, too, and the native novitiate.

The next year, the Maryknoll Sisters undertook to staff a large government hospital at Kandy, Ceylon. Starting with the maternity ward, they were to take over various departments gradually, as building and personnel would permit. The Sisters are now in charge of the pediatric section and eye, ear, nose, and throat wards. A 600-bed hospital, the institution averages ten births a day. The monthly average of patients is close to 3,000. It is spread out on a hillside in twenty-five small buildings, on different levels up and down the hill.

Two Sisters started mission work in Galvarino, Chile, in 1950, with a school equipped with lay teachers. This town is far to the south, close to snow-capped mountains and lakes. It is in the Araucanian Indian country, where people and customs are very primitive. Hardly had the Sisters settled and learned the local language, when another school was opened at Chillan, about 150 miles to the north. A few months after that, a third school started at Curepto, still farther north. Early in 1953, a fourth one opened its doors in Buzeta, the slum district of Santiago, capital of the country. In all these schools there were but two Sisters, except in the Santiago house where there were three. The use of lay teachers makes it possible to have schools of several hundred pupils with a small expenditure of personnel. These are all parochial schools, open to every child in the parish.

The year 1951 saw the first departure for Peru. There the Maryknoll Fathers had been building a school and church in a new section of Lima. About half of the people are of the middle class; the rest are very poor. Both classes desire a school where English is stressed, for few people in South America can get good jobs unless they know English. If the poor are to lift themselves from their grinding poverty, they must be able to secure good positions. Working in cooperation with the National School of Social Work, the Sisters conduct a professional social service bureau for members of the parish.

Communist domination of China was responsible for the opening of a convent on Mauritius, an island in the Indian Ocean. It happens that most of the 17,688 Chinese on Mauritius speak the Hakka dialect current around Kaying. When the Sisters were expelled from the Kaying district, the Bishop of Port Mauritius seized the opportunity to ask for Sisters to work on his island. Four Sisters went there in November, 1951. The Sisters have a Chinese center where they instruct catechumens, encourage new converts and help refugees who find life hard in a strange country.

The Maryknoll Fathers staff two fields on Formosa. They asked for Sisters for the mission centers at Miaoli and Taichung. In November, 1953, four Sisters went to Miaoli for general catechetical work. Three others, a doctor and two nurses, landed at Taichung.

Since the opening of the first two missions on the Pacific Coast —in Los Angeles and Seattle—the work on the home front has spread. In 1927, the Sisters went to Mountain View, near San Francisco, to staff the Maryknoll Junior Seminary's domestic department, and to do catechetical work in the district. During World War II, social and catechetical work among Mexicans began in Guadalupe, not far from Santa Barbara. A large program of catechetical work among migrant fruit workers started in Stockton. In 1946, the Sisters staffed San Juan Capistrano school at the famous old mission. And in 1950, three Sisters began professional social service work for the Archdiocese of San Francisco.

In the eastern States, too, works for Chinese and Negroes were initiated as a contribution to mission work in our own country. Chinese centers were opened in both Boston and New York in 1945. In Chicago, in 1952, the Sisters began catechetical work among the Chinese. Previously, in that city, the Sisters of Notre Dame had set up a small Chinese school in two rooms of the Town Hall of Chinatown. In 1953, the Maryknoll Sisters succeeded them in that project. Schools were opened in the Negro district of the Bronx, New York, in 1945; in Tucson, Arizona, in 1952; and two in St. Louis. A social-service group went to Chicago in 1949, and a catechetical group to Houston, Texas, in 1953, for work among Mexicans.

The six "secretaries" have multiplied, until now the Maryknoll Sisters number 1,138. Of this total, three hundred and fifty are "in training." That is, they are either candidates, whose two-and-a-half year period of religious formation is essential; or they are professed Sisters, being trained as doctors, nurses, teachers, or social workers. The Sisters' apostolate for Christ covers much of the globe. It requires the highest religious and professional standards.

Within the space of thirty years, the work that began with two small kindergartens for Japanese in Los Angeles and Seattle has expanded to include three colleges, eight high schools and forty-four primary schools. The 13,000 pupils come from nipa huts, bamboo and mud and brick dwellings. Most of them speak languages few Americans know, but they receive the same careful training in religion given to little Catholics from America's comfortable homes.

The Sisters' dispensaries treat 47,000 patients each month; three hospitals and a sanatorium treat the underprivileged (and under-nourished, as well) of as many nations. Professional social service workers go out from five centers.

In a few paragraphs such as these, it is only possible to present a brief historical sketch of the work of the Maryknoll Sisters. To tell the story of their heroic deeds and great achievements of charity, would require a volume in itself.

One word more, however, should be added, and that is for the purpose of making the record clear. As required by canon law, the Maryknoll Sisters are a separate community, governing themselves and raising their own finances. It is often assumed that the Maryknoll Fathers are responsible for the support of the Sisters. This is not true. Those Sisters who work directly under the Fathers, either at home or on the missions, are supported by the Fathers; but the tremendous costs for maintaining the Sisters' convents in the United States and the large expenses for training Sisters, must come from funds that the Sisters themselves raise. The priests and Brothers constitute the *Catholic Foreign Mission Society of America*. The legal title for the Sisters is *Foreign Mission Sisters of St. Dominic*. Gifts and other communications intended for the Sisters should be so specified.

Some day some historian will chronicle a full record of both communities. In that work, the pages concerning the deeds and development of the Maryknoll Sisters will be glorious ones. There will be portrayed American womanhood at its finest. The prayers of every Maryknoll Father include one of thanks to God for the Maryknoll Sisters. May the Great Missioner continue to bless them, and may the Maryknoll Sisters continue to grow in the spirit of their foundress, Mother Mary Joseph!

31

The Training of a Missioner

Missioners are not born, they are made—and into their making go long years of training. The formation of a missioner is a process developed through the centuries by the Church, and the training of missioners is the primary reason for the existence of such societies as the Catholic Foreign Mission Society of America—commonly known as Maryknoll. This training falls into three categories: first, the training must form the priest; secondly, it must form the missioner; and thirdly, it must form the Maryknoller. At the initial glance, these categories might seem to be repetitious or mutually inclusive. Actually, they are three completely different things.

The Priest. The purpose of every seminary is to train priests. The seminary provides that mental and physical preparation necessary to produce competently educated men of God. In addition, at the apex of this training is the sanctification of the individual candidate. He cannot be just an educated man; he must be a holy man. He is to become "another Christ"; he will deal in the things of God and he will show Christ to his people. He cannot, therefore, be an actor imitating Christ, but must so transform himself that he can say with Saint Paul, "Not I, but Christ lives within me." Virtue must become a habit, and Christ-like actions must be automatic rather than deliberate.

In his mental training, the seminarian studies many things. His philosophy course trains him in the methods of using logic and of applying the principles of psychology. He is taught to become a man of thought. He must know all the arts taught in a regular college, plus an amplitude of ecclesiastical subjects. There are four years of moral and dogmatic theology. He studies Church history, canon law, liturgy, pastoral theology and sacred Scripture—for all of these will be tools of his profession. His studies give him not only remote knowledge to be filed away, but also the equipment that will be needed in his life as a priest.

Studies for the priesthood take a long time. After the high school course has been finished, there are four years of college training, and four more years of university work. Maryknollers have the addition of another year of training, as will be discussed later. Thus it takes nine years to become a Maryknoll priest—the same length of time it takes to become a doctor.

The Missioner. Training at Maryknoll is designed not only to create priests, but a special type of priest—the missionary priest. For this purpose special subjects are added to the usual seminary course of study, or are taken up in extra curricular activities. Languages are stressed. There is a course in missiology, which treats of mission history and mission methods. Each seminarian spends one summer vacation working in the clinic of a large city hospital, to gain a knowledge of practical medicine. In addition, the regular seminary subjects are slanted towards future needs in the mission fields.

A large part of the training is subtle and is noticeable only upon reflection. For example, in every Maryknoll house, an hour a day is set aside for a period known as "manual labor." Not only does this period save money, which can be used directly in mission work; it also prepares the seminarian for jobs he will be called upon to perform in the mission field where little trained help is available. Knowledge gained while the seminarian works as a plumber or electrician or farm hand will stand him in good stead in later years. In addition, manual labor gives the missioner an understanding of the laborious life of the people among whom he works. Understanding is the first mark of leadership.

THE MEANING OF MARYKNOLL

Recreation periods are spent out of doors in all sorts of athletics that harden the body for mission trails ahead. There are special free days known as "hike days" when the students take long walks, are served their lunches in the field, and then arrive back at the seminary in time for supper. These walks are preparation for the sick calls and other journeys that will some day be taken. In many different ways this training of the missioner goes on unnoticed. One might not expect silence at meals to be a part of preparation for a mission career—but it is. While the students eat, a fellow student reads to them from books especially chosen to form minds and hearts in mission tradition.

Even after the young apostle is ordained the training continues. His first year in the mission field is spent in a language school, where he learns the idiom and customs of the people among whom he will work. When this year is over, he does not immediately blossom out into a full-scale missioner; instead he is assigned to assist an older and more experienced priest, who is expected to guide him through the perilous shoals of transition and adaption to a new work. Thus the molding of a missioner is a long and calculated process.

The Maryknoller. Every mission society has its own spirit and traditions—a personality, so to speak. The seminarian at Maryknoll is trained to be not only a priest and a missioner, but also a Maryknoller. In forming a personality one deals with intangibles that are not easy to describe, but the finished product is there and is recognized as "the Maryknoll spirit." The pattern of his personality was established by Maryknoll's co-founder, Bishop James Anthony Walsh.

One whole year of training is spent at the Maryknoll Novitiate, where the seminarian undergoes intensive spiritual training to the exclusion of everything else. The novice is modeled after Jesus Christ, the First Priest. He is trained in Maryknoll practices and traditions. He studies Maryknoll history, and the Maryknoll Constitutions under which he will live. The Society's rule is explained to him in detail. Through prayer and spiritual exercises, through spiritual reading and meditation, the seminarian strives to make himself into the pattern that is Maryknoll's.

Bishop James Edward Walsh has written a classic essay called "Description of a Missioner." In it he says that, if the missioner is to succeed, he must appear like a saint before his people. Then Bishop Walsh goes on to say that it is easier, actually, to become a saint than to pretend to be one. The year of spiritual training received in the novitiate is designed to start the aspirant missioner on this path to sainthood.

Very often boys and young men come to Maryknollers wondering whether or not they have a vocation to the mission life. In talking to them, one gets the feeling that they are looking for some tangible sign of God's calling. Saint Paul received his vocation when he was knocked off his horse by the hand of God, and then heard God speaking to him from the heavens. But such a direct calling is very rare. Actually God presents His challenge in a much more indirect way, as a rule. He merely plants in the heart of a boy a vague desire to serve God. The Maryknoll co-founder, Bishop James A. Walsh, composed an eight-point check list for young men to use in determining whether or not they have the call to Maryknoll.

These points are:

1. *Age*. The student must be in high school, or at such an age that he can finish his seminary course before he reaches thirty-five.

2. *Health*. Good health is a necessity of mission life.

3. *Zeal*. The applicant should have zeal for souls, zeal to spread the kingdom of God, zeal to help other people.

4. *Intelligence*. He should have at least average intelligence, which will enable him to master his studies and a foreign language.

5. *Common sense*. This means good, old-fashioned "horse sense" which many a genius lacks.

6. *Generosity*. He must be prepared to go "the whole way" for Christ. He must be ready to give freely of himself so that he can serve his people.

7. *Sense of humor*. He must not be a "stuffed shirt" or a person who takes himself too seriously.

8. *Piety*. Since he is to become a spiritual man, he must have an inclination towards things of the spirit.

Young men who possess these qualifications have the material from which the missioner can be made. He is advised to talk the matter over with his pastor or confessor, who will advise him further. If after such discussion he still feels that he wishes to carry out the idea, the next step is to make application to enter the seminary. Not every boy who enters the seminary makes the final step to ordination. He may discover along the way that he hasn't the qualities for a mission vocation, or for the specific Maryknoll vocation, or seminary professors may decide that he lacks the necessary qualities. Leaving the seminary does not mean failure. The seminary exists solely as a training and testing ground. Mission life is difficult and it is better to learn that a young man is not adapted to such a life before he takes the final step than afterwards, when nothing can be done to change his state in life.

After the young man applies to Maryknoll, he must undergo a physical examination. Then he takes an entrance examination, which gauges his character and mental abilities. These examinations are designed to screen applicants so that only those who have the mental and physical abilities to carry out the duties of a missioner will be accepted. If he passes these tests successfully, he is then accepted and assigned to one of the Maryknoll training houses in the United States.

A good Catholic woman once asked her nephew why it took so many years for a seminarian to learn how to say Mass. She supposed that this was the whole purpose of seminary training. As mentioned earlier in this chapter, the course of studies in a seminary is long and full. Actually a student does not learn to say Mass until his final year before ordination. A day in a seminary is a busy one. At Maryknoll's major Seminary, for example, students rise at 5:30. At 5:55 they are in chapel for morning prayers, meditation, Mass and thanksgiving. Then at 7:10 they go to breakfast, which they eat to the accompaniment of reading. At 7:35 they finish breakfast and do morning duties, such as sweeping floors, cleaning classrooms, and the other jobs of keeping the house tidy and neat.

At 8:00 they have a period of study; then they go to classes for the rest of the morning. Shortly after noon they are in chapel for reading of Scriptures and other spiritual exercises. At 12:30 they go to the refectory for dinner, and except on "free" days, the meal is eaten in silence as a student reads from some spiritual book. Dinner ends at 1:00 and ten minutes later the students spread out over the Seminary grounds for an hour of manual labor. This is followed by an hour of recreation, the sports depending upon the season.

Before 3:30 the students are back in the Seminary and on their way to classes. Shortly after 5:00 classes end, the seminarians in small groups walk around the property reciting the Rosary. This is followed at 5:30 by spiritual reading, which is actually a conference by the spiritual director, the rector, or some guest. At 6:00 the seminarians are in the refectory again for the evening meal and more reading. Evening recreation follows until 7:10, and is usually out of doors unless the weather forbids. On "free" nights the students are allowed indoor recreation, and it usually lasts longer. Then follows a study period until 9:00, when night prayers are said in common. After this exercise, each student takes care of his own private devotions and continues study until the signal for lights out at 10:00. The day has been full and everyone is glad to get to bed for the morrow's early rising.

Because Maryknoll is a national institution, it draws its seminarians from all walks of life and from all parts of our country. Many Maryknollers attended college elsewhere before coming to Maryknoll. A few of the schools represented at Maryknoll include Notre Dame, Harvard, Yale, Georgetown, Fordham, Manhattan, Boston, Holy Cross, Minnesota, Villanova, the United States Naval Academy, and many others. Some Maryknollers have been doctors, policemen, actors, firemen, baseball players, salesmen, business men, aviators, chemists and so forth. The majority, of course, are the ordinary young men from high schools and colleges across the country.

Records at Maryknoll show that its members come from twenty-three archdioceses, ninety dioceses, and forty-six States—plus Alaska, Canada, and the District of Columbia. They come from big cities and small towns, from farms and from highly industrialized areas. Some come from well-to-do families; others from families in humble circumstances. They are a true cross section of America, and they give Maryknoll the national character its founders intended.

At the cornerstone laying for the permanent chapel at Maryknoll headquarters in 1953, Bishop Lane predicted that because students had entered Maryknoll in such large numbers after World War II, the number of priests in the Society would be doubled within ten years. Maryknoll's growth has been rapid and since the end of the war, several minor seminaries have been opened. Today these seminaries are scattered across the United States.

Maryknoll Seminary. Located at the national headquarters called "Maryknoll" on the outskirts of Ossining, New York, is our major Seminary, to which students from all the other training houses are funneled. This Seminary was established in 1912, and today consists of an imposing group of buildings high above the Hudson River. Students here must have had two years of philosophy before entering. The Seminary gives a four-year training in theology and allied subjects. Here the seminarian is ordained, and from here he leaves for his mission post.

Maryknoll Novitiate, Bedford, Massachusetts. With a student capacity of one hundred, the novitiate gives one year of special spiritual training after the completion of philosophy. All future Maryknollers must take this course before being admitted to membership in the Society. The novitiate is located about a half-hour from Boston, in the historic Lexington and Concord area. The novitiate was established in 1933.

Maryknoll College, Glen Ellyn, Illinois. The property for this college was bought in 1944, but it was not until several years after the war that the present colonial buildings were erected. The present college has a capacity of three hundred students, but additional building is planned to accommodate one hundred more. Courses here are equivalent to those of a senior-arts college, with the last two years of the four-year course devoted to a major in philosophy. The college is located west of Chicago, about an hour's drive from the Loop.

Maryknoll Junior Seminary, Clarks Summit, Pennsylvania. In 1913, Maryknoll opened its first preparatory seminary in America in the diocese of Scranton. In 1919 the cornerstone for the present junior seminary was laid. Located in the rolling Abington Hills, not far from the city of Scranton, this junior seminary is familiarly known to all Maryknollers as "The Venard." It was named after Blessed Theophane Venard, a young French missioner who was martyred in Indo-China. The student capacity of this school is one hundred sixty and it offers four years of high school training. Connected with the junior seminary is a school for special students, maintained for high school graduates and college students who have a deficiency in Latin—an important seminary requirement. Students are graduated from here to the Glen Ellyn college.

Maryknoll Junior Seminary, Mountain View, California. Located south of San Francisco, near Los Altos, this is the second oldest Maryknoll preparatory school. The property was purchased in 1924; the building erected in 1927. It has a capacity of eighty students, and it accepts boys from the Pacific Coast and Rocky Mountain states. Courses offered here are at the high school and junior college levels. Students from here go on to the college at Glen Ellyn.

Maryknoll Junior Seminary, Cincinnati, Ohio. This small seminary was opened in 1929, on property adjoining St. Gregory's Preparatory Seminary of the Archdiocese of Cincinnati. Maryknoll students live at the junior seminary and study at St. Gregory's. Courses include four years of high school and the first two years of college.

Maryknoll House of Studies, St. Louis, Missouri. Opened in 1938 as a junior seminary, this house serves as a residence for Maryknoll students who attend Kenrick Junior Seminary of the Archdiocese of St. Louis. It also provides classes of its own. Its work covers the four years of high school and the first two years of college. Plans have been drawn up for eventually building a new junior seminary in the St. Louis area.

32

Spreading an Idea

It was a windy day in Denver. The high school lad hurrying down
the street to catch a departing trolley car didn't even take time to
throw away the piece of paper that blew against his leg. He
just pulled it off and kept running. Once aboard the car and out
of the path of the wind, the boy threw himself into a seat. Only
then did he realize that he was still clutching the paper that the
wind had tossed against him.

He opened the paper and smoothed it out. It was a page from a
magazine called *The Field Afar*. With the curiosity of youth, he
began to read the wrinkled sheet. The page told of the experiences
of a priest in China, and a small inset on the page asked that
American boys give their lives to the work of the foreign missions.

The high school lad thought about the page, all the way home.
That night he wrote to Maryknoll for further information. In a
few months' time, he was at Maryknoll. Today he is a missioner in
Peru—a long way from a stray bit of paper in Denver.

The origin of this priest's vocation is a little more dramatic than
most—but there was one thing in common with a majority of
Maryknollers: they were attracted to Maryknoll through reading

our monthly magazine, *Maryknoll-The Field Afar*. It is no exaggeration to say that *The Field Afar* built Maryknoll. The secret behind any success that Maryknoll has had, and the reason for the rapid growth of the Society, are found in this little magazine, which since 1907 has been striving to make the missions a part of every Catholic American's life.

Every year a Maryknoll survey is made of our new students, to determine the sources of their vocations. Each year the results are the same. Over sixty per cent of them were introduced to Maryknoll, and had the missions personalized to them, by *Maryknoll-The Field Afar*.

"My mother subscribed to *The Field Afar*," wrote one student. "When I thought of being a missioner, the magazine made me think of Maryknoll."

"I first learned of Maryknoll by reading the magazine, *The Field Afar*," writes another. "After reading the magazine, I was inspired to be a missioner."

Sometimes it takes years of patient cultivation by the magazine before the results are apparent. This was true in the case of a young Navy veteran. He told us: "Although I received *The Field Afar* since I was twelve, I never seriously thought about joining Maryknoll until I served with the Navy's Antarctic Expedition of 1946-47. During the four months with the expedition, I had a lot of time to think what God wanted me to do with my life."

One warm, spring day in New Rochelle, New York, the pupils of the eighth grade of St. Joseph's School were acting up while their teacher was out of the room. A stocky Italian boy, "Chink" Romaniello, was the ringleader of the disturbance. Returning suddenly to the room, the teacher caught Chink about to throw an eraser at the head of a fellow pupil.

"Go sit in the cloakroom for the rest of the afternoon," Sister commanded. Then handing him a copy of *The Field Afar*, she added, "Read this and see what men do with their time."

After school had been dismissed, the Sister called the boy back into the room. "And now what do you think of yourself?" she inquired.

"I think I'll be a missioner," the boy answered.

Today Monsignor John Romaniello is an outstanding veteran of South China mission work. Countless thousands who have passed through his dispensaries and relief stations can thank a casual introduction to a little magazine, for the help they received.

But the work of *Maryknoll-The Field Afar* is not just one of populating foreign countries with missioners. The magazine was founded for the purpose stated in its first issue: "To deepen and widen the mission spirit of the United States, and ultimately to establish a foreign mission seminary." The latter purpose was accomplished when Maryknoll began in 1911. The former purpose continues to this day. Every mail brings requests from priests and Sisters all over the country, asking for copies that they may distribute to help awaken in their people and pupils a love for the mission work of the Church.

"I was one of the original subscribers to the little paper Father James Anthony Walsh started in 1907," wrote a pastor recently, "and I haven't missed an issue since. It has been the greatest privilege of a long life to have had a small part in the growth of Maryknoll, and because of this, to have helped the whole mission movement in the United States. We are having a little mission exhibit in our school, and I should like some copies of your magazine to distribute. Many boys and girls from this parish have gone to Maryknoll and other missionary groups, after having encountered your publication."

The archbishop of a large Midwestern archdiocese wrote to us recently, stating that he would like to see *Maryknoll-The Field Afar* in every home in his archdiocese. "The more our Catholic people can be taught to think of the Catholic Church as a world Church, the more will this archdiocese be blessed," he declared. "The very foundation of Christian activity is a consideration for all the people of the world. I know no better way to bring this fundamental truth home to my people than through a consistent reading of your magazine."

The Field Afar has three purposes. Two of them have already been mentioned: to be a source of vocations to the missions, and to provide schooling in the mission ideas of the Church. The third purpose of the magazine is to gather the spiritual and material support necessary for the training of Maryknoll's missioners and the development of mission work in foreign fields.

To those whose work brings them into contact with this third function of our magazine, the day's mail is always inspiring and humbling. The sacrifices that many American Catholics make to support the mission work of Maryknoll are hard to believe. It is not infrequent to have someone send in his or her *last* dollar, because that person feels that there is someone, somewhere, who is worse off than he or she is.

"The enclosed is a little gift for some missioner's Thanksgiving," says one letter. "I lost my job in July and haven't found anything yet, but I thought that, if I make this sacrifice for some missioner, his prayers may help me."

"I'm an old man, Father," says another letter, "and I have just been given a pension of $30 a month. I asked my daughter if she would mind if I sent it to you to help the missions. She said, 'What we never had, we'll never miss!' Do not thank me, because it is so little to show my gratitude for what the missioners are doing as my representatives in far-off lands."

Even children are inspired by the magazine to do their bit for the missions. "Dear Father," says the letter of one youngster, "my name is Frederick Langeslay. I am only a paperboy and I haven't much money, neither have my folks. Please use this for the missions."

And so it goes, on and on, letter after letter. A book could be written on what people do to help the work of the missions because of reading *The Field Afar*. To them, Maryknoll is God's work. The following extract from a letter by a student in a large diocesan seminary sums it all up.

"Christ's command to teach all nations was given to each of us in a personal way. One cannot be a good Catholic without being mission-minded. For reasons of health, I cannot go the whole way and become a missioner, but I promise that, after I am ordained, I will do everything in my power to make the work known and loved. Probably the best way this can be done is by encouraging people to subscribe to your little magazine. It was from the pages of the Maryknoll magazine that I learned about the needs of men over the earth. It was from the same magazine that I received my vocation, under God's grace. No other publication breathes the same spirit."

The editors of *Maryknoll-The Field Afar* are pleased with the increasingly large number of Sisters who are using the magazine in connection with their classroom work. "The magazine should be in every Catholic school, since it teaches geography and history in such an appealing way," wrote one Sister. Another declared: "Our children are becoming more and more world-conscious, yet our textbooks are still quite heavy and dry. I began using your magazine to supplement the regular work. My, how it sparked interest! It made the class come alive, and it gave real meaning to what the children were studying."

Today, *The Field Afar*, besides telling of the activities of Maryknoll's missioners, keeps calling for: (1) a knowledge of, and regard for all the peoples of the earth, our brothers in Christ, and our responsibility to promote the welfare of all mankind according to Christian ideals; (2) devotion to the Church's task of carrying to all non-Catholics Christ's teachings.

"As Maryknoll grew," declared Cardinal Stritch in Chicago, "so grew the mission spirit in America." To paraphrase His Eminence, it can be said, "As *The Field Afar* grew, so grew Maryknoll." For the magazine has proved itself the lifeblood of the Society. Without it, there would have been no Maryknoll. If some unforeseen occurrence were to suddenly curtail our magazine's publication, the work of Maryknoll would likewise be brought to a standstill.

The task of *The Field Afar* will be great in the years to come. There is so much yet to be done! The hope has been expressed that some day the Church in America will send a thousand missioners a year out to the world. Impossible? Once it seemed impossible for America to send even ten! *The Field Afar* will continue to cooperate towards that high goal.

It has been part and parcel of Maryknoll's thinking that the Society's purpose was not solely that of training missioners and supporting them on the field, but also one of education to World Christianity. It was a heritage left to Maryknoll by Bishop Walsh and Father Price, who envisioned America as a vital and vigorous leader in the world mission apostolate. But before action occurs, the doers must be sincerely convinced of what they are to do. The Maryknoll founders advocated and practiced a conceived and systematic education of American Catholics in things missionary. This mission education should reach into the pulpit, the classroom and the home. It should enlist the aid of all forms of communication—radio, television, the press, motion pictures. With this in mind, Maryknoll early set up a mission education bureau, aimed at supplementing the work of *The Field Afar*. It was a unique organization in which priests and Sisters worked systematically to supply all Catholics with the full message of their Church in order to make them mission minded. Today this group has

grown to considerable stature, but the job which it has set
for itself is far from done. The aim of the mission-education
department is to put material on the world apostolate into every
walk of Catholic life. The plan has met with encouragement
from Catholic teachers and Catholic homemakers, who realize the
need of emphasis of an understanding and love of the entire
human race based on spiritual and not mere humanitarian motives.

Bishop James Anthony Walsh began a program of mission
education through literature even before the founding of Maryknoll. The Catholic Foreign Mission Bureau in Boston published
books and pamphlets aimed at creating a world consciousness.
After he founded Maryknoll, he set aside some of his best personnel for this work. Today, the mission education department
puts out books for general reading, school textbooks, juveniles,
filmstrips, religion aids, program packets, area studies, teaching
cards, posters, and so on.

One of the most successful ventures is a series of Catholic
geographies, now used as the official text in a large number of
schools. These geographies have pioneered a whole new concept
in the teaching of geography. Formerly in school geography the
emphasis had been on physical geography with little attention to
the spirtual lot of the people of the earth. The Sadlier geographies
on which Maryknollers have worked are social geographies into
which have been integrated a proper consideration of the spiritual
welfare of all peoples throughout the globe. Teachers have written
to Maryknoll that their pupils are so entranced by the books that
they take them home just to read. Some half a million of these
geographies are in use. The same catholicity of outlook should, our
editors contend, be applied to religious courses and other fields
in education.

Another development has been the creation of an Information
Bureau, which is prepared to supply background material to
teachers, students, publishers, lecturers, and so on. Large national
magazines frequently call upon the Information Bureau for facts
connected with some article being published. The Information
Bureau has a large selection of photographs available for loan.
Through the work of this bureau, information on the world apostolate is spread abroad.

The education division is also responsible for World Horizon
Films, a subsidiary organization that produces motion pictures on

mission subjects. The films are kept short, educational values are considered in each film, and the films are high in human interest. These motion pictures have been shown in schools and parishes all over the United States, but their greatest use has been on television where they have played on national hook-ups to millions of people. A desk at Maryknoll is kept busy handling requests from television stations and other users for prints of the various films.

A unique factor of this mission education program is that it is not aimed at the promotion of Maryknoll but of the Church's world-wide mission cause. Maryknoll sees it as part of its apostolate to promote an interest in the world missions. It is largely because any pronounced particularism is absent from its productions that the educational program has been accepted and its offerings used all over the country.

"We are trying to give the Catholic American people a strong sense of belonging to a world-conscious Church, rich in mission history," says Father John J. Considine, of New Bedford, Massachusetts, who is the architect and director of today's educational program, and a prominent mission authority. "This means more than a casual acquaintance with miscellaneous historical or current missionary events. It means a rounded knowledge of world missions through: (1) a grasp of modern-day world geography; (2) a systematic acquaintance with the constitutive parts of the human race; (3) a comprehension of the socio-economic problems of the human race; (4) a familiarity with the Church's world activities among the human race, as well as an appreciation of the impact of other religions and anti-religious forces on the human race; (5) an understanding of the Church's theological teaching on its world-wide mission."

A glance through one of the Maryknoll catalogues listing aids for priests, parents and teachers gives an idea of how this program is being carried on. *I Make the Stations of the Cross* is a dynamic presentation of the Way of the Cross through large teaching cards, aimed to show the personal participation of every Catholic. *The Religion Teacher and the World* are books to be used as supplementary doctrinal matter for catechism courses, broken down into three grade levels. *World Kinship Fun Packets* contain games, songs, plays, make-it-yourself projects, and so on. The catalogue contains a selected book list under the title "Books with World Vision." These books embrace biography, juveniles and adventure stories at all age levels, books on specific world areas, books for Catholic Action, books of reflection, books in Canon Law, and so on.

Speaking before a group of Sisters, Father Considine amplified the reasons for Maryknoll's activity in the mission education field. He said in part:

"It is of capital importance to establish that the missionary idea will not flourish spontaneously of itself. True, the teachings of the Church clearly proclaim that Christ's message must go to all men, that every recipient should pass it on to his neighbor. A popular application of this teaching, however, has not existed among any great segment of Catholics since Apostolic times. There have been whole centuries in history when no tangible missionary effort has been evident anywhere in the Church.

"In our own land, great though our Faith is, we hear our children sing blithely of the Christ Child who came for all and yet Christmas is a forgotten feast so far as recognition of its missionary significance is concerned. Our Catholic millions devoutly celebrate Passiontide each year and gladly proclaim the Risen Christ of Easter but ignore almost completely the angelic exhortation of Easter morn to 'go and tell.'

"By what almost seems a diabolical conspiracy, words no longer carry their obvious meaning, prayers in the Church no longer convey their significance among those who use them. Millions, for instance, read the beautiful, all-embracing sentiments in the Mass, learn the parables, accept devoutly the teaching of the Second Great Commandment. 'Thou shalt love thy neighbor as thyself,' and yet it never so much as enters into their minds that their Catholic life is incomplete unless they carry Christ's message to others as well as live it themselves.

"The remedy lies in carefully conceived, systematic education that will remold the Catholic social concepts to the apostolic pattern. This must be done principally through the pulpit, the classroom, the home. It must reach the specialized groups such as seminarians and novices. The instruments employed must be books, periodicals, the press, movies, radio and television, audiovisual aids."

Thus through its magazine and its mission education program, Maryknoll attempts to do its part in bringing to all American Catholics the full message of Christ.

This then is the story of Maryknoll—a story of achievement spanning fewer years than the lifetime of a man. From a dream imagined in the pine-clad hills of North Carolina and on the twisting, narrow streets of Boston, reality was born. But the crown of accomplishment and sacrifice belongs not exclusively to the priests, Brothers and Sisters of Maryknoll. It belongs in great degree to the mothers and fathers who have given sons and daughters to work in fields remote and foreign. It belongs to the clergy of America from whose ranks Maryknoll came, and whose loyal support enabled the Society to increase and fructify. And it belongs in a special degree to all those Americans who bought the stones that built the seminaries and churches and hospitals; who found the fare of the missioner to the Orient, or Africa, or Latin America; who furnished the medicine, the school books, the horses, and the thousand and one things so necessary for mission work.

To all of these people does Maryknoll belong. In all of them does Maryknoll find its real meaning.

Index

Aborigines, Formosa, 265
Adogo, Queen of Sherati, 258 ff
Africa, Maryknoll in, 252 ff; Tanganyika, description, 252 ff; languages, 253; names, 254 ff
Aglipay, Bishop, 71
Agneta Chang, Sister M., 86, 93, 301
Agricultural school, Molina, Chile, 230 ff
Ainu race, 183
Albert Staubli, Brother, 76–77, 279, 280, 287 ff
Albouy, Bishop Paul, 151
Allie, Rev. Arthur F., 235, 248
Amazon headwaters, 202 ff
American fliers, aided by missioners, 153 ff; helped by Maryknollers in Wuchow, 111
American Medical Commission, 210
American Missionary in Alaska, An, 28
American Presbyterian Mission, 66
Andre, Rev. Gabriel, S.S., 24–26
Animals, Musoma, Africa, 258; Pando Vicariate, 202 ff
Annals of the Propagation of the Faith, 27
Antigua, Guatemala, 244–245
Antonia Maria, Sister, 299
Antu, 123
Antung, 120, 128
Aodani, 184, 186
Aoyagi, 182
Approval, official, of Maryknoll, 47, 294
Approval of Maryknoll Sisters, 296
Araoz, Senorita Maria Rosario, 223
Araucanian Indians: Chile, 226
Arequipa, Peru, 222
Atab, 138
Aymara Indians, 209

Bagalawis, Dr. Artemio, 70, 71, 76, 79
Baguio, 138; Maryknoll Sisters in, 302–303
Bakuria Tribe, Africa, 260 ff
Bangoreme Tribe, Africa, 256
Barile, Doctor, 52

Bataan, 135, 136, 138; death march, 137
Bauer, Rev. Thomas J., 274
Bayless, Rev. Louis I., 252–253
Beatrice, Sister, 89, 91
Becka, Rev. Frederick, 117–119
Benedictine Abbey, Belmont, N.C., 16
Beni River, 203, 207
Benziger, Bishop, 34
Bernadette Sobirous, 46, 56, 64
Bethany Convent, 309
Bianchi, Bishop Lawrence, 102, 279
Big Six (catechist), 116
Bilibid Prison, 137
Birth Control, Japan, 179
Blaber, Dr. Harry, 70
Blessed Sacrament, 85, 193; hidden, 162
Blessed Virgin, 46, 56, 58, 64, 197
Blind, work for in Soloma, Guatemala, 242
Blois, Bishop, 121, 128
Blue Cloud County, 116
Boesflug, Rev. Clement P., 182
Bolivia, 201 ff; Dioceses, Maryknoll work in, 209 ff; Maryknoll in, 201 ff; statistics, 202
Bonner, Rev. Raymond J., 201, 207–208
Booth, Rev. William R., 89, 90, 92, 95
Boston, 21, 22, 34, 41, 43, 49, 190, 191, 193; Chinese work in, 149; Propagation of the Faith, 34
Boston College, 22, 24
Boston College High School, 22
Boystown, Chile, 230, 235 ff
Boxer Rebellion, 120
Brainwashing, 7; and Father Greene, 164 ff
Brannigan, Rev. Joseph E., 252–253, 260
Bratton, Rev. Edward, 254
Bridge, Rev. Francis A., 123–124
Bridgeport, Conn., 147
Brigita, Sister M., 304
Brookline, Mass., 85
Brooklyn, 2, 89, 93, 99, 149, 178

Brothers (Maryknoll), beginnings, 49; 283–291; description of vocation, 291; novitiate, 286; training of, 286
Brown, Rev. Charles A., 210
Bruneau, Rev. Joseph, 28, 60, 192
Buddhism, Japanese, 146
Buena Paz, Chile, 232
Buffalo, N.Y., 148, 177
Burns, Rev. Clarence J., 124 ff; 125
Burns, Rev. Constantine F., 289
Burns, Rev. Lawrence J., 209
Bush, Rev. Harry M., 99–100
Buzeta, Chile, 229–230
Byrne, Rev. Patrick J., 82 ff; 169 ff, 177, 190–191; American occupation of Japan, 170–171; raised to rank of Monsignor, 170; resigns, 170; Apostolic Delegate to S. Korea, torture and death, 87–92

Cachuela Esperanza, 208
Cairns, Rev. Robert J., 72 ff, 271
Calacala parish, 209–211
Calvary in China, 161
Cambridge, Mass., 22, 25
Canton, China, 5, 59, 64, 71, 116, 154; and Bishop Ford, 1 ff; federal prison described, 6–7; People's National Prison, 1 ff
Cantwell, Bishop James, 298
Cappel, Rev. Joseph C., 229
Carey, Rev. Thomas J., 212
Carmelite Sisters, 91
Carmencita, Sister, 138
Carroll, Bishop John, 23
Carroll, Monsignor George M., 89, 92; appointed Apostolic Administrator of Pengyang Vicariate, 93
Cashin, Rev. William, 53
Cathedral College, N.Y.C., 2, 49
Catherine, Mother (sister of Fr. Price), 17
Catholic Center, Kyoto, 176
Catholic Central Bureau, 275
Catholic Charities, Japan, 179–180
Catholic Club, Tokyo, 179
Catholic Emperor of China, 150
Catholic Foreign Mission Bureau, 28 ff, 34, 46, 49, 327
Catholic Foreign Mission Society, 9, 34, 51; title explained, 48; exclusive name, 189
Catholic Missions, 28
Catholic News, N.Y.C., 191
Catholic Press, 133

Catholic Students' Conference, 133
Catholic Students' Mission Crusade, 190
Catholic Synodal Commission (China), 108
Catholic University, Washington, 31, 32, 45
Catholic Welfare, Hong Kong, 300
Cavin Indians, 203–205
Cavinas mission, Bolivia, 203–207, 209
Cebu, 141; Maryknoll work, 134
Ceylon, Maryknoll Sisters in, 311
Chaaiwan Refugee Area, 280
Ch'a Kou, 120
Chambon, Archbishop, 169
Chang Ho Wun parish, 94
Chang, John, 86–87, 93; see: Agneta, Sister M.
Changpai trail, 124
Chatron, Bishop, 34
Chiantla, Guatemala, 248 ff
Chicago, Ill., 134, 157, 180; Maryknoll's Chinese parish, 149, 320
Childs, Captain, 12–13
Chile, description, 225 ff; Chillan, 228; educational work of Maryknoll Sisters, 311; Maryknoll in, 225–237
China, 59, 62, 66, 71, 96, 102, 114, 141, 199; North, 76; South, 68, 70, 150
China Missionary Bulletin, 274
Chinese Catholic Club (Hong Kong), 278
Chinese, loyalty of, 4, 79; petition Reds to release Bishop Ford, 3
Chinese Sisters, Kweilin, 159–160
Chinnampo, 83–85
Cholchol, Chile, 228
Christian Brothers, 50
Christ's mission methods, 173–176
Chuanhsien, 155–157
Chung Chong Pouk To (Korea) assigned to Maryknoll, 94
Chunggangjin, 91
Chungking, 112, 114, 116
Chungking Listening Post, 116
Church, condition of in Chile, 235 ff
Cincinnati, Ohio, 191; Maryknoll in, 321
Clare, Sister Mary, 91
Clarks Summit, Pa., 53, 82, 103; Maryknoll in, 320
Cleary, Rev. Donald C., 218
Cleary, Patrick H., 82

Clement Hansan, Brother, 287
Cleveland, Ohio, 143
CNRRA, 71
Coleman, Rev. William J., 231 ff
Collegio San Ambrosio, 221
Collins, Rev. William J., 252
Columba, Mother Mary, 309
Columban Fathers, 134, 141, 190, 303
Columbus, Indiana, 52, 66
Communism, Chile, 234; Fushun, 129 ff; Kweilin, 158 ff; methods of search, 3; religion in China, 3; Wuchow Diocese, 117
Communists, attitude to God, 5; attitude towards religion, Manchuria, 130; blackmail (see: Paschang, Bp. Adolph A.), 77; brainwashing, 7; constitution adopted by Communists, 1948, North Korea, 88; demonstration—Tungan, 163; interrogation—Tungan, 164 ff; jail, 6–7; Kyoto, 171, 173, 186; Legion of Mary, 157 ff; and Mary—Tungan, 166; and Maryknollers, 76 ff; and Maryknoll Sisters, 298, 299, 300, 301; mass demonstrations against foreigners, 4–6; methods of search, 3; and N. Koreans (see—Pengyang, loyalty of N. Koreans under Communists), 88; North Korea under, 89; propaganda, 3; public trial (see: Paschang, Bp. Adolph A.), 77; trial—Tungan, 163 ff
Conaty, Father, 20
Congregation of the Charity of the Sacred Heart, 110
Conley, Lawrence A., 75
Connors, Rev. Frank, 69
Connors, Rev. Joseph W., 93, 95
Conquista, Bolivia, 208
Considine, Rev. John J., 193 ff, 328–9
Constance, Sister M., 303
Constancis, Rev. Joseph, 105
Constantine, Catholic Emperor of China, 150
Constitution of Japan, 176
Contero school, Chile, 227–228
Convents of Maryknoll Sisters, 306
Conversion, Mass, in Wuchow, 116 ff; inspired by Fr. Jerry Donovan's death, 127; Kyoto, 178; Tokyo, 179
Corazon, Sister M., 299
Corregidor, 134
Cortland, N.Y., 145

Cothonay, Rev. Bertrand, O.P., and Maryknoll, 29
Cotoca parish: Bolivia, 211
Cottonwood, Idaho, 179
Coulehan, Father John M., 144
Covington, Ky., 112, 158
Cowan, Rev. Vincent M., 226 ff
Coyos, Rev., 92
Crane, Rev., 30
Cresco, Iowa, 156
Cronly, J.M., 14
Cumberland, Maryland, 144
Cummings, Edith, 135
Cummings, Rev. William T., 134–138
Cunningham, Rev. Vincent A., 215
Curepto, Chile, 229
Curran, Rev. John F., 277 ff
Cuzco, seminary in, 220

Dairen, Manchuria, 120, 121, 122, 128, 129
Daley, Rev. Timothy, 139
Damien Walsh, Brother, 254, 286
Danehy, Bishop Thomas J., 201, 206, 207, 208; consecration, 205
Daniel Doherty, Brother, 286
Davao, 79
Davis, Rev. Leo, 121
Deaf and dumb, Kyoto, 178
Death of Bishop James A. Walsh, 195
Death March (Korea), 89 ff
Dempsey, Rev. Arthur F., 113–114
Departure Ceremony, 60
De Paul, Sister Mary, 307
Dickson, Dr., 66
Dietz, Rev. Frederick C., 108, 109, 179, 271
Dispensary work, Cavinas, 204; Korea, 300–301; Huehuetenango, Guatemala, 251; Soloma, Guatemala, 242
Dissez, Rev., 38
Divine Word Fathers, 141, 190
Dominicans, 29, 48, 180; German, 98; Sisters, 296
Donaghy, Bishop Frederick A., 110 ff, 115, 116, 289, 290, 299
Donovan, Father Jerry, 126–127, 208
Donovan, Rev. John F., 103
Dorchester, Mass., 161
Downs, Rev. William, 66
Drought, Rev. James, 71, 97, 132–134, 194, 195

Duchesne, Rev. Paul J., 275 ff, 281–282
Ducoeur, Bishop, 108
Duffy, Chaplain John E., 138
Dunn, Rev. James, 41
Dunn, Bishop John J., 18, 60, 191–192, 296
Dunne, Rev. Martin P., 229
Dwight School, 21, 22
Dwyer, Mary, 294–296
Dyer, Rev. James, 36, 39, 42

Early Church, mission methods, 173
Edmonds, Rev. Stephen B., 279 ff
Education, Bolivia Dioceses, 210; Chile, 226 ff; Lima, Peru, 223 ff; Pando Vicariate, 208; Puno, Peru, 220
Educational work of Maryknoll Sisters 299 ff; in Philippines, 302 ff
Eggleston, Rev. William J., 185
Eijk, Mary P. van, 251
Elenita, Sister, 85
Eleventh Airborne Division (U.S.A.), 139–141
Elliott, Rev. Walter, C.S.P., 27, 34, 38
Elma, Iowa, 84, 145
Elmhurst, N.Y., 112, 149
Emergency Relief Council, Hong Kong, 103
Emmitsburg, Md., 49
Emperor of China, Catholic, 150
Entrance requirements, Maryknoll Brothers, 286
Escalante, Bishop Alonso E., 201 ff
Eucharistic Congress, Montreal, 29, 30
Eucharistic Congress, Philippines, 133
Eunice, Sister Mary, 306
Eusebe, Sister, 63

Fage, Rev. Peter, 180
Falconio, Archbishop Diomede, 44
Fall River, Mass., 74, 82, 111, 133
Farley, Cardinal, 28, 29, 44, 48, 53, 196
Farmer, Rev. F. X., 108
Fedders, Rev. Albert V., 112 ff, 113, 158, 290
Feeding poor, Kyoto, 171–173; Lima, Peru, 224
Felix Fournier, Brother, 286
Felsecker, Rev. Harold J., 178
Fidelia, Sister M., 296

Fidelis Deichelbohrer, Brother, 286
Fidelis, Sister M., 303
Field Afar, The, 19, 33, 34, 46, 49, 54–55, 57, 199, 293, 294, 296; founding of, 28, 29; role of in Maryknoll's work, 322 ff
Finn, Father William, 26
First Departure Group, 60
First Departure of Maryknoll Sisters, 298
First General Chapter, 71
First Maryknollers in Japan, 169
First mission field, 59
First students, 49 ff
Fitzgerald, Rev. James W., 211
Flagg, Dr. Paluel J., 52, 53, 54, 60
Fletcher, Rev. William A., 133
Flying Tigers, 153, 156
Foody, Rev. Stephen P., 229, 232
Ford, Austin, 2
Ford, Elizabeth, 2
Ford, Francis X., 49, 51, 54, 60, 63, 96, 97 ff, 101, 102, 103, 105, 269, 279, 299; biography, arrest, torture, imprisonment and death, 2–9; consecration of by Bishop James A. Walsh, 192; parents, 2; prayer by, 96
Fordham University, 127
Foreign Mission Brothers of St. Michael, 283–291
Foreign Mission Sisters of St. Dominic, 292 ff
Formosa, 149 ff; description, 264; Maryknoll Sisters work in, 312
Francis Wempe, Brother, 287
Franciscans, 167
Franconia, 46
Freri, Msgr. Joseph, 26, 27, 28
Freuler, Rev. Charles, C.M., 284
Fritz, Rev. Gorden N., 203–205, 209
Fu Jen University, 155
Fukien Province, 98
Fumasoni–Biondi, Cardinal, 191
Furuya, Bishop Paul, 170 ff, 180, 185
Furuya, Mr. and Mrs. (Bishop Furuya's parents), 180
Fushimi, 185
Fushun, 122, 127, 128, 208; bandits, 122; Communists, 129 ff; history and description, 120–121; industrial schools, 122, 127; Japanese work, 121 ff; loyalty of Chinese, 124, 125; mission methods, 121–129; native clergy, 121, 129–130; old folks

home, 122; orphanage, 122; Prefecture Apostolic, 124; statistics, 121, 122, 127; Vicariate Apostolic, 127; weather, 123, 124, 125, 126; World War II, 128

Gallagher, Dr. and Mrs. Frederick, 10, 11
Galvarino, Chile, 229
Garvey, Rev. Jerome P., 229
Gaspard, Rev. Raymond A., 77
Gate of Heaven Leper Colony, 70 ff, 73 ff, 76, 78
Gauthier, Rev. Alphonse, 62
Gemma, Sister M., 296
General Chapter (Hong Kong, 1936), 198
Geographies, Catholic, 327
Geselbracht, Rev. Howard C., 157
Gibbons, James Cardinal, 44–45, 86
Gishu, 82
Gilmartin, Rev. Gregory, 162
Glass, Rev. Lloyd I., 156, 157
Glen Ellyn, Ill., Maryknoll in, 320
Glynn, S. M., Rev., 185
Goiter, Formosa, 266 ff
Gombert Brothers, 89, 91
Gounod's *Departure Hymn*, 60
Gonzaga, Brother, 207–208
Good, Rev. Albert E., 252, 253, 254 ff, 258 ff
Gotti, Cardinal, 59; approves foundation of Maryknoll, 47 ff
Graham, Rev. Ambrose C., 203, 209
Greene, Rev. Robert W., 161 ff
Gregoria, Sister M., 85
Gripsholm, 85, 128
Grondin, Monsignor J. Gerard, 209, 252, 263
Guatemala, description, 238 ff; Maryknoll in, 238–251; Maryknoll in (statistics), 250–251
Guebriant, Bishop de, 59, 60, 64
Guerrillas, Tungan, 165

Habenicht, Rev. James F., 183
Hachijo, Michael, 179
Hachijo, Viscount Takamasa, 179
Hahn, Rev. Joseph A., 203
Haid, Bishop, 32, 39, 41; connection with Father Price, 16
Hakka, 97, 101; Formosa, 269
Hanna, Archbishop, 136
Hannon, Rev. Austin, 133
Hanscom, Miss, 293

Harvard University, 23, 24, 131
Hayes, Patrick Cardinal, 296
Hawaii, 142, 189; education, 142 ff; Maryknoll Sisters, 142; Maryknoll Sisters work in, 304, 305; Maryknoll work in, 142–146; mission history, 142–143; mission methods, 143 ff; native clergy, 146; Protestants, 143; statistics, 142, 144
Hawthorne, N.Y., 29, 48–52; Maryknoll in, 48 ff; and Sisters, 294
Hawthorne, Mother Rose, 48
Health, Guatemala, 238, 242
Health education, Pando Vicariate, 205
Health statistics, Pando Vicariate, 204, 205
Heiwa-mura, 181 ff
Hermit Kingdom, 80 ff
Hessler, Rev. Donald L., 274
Hierarchy of U.S. approves plan to start Maryknoll, 45 ff
Hikeda district, Sapporo, 183
Hilbert, Rev. Charles, 102, 269
Hill, S.M., Father, 185
Hilo, Hawaii, 145
Hirschboeck, Rev. George J., 176, 185 ff
Hoban, Bishop Edward F., 53
Hochelaga Convent, Montreal, 20
Hogan, Abbe, 24
Hoignan, 75
Hokkaido, 183
Hollger, Brother Ernst, 49
Holy Family Seminary, Wuchow, 117
Holy Rosary Church, 94
Hong, Bishop Francis, 86, 88, 92, 141
Hong, Rev. Callistus, 84
Hong Kong, 59, 63, 66, 71, 77, 78, 79, 102, 115, 120, 149, 153, 158, 161, 162, 189; history, description, 270 ff; Maryknoll in, 279–282; Maryknoll Sisters work in, 298 ff
Hong Kong Standard, 277
Honolulu, 143; Diocese of, 146
Hopei mission, 126, 127
Hostel work, Kyoto, 178; Philippines, 132–133; of Maryknoll Sisters, Philippines, 304
Housing for refugees, Hong Kong, 277
Ho-yun, 6
Hsingan, 154 ff; mission, 155
Huehuetenango, Guatemala, 248
Hughes, Rev. J. Russell, 134, 139

Hunan Province, 156
Hunt, Idaho relocation camp, 149
Hunt, Rev. Joseph, 85
Hurley, General Patrick, 156
Hyacinth, Sister M., 138–140
Hyatt, Rev. James F., 176

I Make the Stations of the Cross, 328
Iburi district, Sapporo, 183
Ide, 184, 186
Igorots, 303
Imelda, Sister M., 277, 280
Immaculate Heart, Sisters of the, 68; (Kongmoon) 298
Immaculate Heart of Virgin Mary, Sisters of, 266
Incas, 213
Inchon, 90
Indians, Bolivia, 203–204, 209, 210; Guatemala, 238 ff; Puno, Peru, 213, 216–221
Industrial School, Soloma, Guatemala, 243
Information Bureau, Maryknoll, 327
Innisfail, 207
Institute Leo XIII, 234 ff
Inter American Agricultural Service, 211
Iramba Mission, 256–257
Irish World, 2

Jacaltenango, Guatemala, 247–248
Jacksonville, Fla., 192
Jacques, Rev. Armand J., 128, 154, 155, 265
Jamaica Plain, Mass., 190
Japan, 58, 60, 87, 102, 137, 189; Maryknoll in, 177 ff; mission history, 167–169
Japan-China war (see: Kongmoon, Japan-China war), 72 ff; Kweilin, 152 ff; Wuchow, 110–111
Japanese Army, 68
Japanese, work, Los Angeles, 146–148, 298; Seattle, 298
Japanese school, Lima, Peru, 223
Jasper, Indiana, 161
Java, 102
Jefferson, Sgt. Curtis, 137
Jesuits, 141, 150; scholars, Formosa, 268
Joan Marie, Sister M., 1–9
John, Saint, 57
John, the Apostle, Saint, 54

Joseph, Mother Mary, 195, 296 ff, 304, 306, 309, 313
Joseph, Saint, 197
Joseph, Sister M., 296 ff
Joyce, Rev. John J., 72–73
Juan Mateo, 240 ff
Judge, Rev. William, 46
Jungle, Bolivia, 202 ff
Jungyun, 116

Karlovecius, Rev, Anthony J., 185
Kaschmitter, Rev. William A., 179
Kaulungtsai refugee mission, 279
Kawanishi, 185
Kaying, 96–106, 189, 192; cathedral, 4; Communists and Maryknollers, 1; Communists (in twenties), 98; Communists, 106; co-operatives, 104 ff; education, 102; expulsion by Communists, 106; history, 97 ff; hostel work, 101; intellectual apostolate, 101; Maryknoll Sisters, 100–101; Maryknoll Sisters work in, 298 ff; mission methods, 97, 101–106; native clergy, 4, 97, 101–102, 105–106; Prefecture Apostolic, 98; refugee work, 102–103; rice bank, 103; self-help programs, 104; statistics, 99, 105; Vicariate Apostolic, 101
Keelan, Rev. Francis X., 153
Keelung, Formosa, 264
Kelly, Rev. James F., 190
Kennelly, Rev. Robert P., 77
Kenrick Junior Seminary, 321
Kentucky, 107, 120
Kevin Grimley, Brother, 287
Kiernan, Rev. Thomas V., 145
Kim, Blessed Andrew, 81
Kim, John, 95
Kim, Rev., 83
Knotek, Rev. Wenceslaus F., 156–157
Kochow, 75
Kongmoon, 62–68, 71, 73, 74, 76, 84, 110, 189; Japan-China war, 72 ff; lay apostles, 70 ff; chapel, 289; communism, 76 ff; history, 62 ff; methods, 67–79; relief work, 75–76, 78; statistics, 62
Korea, 59, 80–86, 132, 145, 169, 189; Maryknoll Sisters work in, 300–301; mission history, 80 ff; persecution, 81; statistics, 81
Kouen, Francis Xavier, 81

Kowak Mission, Africa, 253
Kowloon, 270, 271, 272
Kress, Rev. William S., 143, 146
Krock, Rev. George L., 249 ff
Kunming, 112
Kuomintang, 109
Kupfer, Msgr. William F., 266, 268
Kwangsi, 108–109, 111–112, 151,
    155; contrast with Kwangtung, 107
Kwangtung Province, 59, 62, 79, 108,
    109; contrast with Kwangsi, 107;
Kwangtung International Relief Com-
    mittee, 103
Kweilin, 110, 161, 162, 163, 189;
    Boystown, 156; Chinese Sisters,
    159–160; Communists, 158 ff; con-
    trasted with Wuchow, 151; dispen-
    sary, 157; flood control, 157;
    Foundling Association, 155; history,
    description, 150–151; Japan-China
    War, 152; Legion of Mary, 157 ff;
    mission methods, 152–155; Prefec-
    ture Apostolic, 150 ff; refugee
    work, 152–160; rice bank, 157;
    split from Wuchow, 151; statis-
    tics, 154, 157, 160
Kyoto, 167, 186–187; history and de-
    scription, 169 ff
Kyoto Imperial University, 176
Kyoto Mission, 169
Kyoto, Prefecture Apostolic, 170
Kyoto, Vicariate Apostolic, 180

Laai, Rev., 118–119
Lacroix, Rev. Arthur, 151, 154
Lacson College, 134
La Farge, Oliver, 245, 246
Laipo, 159, 160, 162
Laity and Maryknoll, 324
Lane, Rev. John I., 28, 49, 52
Lane, Bishop Raymond A., 54, 120 ff,
    127, 128, 129, 141, 207 ff, 319; as
    Superior General, 199–200
Langeslay, Frederick, 325
Languages, Africa, 256
Language school, Arequipa, Peru, 222
LARA, 178
Larmour, Victoria, 294
Larrain, Bishop Manuel, 230, 234
La Salette Fathers, 141
Last testament of Bishop James A.
    Walsh, 196 ff
Latin America, why Maryknoll went
    to, 201
Lavanoux, Maurice, 284

Lavery, Rev. Hugh, 147 ff, 148
Lawler, Rev. John J., 210, 222 ff
Lawrence, Mass., 127
Lay Apostles, 70; Kyoto, 173, 178
Legion of Mary, Japan, 178; Kweilin,
    157–159
Lenahan, Rev. John F., 250 ff
Lenin, 186
Lepers, work for, Kongmoon, 69 ff
    (see: Sweeney, Rev. Joseph A.)
Li, Joseph, 278
Life, 28
Lima, Peru, Maryknoll work in, 222 ff
Linkiang, 122–123
Lintaan, 67
Lipa Diocese, 141
Lipa School, 303
Liturgical Arts, 145, 284
Liu, Francis, 126
Los Angeles, "Little Tokyo," 148;
    Maryknoll Sisters work in, 147,
    298; Maryknoll work for Japanese,
    146–148; vocations from Mary-
    knoll, 148
Los Banos, 139, 140
Los Hombres del Mañana, 235
Lost Christians of Japan, 168–169
Loting, 59, 63, 66–67, 74, 77, 108;
    chapel, 288
Lourdes, 55, 71
Lourdes and Father Price, 46, 47, 48,
    51
Loyalty of Chinese, Fushun, 124,
    125; Japan, 168–169; Korea, 85
Ludden, Mr. (Consul at Mukden),
    126
Ludwig, Rev., 99
Lumen News Service, 179
Luos, 253
Luzon, 138–139, 141
Lyons, Rev. Francis X., 213 ff

Macao, 62, 74, 78, 81, 274
MacArthur, General Douglas, 90, 94,
    133, 135, 171
Mainichi, Tokyo, 172
Maisonneuve, 20, 30
Malaria, Peru, 218–219
Malenkov, 186
Malone, Rev. Patrick F., 99
Malone, Rev. Thomas J., 275
Mam Indians, Guatemala, 241, 244
Manchuria, 59, 76, 81, 82, 120 ff,
    124, 132, 189

Manchuria Daily News, 147
Mandarin language, 151, 156
Manhattan College, 87
Manila, 70, 71, 131, 132, 133, 134, 135, 141; hostel work, 132–133
Manning, Rev. James T., 266
Manning, Rev. James V., 234 ff
Manpojin, 90
Manual labor, Maryknoll seminaries, 315
Marcelline, Sister M., 299
Maria Corozon, Sister, 299
Marist Fathers, 185; Kyoto, 180
Mark, Sister M., 277
Marks, Lt. Mortimer, 111
Marquette University, 94
Marsden, S.M., Father, 185
Martyrs, Japan, 168
Mary, 198; Bp. Furuya's parents die before her shrine, 180; and Brother Gonzaga, 207, 208; hated by Communists, 166; and Japanese Catholics, 168; pilgrimage to her shrine, Chiantla, Guatemala, 248 ff
Maryknoll, 49, 52, 53, 58–60, 59, 64; approved by *Propaganda Fide,* 47; beginnings, 30 ff; beginnings of in Rev. T. F. Price's mind, 31 ff, 37; beginnings of in mind of Bp. J. A. Walsh, 29, 34; defined in human terms, 9; its debt, 330; and Eucharistic Congress (1910), 29; first mission field, 59 ff; in Kweilin, 151; on Formosa, 264–269; foundation, 43–51; missioners, training of, 314 ff; Novitiate, 320; official title explained, 48; and other U. S. Mission Societies, 190; Philippines, 132 ff; in Peru—statistics, 224; poetic description, 199; in Puno, 212 ff; Seminary, 320; spirit, 316; Teachers College, 307; training houses in U.S., 320 ff; work in Bolivia Dioceses, 209 ff; work in Japanese relocation camps, 147, 148, 149
Maryknoll Brothers, 52, 283–291
Maryknoll College, Manila, 302
Maryknoll, The Field Afar, role, 322 ff
Maryknoll General Chapter, 129
Maryknollers, Bp. J. A. Walsh's last testament to, 196 ff; under fire, Hong Kong, 272 ff
Maryknoll Sisters, 132, 133, 138, 139, 185; Africa, 310–311; Bolivia, 203; Carolines and Marshalls, 310; Cloister, 307; Formosa, 268; Hawaii, 304, 305; Hong Kong, 277, 279, 280; Japan, 307 ff; Kandy, Ceylon, 311; Kaying, 96; Kyoto, 180; Latin America, 308 ff; Lima, Peru, 224; Manchuria, 305, 306; Mauritius, 311, 312; Mindinao, 303; Motherhouse, 306–307, 309; Novitiate, 310; Panama, 308, 309; Pando Vicariate, 204, 205; Pengyang, 84, 85; separate community, 313; Siuna, Nicaragua, 309; South Korea, 93, 94; U.S., 312; Wuchow, 110; medical work—299 ff; Bolivia, 308; Philippines, 304; clinic, Pusan, 94
Maswa-Shinyanga, 263
Matsudaira, Mrs. Theresa, 149
Mayan Indians: Guatemala, 241
McCabe, Rev. Edwin J., 155, 156, 158
McCabe, Rev. Joseph, 52
McCann, Thomas, 49
McCarthy, Rev. Edward, S. C., 134
McCarthy, Rev. William R., 139, 141
McClear, Rev. J. Edmund, 238 ff
McCormack, Rev. Joseph P., 121
McCormick, Rev. James A., 103–104
McDermott, Rev. Thomas F., 229
McGlinchey, Father Joseph, 46
McGurkin, Rev. Edward A., 128
McKay, Rev. Francis A., 227–228
McKiernan, Rev. Michael J., 149
McKillop, Rev. Michael J., 178
McLaughlin, Rev. James E., 290
McLeod, Rev. Daniel J., 246
McLoughlin, Rev. John M., 112, 114, 149
McNicholas, Archbishop John T., 58, 191, 196
McNiff, Rev. James F., 231–232
McShane, Rev. Daniel, 52, 53, 65, 67, 77
Meaney, Rev. Joseph P., 212, 215–218
Medical work, Bolivian Dioceses, 210, 211; Pando, 204; Puno, Peru, 216–219
Men of Tomorrow, 235 ff
Mercy, Sister Mary, 85, 94, 300, 301, 308 (see: Pusan Clinic)
Mercy, Sisters of, 17

Meyer, Rev. Bernard F., 60, 63, 67, 108 ff, 113, 115, 272, 274
Mexican Foreign Mission Seminary, 205
Miaoli, Formosa, 269
Milan Foreign Mission Society, 26, 47, 102
Mill Hill College, 46
Mill Hill Foreign Mission Society, 26, 28, 32, 34, 52; Tyrol, 47
Milwaukee, Wis., 94, 176, 178
Mission Education, 57, 187, 190, 329; Maryknoll fosters, 324; Maryknoll's program, 328, 329
Mission History, Japan, 167–169
Mission Literature, 58
Mission methods, Chile, 226 ff; Christ's, 173–176; Fushun, 121–129; Guatemala, 241; Kongmoon, 67; Kyoto, 178–179; Musoma, Africa, 256–257, 262; Father Price's, 15 ff; Tienchung, Formosa, 266; Kyoto, 170 ff
Missioner, description of a, 316 ff
Missioners expelled from China, 274
Missions Etrangeres de Quebec, 128
Missions, logical basis, 188–189
Mitsukoshi Dept. Store, 179
Miyako Shinbun, 172
Modern Martyr, A, 28
Moikong River, 105
Moira, Sister M., 299
Molina agricultural school, 230 ff
Montreal, Canada, 34, 104; Eucharistic Congress (1910) and Maryknoll, 19; Eucharistic Congress and Fr. J. A. Walsh, 29
Mooney, Edward Cardinal, 196
Mooney, Rev. Joseph J., 185
Moore, Rev., 14
Morita, 181 ff
Morning Star School, 76
Morris, Rev. John E., 82, 84
Morrissette, Rev. Dominic J., 234
Moslems (Moros), 131
Motion pictures, Maryknoll, 327–328
Mount Misti, Peru, 222
Mt. St. Mary's College, 49
Mountain View, Cal., Maryknoll in, 321
Mukden, 120, 121, 128
Mulcahy, Rev. William P., 275
Mulligan, Rev. Francis J., 228
Mundelein, George Cardinal, 134
Murphy, Rev. Maynard, 104

Murray, Archbishop John G., 196
Murrett, Rev. John C., 148, 177–178
Mutel, Bishop, 59
Musoma: Prefecture Apostolic, 252 ff; statistics, 262

Nagasaki, Japan, 168
Nakamura-san, 181 ff
Nanking, 108
Nanning, 111, 151
Nara, 186
National Catholic Committee of Japan, 178–179
National Cathloic Welfare Conference (U.S.), 178, 199 (See: War Relief Services)
National Safety Force, Kyoto, Japan, 185
Nationalists, Chinese, 265
Native Clergy, Bishop Ford, 4; Bolivian dioceses, 211; Brothers, 83; China, 166; Formosa, 268; Fushun, 121, 129–130; Kaying, 97, 98, 101–102, 105–106; Kyoto, 169–170, 176, 178, 179, 180; Maryknollers foster, 83; Chile, 226, 228; Puno, Peru, 219 ff; Philippines, 132, 141; shortage of, Bolivia, 202; Chile, 226 236; Puno, Peru, 213 ff; and Bishop J. E. Walsh, 68; Maryknoll Sisters foster, 298 ff, 301; Africa, 311; Japan, 307; Manchuria, 306
Native Sisters, 83; trained by Maryknoll Sisters, 298 ff
Native Teachers, use of: Philippines, 303
Nazareth, N.C., 17 ff, 32, 36, 38, 39, 41, 46
Nevers, France, 47, 48, 56, 64
New Bedford, Mass., 133, 193, 210
New Bern, N.C., 25
New Britain, Conn., 69, 84
Newport, Minn., 203
Newport, R.I., 103
New Rochelle, N.Y., 151, 152
New Southern Star, 102
Newton, Mass., 151
New York, 41, 44, 46, 53, 191, 196, 201
New York Chinatown, Maryknoll work in, 149
New York City, 48, 50, 52, 89, 121, 134, 138–139, 203, 210
New York Times, 281

Ngaimoon, 70 ff
Ngau T'au Kok Refugee camp, 278
Niedhammer, Bishop, 309
North Carolina, 42, 44, 46, 60
North Carolina Apostolate, 15 ff
North Carolina State College, 17
Norwalk, Conn., 77, 149
Notre Dame University, 134
Nugent, Rev. Irwin D., 162, 163
Nyegina, 253

Oakland, Calif., 209
Oberlin, Ohio, 108, 179
Oblate Fathers, 141
Occupation, American, Japan, 171
O'Connell, William Cardinal, 13, 29, 30, 34–35, 43, 44, 46
O'Connor, Rev. Michael J., 264, 266
O'Dea, Bishop, 298
O'Doherty, Archbishop Michael J., 132, 133, 302, 303
O'Neill, Rev. Francis, 269
O'Neill, Rev. Joseph J., 201
Only A Veil, 192
Operation Goiter, Formosa, 266 ff
Oriental Exclusion Act, 147
Oriental Work in U.S., 142 ff
O'Rourke S.J., Rev., 39
Orphanage, Yeungkong, China, 298
Orphan Boy, The, 17
Osaka Diocese, Japan, 169, 180, 186; part given to Kyoto, 169–170
O'Shea, Bishop William F., 51, 84 ff
Ossining, N.Y., 50, 195, 320

P.O.W. Camps, Korea, 93
Pai, Rev. Maurus, 129, 130
Pai, Michael, 129
Pakhoi, 116
Pakkai, 74, 76
Pando, assigned to Maryknoll, 201; becomes Vicariate Apostolic, 202; history and description, 201 ff
Panquehue, Chile, 229
Pardy, Rev. James V., 93–94
Paris, Bishop, 59
Paris Foreign Mission Society, 24, 26, 28, 32, 62, 82, 92, 97, 105
Parochial schools, Chile, 226 ff; Lima, Peru, 223; Maryknoll Sisters in Latin America, 308 ff
Paschang, Bishop Adolph, 71–78
Paul, Saint, 196
Paul, Sister Mary, 298
Paulhus, Rev. Anthony, 74

Pearl Harbor, 73, 85, 128, 134, 136
Pedro II, Emperor of Brazil, 21
Peekskill, N.Y., 114
Peking, 78, 81, 87, 88, 102, 108, 129, 150
Pengyang, Communists, 83, 85 ff; history, 83; internment of Maryknollers, 85; Japanese work, 83, 86; loyalty of Koreans, 85, 88, 90, 91, 92, 94; mission methods, 139–143; native clergy, 83 ff; Prefecture Apostolic, 83; statistics, 83–84; Vicariate, 84
Perpetual Help, Sisters of Our Lady of, 84
Perry, Admiral, 168
Persecution, Japan, 168 ff
Peru, educational work of Maryknoll Sisters, 311
Petipren, Rev. Roy D., 93
Petitjean, Rev., 168 ff
Petteoutsai, 104 ff
Philadelphia, Pa., 207
Philip Morini, Brother, 143–144
Philip II of Spain, 131
Philippine Archipelago, 131
Philippines, 41, 59, 71, 149, 189; and Spain, 131–132; and U.S., 132, 134; during World War II, 134 ff; Eucharistic Congress, 133; history, 131–132; Maryknoll work in, 134; Mission methods, 132–133, 134; native clergy, 132, 141; rescue of missioners by G.I.'s, 139 ff
Pichingal, Chile, 232
Pinglo, 162
Pingnam, 108, 109 ff, 115, 118
Pittsburgh, 126, 127
Pittsford, Vt., 115
Pittsfield, Mass., 93
Pius X, Pope, 47
Pius XI, Pope, 190, 191
Pius XII, Pope, 84, 149, 278
Pocantico Hills, 48–50
Porres, Blessed Martin de, 222
Port Arthur Territory, 121
Pospichal, Rev. Hubert M., 84, 144–145
Portezuelo, Chile, 226 ff
Powers, Father George C., 144
Pravda, 3
Prendergast, Rev. Thomas J., 184
Price, Alfred Lanier, 11
Price, Clarissa Bond, 10 ff; death, 14
Price, Joseph, 11

Price, Rev. Thomas F., 23, 30, 44, 45, 47, 48, 49, 53, 56, 62, 65, 199, 271, 294, 326; and Bishop Haid, 16 ff; and Mary, 13; Apostolic work in North Carolina, 15–18, 38–40; assignment to Orient, 60; beginnings of Maryknoll, 19; correspondence, 31–42; devotion to Blessed Virgin, 14; devotion to St. Bernadette, 64; early life, shipwreck, seminary days, 10–18; first contact with James A. Walsh, 20 ff; foundation of Maryknoll, 43; founds *Truth*, 16–17; last days, 63 ff; mission methods, 15 ff; spirituality, 55–57; Tar Heel Apostle in Wilmington, N.C. and Raleigh, 15–18, 38–40; vocation, 11
Promotion methods, 49, 54
Propaganda Fide, Congregation of, 83, 252
Propagation of the Faith, Society for, Boston, 26 ff
Protestants, Chile, 236–237
Protestants praise Catholic flood relief, 186
Proulx, Benjamin, 272
Providence, R.I., 155
Providence, Sisters of, 266
Puno, history and description, 212 ff; program, 219–220
Pusan, 90, 94–95; Clinic, 94, 301
Pyek, John Baptist, 81
Pyongyang (see Pengyang)

Quechua Indians, 209
Quincy, Ill., 149, 178
Quinlan, Msgr. Francis, 89–90, 92
Quinn, Rev. Carroll, 78–79
Quirk, Rev. Thomas N., 126, 258

Rachel, Sister M., 194
Raymond, Rev. Antonin, 284
Readers Digest, 73
Rebecca Clyde, 10 ff
Recollections of Seventy Years, 13
Redemptorist Fathers, Kyoto, 180
Redmond, Juanita, 136
Refugee work, Korea, 89, 93–94, 301; Kweilin, 153–160
Refugee work by Maryknoll Sisters, 300
Refugees, Hong Kong, 275
Regan, Rev. Joseph W., 153, 159

Reilly, Rev. Peter A., 111, 279, 289, 290
Reinhart, Rev. Joseph A., 260 ff
Relief work, Hong Kong, 276 ff; Japan, 178; Kyoto, 178, 183 ff; Wuchow, 190 ff
Religion Teacher and the World, 328
Relocation of Japanese, 147, 148, 149, 171
Renaico, Chile, 228
Repatriation of Maryknollers on Gripsholm, 128
Restaurant Guild, Kyoto, 172
Rhee, Syngman, 87, 88
Ri, John, 90
Ri, Peter, 81
Riberalta, 202, 203, 205, 208, 209
Riberi, Archbishop Anthony, 77, 275
Ricci, Mateo, 62, 81
Riganti, Monsignor, 275
Ro, Bishop Paul, 85, 89, 94
Robinson, Rev. Delbert W., 256, 257
Rochester, N.Y., 102
Rockefeller, John D., 48, 50 ff
Rogers, Miss Mary, 51, 292–297; buys Sunset Hill property, 50; (see Mother Mary Joseph)
Rogers, Patrick, 293
Romaniello, Monsignor John, 151–154, 323
Rome, 41, 45, 47, 48, 53, 59, 60, 64, 83, 93, 110, 168, 191, 196; Revs. J. A. Walsh and T. F. Price in, 46 ff
Romulo, General Carlos, 133, 134, 135
Roosevelt, Franklin D., 133, 137
Rosana Mission, Africa, 260 ff
Rose of Lima School, Saint, Lima, Peru, 223
Rose Victor, Sister, 299
Roxbury, Mass., 111, 147
Rural Apostolate, Kyoto, 173 ff
Rusk, Dr. Howard, 281
Ruth, Sister M., 296
Ryang, Rev. Peter, 83
Ryou, Rev., 89

Sabengo Air Base, 89
Sacraments go underground, 91
Sacred Congregation of Propaganda Fide, 124, 191, 201
Sacred Heart Church, Brooklyn, 2
Sacred Heart Church, Hawaii, 144

Sacred Heart Church, Raleigh, N.C.,
16
Sacred Heart Fathers, 143–144, 305
Sacred Heart Hospital, Toisham, 71,
299
Sacred Heart of Mary Sisters, 268
Sacred Heart Parish, Hawaii, 143
Sacred Heart Review, 25
Sacred Heart, Sisters of the (Wu-
chow), 299
Sadlier geographies, 327
St. Albans, L.I., N.Y., 201
St. Charles College, Md., 11, 14
St. Francis, Teaching Sisters of, 226
St. Francis Xavier Church, Kyoto,
169, 171
St. Gregory's Seminary, 321
St. James Academy, 303
St. John's Seminary, Brighton, 23 ff
St. Joseph of Carondelet, Sisters of,
180
St. Joseph's Parish, Hawaii, 145
St. Joseph's School, Pittsfield, 284
St. Joseph's Seminary, Yonkers, 18, 52
St. Louis, Mo., 183; Maryknoll in,
321
St. Mary's Hall, Manila, 133, 304
St. Mary's Seminary, Baltimore, 14,
18, 23, 26, 31, 36, 39, 66, 82
St. Michael, Foreign Mission Brothers
of, 283–291
St. Patrick's Cathedral, New York,
196
St. Patrick's, Roxbury, 25 ff
St. Paul de Chatres, Sisters of, 89
St. Paul's Hospital, Manila, 63, 132,
304
St. Rita's Hall, Manila, 132, 133
St. Teresa's building, 295
St. Therese Mission, Chicago, 149
St. Vincent de Paul Society, Kyoto,
171 ff, 173 ff; Japan, 178
Salesian Fathers, 149
Sanchez, Don Jorge, 231, 233
Sancian Island, 59, 62, 65, 72 ff, 76,
167
Sandman, Rev. Walter J., 232
San Francisco, 58, 66, 134–135, 146
San Jose, Bolivia, 208
San Juan, Puno, 221 ff
Sanko College, 177
Santa Cruz, 211
Santa Cruz Church, 134
Santa Eulalia, Guatemala, 245 ff
Santiago Prison, Philippines, 138

Santo Tomas Internment Camp, 139
Santos, Bishop Rufino, 141
Sapporo Diocese, 183
Saturday Evening Post, 152
SCAP, 178
Schiff, Rev. John M., 263
School Sisters of Notre Dame, Kyoto,
180
Scranton, Pa., 53, 66, 121
Seattle, 148, 176; Maryknoll work in,
148
Secretaries, The, 49–50
Self-help programs, Guatemala, 251;
Pando, 205, 208; Puno, Peru, 221–
222
Seminarian at Maryknoll, his day,
318 ff
Seminarians (U.S.) and Father Price,
18–19
Seminary, Puno, Peru, 220 ff
Seoul, 59, 81, 82, 85, 88, 89, 94;
Maryknoll work in, 89; Maryknoll-
ers begin work in, 86
Serengeti Plains, 252, 257
Shahan, Msgr., 32
Shambaris, Rev. Edmund T., 180
Shanghai, 59, 78, 102, 153, 199
Shantung Province, 121, 153
Shea, Nora, 294–295
Sheridan, Rev. Robert A., 133, 134,
139
Sherry, Dr. John L., 71
Shiga County, Japan, 169
Shingishu, 82
Shrines, Kyoto, 169
Shumkai, 116 (see: Blue Cloud
County)
Siaoloc, 103–104
Siberia, 183
Silver Virgin, Chiantla, 248 ff
Sing Sing Prison, 53
Sino-Japanese War, 163
Sister Catechists of Our Lady, 299
Sister Doctors, 299
Sisters of Providence, 268
Sisters, work of in early days of Mary-
knoll, 296
Smith College, 293, 294
Smith, Rev. James F., 149
Smith, Rev. Richard J., 229
Social Service work of Maryknoll Sis-
ters, Hawaii, 305
Society for the Propagation of the
Faith, Boston, 292 ff
Solano, Saint Francis, 222

Soloma, Guatemala, 239 ff
Sommer, Rev. Paul J., 247–248
Sorachi, Japan, 183
South China, 63, 132, 133
South China Sea, 73
South Korea, Apostolic Delegate, 87 ff (see: Byrne, Bp. Patrick J.); invasion of, 80; Maryknoll's work in, 93–94; refugee work, 89, 93–94
Spain, 97, 133; and Philippines, 131–132
Sparks, Captain, 137
Spellman, Francis Cardinal, 94, 201, 279
Spiritual Exercises of St. Ignatius, 42; and Rev. T. F. Price, 37, 39–40
Sprinkle, Rev. R. Russell, 111, 112, 115
Stalin, 186
Stanley, Hong Kong, 271 ff
Stanton, Rev. James F., 28
Statistics, Maryknoll in Bolivia, 202; Chile, 235; Fushun, 121, 124, 127; Guatemala, 250–251; Hong Kong, 274, 275, 276, 280; Kyoto, 170, 173; Africa, 253, 254; Peru, 223–224; Maryknoll Sisters, 312–313
Steinbach, Brother Frederick, 287
Steinbach, Rev. Leo, 171 ff, 176
Story of Juan Mateo, The, 239 ff
Stritch, Cardinal, 326
Sullivan, Sarah, 294
Sulpician Fathers, 23, 24, 25, 34
Sumatra, 102
Sunchong, Chapel, 289
Sunset Hill, 54, 195–196
Sunset Hill property, 50 ff, 52; purchase, 295
Sunwui, 70–71
Sun Yat-sen, Doctor, 271
Support, U.S. Catholics, 224
Swatow, 98
Swatow Vicariate, part given to Maryknoll, 97
Sweeney, Bishop James T., 145–146
Sweeney, Rev. Joseph A., 69–70, 72–73, 76, 78–79, 84, 122–124
Sweeney, Rev. Leo, 84
Szupingkai, 128

Taaiwan, 159, 264 ff
Taichung, Formosa, 266; statistics, 268
Takahashi, Rev. Thomas, 148
Talbot, Major Albert, 137

Talca, Chile, 229
Tambopata valley, Peru, 218 ff
Tanchuk, 110, 112, 118
Tanchuk seminary during World War II, 113 ff
Temuco, Chile, 236
Tennien, Father Mark A., 115 ff, 116, 117, 275
Teresa, Sister M., 295
Teresians, 52, 295
Theophane, Sister M., 296
Theophane Walsh, Brother, 147
Third General Chapter, 199
Thoughts from Modern Martyrs, 28
Tibesar, Rev. Leopold H., 121, 149, 178–179
Tienchung, Formosa, 266 ff
Tientsin, 122, 129
Tiger, The, 91
Titicaca, Lake, 213
Toishaan, 69, 75; hospital construction, 289
Tokugawa Ieyasu, 179
Tokugawa, Michael, 179
Tokuhisa, Rev. James S., 148, 184 ff
Toledo, Ohio, 124, 138
Tomizawa, Bishop Benedict, 183
Tonkin, 59
Toomey, Father John J., 133
Topong, 290
Tosei News Service, 179
Tour, Rev. Jean, 64
Transfiguration Church, New York City, 149
Tracy, Dr. Joseph V., 26
Trade School, Molina, Chile, 234 ff
Training of Maryknoll Missioners, 52 ff; 314 ff
Transcript, Hartford, 191
Travel, Pando Vicariate, 205; Puno, Peru, 212 ff
Tributes to Bp. James A. Walsh, 196 ff
Trinita, Sister M., 304
Trinita Logue, Sister, 138
Troesch, Rev. John C., 271 ff, 273
Trube, Rev. Howard D., 279, 282
Truth, 16, 17, 18, 33
Tsiou, Rev., 81
Tungan, 162 ff
Tungchen, 63, 66, 108
Tunghua, 124, 125, 126
T'ung Hwa, 122
Tung Tao Tsuen refugee mission, 279
Turibius, Saint, 222

Ujidawara, 172–173
Una, Sister, 138
United Nations, 87, 92, 93, 133
University of the Philippines, 134
University of Santo Tomas, 71, 131
Urakami, 168

Valladon, Rev. Walter J., 209
Valtorta, Bishop, 273
Vatican, 47, 127, 191
Venard, Blessed Theophane, 24, 28, 47, 59
Venard College, 53, 320
Viatorian Fathers, 180, 268
Victoria (see Hong Kong)
Victoria, Lake, 253
Victoria Francis, Sister M., 305
Villemot, Rev., 89, 91
Vocation, indications of, 316; due to Maryknoll, The Field Afar, 322; from Maryknoll in Los Angeles, 148; inspired by Fr. Jerry Donovan's death, 127; Kyoto, 176; in mind of Bishop J. A. Walsh, 188–189; recruitment, Puno, Peru, 219–220
Vogel, Alphonse S., 52
Voice of San Juan, The, 221

Wakefield, Mr. J., 277
Waldie, Rev. John A., 213
Walker, Rev. Frederick P., 228
Walsh, Hannah Shea, 22
Walsh, James, 22, 23
Walsh, Bishop James Anthony, 19, 21–30, 44, 47–51, 53–63, 64, 109, 110, 187 ff, 190, 200, 283, 292–294, 303, 317, 324, 326, 327; conferences, 59; consecrates Bishop Ford, 192; correspondence, 31–42; first contacts with Father Price, 20 ff; first trip to Orient, 58 ff; foundation of Maryknoll, 43; in the early days, 57 ff; tributes to, 196 ff; years up to foundation of Maryknoll, 21–29
Walsh, Bishop James Edward, 49, 51, 52, 60, 65, 66, 67, 68, 71, 108, 188, 271, 287 ff, 316 ff; as Superior General, 198–199
Walsh, Rev. Thomas S., 236
War Relief Services N.C.W.C., 89, 94, 267, 269; Hong Kong, 275
Washington, D.C., 41, 43, 44, 82, 87, 169

Waterbury, Conn., 139, 162
Wazuka Village, 184 ff
West River, 62, 111
White Fathers, 252, 253
Wholean, Mary Louise, 294, 296
Wiju, 81
Wille, Rev. Arthur H., 254
William Neary, Brother, 284 ff
Williams, Archbishop, 26, 27, 28, 34
Wilmington, N.C., 10 ff, 14
Windsor Hotel, 30
Windsor, Ontario, 128, 154
Witte, Rev. Clarence J., 185, 248
Wong, General, 75–76
Wong, Margaret Mary, 158
Woo Feng, 265
Worcester, Mass., 73
World Christianity, 328, 329; Maryknoll's work for, 326 ff
World Horizon Films, 327–328
World Kinship Fun Packets, 328
World War II, 76, 102, 200; Fushun, 128; Maryknollers, Hong Kong, 271 ff; Maryknoll Sisters and, 304; and Philippines, 134 ff; Wuchow, 111–114
Wu, Doctor John, 153
Wuchow, 108, 109, 111, 112, 145, 151, 189, 289; bandits, 108; canonically erected mission, 109; Communists, 117–119; contrasted with Kweilin, 151; diocese of, 159; Japan-China war, 110–111; Maryknoll Sisters, 110 ff; mission methods, 110 ff; native clergy, 110; Prefecture Apostolic, 109; refugee work, 111; relief work (postwar), 115; Vicariate, history and description, 107–119

Xavier, St. Francis, 2, 59, 62, 65, 167 ff
Xavier, Sister M., 296

Yalu, 81, 82, 90, 91, 93, 120, 122
Yang, Rev. Paul, 269
Yangtze Valley, 152
Yaos, 114
Yap, John (seminarian), 97–98
Yengyou, 82, 85
Yeungkong, 59, 62–63, 65, 68, 96
Yungli, 150

Zaculeu, City of the Dead, 244–245
Zanin, Archbishop Mario, 109